YOU DECIDE! THE FUTURE OF SCOTLAND

Judgement Dave

You Decide! The Future of Scotland
By Judgement Dave

Helneaux Farkier
Published by Helneaux/Farkier

ISBN: 978-0-9930125-1-8

Also available for Kindle (ISBN: 978-0-9930125-0-1)

This is a work of fiction. All characters, companies, private organisations, deities and countries are fictitious. Heck - even the United Kingdom is probably fictitious. I'm not even certain that I'm real, let alone you, dear reader, but that's a totally different existential ballgame.

Of course, having said that, this whole book is about exploring some of the events in an infinite multiverse, and if there is an infinite multiverse (hint: there is - I've travelled it during research) then everything that is possible has happened/will happen/is happening somewhere. So if I write about a 78 year-old, one-legged, lesbian dwarf from Aberdeen, with a subnormal IQ, called Maureen Pernickety then I think I'm making her up, but she does actually exist in an infinite number of other parallel universes and times. Yikes - I hope she doesn't get transdimensional lawyers to sue me for defamation - after all she really does have a subnormal IQ. That's fact.

For Democracy
For Freedom
For God's sake… why?

Foreword

This is a special book.

It's special because it's the only book tenuously linked to the Scottish referendum that actually has bugger all to do with reality and can be equally enjoyed by people of any land, not just Scots.

It's special because its lack of facts and realism make it as irrelevant and irreverent 10 years after the referendum as it is in the run-up to the vote.

It's special because it lets you explore how you would vote on the day of the Scottish referendum and, as the author has travelled through time and space and infinite parallel dimensions to research it, it shows you the effects the vote has on the futures of Scotland, the United Kingdom and the entire world.

I hope you'll agree that all the above makes this book pretty damn special already. But that's not all. It's special in other ways too.

Many books take years of restless toil to write. This one didn't - it's special. It only took mere months without sleep.

Many books take ages to get published as every word is edited to death to make sure it's the write word and their are no gramma ore speling misstakes. This one didn't - it's speshial.

Many books try to say things that are important or thought-provoking. This one doesn't - it's special.

But its specialosity goes further than that.

What other book cashing in on the Scottish referendum, or any other topic ever, features* hot sex, kilts, quantum physics, Earl Grey tea, romance**, hot sex, goblin-banshees, broken 4th walls, unicorns, hot sex, deadly hemorrhagic fevers, Alex Salmond, time travel, a 100% money back guarantee (conditions apply), a thoroughly deluded author and hot sex?

What other book is so ideally suited to a quick read on the loo?

Finally, and most importantly: What other book helps Judgement Dave's children not starve???

You know you want to read this. You know it's the right thing to do. You know that buying this book is the answer to the question '*What would Jesus do?*'

* Please be aware that 'features' is being used as a synonym for 'includes' much as 'special' may be appearing as a synonym for 'puerile'.

** Romance not included, but you can always read this in bed when your partner has fallen asleep. I think that counts.

Forewarned

Just in case you haven't realised by now. This book may be very puerile in places. [Places! Where isn't it?]

It contains plenty of potty-mouthed language to the extent that if you're someone who never swears then reading it aloud will sometimes sound like you're saying words at random every 20 seconds or so.

Okay - it's not actually *quite* that bad. But this certainly isn't a book for minors, miners, minah birds or elderly aunts with weak hearts and delicate ears.

If you do let your children read it then don't be worried that I'm introducing them to foul language (unless they're very young, in which case I'm not certain that I'm the one with the problem).

I probably haven't taught them any new words, whatever little darlings you believe them to be. I actually learnt many of the expletives and slang used in this book from teenagers on public transport, but don't tell them - they may try claiming royalties.

It also contains really hot sex. So hot that you may be surprised.

But, in all, seriousness: this book may not be suitable for maiden aunts or infants.

YOU HAVE BEEN WARNED

On the other hand if you would describe yourself as having a sick or weird sense of humour, enjoy adult comics, blue comedians or just trying out new experimental books then you may really like it. Good luck :)

Introduction

On the 18th September 2014 Scotland goes to the polls to decide whether or not it should become an independent country separate to the United Kingdom. Most people born in the UK, 16 years old or older and living in Scotland at the time of the referendum get to vote. But this important decision affects all of the UK.

So what if you're Scottish but not currently resident in Scotland? What if you're not quite 16 yet? What if you're an interfering sassenach? What if you just can't be arsed to vote?

Well now you too can have your voice heard as **You Decide! The Future of Scotland**.

Well, the future of *a* Scotland…

All the possible outcomes presented in this book have actually, really, really, honestly, totally, truly, really, really happened in one or more parallel universes. They might even happen in ours.

Advanced research by the author involving various quantities of time travel, visiting parallel universes and strong alcoholic drinks[1] has revealed all possible outcomes for the future of Scotland, England and the United Kingdom.

So now, whether you won't have a say in the real referendum or just want to explore the ramifications and knock-on effects of possible votes, you can vote here as **You Decide! The Future of Scotland**, safe in the knowledge that if it all goes tits up it's someone else's reality that got screwed.

What the heck is 'You Decide!'?

Remember back in the 1980s when there were loads of children's books with names like '*Select Your Own Shitty Story*', '*Farting Fantasy*' or '*Another-Book-Series-That-I-Probably-Can't-Mention-as-it-is-Protected-By-Trademarks*'?

These books were different as they were nonlinear. You wouldn't just read them sequentially from page 1 to page 2 to page 3 and so on to the end. No. They let you choose your own flow of the story by reading a section then being offered a choice of which section to go to next. So instead of just reading a single story that the author had created, these let you create your own personal story. You didn't have to put up with the protagonist doing something you thought was stupid, you could chose for them to do what you wanted them to do.

If you don't remember them, they went something like this…

1. The Dangerous Dungeon

You spent last night in a rowdy tavern, knocking back a couple of flagons of dragonmead and flirting with the scantily-clad, buxom, elven barwench before retiring for the night (though sadly not with the pointy-eared minx).

This morning, broadsword in hand[2], equipment and provisions safely in your backpack you approach the entrance to the dungeon of infinite riches or eternal doom…

You know that entering the dragon's lair and escaping with its hoard is going to test your strength, your courage, your intelligence, your will - in fact every aspect of your being is going to be scrutinised by fate and there is a good chance that you will not escape with your life, your soul and your genitalia intact.

Thinking about the dangers ahead, you suddenly wish that you'd gone to the toilet before setting off.

Quickly swallowing two Imodium and casting those thoughts out of your mind, you sneak past the inebriated orc guards sleeping at the entrance, and, entering the dungeon, you quickly arrive at a T-junction.

Do you go left (turn to section 3) or right (turn to section 2)?

2. You turn right

And you are confronted by a daemonic goblin-banshee which starts screaming an unearthly shriek of hellish shittiness *"ktheaaaarrrrrr!!"*

Do you put your hands over your ears to lessen the ungodly noise (turn to section 5)? Or do you attack the goblin-banshee with your broadsword (turn to section 4)?

3. You turn left

As soon as you turn left you know that there's nothing 'sinister' about the left-hand path, because you enter a room full of riches beyond your wildest dreams!

Really, you thought the dragon would be smarter than to keep all his treasure by the dungeon entrance, but no. It turns out he's a fuckwit and you live happily ever after.

The End

4. You attack the Goblin-Banshee

You lift up your broadsword and charge towards the accursed creature, shouting your fierce battle cry.

"By the power of Fu'Q'Nuck-El!"

And the goblin-banshee easily dodges the attack and then rips you a new arsehole.

You are dead.

The End

5. You place your hands over your ears

And the goblin-banshee kicks you hard in the bollocks.

As you lie on the floor with tears running down your cheeks, gently rocking back and forth, the goblin-banshee mocks your manliness before taking a selfie with you crying in the background. It then posts the picture to instagram and then kills you. Nastily.

You are dead.

The End

[*Please note that the above is the full text of 'Even More Dragon Gold!', Book 327 of the popular 'All the Way to the Bank' series and the direct sequel to 'Dragon Gold!', 'More Dragon Gold!', 'Yet More Dragon Gold!', 'Where do these Dragons Get All this Gold?' and 'You'll Never Guess What The Dragon is Hoarding... That's Right: Gold!'. Used by kind permission of the now-inexplicably-rich author.*]

Now you can probably see how these 'adventures' weren't quite as exciting as normal adult life can be. But, despite that, they gave people a chance to exercise their imagination and explore what could happen depending upon the choices they made.

It was a way to learn valuable lessons about the cause and effect of personal actions. Many university studies have proven that it's mainly because of these books that whole generations have grown up without ever being kicked in the crotch (or given additional excretory orifices) by any supernatural entity.

That's the sort of thing that adults can sometimes still benefit from. Especially when they've got a big decision coming up, like how best to deal with the goblin-banshee in front of them or deciding the future of Scotland and the United Kingdom!

The 100% Money Back Guarantee

Many endings in this book carry a **100% Money Back Guarantee**. Should the events of that ending actually happen to the instance of you (or your consciousness) that has purchased and read this book then, if you meet all qualifying terms and conditions, you may be able to claim back 100% of the cost of this book.

You may be wondering exactly how I can afford to offer such a generous and totally not fake **100% Money Back Guarantee**. Well, here's how:

1. Maybe I can't afford it!

Across the multiverse there's an infinite number of **100% Money Back Guarantee** claims being made against the purchase of this book. There's also an infinite number of copies of this book being sold. But the distribution of sales and refund claims varies from specific reality to specific reality.

In an infinite number of universes nobody makes a single claim and I sell what is technically referred to as '*shitloads*'. I just hope that in these universes I'm making the most of it because there's also an infinite number of universes where so many people claimed that I'm left a penniless ruined alcoholic bum, living on the streets and only ever having a hot meal when someone drunkenly staggers out of a nightclub before vomiting over me and I manage to salvage some warm carrot chunks.

In a way this is meta-**You Decide!** Your decision to purchase this book and possibly to subsequently take advantage of the 100% Money Back Guarantee lets **You Decide! The Future of Judgement Dave**... please don't condemn me to a future of eating semi-digested kebab meat from my beard.

2. Lawyers' cunning stunts

They're used to writing up guarantees for a wide range of products and services. So used to it that they can write them so that they sound good but nobody will ever realistically qualify for them.

They're so good that they offered their own **100% Money Back Guarantee** to me and I thought it looked good until I tried to get my money back for the shoddy job they'd done. Now I really wish I'd studied the small-print and spotted the clause about needing all my great-great-grandparents to accompany me whilst making a claim…

Still - don't let that put you off, maybe you'll be the exception to the rule and you will manage to claim the **100% Money Back Guarantee**.

How to Claim

Each ending that carries the **100% Money Back Guarantee** states any terms and conditions that may apply in the case of that specific ending actually happening to you in your reality. All claims must be made in person, within 14 days of the ending happening. You are only eligible to claim for eventualities that are realised by the specific you making the claim and may not claim for events that may happen to 'equivalent yous' in their own specific reality segment of the multiverse.

See it's more seeemple than teaching a meerkat to speak English with a dodgy Russian accent.

The Dead Cat Factor

The author knows that anyone interested in choosing the future of the United Kingdom obviously has a keen grasp of quantum mechanics and probably leaves food and water out for Schrödinger's Cat.

It's even possible that you've occasionally found small quantities of hairballs, sick and faeces around your home, when the cat has left its box for a prowl. Coincidentally, this usually happens after you've been out with your mates for twelve pints, a curry, six more pints, a couple of stronger nightcaps and then a kebab, before mysteriously teleporting yourself through time and space to instantaneously arrive the next morning, fully dressed, in your own bed.

Bearing this is mind, this book contains no explanation of collapsing wave packets, relativistic temporal travel or why Americans say 'math' not 'maths'. You either understand it already or, like Piers Morgan's success, it's a mystery of the universe that may never be properly explained.

But occasionally in this guide to infinite possibilities[3] there are places where two or more outcomes are possible, apparently at random. Here you'll get to decide just how well the cat is when you look in the box…

Oh okay - it's just a way of picking a random(ish) outcome. I could have just said that straight off instead of trying to fob you off with all that bollox, but I'm getting paid by the word for this.

You don't really want my children to starve, do you?

You are...

In the rest of this book, whilst **You Decide!** what happens, you won't actually be 'you'.

You'll be doing a little bit of roleplaying as 'you' are a twenty-something Scottish male who lives in Scotland and is eligible to vote in the referendum[4]. This probably won't impact too much on the story, but if you get asked to make a decision and think *"Well I wouldn't do* ***any*** *of those things"* then rest assured that whilst you wouldn't the Scottish 'you' of the book would, and indeed must to progress the story.

For anyone worried about me describing this as a little bit of roleplaying, don't worry. You won't need loads of many-sided dice, a games master or the ability to bore strangers with your love of Tolkien and intimate knowledge of hobbit mating habits[5]. However you will need the willing suspension of disbelief especially if you read that you do something incredible.

It's probably for the best that you are 'you' (the story you) and not you (the real you, if you get my drift), as the first part of **You Decide! The Future of Scotland** concerns the day of the election and depending upon what choices you (and the cat in the box) make for 'you' it could end up being quite a terrifying experience. Especially if the real you is from the English home counties and not used to life or death situations in the barren expanses North of Watford.

Throughout all of this, please remember that these things have actually really truly etc. etc. happened to someone elsewhere in the multiverse. They must have, because the alternative is that I, the author, am truly mad.

And I know that I'm quite sane as the neighbour's dog told me.

—— **Section 001** ——

Your adventure starts when you begin to wake up (go to **Section 059**)

Pssst! You! Yes you!
If you've read through ***You Decide! The Future of Scotland*** *a few times and want to use a time warp to jump to further in your story, just continue on to* ***Section 002***

—— **Section 002** ——

Hi folks! You're here because you've read this book a few times and want to skip some of the earlier parts for this read through.

Unless you've gone back a lot to explore alternate options, there's bound to be sections in the earlier parts of your stories that you've not seen, but you're probably right to skip them for a while then find them in a reread in a few months time. It'll all seem new then, and still be as totally irrelevant to current affairs!

As you do want to skip some parts, thanks to the magic of time travel technology, you can use the rest of this section to choose to jump to when you get dressed or when the result of the vote comes in…

Jump to Getting Dressed (go to **Section 230**)
Or jump to when the 'Yes' vote wins (go to **Section 069**)

—— Section 003 ——

You open the door and you're greeted by the sound of a music system blasting out 90s pop music. You recognise the track as the biggest hit that *2 Unlimited* had - you think it was called *No Limits*. It only takes a few moments for you to realise that something's wrong: the CD or record seems to be stuck in a loop. It just keeps repeating part of the chorus.

No no. No no no no. kzt No no. No no no no. kzt No no. No no no no. kzt No no. No no no no. kzt No no....

Oh! Suddenly you realise what it is - it's not a broken music player but an intentional loop acting as a slightly less than subliminal hint about how to vote.

You can't help but smile as you around the room and see it's adorned with union flags and graphical reminders of the long and great history that Scotland has shared with the rest of the UK.

You go to exchange pleasantries with the lady (dressed in an equal mix of red, white and blue) behind the desk dealing with addresses including your home, but she smiles widely at your attire and greets you like a long-lost brother. Once you've confirmed your identity, she says "You're doing us proud, laddy", gives you your ballot paper and points you in the direction of the small individual booths that you can go in to cast your vote in private.

As you walk across the room to the polling booth, it is with the weight of a country's destiny bearing down on your shoulders… (go to **Section 184**)

—— Section 004 ——

You get some funny looks on the way, but most people seem to accept that on such a momentous day some people might dress up and treat it like some sort of party. At least there's no trouble and eventually you get to the polling station, walk up to the doors and pause.

You always thought that polling stations are places full of wonder and promise for the future. The almost-mystical locations that can alter a nations fate. Each one a powerful nexus where all possible destinies of the country intersect, just waiting for the public will to select one single possibility and to transform it into reality. Places of truly amazing, almost miraculous, transformative power.

But really they are just local primary schools that have swapped the kids for a naff sign saying 'POLLING STATION'.

Finally you approach the doors and prepare yourself to step inside.

DEAD CAT TIME

Yes it's time to peek inside Schrödinger's box and see how well Jess is…

Hello Jess. Where's Pat? (go to **Section 013**)

or Hello Pat. Where's Jess gone? (go to **Section 168**)

or That's not a cat that's George Galloway! (go to **Section 177**)

or Jess is curled up asleep, blissfully unaware of their role in the future of Scotland. (go to **Section 036**)

or Postcat Jess. Postcat Jess. Postcat Jess has left a mess! (go to **Section 366**)

or OMG! Jess is dead! Pat will be upset. (go to **Section 288**)

—— Section 005 ——

Immediately the costume of a giant haggis literally leaps out at you. Not literally 'literally', of course, it only really leaps metaphorically, so you only need to imagine yourself jumping out of it's way rather than really jumping to safety.

You examine the costume. It looks perfect.

You've always secretly desired to be a haggis - playing in the wilds of the highlands. They enjoy a freedom of expression that humans just can't achieve. They're somehow more in-touch with nature and more full of life for it. Yes - goodbye rat race world of wage-slave people, for today, if not any other day, you'll be a haggis!

You can't stop grinning as you pay the shopkeeper for the costume then enter the changing room to get changed there and then. You keep smiling even when you get confused about which of the haggis' 17 legs you're meant to use for your own arms and legs. Finally, you figure it out and before long you leave the shop; the happiest haggis in Scotland is heading to the polling station. (go to **Section 259**)

—— Section 006 ——

The nurse greets you with the words "God - not another one" and a look of exasperation. "Take a ticket and sit down in the waiting room. If I hear a bloody peep out of you I'll get security to kick you out. Right?"

You're too fragile to put up much resistance, so you agree weakly and take a ticket from the machine the nurse indicated on the wall.

Hmmm - number 23. That's not great. Oh well they probably keep it running day after day, for all you know you might only be the third or fourth person to come in today.

You go over to the entrance to the waiting room and walk in…

"Bloody hell." You were right that they must keep the tickets just cycling day after day, but it obviously clicked around again this morning as there must be 40 or 50 people waiting here. All with the tell-tale blue faces of *Fatal*

Facial Azuritis.

You wait and wait, and eventually the doctors get around to looking at you. They can't make a definite diagnosis yet, this disease is something new to them, but the prognosis is not good. They work around the clock but you are running a temperature, feel sick and are just getting worse.

Eventually, despite all their help, you slip into a coma.

Over the next few days it doesn't seem to matter what the doctors and nurses try to do for you, you just keep on deteriorating. The referendum that seemed so important to you is all but forgotten as your body suffers the devastating onslaught of the strange disease. You know that the end is near.

It's odd but this wasn't how you thought you'd die. You'd always hoped you'd go out as the result of a really hot kinky sex game gone wrong, two or three famous actresses and bunny girls dying with you. Lots of really really hot sexy sex going on and everyone with tremendous, orgasm-fuelled smiles on their faces…

If you still had the energy and consciousness to smile, then thinking about your preferred death-by-orgy would have brought a wide azure grin to your blue face. Instead you pass away with a neutral-expression cast in the sickest hue any face has ever seen.

As the last remnants of consciousness slip away you hear the doctor say "I'm calling it as 10 past midnight. The first ever death from *St Andrews Cross Disease.*"

St Andrews Cross? St Andrews Cross! How dare they call it that. You're the one dying, the one with milliseconds of thought left as your brain goes into it's final sleep. The very least they could do was to name the disease after you. But no, they're calling it St Andrews Bloody Cross.

Well it may be the case that St Andrew's Cross but you're fucking furious.

The End

Should it actually happen in your reality, this ending is <u>NOT</u> covered by the 100% money back guarantee. Mainly because the publishers and everyone else on the planet is soon dead from St Andrew's Cross Disease so there's nobody left to pay you the refund.

—— Section 007 ——

September 18th 2018

You can't help but be tense in the control van, if this officially-unsanctioned break-in goes astray then you'll be hung out to dry. Holyrood will be forced to deny all knowledge of you and your operation. Admitting that you're spying on your old friend is something Scotland can never do.

So here you sit, nervously concentrating on the equipment in front of you. Telecommunications letting you observe and direct the operation almost as if you were there. You see everything your operative sees. Hear all that they hear.

Special Agent 0087 is in a nondescript brownstone building in Newcastle. Officially it's a small regional office of *Britannic Mass Haulage*, but you know it's a front for the subsection of English MI6 keeping an eye on their newly independent neighbours.

You're still not convinced your operative is the right man for the job, but he's all you had available. You remember back to when you first met him, about a year ago when you'd just joined the service.

Your immediate boss had called you to his office to meet your new partner. When you got there M was sat opposite an elderly man in a tuxedo, drinking some sort of cocktail with an olive in it. As you entered the stranger put down his drink and, over the course of 20 seconds, slowly stood up and put out a hand.

"Pleashed to meet you. The name's McBond, James McBond. Shpeshal agent double-ohhh-sheven" he said shaking your hand.

Your supervisor quickly corrected him. "Look Mr Connery, we've been over this before; you are not James McBond and you're a bit old to still be 007."

"If I'm sho old why doesh Shcotland need me? Why choose an eighty-sheven year old man?"

"Your time playing a secret agent on screen makes you Scotlands most experienced spy, we've no training budget and desperately need to know what England is up to."

"Fair enough. But I demand the cover name of McBond and a designation that shtill uses my dishtinctive pronounciation of esshess."

You finally spoke "I'm honoured to meet you sir. You're 87 you say? I'm impressed."

"Yesh, eighty-sheven - and I shtill have my own teeth, you know."

That was quite a memorable introduction. It's not everyday you get to meet a living legend. But now you've been working with him for a year and know that it doesn't matter how famous you are, but how good you are. Unfortunately you're not certain he's anywhere near as good as he thinks he is. The ravages of time haven't passed him by.

Back in the control van, or mobile operations room, you watch 0087 try to open the wall safe. He's having problems with his arthritis but, slowly and painfully, he's getting there.

Eventually he's in and after a couple of minutes photographing the documents inside the safe is shut once more and it's time for extraction.

0087 grips his walking aid and starts racing towards the open window and awaiting rope. You'll give him his due, for an old man he can still rappel well.

Then, unexpectedly, alarms start to blare out in the building. No! You realise what has happened: in his haste to leave he's forgotten about the laser beams crisscrossing the floor and zimmered straight into one.

You don't have time to plan an alternate escape as suddenly the door to the office is thrown open and in burst several men in pinstripe suits. As they subdue your agent you notice that most are wearing glasses and all are armed.

Through the comms link you see one of them step forward, carrying a black suitcase alongside the Heckler & Koch sidearm.

"So Sean Connery, at last we meet face to face" says the suitcase man.

"I don't know who you think I am, but you're mishtaken. I'm McBond, James McBond. You have me at a dishadvantage ; you know who I am, but I don't know you."

"Ah Mr… McBond, all will become clear in time. You made a mistake thinking you could get away with breaking in here. Now you will pay. We will extract everything we want."

"Do you exshpect me to talk?"

"No Mr McBond, I expect you to pay the taxes you still owe."

Shit! Your bosses should have known better than to use an old UK tax exile as an asset in field-ops. HMRC are far better organised than MI6 and they *always* get their man.

With your operation blown you shut off the telecom link and get into the drivers seat. The political fallout to Scotland could be terrible, but you'll deal with that when you get back to Edinburgh. If you make it back, that is.

That seems unlikely as several cars with flashing blue lights screech to a stop around the van and armed HMRC accountants swarm out of them to surround you.

You curse your government. If only they'd assigned a bigger budget for espionage then things could have been so different and you wouldn't be about to officially disappear off the face of the Earth.

The End of the beginning

Should it actually happen in your reality, this ending is NOT covered by the 100% money back guarantee. You don't officially exist anymore.

—— **Section 008** ——

The coin flies up...

And then comes back down again landing clearly on 'Tails'.

That's interesting. You're fairly sure you'd decided that tails is a NO vote, so you pick up the teeny tiny pencil and place a cross in the 'NO' box.

You fold the ballot paper and happily stroll out of the booth, walk across the floor and pop the folded ballot in the box. You exchange knowing nods with the station attendants. You know and they know that you have fulfilled your democratic duty.

It's surprisingly easy when you use a coin and don't worry too much about political arguments. You hardly know why people treat it as such a big deal.

You go home and carry on as normal until the results are announced. (go to **Section 321**)

—— **Section 009** ——

"That's not good enough" you say to the doctor, "I want a second opinion."

"Of course you do, it's not enough to just waste my time, is it? Well follow me and I'll take you to another doctor." He walks out of the examination cubicle and you follow him to another.

DEAD CAT TIME

I wonder if little twinkle wants any food?

Oh I guess not - she's dead. (go to **Section 343**)

or Oh you were hungry weren't you? (go to **Section 151**)

or Ow she clawed at me! (go to **Section 026**)

—— **Section 010** ——

On a 24hr news channel you see footage repeating a recent exchange from Prime Minister Questions in Westminster.

The leader of the opposition is quizzing the PM, "Prime Minister, will you explain exactly what you're planning to do about the West Lothian question?"

"I've solved that one already. Why don't you ask me something tricky for a change?"

"Really? When many great political minds before you have struggled over the issue? You must be a genius!"

Laughter from the opposition benches

"Oh thank you - it was really quite simple for a Bullingdon boy."

"Well don't keep us in suspense - tell the house what your answer to it is."

"After thinking about it for several hours, I've come to the conclusion that West Lothian is *actually* part of Scotland and not some fantastic creation of C S Lewis or Tolkein. And you'll be glad to know that Wikipedia backs me up on that."

Murmurs of 'ahhhh' and 'so it is real' rise from the benches behind the PM.

"And how exactly does that help decide Scottish MPs voting rights on English affairs?"

"Well obviously it doesn't. Why? Should it?"

"Of course it should, that **is** the West Lothian Question. The question of Scottish MPs voting rights on English issues in Westminster."

"That's really the question? I always thought it was *Is West Lothian a real place and if so, where is it?*"

The government benches echo with calls of 'quite right', 'so did I' and 'here here' whilst the opposition fling boos and calls of 'shame' back at them. You spot two or three cases of money changing hands as Conservative MPs from Southern England, who bet against it being a real place, pay up.

You decide to turn off the show. Changing channel you're glad you've managed to get rid of the English 'home counties' idiots in Westminster.

Do you now watch Food+ TV (go to **Section 056**)
or Maybe try ScottishLivingTV (go to **Section 122**)

—— Section 011 ——

You wait...

You're already bored of waiting. The only thing to do is worry or watch the other people, but that's just annoying.

Take those two youths over by the blood donor poster for example.

"A pint! That's most of me arm innit!"

"No idea mate - I don't do that old pints and ounces shit. Ain't a pint just under half a litre?"

"No idea - it's just a quote from some old Alfred Hitchcock film me gran told me about once. Hitchcock's in hospital an' he sees a poster asking for blood donors to give a pint an' he says 'A pint! That's most of me arm innit?' Me gran thought it were proper funny."

"I s'pose people used to laugh at anything after the war."

Thankfully at this point your name is called by the nurse from reception and she leads you through to an examination cubicle.

DEAD CAT TIME
Has anyone fed Tiddles today? No? I'll see how he is then.

He's fine and ready to play! (go to **Section 320**)
Or He's fine and ready for some food! (go to **Section 151**)
Or He's fine… if you didn't want a living cat. (go to **Section 343**)

—— Section 012 ——

September 18th 2022

Despite several delays due to bad weather, the World Cup Final is finally here and it just happens to be on the 8th anniversary of *Yes-day*. What a great omen for Scotland, who enter the final with a real chance to win a historic victory on home soil. All they're got to do is beat the United Arab Emirates and that shouldn't be too hard as they've only made it this far by fluke.

It's still a goal-less game when, in the 3rd minute of stoppage time, McAdam sends a perfect pass straight to your feet at the halfway line. You turn and start running the ball downfield. You beat one man on the turn, a second with sheer pace before flicking the ball up and over the last defender in your way. Racing around him you get to the ball just in time to volley it with a stunning scissor-kick from just inside the penalty spot.

The shot looks good but the UAE keeper's diving towards it. The next couple of seconds seem to last an eternity as the keeper closes in on the ball that is slowly curling away from him. Finally the keeper gets to the ball, but only with the very tips of his fingers, not enough to do anything except to deflect it perfectly into the top right corner of the goal.

GOOOAALLL SCOTLANNNNNND!!!!!

That's all it takes for you and Scotland to win the cup.

You're so glad that you took up football seriously after Scotland was awarded the World Cup Finals back in 2014. That would never have happened without an Independent Scotland.

But sadly, despite getting the cup, sports and health funding was never the priority it should have been in Scotland although the video game industry is now leading the world. That's why your winning goal is only seen by you and your mate Andy in that Cup Final game of *Fuckin' Soccer 2022* on the Playstation 6.

Of course it's not really called Fuckin' Soccer. Officially it's ProCreation Soccer 2022, the football game funded by the Catholic Church to directly compete with the Pro Evolution Soccer franchise.

But despite having Vatican funding, you're proud to say that, partly because of the tax breaks available, the game itself was developed by a wholly Scottish company based in Silicon Glen. And they did an excellent job. Although making a great game wasn't the only reason that PCS '22 had become the undisputed genre leader.

In truth Pro Creation Soccer was only slightly better than Pro Evolution Soccer, but it became far, far more popular due to the Catholic Church decreeing that all good Catholics should play video games and then making playing the rival game a cardinal sin.

Game-wise there was so little difference except that, off the pitch, the players are perfect computer-generated Christian role-models who don't covet anyone's wife and certainly don't take part in spit roasts in hotel rooms.

The only other minor difference being that it's the only video game to feature the unbeatable Vatican first XI team made up of the last 10 popes and featuring their star-player, God, who seems to be almost everywhere on the pitch at once and, unlike Maradonna, uses his literal hand to score goals.

Despite that, it's still only a video game and it's still Scotland's only chance to win the Jules Rimming trophy. But, as your onscreen pixellated form crosses themselves and says a prayer before raising the trophy you think 'at least you *did* win it' and at least it was in a Scot-developed game.

Virtual Scotland is virtually proud of the computer-generated virtual you. And *really* proud of it's real games industry.

The end of the beginning

Should it actually happen in your reality, this ending is NOT covered by the 100% money back guarantee. It's the end of this read through or exploration of what may happen to Scotland, but it's not the end of your story or the story of Scotland. It is not the end. It is just the end of the beginning. Or maybe the end of the middle or beginning of the middle or it might be the end of the beginning of the middle or the end of the end of the beginning of the middle.

Winston Churchill made this type of thing look easier than it is. Honest.

—— Section 013 ——

You open the door and you're greeted by the sound of a music system blasting out 90s pop music. You recognise the track as the biggest hit that *2 Unlimited* had - you think it was called *No Limits*.

It only takes a few moments for you to realise that something's wrong: the CD or record seems to be stuck in a loop. It just keeps repeating part of the chorus.

No no. No no no no. kzt No no. No no no no. kzt No no. No no no no. kzt No no. No no no no. kzt No no…

Oh! Suddenly you realise what it is - it's not a broken music player but an intentional loop acting as a slightly less than subliminal hint about how to vote.

You look around the room and see it's adorned with union flags and graphical reminders of the long and great history that Scotland has shared with the rest of the UK. You're really beginning to get the idea that this polling station may be slightly biased towards the 'NO' vote.

You're greeted by the lady (dressed in an equal mix of red, white and blue) behind the desk dealing with addresses including your home. She looks you up and down in disbelief, shakes her head and says "Well it takes all sorts I suppose". Once you've confirmed your identity, she says "You know what's the right thing to do, laddy", gives you your ballot paper and points you in the direction of the small individual booths that you can go in to cast your vote in private.

As you walk across the room to the polling booth, it is with the weight of a country's destiny bearing down on your shoulders… (go to **Section 119**)

—— Section 014 ——

You soon arrive in the future of H G Wells The Time Machine and are disappointed to see that it isn't a world full of ignorant childlike Eloi and troglodyte Morlocks. That's so bad of H G Wells to mislead his readers like that - you absolutely hate authors who lie and don't do proper research, especially when it comes to time travel.

Instead of Wells' future world you find a wasteland with no apparent life. However, a closer look shows that it's not lifeless - where cockroaches fell microbes still survived.

You'll never trust an author again.

The End

Should it actually happen in your reality, this ending is covered by the 100% money back guarantee. Really it is. Sure you can have a refund. Trust me it's already on it's way to you.

—— Section 015 ——

The four of you leave the bar and head over to The Raj Tandoori Curry House.

Conversation is a little odd as you and Kelly keep talking about politics and the Andy and Mark keep on making crap jokes (most of which are blue), boasting about their various exploits (in everything from sport to women) and apologising for being dicks earlier. As before, every time they apologise it's as if it's the first time they've done so and they buy another drink.

You think it's probably a relief when the food arrives and conversation slows as you all tuck in to various spicy concoctions.

You say that '*you think it's probably a relief*' because, now that you're awake again this morning, you can't actually remember whether it was or not. You recall ordering food and being apologised to with a third round of shots, but everything gets a bit hazy after that. And by hazy you mean that the memories are non-existent.

Getting into the shower to freshen up you just hope you didn't make a complete dick of yourself in front of Kelly. (go to **Section 120**)

—— Section 016 ——

Entering the bathroom you catch a glimpse of yourself in the mirror and are horrified to see that your face has a strange, sickly, bluish tint which clashes badly with your bloodshot eyes. If yours isn't the visage of someone at death's door then you don't know what is.

"**Nooooo!** I'm too young to die."

Your life starts to flash before you. All the good times, all the bad times and all the *so-mediocre-they're-not-worth-describing-in-any-sort-of-book-even-a-You-Decide!* times.

It's quite depressing to realise that it's the boringly mundane times that made up 99.423% of your life[6]. That's not what life was meant to be. Where were all the fun times? Oh that's right, they were missed whilst you were busy frittering away your life at work or school.

A wave of fresh resolve washes over you. You are not going out like this. You are going to beat whatever disease has struck you down and then you are going to start living. Actually living. If today's referendum can give Scotland a new lease of life then, by god, today can also give you the strength and determination to carry on and have a real life.

You go back into the bedroom to look for your phone, deep in panicked thought.

C'mon phone. Where the hell did I leave you? I need to call the doctors. No, wait. What am I thinking? They won't be open for hours. I need an ambulance.

Most people only see a hospital's A&E department because of the accident part. Very few need it because of a true life-threatening emergency. But then very few people, if anyone, has ever developed *Severe Facial Cyanitis* or whatever it is you have. In fact you could be the very first case known to medical science. You're going to be famous. Either this is an untreatable plague that will kill mankind and you'll forever be known as patient zero or you will pull through and survive and when you do they'll probably name the disease after you.

But first to find that phone, call an ambulance and actually beat the disease.

Then you notice that your pillowcase also has a strange bluish tint.

Oh My God! Whatever I've got must be making my body disintegrate. My sweat, my blood, all my internal organs must be turning blue and seeping out through my skin. This disease is worse than I thought. Where is my bloody phone?

You know you had it whilst you were watching the film before bed as you kept posting patriotic tweets every few minutes. But then that film does bring out the true Scot in you, that's why you love it so much. Watching it has become some sort of ritual for you.

Oh…

Oh… Of course!

You were watching Braveheart again last night and, as usual, painted St Andrew's saltire on your face. And then, as usual, enjoyed a few single malts. And then, as usual, felt a bit tired - too tired to remove the design from your face before hitting the sack. And so now, again as usual, you've woken up and convinced yourself you've contracted a fatal tropical disease. Will you never learn?

At least this time you didn't get as far as A&E. That was embarrassing when that happened.

Both times.

You're still pretty sure that the second time you didn't really need the un-anaesthetised rectal endoscopy but Dr Cook insisted and you trusted him as he was the same doctor you had the first time you went to the hospital. Although he did seem a bit more stressed out than he did the first time and he kept swapping between irritation and laughter whilst treating you. But then that's the life of an NHS hospital doctor; he'd probably already been on duty for 40 hours straight.

Fortunately he calmed down and seemed a lot less stressed after he'd given you the anal probe.

He even apologised for forgetting to lubricate it first.

Thinking about it, maybe you should still go to hospital and get checked out. (go to **Section 319**)

or You can't believe you did it again. Get cleaned up and hope no-one ever finds out. (go to **Section 379**)

—— Section 017 ——

You pick up the teeny tiny pencil...

And you're not sure exactly why, given you'd been supporting the union up until now, but you make a cross in the 'YES' box.

Immediately you wonder if you have done the right thing... It doesn't really matter if you have or not. You've done it - and that is that.

You fold the ballot paper and, trying not to make eye contact with anybody, walk across the floor and pop the folded ballot in the box. You exchange knowing nods with the station attendants. You know and they know that you have fulfilled your democratic duty.

For such a momentous historic vote it all seems like an anticlimax now. You just hope that you chose correctly.

All you can do is go home and carry on as normal until the results are announced. (go to **Section 321**)

—— Section 018 ——

You open the door...

And almost immediately know that you've entered the wrong room because you come face to face with a sleeping goblin-banshee.

You exit the room quickly before it wakes and rips you a new arsehole and decide to look for the polling station behind a different door. (go to **Section 083**)

—— Section 019 ——

Maybe just this once...

You consider the situation. Where's the real harm in having a little light relief? Is anything about the referendum so serious that you can't occasionally joke about it? Life can become depressing if you take everything too seriously... Maybe the only thing that should remain taboo is the mix of vodka, white wine and tropical fruit juice that your mum used to drink to help her forget.

No; you aren't being asked to laugh about celebrity nonces, deadly disease or blacking up and singing *De Camptown Races* in an insulting accent. Nothing like that. All you are doing is having a chuckle about your own future. Surely there can be nothing wrong with that?

With that thought in mind you laugh at the drunk's bad pun and before long others are laughing too. Although much of it sounds like forced, fake laughter, the drunk and his mate don't seem to notice; the punster grinning like he's the funniest, most successful stand-up ever and his mate patting him on the back and saying "nice one mate" again and again.

Repeating it in the way that only the pissed can.

Before long they both sit down, crack open a can of lager each and seem happy enough to pay attention to the debate without causing any more interruptions.

Happy that any potentially explosive pun-based incidents have been avoided, you also enjoy the rest of the debate. (go to **Section 365**)

—— Section 020 ——

You arrive at the Polling Station without anything interesting having happened to you. That's the type of thing that happens (or rather doesn't happen) when you wear normal clothes and make normal decisions and do your best not to be weird or wacky or to stand out in any way, shape or form.

That's *why* you wear normal clothes.

Even though you don't want to stand out or make waves, and genuinely enjoy being what some would call boring but you prefer to call 'normal', some minuscule part of you wonders if it wouldn't be more fun to occasionally just let go and do something unusual and unexpected.

Maybe something wacky like waiting for your boss to ask if you've done the monthly sales report and saying '*no*' when you have, of course, done it already. Or something really hilarious like saying '*oh you look different today*' when a coworker sits in someone else's chair. Or maybe go totally crazy and read a **You Decide!** book but pick interesting choices rather than the boring humdrum ones you'd probably do in real life…

Oh but the very thought of such lunacy starts to give your heart palpitations. Those crazy things are for another day. Right now you've got voting to do.

You walk up to the doors and pause.

You've always held the belief that polling stations are special places, places that give birth to democracy. Almost like the womb of the democratic process that's so important to the long term marriage between citizens and state. And just like many long term marriages, every four or five years the public and politicians are allowed to spurt into the polling womb, each political spermatozoa hoping to be the lucky one that fertilises the egg of public consensus and is carried to a full term of office.

Okay it's not the best ever analogy, but it's one you've always thought apt. Polling stations are the womb of democracy. Which is particularly ironic given that most people end up being shafted and so many politicians turn out to be cunts.

Of course in reality they aren't special places but are just local primary schools that have swapped the kids for a naff sign saying 'POLLING

STATION'.

Finally you approach the doors and prepare yourself to step inside.

DEAD CAT TIME

Yes it's time to peek inside Schrödinger's box and see how well Jess is... but since we know you like things to stay normal, without any surprises, we'll give you some hints.

Hello Jess. Where's Pat? (HINT: This is the way to get to a weird room that you probably won't like. We're not lying.) (go to **Section 098**)

or Thankfully everything about the cat looks normal. Totally and utterly normal. (HINT: This is the option that goes to the normal polling station. Honestly.) (go to **Section 372**)

or Where's he gone? (HINT: This is a very pro-independence polling station. Really.) (go to **Section 264**)

or That's a penguin in disguise! (HINT: This is the pro-Union polling station. It is.) (go to **Section 127**)

or Jess is curled up asleep and blissfully unaware of the part he's playing in the future of Scotland. (HINT: Another weird room you won't like.) (go to **Section 200**)

or OMG! The cat's dead! (HINT: This is an odd polling station that you probably won't enjoy.) (go to **Section 293**)

—— Section 021 ——

September 18th 2019

After *Yes-Day* the new Scottish government did something that politicians never do, no matter what party or country they are from. They took the brave step of being totally honest with the public.

Realising that modern people's affluence and relative longevity has made the tsunami of laziness and obesity far too strong to fight, Holyrood decided not to throw money down the drain promoting healthy living but to spend it on making fatties feel better about themselves so that depression and anxiety didn't add to their problems.

Advertising campaigns spreading a positive message to unhealthy overeaters were soon rolled out across the land and many were so well received that they immediately entered the public consciousness.

'*Fat is Phat!*' made being extra-extra-plus-sized into something so cool that Will.i.am put on 5 stone just to stay popular in Scotland. '*Lips up, Fatty!*' encouraged the morbidly obese to curl the edges of their lips into smiles (pointing out that smiling uses more energy than frowning and so counts as exercise). '*Big Boned Means Big Boners*' tried to boost the self-image of fat men by making them appear more sexually attractive. This worked despite the logistical problems of attempted intercourse between two people each with 60 inch+ waists, buttocks and thighs to match, but a male with an average sized cock.

The campaigns worked so well that today, on the fifth anniversary of *Yes-Day*, the government is pleased to announce the latest findings of the UN Happiness Survey. Scotland has risen rapidly to become the happiest nation on Earth!

And whilst everybody is celebrating that, it's easy for the government to brush the 34 year average life expectancy under the carpet...

The End

Should it actually happen in your reality, this ending is NOT covered by the 100% money back guarantee. Bah! You lot. What are you like. Yeah - you bought a book you don't like. Yeah - you can't fit through normal-sized doorways. Yeah - you're dead before you're 40. Think of me for once - I'm miserable and probably going to live for at least 2 more years. I'm keeping the money.

—— Section 022 ——

"Thanks but I think I'll pass this time" you say to the punster.

"What about you, Lassie?" he says to Kelly.

"Who you calling Lassie? I'm no a dog and I think I'm fine here" she quickly replies.

"Nae probs - see you round" he says and he and his friend start heading towards the bar's exit.

"What a pair of dicks - I thought they'd never go and leave us alone." You say to Kelly.

"Whaddyou mean 'leave us alone'? We're just talking politics. Are you hitting on me?"

"Sorry I just thought-" you're cut off as she calls you a 'fucking jerk', then stands up and goes running off after the punsters.

"Guys - Changed my mind. Think I will come for a curry after all."

Nice one. Well done. You ruined any chance you might have had there.

It's annoying that you can debate eloquently all night displaying incisive reasoning and a mastery of the English language, but as soon as you talk to a girl you stumble about like a brain-damaged stilt-walker whose 'feet' may be 3 metres away yet he still demonstrates a stunning knack for somehow getting them in his own mouth.

At least you talked to Kelly and she might even talk to you again if she puts the end of the night down to drink on both your parts. If you're lucky she won't even remember getting upset at you. And if she does remember and never talks to you again, at least there's nothing she can do to take the memory of her cracking pair of points out of your mental bank.

This brings a smile to your face this morning as you decide to make a withdrawal from the bank and a deposit in the shower, before freshening up. (go to **Section 120**)

—— Section 023 ——

Sometime in 2014...

You're just completing the final transaction to purchase the strange book you've been thinking of reading. Within seconds the transaction is complete and before the minute is out you prepare to read **You Decide! The Future of Scotland**. You open the book and start reading. (go to **The Foreword**)

—— Section 024 ——

Entering the bathroom...

You catch a glimpse of yourself in the mirror and are horrified to see that your face has a strange, sickly, bluish tint which clashes badly with your bloodshot eyes. If yours isn't the visage of someone at death's door then you don't know what is.

"**Nooooo!** I'm too young to die."

You turn away from your reflection, but as you do you're sure you saw a tiny movement in the mirror... a slight twitch of the shower curtain. Surely someone isn't hiding there? You live alone - there is no-one to hide there.

Bracing yourself, you turn to the shower and with one swift motion whip the curtain to the side.

"Cockmunching shitsticks!"

Your sudden outburst comes as no surprise to the goblin-banshee who dives forward, slamming you into the sink hard enough to crack the porcelain. You slip to the floor, fighting hard to keep hold of consciousness.

"But you're not re... real..."

The goblin-banshee wastes no time in ripping you a new arsehole, before dismembering you and proceeding to beat you to death with your own penis. Your last thought as life slips away from you is one of pride that your dick, even when flaccid, was still big enough to beat someone to death. But then, your dying mind hasn't accounted for the significant blood loss...

The End

Should it actually happen in your reality, this ending is NOT covered by the 100% money back guarantee. We were all sympathetic to your plight and were thinking of sending you a refund without you even asking for it until you said "Cockmunching Shitsticks!". No matter how scared or shocked you are by the goblin-banshee, there's no need for language like "Cockmunching Shitsticks!", "Friggin' Cumbucket" or "Pissing Wankstain". If you can't express yourself without resorting to phrases like "Cockmunching Shitsticks!" then maybe it's a good thing that the goblin-banshee removed you from the world.

—— Section 025 ——

You pick up the teeny tiny pencil...

And make a decisive cross in the 'NO' box.

It was a no-brainer really. You came out to vote supporting the union and you're convinced it's the right thing to do.

You fold the ballot paper and, trying not to make eye contact with anybody, walk across the floor and pop the folded ballot in the box. You exchange knowing nods with the station attendants. You know and they know that you have fulfilled your democratic duty.

For such a momentous historic vote it all seems like an anticlimax now. You just hope that your countrymen and women all see sense and vote as well as you have.

All you can do is go home and carry on as normal until the results are announced. (go to **Section 321**)

—— Section 026 ——

You enter the examination cubicle with Dr Nassir, who hands your notes to the other doctor who was already there waiting. He then explains who you are before he leaves. Doctor McNulty scans your notes then looks you up and down.

"You're not happy with my colleague Dr Nassir's assessment of you having *cerebral faeces syndrome*? You want a second opinion do you?"

You reply that you do, whilst thinking that at last you've got a good Scottish doctor.

"Well quite right, too. Looking over your notes and past visits I think it's safe to say that you also display the symptoms of *acute cubital anal disambiguation failure*, and that's not good. Not good at all."

The news leaves you stunned into silence. You think of all the things you'd planned to do in life that are impossible now you have a cute annulled... err thingy...

"What does that mean doctor? Is there a common name for it?"

He looks at you with a compassionate sadness in his eyes and gives it to you straight.

"Well it means that you have real difficulties telling your arse from your elbow. That's why you think that you, some numpty who's just walked in off the street, have the right to question a doctor who's trained for 7 years and practiced for 5 more."

He carries on talking at you for 5 more minutes, but, to be honest, the shock hit you badly and you didn't really take in anything other than the first sentence. In fact, you didn't really hear much past 'real difficulties'.

Do you ask for time to let the shock sink in (go to **Section 121**)
or Ask for a third opinion. (go to **Section 274**)

—— Section 027 ——

September 18th 2015

The studio lights dim and Ant or maybe Dec, it's certainly one of them, announces "The winner of The Rex Factor, Scotland's search for a new monarch is…" Then they wait for dramatic tension.

Then they wait a bit more.

Then you start to wonder whether the autocue has stopped working.

Then they still haven't announced the winner.

"**Alun Robertson!**"

Of course it is. Alun steps forward in his white jump suit, a thousand rhinestones glinting in the studio lights, lifts off his sunglasses and says "Ah thankyouverymuch" before jerking his hips to the side.

You don't think it was really fair to the other contestants to let Aberdeen's top Elvis impersonator enter the competition. People already love his music and how could they resist the chance to make The King the king?

Oh well - you've no idea how this bodes for the future of Scotland, but you do know that the king's Christmas message should be really entertaining.

The End of the beginning

Should it actually happen in your reality, this ending is <u>NOT</u> covered by the 100% money back guarantee. You're not the king, I don't need to explain to you why it's not covered.

—— **Section 028** ——

You take a deep breath and, planting your feet firmly on either side of the stone, you take a strong two handed grip on the hilt of the sword and start to pull as hard as you can.

You pull and strain and strain and pull and pull until finally, with a massive strain and a forceful pull, you feel something pop out. Not the sword popping out of the stone but something popping out of you…

"Ow bloody hell!" you cry as you fall to the ground feeling the pain of a hernia.

The crowd gasps and someone in long robes rushes forward to aide you.

"Take some of this potion, sire" he says bringing a small vial of liquid to your lips.

"I'm not drinking that - it stinks."

"It may smell foul and taste almost as bad, but it will make you well again, so you will probably like it. Mayhaps not a lot, but you will like it."

Suddenly, with that last utterance, you realise that this man must be Merlin, the court magician.

Now knowing that the legend of the sword in the stone is true, you reason that the legends about Merlin must also be true. Here, knelt beside you, aiding you, could be the most powerful magician the world has ever seen. Surely just one sip of his potion and you will be back on your feet.

You drink the potion and wait to feel magically better.

And wait.

And you wait.

And then you start to feel a strange burning throughout your body. Every nerve ending is on fire. Your eyesight starts to dim. Everything sounds distant. Oh fuck - maybe the legends about Merlin weren't true.

Within minutes, you are dead.

The End

This ending is <u>NOT</u> covered by the 100% money back guarantee should it actually happen in your reality. If you're really stupid enough to put faith in a Paul Daniels wannabe based upon legends, dodgy TV series and Disney films then you really deserve everything that happens to you.

—— **Section 029** ——

You open the door and almost immediately know that you've entered the wrong room because the constant stream of inhuman screams and the charnel stench convince you that you have arrived in some sort of slaughterhouse.

That shocks you. But what really horrifies you is the realisation that this is no normal slaughterhouse for pigs, or sheep or cattle. No. Upon seeing that the processing line is manned by a collection of well known politicians, your old teachers and bosses you realise that this is the abattoir of your dreams.

You exit the room and decide to look for the polling station behind a different door. (go to **Section 083**)

—— Section 030 ——

Seeing BBC1 on a weekday daytime, your expectations plummet. But then you are surprised to see it's not a programme about making money from auctioning junk, a crap daytime quiz or *Doctors*.

Instead, seeing the title on the TV guide, you realise it must be a cribs style show looking at the many properties owned by 1980s/90s rap and dance sensation MC Hammer.

Your optimism is soon dashed as you realise that it's not that, it's just a Scotland-centric series of the property porn that makes up the BBC1 daytime output that isn't junk-auctioning rubbish, crap quizzes, the news or *Doctors*.

Still it's on now so you may as well watch a few minutes of *Homes Under McHammer*.

After a few minutes you're quite pleased that you did, as it helps you realise the many benefits of living in Scotland now that it has gained independence. You just hope that this isn't shown on TV across the rest of Britain or you could see a flood of sassenachs trying to buy property up here.

You eventually decide to turn off the TV and start to think about your future and the future of Scotland, and where the priorities lie for both of you.

Do you hope the government concentrates on the impending food crisis whilst sending a 'Buy Scottish!' message (go to **Section 079**)

or Spotting a chance to make some money, do you start investing in Scottish property (go to **Section 371**)

or Forget property! Something must be done about the impending food crisis and you know you're the person to do it (go to **Section 203**)

or Something needs to be done about the food crisis, so maybe you should start researching new foodstuffs (go to **Section 135**)

or I don't want to think about all this - just give me something random! (go to **Section 375**)

—— Section 031 ——

Thirty minutes later as you walk up to your front door, you're feeling wonderful. Of course you weren't going to die - it's just the daft way you painted your face. How could you have been so stupid?

Again.

Why oh why did you overreact like that? You should have known better after the last two times. This really does weigh heavy on your mind as you open your front door and Tilly comes bouncing up to you, glad to see her owner back home.

"Hiya Tilly! Good girl, who's a good girl? Shall I put you out some food?" you say whilst giving her a friendly rub down her back. You stop rubbing her back and gather up several handfuls of her fur - she's malting with the hot weather. Tilly doesn't want you to stop and keeps rubbing her head against you.

"No stop that - don't get carried away you'll hurt me with your horn."

You back off dismayed that you're covered in bright pink fur. You love Tilly, but hate having to use the pet hair roller on your clothes every five minutes. Still, in the great scheme of things, it's a small price to pay for having such a friendly unicorn.

You go to the cupboard in the kitchen where you keep the roller, hitting play on the phone as you walk past it.

"You have 3 new messages. Message one, 10:00 am Thursday." Announces the metallic voice before changing to what sounds like a young woman with an American accent "Hi. I'm calling from Mr Spielberg's office. Will you call as soon as you get this message." BEEP!

"Message two, 10:37 am Thursday." Then an irritated American male "Goddammit!" BEEP!

"Message three, 10:53 am Thursday." Followed by the same voice as the last message. "Look stop playing hard to get and call me. Schwarzenegger and Stallone are both pulling out unless you're in. We'll add a couple of zeroes to your fee. Hell you want a Caribbean island as a sweetener? You got it. Whatever you want - you got that too. Just agree to the role. You're box office gold and we need you." BEEP! "End of messages."

You've never heard Stephen Spielberg so irritated.

"Oh just a second... that's not right" you say out loud. The roller is in the cupboard to the left of the sink. You could have sworn you put it away in the cupboard directly under the sink when you last used it.

That's really weird. Rollers don't just move from cupboard to cupboard all by themselves. Not in real life. Oh, of course... This must be a dream.

Oh Bum. That means you're still asleep. Suppose you'll wake up sometime... (go to **Section 047**)

—— Section 032 ——

September 18th 65 million years BC

You arrive in the cretaceous period to a blazing sun and air that tastes fresher than anything you've ever experienced. You've appeared near the top of a hill in quite dense woodland, although, looking up towards the crest of the hill it seems that you're near the edge of the trees.

You walk up towards the hilltop and when you get there, emerging from the woods you set eyes upon a large plain spreading out below you. It's covered in low level plants and something else, perhaps the most amazing sight you've ever seen (or at least the most amazing you've seen since breakfast).

Grazing on the vegetation is a large herd of dinosaurs. You think back to the dinosaur books you read as a kid trying to identify what species they are.

They're not purple and irritating as fuck, so they aren't Barnies. They're on 4 legs and don't have long necks, so they're not brontosaurs. They don't have the bony plates down their back so they're not stegosaurs. They look a bit like Triceratops, but instead of 3 horns they have the large nose horn and 6 spikes out of the top of their bony neck frill. Styracosaurs - that's what they are!

Wow look at them! Magnificent massive beasts the like of which the world hasn't seen for millennia. Each one is bigger than a whole herd of cattle and they… Just a second… Each single Styracosaur is bigger than a herd of cows, which means they could feed as many people as a couple of herds of cows. And there are hundreds of them here in just this one herd of Styracosaurs.

Maybe this is the solution to modern hunger. Use the time travel technology to farm dinosaurs in the past and then transport the meat back to the 21st Century.

You return to the present to prepare a business plan - one that will place both you and Scottish technology as the saviours of mankind.

Two months later you're back in the past, mounted on the saddle of your Iguanodon steed, guiding a herd of Styracosaurs towards the dining rooms of the future.

It suddenly strikes you that this all seems vaguely familiar. You search your mind for a minute before hitting upon the source. It's almost like… *Flesh* in the British comic *2000AD*! Of course. It was pretty much the same scenario, even down to farming Styracosaurs in 65 million BC when they actually lived around 75.5 - 75 million BC…

Your already unbelievably-low respect for the **You Decide!** author sinks even further as you come to the conclusion that he's probably just ripping off comics from his youth. Then, from out of nowhere, almost as if written there by somebody else, the realisation hits you that he can't be ripping off comics that were published in 1977 since this is really, really, actually, truly happening to you in 65 million years BC.

Phew! That's a relief. 2000AD must have based their story upon your reality.

With your mind settled, your respect for the author at an all-time middling and your eyes peeled for a pissed-off one-eyed Tyrannosaur, you drive the herd of Styracosaurs onwards towards the Trans-Time base to return them to the starving megacities of the modern world.

The End

Should it actually happen in your reality, this ending is NOT covered by the 100% money back guarantee. By working out how to feed the world (which you did all by yourself and you weren't helped by any Betelgeusian called Tharg) you're the saviour of mankind. You probably have riches beyond your wildest dreams *and* you get to ride dinosaurs! Who cares if you get a couple of quid back?

—— Section 033 ——

September 18th 2024

You check over your pressurised suit one last time before speaking into the helmet mic. "Kirkcaldy Control this is Golden Eagle. I'm about to leave the command module. Over."

You wait for Kirkcaldy Mission Control to reply. And you wait. Any minute now. That's the problem with being the first man on Mars. SciFi films are always forgetting that radio waves take about 4 minutes to travel between the Earth and Mars, and that's when they're close to each other. If they're on opposite sides of the Sun it can take about 21 minutes. And that's one way. To hold a conversation you're looking between 8 and 42 minutes from asking a question to getting the response back. That makes any conversation pretty stilted and telephone sex practically impossible.

One of the biggest problems with exploring the red planet wasn't upsetting Roman gods of War or little green men but taking enough equipment that the mission was self-sustaining. It takes an extraordinary amount of energy to transport matter from Earth to Mars, so it wasn't practical unless some way was found to reduce the equipment that astronauts would need to take with them.

Sure it had been possible for a few years to get a man to Mars, but the SASA (Scottish Aeronautics and Space Administration) aim was to get a man to Mars alive and able to survive there. That's a much harder task. If nothing else you need a ridiculous amount of equipment and supplies just to produce edible food.

The big breakthrough came when chemical analysis of Martian rock samples acquired by robotic probes revealed that it could provide 98% of the nutrients needed to support human life. The only thing required to unlock this wonder food was to scientifically treat the rocks in high-temperature oil, a process that was most efficiently performed after cutting the rock into small ingots.

The only problem had been in naming the miracle foodstuff in such a way to avoid trademark infringement or being associated with decades of Scotophobic jokes. *That* task had taken much longer than it took scientists to discover how to process the rocks, but eventually Scottish ingenuity had prevailed.

And so now here you are, exactly 10 years after *Yes-Day* made SASA possible, about to be the first man to step onto the surface of Mars, and you're doing it on a diet of nothing but Deep-Fried Martian Bars.

Finally Kirkcaldy Control give you the go ahead.

You leave the command module, careful descend the ladder and finally step foot on the surface of Mars eager to plant the St Andrew's Cross flag and claim the planet for Scotland and the good of all Mankind.

Right now there's nothing, not even the clash between the blue flag and the red rocks, that can stop you being the proudest Scot in the universe.

The End

Should it actually happen in your reality, this ending is <u>NOT</u> covered by the 100% money back guarantee. You're a hero to the whole of planet Earth. Do you really want to ruin that image by pettily asking for a few quid back? Do you?

You do?! Really.

Well tough it's not going to happen.

—— Section 034 ——

You leave home with all 5 dogs eager for their morning walk. You sometimes just go around the block and let them 'do their business' but the referendum's made today a special day for you so why not treat the doggies as well?

You'll take them to a local park for a nice long walk and a chance to play fetch. You love playing fetch with your dogs nearly as much as they seem to like playing it with you. Each dog has their own toy and they're all very well trained to only ever try to return their own specific toys. It's important that even dogs are polite to each other when they're representing the countries of the Union.

Gwen has a squeaky red plastic dragon; Hamish a big green Nessie which used to squeak until he savaged it; Paddy loves his squeaky bomb-shaped toy just as much as Tommy loves his squeaky red telephone box. Britannia doesn't have a squeaky toy. For her you had custom-made 7-sided frisbee printed to look just like a 50p coin with the picture of Britannia on it.

You're happily playing with them on the playing fields at the park, when, in the distance, you see someone half-stagger onto the pitch. Something doesn't seem quite right about them so you carry on playing fetch, but keep an eye on the odd man.

As he continues his odd stagger towards you, you realise that he seems to have a strangely blue face and his almost-unaware gait is reminiscent of nothing less than the zombies in TV programmes like *The Walking Dead.*

Do you call the dogs back to you and quickly leave (go to **Section 195**) or Carry on playing with them (go to **Section 402**)

—— Section 035 ——

Aaaaaaargh!

You can't stand thinking about it for soooooo long.

The stress is just too much. How are you meant to decide the future of an entire nation? It's not fair - you're only human. What if you make a mistake? What if you end up wrecking Scotland's future. What if you do that and the press finds out it was all your fault? You'll be hounded in the street. People will throw things at you. You'll probably be regarded lower than Rolf Harris or Stuart Hall. OH GOD!

You can't take it…

You pick up the teeny tiny pencil and go to put a cross in a box to get it over with, but instead a sudden panic makes you accidentally draw a picture of a dog urinating against a tree across your ballot paper.

Hmmmm… I suppose that counts as a spoilt paper.

Trying to salvage some slight respect rather than looking like a complete mentalist, you draw the word 'Tories' on the dog and 'Scotland' on the tree. You've still spoilt your paper but at least now it looks like some sort of political comment rather than just a bad stress reaction.

You fold the ballot paper and, without making eye contact with anybody, walk across the floor and pop the folded ballot in the box. The station attendants say something, but you ignore them and walk out quickly, embarrassed that they somehow know what you did.

For such a momentous historic vote it all seems like an anticlimax now.

All you can do is go home and carry on as normal until the results are announced. (go to **Section 321**)

—— Section 036 ——

You open the door and almost immediately know that you've entered the wrong room because you have walked onto some sort of model village, only it's not a village it's more like a model city.

The detail is amazing; there are skyscrapers, parks, docks, even little radio controlled cars and boats. You stomp over a building to pick up a toy bullet train.

Oh wow! The detail is even more impressive when you look at it really closely. There's even small model people at just the right scale.

Then you realise that some of the model people are running about. And making quiet model-volume screams.

"Wow! Just wow!" you think, "The models even act like real people. What will the Japanese think of next?"

Maybe you're feeling a bit dim today, but it takes about 5 minutes, and an untold loss of life, before you realise that they are not models but real people that you are terrorising and killing.

You're not sure exactly what the door you came through did, but you do know that even Alice didn't have it this bad when the looking glass altered her size.

You exit the room as quick as you can, to avoid more bloodshed, and decide to look for the polling station behind a different door. (go to **Section 083**)

—— Section 037 ——

You wait...

You're already bored of waiting. The only thing to do is worry or watch the other people, but that's just annoying.

Take those two youths over by the blood donor poster for example.

"A pint! That's most of me arm innit!"

"No idea mate - I don't do that old pints and ounces shit. Ain't a pint just under half a litre?"

"No idea - it's just a quote from some old Alfred Hitchcock film me gran told me about once. Hitchcock's in hospital an' he sees a poster asking for blood donors to give a pint an' he says 'A pint! That's most of me arm innit?' Me gran thought it were proper funny."

"I s'pose people used to laugh at anything after the war."

Thankfully at this point your name is called by the nurse from reception and she leads you through to an examination cubicle.

DEAD CAT TIME

Has anyone fed Tiddles today? No? I'll see how he is then.

He's fine and ready to play! (go to **Section 151**)
or He's fine and ready for some food! (go to **Section 343**)
or He's fine... if you didn't want a living cat. (go to **Section 133**)

—— Section 038 ——

September 21st 2014

Within days of *Yes-Day*, President Salmond had access to military might possibly equal, or even greater, than the rest of the UK (rUK).

It wasn't clear quite how Scotland compared to rUK as the split of assets, both military and domestic, was complicated and negotiation was ongoing.

President Salmond certainly had access to the Trident nuclear missile launch codes and he was making a case for getting half the army, navy and air force. The situation was chaotic and the UKs military had no idea who they belonged to.

Scotland seized it's chance in the confusion. Learning from Sun Tzu who said "When the enemy is confused do not hesitate to kick them in the bollocks", President Salmond ordered the UK military to invade England in the name of the independent Scotland.

The offensive had the full support of Scottish nationalists still present in the British military. Support in the rest of the military was split pretty much 50-50, sometimes within the same regiment resulting in military units fighting themselves but unsure why they were doing it. In at least twelve cases of mental disorder the split was in the same person leading to self-inflicted injury.

In the general confusion, the small core of Scottish loyalists was enough to steam-roll through England on course for London.

Learning from the Russian President Vladimir Putin, President Salmond claimed that his military forces were across the border due to a navigational accident right up until his tanks finally pulled up at the gates at the end of Downing Street. It seemed a bit petty pretending at that late point, so he came clean and declared England's capital under his rule.

By midnight the whole of rUK belonged to Scotland.

Of course there were international repercussions, but again President Salmond had learnt from Mr Putin and easily avoided too much fuss by controlling both nukes and something that other countries rely on. Unlike Russia's gas, for President Salmond this was the financial institutions in the City of London. This gave him so much international clout that even Mr Putin was slightly wary of upsetting him, as too much Russian money was secreted away in the square mile.

Edinburgh ruled over the country officially called ***The United Kingdom of Scotland, Wales and Northern Ireland I Think That's All I didn't Forget Anyone Did I? Oh Yes - England Haha!*** For the next 500 years.

After 500 years England voted for independence spurred on by the mostly-fictitious film *MediocreHeart*, which told the tale of how, in 2023 the rebel leader Ed Miliband painted half his face red, the other half white and made a rousing patriotic speech about fighting for English independence:

"*They may take our things and other things, in fact pretty much everything, but they'll never take our freedom - only they sort of did, didn't they... well they'll probably never make us cry... again... especially if my brother David helps us.*"

And to think that the speech was beefed up for the film. It's no surprise the English rebellion of 2023 failed.

The End

Should it actually happen in your reality, this ending is NOT covered by the 100% money back guarantee. You've got control of the kingdom.. You're just never happy are you?

—— **Section 039** ——

You open the door and the first thing that you notice is that you can hear what sounds like a cold war numbers station playing from a nearby radio. There are bursts of some classical music interrupted every minute or so by a child's voice reading out a series of 27 numbers and colours. Every minute it is the same sequence that the child says.

Sat behind the desk waiting to hand out ballot papers is a gorilla in a traditional male Greek dress. You walk over to it and once you have confirmed your identity, the gorilla gives you your ballot paper, points to the individual polling booths and says "You can vote over there, then put the folded ballot paper in this box when you've finished" in perfect Swahili.

Of course that's not the weird bit.

It's not weird that there are 10 pairs of ballroom dancers dancing to the numbers station, each with a number on their back and a man-sized fly judging them. It's not weird that the obviously female gorilla is in male dress and is wearing different colour eye liner on each eye. It's not weird that neither shade matches her skin tone. It's not even weird that the dancers are dancing in 4/4 time but the classical music is clearly a waltz.

The weird bit is that you understood the gorilla perfectly well and you don't even speak Swahili.

As you walk across the room to the polling booth, it is with the weight of a country's destiny bearing down on your shoulders… (go to **Section 393**)

—— **Section 040** ——

You back away…

Retreating from the primitives noises. You've no idea who or what is up ahead, but there's definitely a group and you'd rather play the odds and head back towards the gigantic, but presumably solo, creature behind you on the path.

But as you cautiously back away as quietly as you can, you step on a twig that cracks loudly. Immediately the primitives stopped their grunting for a moment before they start lots of quick hushed grunts that you can only just make out.

If you didn't know any better you'd say that the grunts was some sort of primitive language, although you never heard any modern tribe using language anywhere near so animalistic.

Suddenly you hear movement from the apemen - they've obviously heard you and are coming to get you. You start running again. Running as fast as you can whilst looking back over your shoulder for your pursuers.

You can't help but think that looking back may have been a mistake as you run headlong into a Tyrannosaurus Rex which takes no time at all in grabbing you in its jaws and whipping its head from side to side, rending your flesh asunder and snapping your spine as if it were no more than the twig you broke just moments ago.

Yes, in retrospect, running back along the path and not looking where you were going was probably the wrong thing to do.

You are dead.

The End

This ending is covered by the 100% money back guarantee should it actually happen in your reality. To reclaim the cost of your book please personally present the publishers with irrefutable evidence of your death at the hands, or rather teeth, of a Tyrannosaurus Rex in the early dawn of mankind alongside proof of purchase. This offer is voided by travelling back to the present or any return to life or sentience by any method including but not limited to advanced scientific methods, CPR, homeopathy, reincarnation, magic, OCP cyborg programmes, rites involving essential saltes and supernatural possession.

—— Section 041 ——

HAM TV is showing one of it's usual cheap documentaries full of complete rubbish. It's odd that History And Myth Television markets itself as 'No porkies, just HAM' when it's usually full of porkies and unsubstantiated claims.

Today's show is looking at the history of ancient Britain and some of the monsters that (according to the show) almost totally utterly irrefutably existed and roamed the countryside. These range from the benevolent Loch Ness Monster, through the giant haggis of Aulde Dundee to the petrifying cockatrice, evil goblins and wailing banshees. Finishing with the near-total godless evil of the goblin-banshee, once thought to roam the land until vanquished by King Arthur and the Knights of the Round Table.

The idea of earth and fertility deities is mentioned. The green man figures heavily as does the ancient practice of human sacrifice to appease the gods following a particularly bad harvest. It all seems barbaric that people used to believe in this, but you suppose the ancient gods were no crueller than a supposedly loving god that drowned the world in a hissy fit, and many people have no issue with believing in the power of the latter.

You eventually decide to turn off the TV and start to think about your future and the future of Scotland, and where the priorities lie for both of you.

Inspired by HAM TV do you personally go looking for Nessie (go to **Section 401**)

or Do you devote your life to theoretical research into time travel, in the hope that one day you could use it to travel to the past chasing the beasts of myth (go to **Section 249**)

or Maybe you could use Scotland's mythology and natural beauty to relieve gullible idiots of their money (go to **Section 187**)

or I don't want to think about all this - just give me something random! (go to **Section 375**)

—— Section 042 ——

Suddenly...

The doors of reality burst open and, knowing that this section is not linked to anywhere in the book, the author takes advantage of the supposed privacy to let his real thoughts spill out.

If you're reading this in the Kindle version I either fucked up a link or you were turning pages rather than using the links and back to navigate between sections. You may have been doing that looking for Easter eggs like this - if so Well done!

Given that this book jumps about and (hopefully) plays a little with 4th walls and notions of reality it makes some sort of sense that the supposed Foreword/Afterword/FAQs/About the Author/etc. are all fictions, made up with very little truth between them. Whilst here in the middle of what most would consider the fiction is a section of truth. Having said that... it's all truth in some reality, remember.

But in the reality that I think we both probably exist in, I'd like to say thanks to the very small number of people who read early versions of my mindspasms. It wasn't easy getting my head around the flow of the book (seriously - you should see my multicoloured flowcharts covering several sheets of A1 in rollerball scrawl...) and they often had to read half finished, disjointed segments with broken links and lots of parts ending abruptly with a *[TBC]* or *To Be Continued*.

I'd also like to thank you for buying this book and obviously reading at least some of it to get to this page! Hopefully you've been enjoying it, in the main. I know that not all parts will appeal to all people, but they say write what you know so it was inevitable that I did a dimension-hopping, time travelling mix of bad puns, toilet humour and assorted mindfuckery.

Please keep an eye out for my next works. I've a collection of short stories and oddities currently in the works and a dark humour novel set firmly in reality. I know that you should enjoy them as:

If you enjoyed this, then some of the humour will obviously be similar as it's from the same deranged mind, but should be more cohesive and less puerile.

If you didn't enjoy this, then you'll find the other works more cohesive and less puerile, though with some elements of similar humour.

That just leaves people who really love the disjointed swearing and knob gags not liking my new works so much, but they're already fully served by many comedy clubs and TV shows.

By the way, you can hopefully find out about my future works at http://www.judgementdave.com or @Judgement_Dave at http://twitter.com/Judgement_Dave - I may even get a mailing list going soon…

Take care & have fun wandering through the multiverse, wherever it may take you!

Dave

—— Section 043 ——

September 18th 2022

In the years after *Yes-Day,* Scotland managed quite well despite the pressures of many people from the South of England moving North of the border as rising sea-levels swallowed much of the Home Counties.

Luckily feeding the masses of environmental refugees, many of whom had lost everything, was no great issue as an enterprising Scottish company had recently devised a wonderfood that was well on it's way to solving the world's hunger problem.

Soyalent's breakthrough was a range of colour-coded products made from a secret formula of soya mix and other additional foods to vary the texture and flavour. The company was booming after launching the Haggis flavoured Soyalent Brown and Neeps and Tatties White flavour and needed as many people as possible to work in it's ever expanding Haggis and vegetable farms.

This was the perfect chance to kill 2 birds with one stone - the dispossessed Southerners from around London were given jobs and housing in the gigantic Soyalent farms. Production soared and everyone was happy.

But then the company launched a mysterious new product Soyalent

Green.

Nobody knew what it contained as the recipe was a closely guarded secret, but surprisingly it sold very well in Scotland and was soon launched worldwide. Then one day, the newspapers broke with the front page story that blew the lid on the secret ingredient that was so unpalatable to many that hearing the news was enough to turn some people's stomaches.

But despite Soyalent Green being made from sprouts, sales remained high even after it started listing it on the packet.

Soyalent continued developing new products like Soyalent Blue, Yellow and Tartan, each formulated to a top secret recipe. It continued to expand it's farms and workforce. It continued it's march towards eradicating all world hunger.

Everything seemed fine.

Until 5 minutes ago.

Then, you were disturbed by a banging on the door of your abode.

You answer the door and your friend, who works at the Soyalent Factory, looks suspiciously like Charlton Heston and hasn't been mentioned until now, bursts into your home in a panic.

"You've got to help me. I think they're after me - I got too close. I know the truth."

"What truth?" you ask.

"The truth the Soyalent Corporation don't want you to know. The oceans are dying. The plankton is dying. We can't feed ourselves on just haggis, neeps an' tatties. It's people. You gotta tell em!" he grabs you in panic and, falling to his knees, shouts "***Soyalent Tartan is People!***"

"Auch is that all, yer numpty? Soyalent Tartan's no people - it's English Tories. Look. It even says so on the packet."

You show him the pack where it clearly states *20% pure English Conservative.*

"Ah so it is... Fry some up then, I'm starving. Not had anything all day as I was worried it'd be unethical to eat people."

You both laugh and enjoy a good Soyalent Tartan fry up - making sure, as advised, that you wash it well first to remove any lingering seediness or stubborn self-interest.

The End

Should it actually happen in your reality, this ending is <u>NOT</u> covered by the 100% money back guarantee. But you should count yourself lucky in other ways. Obviously being alive with a fun friend who works at Soyalent and can get you it cheap... What did you think I meant?

— Section 044 —

You suddenly realise that you really take the whole issue of Scottish independence very, *very*, ***very*** seriously.

You don't really consider it a fit subject matter for any form of humour. Laughing about the referendum and your homeland's future would be like laughing about cancer, sex pests in 1970s light entertainment or racism. And you never do that.

No.

You stopped joking about those things after what happened when your mum raised money for gran's chemotherapy by performing with the Black and White Minstrels. She'd arranged it all by writing to a TV show. If only she hadn't worn a skirt when she received her 'Jim Fixed it for me' badge off the dodgy old bugger himself. She was so traumatised she was happy to be given a shoulder to cry on from that nice antipodean artist playing with his didgeridoo…

No - that taught you to never ever consider serious subjects a laughing matter.

And that's a view that will never change. (go to **Section 353**)

or But then again maybe just this once won't do any harm if you don't tell anyone (as the now-disgraced entertainer once said to your mum). (go to **Section 019**)

— Section 045 —

You open the door and almost immediately know that you've entered the wrong room as someone says "Ah Bozza, about time".

Your eyes adjust to the dim light and you're shocked to see a bulbous mass of jelly-like flesh strapped to a harness above a large map of the British Isles. Surrounding the dangling obscenity stand several leather clad gimp-slaves who occasionally move in to lick and caress the gelatinous abomination. As they do strange liquids, brown, white and golden yellow, occasionally spurt out from the mass, squirting all over the map except for over the home counties.

"C'mon Bozza, get your kit off we've left London for you. It'll feel unloved if it doesn't get some Tory-loving soon."

Suddenly you recognise the voice and realise that you are gazing upon the true form of Prime Minister David Cameron, and the depraved gimp-servants tending to his bloated corpulence are none other than Gove, Hunt, Osborne and The Clegg.

You put on your best Boris impersonation and say "Back in a mo - just realised I forgot to lock my bike. What a silly old fool I am."

"Well hurry up, Bozza, You know I can't fuck the entire country all by myself."

You quickly exit the room and decide to look for the polling station behind a different door. (go to **Section 083**)

—— Section 046 ——

September 18th 2017

After the referendum Scotland soon got it's act together. The power of independence-driven positivity lead Scots to great success in sport, business, culture and progressive tartan design. It's many achievements made it the envy of the world.

It was almost as if luck shone on Scotland. As if fate was being kind. As if the stars were right...

Last month the strange dreams started. Artists, poets, writers and those with any creative leanings started to have weird dreaming terrors that befell them nightly. The worst, most hideous, yet most realistic, nightmares of sleeping gods and tentacular behemoths.

Last week the dreams abruptly ended on the same night a massive earthquake in the Pacific sent Tsunamis crashing into California, South America, Australasia and Eastern Asia. The death toll was enormous.

Today a new island was spotted in the South Pacific. The spotter plane sent to survey it reported gigantic stone buildings whose geometry didn't look quite right, almost as if they had been built by Salvador Dali. The reports were cut short suddenly, mid-sentence and the plane has not been seen since. Airforce press releases are not overly hopefully.

Tomorrow the world ends and it won't matter a damn who has Trident.

The End

Should it actually happen in your reality, this ending is NOT covered by the 100% money back guarantee. Money won't help you. If you can't beat them join them.

Fhtagn! Cthulhu fhtagn! Ïa Shub Niggurath!

—— Section 047 ——

You wake up...

Which is odd as you could have sworn that you'd already woken up today. Oh well - maybe you had a strange dream about waking up. It wouldn't surprise you if you had - you feel knackered, as if you've been living another life instead of sleeping.

"Oh my head. What was I thinking last night? I'm not 18 anymore. I need more sleep... another 24 hours should do. What time is it anyway? Hell... What day is it?"

Just a second; you really do have a strong sense of deja vu...

It's Thursday September 18th isn't it. The day of destiny. The day of the referendum.

I'd best try re-remembering exactly what it was that I did last night.

Did you stay up most of the night drinking single malt and watching Braveheart? (go to **Section 016**)

or Maybe you overdosed on Earl Grey while watching recorded highlights of Last Night of the Proms and Downton Abbey. (go to **Section 126**)

or Were you one of those that went out clubbing and partying and didn't plan on giving the referendum a second thought? (go to **Section 183**)

or Did you spend the night re-reading all the referendum literature and debating the pros and cons of independence with a group of well-informed Scots? (go to **Section 207**)

—— Section 048 ——

September 18th 2015

Before the referendum, the new Scottish government had pledged to get rid of Trident and that was a pledge that it intended to keep. Hopefully before the first anniversary.

The big problem wasn't really the rest of the UK (rUK) so much as it was England. They were refusing to be helpful and trying to insist that Scotland must keep them for now as they had nowhere else to store them. Holyrood insisted that it was more a case of having nowhere else that it wanted them, rather than nowhere to actually store them. But that wasn't Scotland's problem anymore.

An ultimatum was delivered to remove them before September 18th 2015.

So it came to pass that on September 11th the English military forces were allowed into Scotland to remove the nuclear weapons, finally clearing Scottish territory by 20:00 on the evening of the 17th.

So today, the first anniversary of *Yes-Day*, sees Scotland throw it's biggest party since winning independence. Bigger than any Christmas, St Andrew's day, Hogmanay or Burns Night.

It is as if all of Scotland came out to celebrate a year of independence and a nuclear-free Scotland, regardless of whether they'd been for or against independence or nukes a year before.

Sure the first year hadn't all gone smoothly. There were still issues with currency, membership of the EU, membership of NATO, international alliances and trade and so on, but in the main most people are happy that Scotland has its own rule.

The party goes on late into the night and is only really just starting to slowly wind down at dawn the next day.

It was then, at dawn, that the English struck with brutal efficiency.

Fighters dominated the skies over Edinburgh and Glasgow. Tanks rolled over the border facing little resistance from the few extremely-pissed revellers who were still up or the many hungover Scots that awoke from the commotion.

Holyrood was caught over a barrel. It didn't have any nuclear capability to defend itself, but the rUK forces had Trident backing them up if needed… Not having negotiated membership of NATO or the EU really hurt as well, it just wasn't enough trying to call in allies from the International Federation of Salmon Farmers. It looked dire. Even masonic handshakes and Eton old boys contacts didn't seem to help…

Within 11 hours the English invasion had forced Holyrood into submission and within days Scotland became a UK satellite state and the home to it's nuclear deterrent.

Independence was never meant to work out like this.

The End

Should it actually happen in your reality, this ending is <u>NOT</u> covered by the 100% money back guarantee. Ah sorry - you're Scottish aren't you? Under the terms of your surrender to the UK all money back guarantees in **You Decide!** books are now void. Sorry.

—— Section 049 ——

You neck your drink and say "Get us another, will ya mate? About time we have some shots an all."

"Another? No wonder you don't seem bothered about the referendum" said Andy, "you can't drink a vote can you?"

"What you saying? You think I'm a fuckin' alcoholic do yer?"

Andy just says "no. But if it looks like a duck, walks like a duck and quacks like a duck then it is a fella developing drink dependency issues."

Maybe you have had quite a lot to drink because you know Andy's your mate and isn't trying to be nasty, but you really don't like what he's saying and take great offence at it. You give him a little shove and warn him "Watch what yer saying."

But as he doesn't immediately apologise profusely the drink gets the better of you and you start shoving him more and before long things have escalated. (go to **Section 197**)

—— Section 050 ——

ScotParli TV is showing the Scottish parliament debating national defence strategy, whether to actually get rid of Trident and what timescale to do so if they do.

Despite a lot of talk about getting rid of nuclear weapons before *Yes-Day* its suddenly been realised that allowing them to still be stationed in Scotland provides some benefits. Mainly that Scotland can always kick them out if England messes her about and also that it gives Holyrood some say over their use, they could even arrange an effective veto of their use if England ever got uppity and close to the brink of using them.

Maybe it would be better for world peace and Scotland's future if she keeps Trident stationed there. It may also mean that Scotland wouldn't need so many conventional forces as they may need if they got rid of 'the bomb'.

You're sure it's all very interesting, but not as interesting as what's on the other side, so you change channel.

Maybe you see what's on Channel 5 (go to **Section 269**)
or You decide to watch BizBites TV (go to **Section 064**)

—— Section 051 ——

You wake up...

Feeling drained after a night of fitful sleep. Your slumbering mind had been full of wild ideas about delivering a moving speech envisioning a future where your four young children could be judged by the content of their character and *not* by the colour of their skin.

You remember looking down at your children, seeing those eight little eyes gazing back up at you from your youngest girl's face, and wondering why oh why they had been born such mutated freaks with orange polkadots all over their delicate, fur-covered, purple, many-limbed bodies.

Your dream must have been brought on by the St Agur cheese you ate before bed. Why else would you have had such a wacky fantasy? The whole dream was bizarre. I mean, you could understand 8-eyed mutants roaming the earth, it's only to be expected after years of atom bomb tests. You could believe that you'd fight for mutant rights, just like in your X-Men dreams.

That's all quite believable. But there's no way that you want ***four*** children.

"Oh my head. What was I thinking last night? I'm not 18 anymore. I need more sleep… another 24 hours should do. What time is it anyway? Hell… What day is it?"

The bedside clock tells you it's only quarter to seven - far too early to be awake and feeling like this, especially on a Thursday. Just a second… Thursday? Isn't something happening today? No. Not the bin collection - that's tomorrow isn't it?

Thursday, Thursday, Thursday. Nope - nothing's materialising from your still-fogged memory.

Thursday… Thursday… Thursday?

Shit! THURSDAY!

It's Thursday September 18th! It's today. The day of destiny. The day of the referendum.

Whilst still not feeling 100 per cent, or even 54 per cent, you feel the weight of history on you and so somehow manage to leave your bed, still struggling to remember just what it was that you did last night.

Did you stay up most of the night drinking single malt and watching Braveheart? (go to **Section 016**)

or Maybe you overdosed on Earl Grey while watching recorded highlights of Last Night of the Proms and Downton Abbey. (go to **Section 126**)

or Were you one of those that went out clubbing and partying and didn't plan on giving the referendum a second thought? (go to **Section 183**)

or Did you spend the night re-reading all the referendum literature and debating the pros and cons of independence with a group of well-informed Scots? (go to **Section 207**)

—— Section 052 ——

You can't wait around here like everyone else. You could be about to die a horribly painful death. Surely that's more urgent than amateur footballers with sprained ankles, kids with their heads stuck in pans and people missing fingers from industrial accidents.

You just need to make the nurse see it that way.

Do you argue that you may be about to drop down dead. (go to **Section 226**)

or Ask how long the wait will be. (go to **Section 252**)

or Just state that you "need attention right now." (go to **Section 361**)

—— Section 053 ——

September 18th 2025 (ish)

The rain pours down on you as you stand in the centre of the ruined city. Trees grow out of the windows and on the rooftops of the decaying buildings around you. It's amazing how quickly nature can claw back land from mans efforts to tame it. To eradicate it.

You remember standing here when the festival was on, a month before *Yes-Day.* Back then this courtyard was a writhing mass of people coming to and from the many comedy shows at the venue. Now you are the only person here, maybe the only one left anywhere in the former capital, and the writhing mass is made of so many grasses, bushes, trees and the numerous insects, mammals and birds that now call it home.

Everybody knew that *Yes-Day* was making history, but no-one appreciated quite how momentous it was. The beginning of the end followed that day as surely as Spring follows Winter.

Back in 2014, independence brought a host of problems that hadn't been properly addressed during the pre-referendum debates. Not least of these was the question of currency and the Scottish share of UK debt.

Westminster had held firm that they would not allow the new nation to keep on using the Pound Sterling (also known as GBP - the Great British Pound). In return Scotland had refused to honour it's share of the UK national debt.

It was much like a married couple divorcing with a joint bank account and joint debts and one side insisting it wouldn't take it's share of the debt unless it could keep using the joint bank account. Yes much like a divorce, only far, far more bitter and twisted.

The Scottish people didn't seem to fancy moving to the Euro, and it still wasn't certain whether Scotland would automatically join the EU. So what currency would Scotland use? Eventually it decided to create its own new currency and quickly established the central Gaelic Bank with its own coin mint at Stirling.

Even though they kept the initial exchange rate at 1:1, it was a massive job changing from Pounds Sterling (£ or GBP - the Great British Pound) to Pounds Stirling (£ or GBP - the Gaelic Bank Pound). All items and services from Scottish shops and companies had to be repriced at the same number of pounds, causing literally minutes of disruption.

But before long Scots were happily using the Pound Stirling. The problems began shortly after.

The international money markets didn't have high confidence in Scottish financial practices after Scotland refused to honour its share of the UK debt. As a result, the Scottish government faced high rates for borrowing and the value of Pound Stirling dived. This would have been bad for Scotland, but due to international confusion between £ and £, between GBP and GBP and between Pounds Sterling and Pounds Stirling, transactions across the world were accidentally being made using the wrong currency.

Before long the international economy descended into utter chaos. The business world collapsed and food production and distribution went with it. Utility services ground to a halt. Nobody had fuel or food or even basic internet connectivity.

Whole families died - succumbing to famine, dehydration or disease. Many ordinary people committed suicide as they couldn't cope with the new world disorder.

Around the world, bankers and stockbrokers killed themselves - not from shame, like decent human beings might, but because their bonuses were now worthless. But at least they still killed themselves - they say that every cloud…

Still, despite that silver lining everything else in the world turned to shit. So now you stand here. You think it took about 11 years since the referendum to get to this point, but you have no way of knowing in the absence of working watches and calendars.

It took thousands of years to create civilisation but just 11 years for the fall of mankind.

You realise it's ironic that the Scottish independence movement was so spurred on by *Braveheart* and yet it ended up more like the post-apocalyptic *Mad Max*… It's almost as if your fate has been decided by Mel Gibson's life. Oh well, you may be the last human alive for all you know, but at least you never got drunk and offended any jews.

The End

Should it actually happen in your reality, this ending is <u>NOT</u> covered by the 100% money back guarantee. Face it there's no-one alive to refund your money and money's useless anyway. So it's irrelevant whether it's GBP or GBP.

—— Section 054 ——

Oh no! It's a total disaster!

You go to the fridge and realise that you only have one pack of bacon left. That's a mere 8 rashers. It's barely worth it…

Then you realise that there's another 40 or so packs of rashers in your secondary bacon-only fridge. Phew! That was close. A lack of bacon could have seriously ruined your whole day. You're not superstitious but how exactly would the 'Better Together' campaign win if all the baconic omens were against it?

The annoying thing is that when the history books recall the historic victory that the Better Together 'NO' campaign won, it's highly unlikely that any of them will mention the pivotal role you played with your bacon supply.

No. It's infuriating to think that the only mention you'll probably get is in some sort of weird book like a **You Decide!** Or similar.

This really annoys you. You're possibly playing a more important part in keeping the Union together than David Cameron or Alistair Darling.

You only manage to stop feeling angry by eating another 5 packs of bacon.

Once you've had your fill of bacon, you go for a shower to freshen up before you choose what to wear on this eventful day. (go to **Section 258**)

—— Section 055 ——

You wait…

Dum-de-dum. This is boring. You hate queues at the best of times but it's even worse when you're ill and waiting to be seen by a doctor.

Dum-de-dum.

It's amazing how boring waiting rooms are. Almost as if they are designed to make waiting as bad as possible so as to deter people from bothering hospitals with their petty injuries, illnesses and other life-threatening conditions.

Dum-de-dum-de-dum.

DEAD CAT TIME

I'm too bored to even make up a cat name and some possible fates for the cat. Just pick one of the following three boring options.

Option One (go to **Section 289**)
or Option Two (go to **Section 331**)
or Option Three (go to **Section 107**)

—— Section 056 ——

Food+ TV is showing '*Tomorrow's Dinner?*' a programme about the anticipated future food requirements of the world. It makes for alarming viewing, as the human population is projected to grow exponentially but food production, especially meat production, won't be able to keep up.

Dark stuff, but there is light at the end of the tunnel.

One of the possible solutions is to grow artificial meat in labs. Another is to make soya-like miracle foodstuffs. Another 'out-there' idea is to use genetic engineering to make much larger animals to farm for their meat.

An alternate approach would be to try dissuading people from wanting to eat meat, as it's much easier and more efficient to grow food crops, but you don't see much hope of that happening since the horse-meat scandal did little to put people off meat.

You're pleased that there is some hope, but whatever solution is (hopefully) found you know there could be some hard times ahead for humanity.

Which isn't what you want to be concentrating on whilst you're still optimistic for the future after *Yes-Day*, so you change channel.

You start watching BBC1 (go to **Section 030**)
or You turn over to watch SciTech TV (go to **Section 228**)

—— Section 057 ——

Nothing at the shop grabbed you so you decide to save your money and wear the same old BDSM bondage gear you usually wear at weekend parties.

It's odd, but whatever you wear, whether a normal business suit or jeans and tee-shirt, you never feel quite as comfortable as you do when wearing a full-body, studded leather gimp suit complete with ball gag and vibrating anal intruder.

That just leaves the question of which of your many, many, many leather gimp suits to wear, which of your numerous ball gags and which vibrating butt plug from your connoisseur's collection .

As it is such a special day, you finally decide to go with the shiniest, spikiest leather gimp suit, the most-studded ball gag and the Dream Ream Monthly editors pick 2013 - the 10-speed 8-inch rectal wrecker, choice of royalty and TV celebrities alike.

You put it all on and gaze in the bedroom mirror. Yes the outfit's overall appearance is just right. It makes it clear that you're confident, adventurous and playful in a slightly scary way.

But most of all it states that you're a totally and utterly depraved deviant. Just the look you wanted.

Eventually, when you feel sexy and dominant enough, off you go to the polling station (go to **Section 300**)

—— Section 058 ——

On Gaia TV there's a show about how mankind has been mistreating planet Earth and discussing whether or not it's too late to save our home.

You're undecided about global warming. It's hard to really know what effect man has had on the planet's climate as it's hard to define a fixed climate for the planet.Despite that, irrespective of whether global warming is man-made or down to entirely natural solar and planetary fluctuations, you've always found it hard to decide if it's net effect for the planet is good or bad.

On the bad side it could be the start of an ecological disaster that kills off much of the planet's current life.

On the good side it's certainly made people more environmentally aware, so may actually lead to us avoiding future ecological disasters that kill off much of the planet's life.

On the bad side, it could mean higher temperatures and more sunshine and so more skin cancer for your redheaded countrymen.

On the good side, higher temperatures and more sunshine would mean that you could wear a kilt without freezing your giblets.

On the bad side, rising sea-levels could see lots the English home counties disappearing under water.

On the good side, rising sea-levels could see the English home counties disappearing under water.

Overall it's a really complex problem, with multiple possible causes and effects.

Eventually you decide to change channels.

Do you watch BBC1 after crossing your fingers and hoping it's showing something other than property porn, junk being auctioned, a crap quiz or Doctors. (go to **Section 219**)

or Should you turn over to Skye Living+1 (go to **Section 390**)

—— Section 059 ——

You wake up...

You feel groggy, from a troubled night of strange dreams, made even stranger as you can't actually remember eating cheese before bed.

Whilst you were sleeping, someone has set up a highland games meet in your head and legions of Morris dancers have crashed it, starting a bloody battle of handkerchiefs versus cabers.

"Oh my head. What was I thinking last night? I'm not 18 anymore. I need more sleep… another 24 hours should do.[7] What time is it anyway? Hell… What day is it?"

The bedside clock tells you it's only quarter to seven - far too early to be awake and feeling like this, especially on a Thursday. Just a second… Thursday? Isn't something happening today? No. Not the bin collection - that's tomorrow isn't it?

Thursday, Thursday, Thursday. Nope - nothing's materialising from your still-fogged memory.

Thursday… Thursday… Thursday?

Shit! THURSDAY!

It's Thursday September 18th! It's today. The day of destiny. The day of the referendum.

Whilst still not feeling 100 per cent, or even 54 per cent, you feel the weight of history on you and so somehow manage to leave your bed, still struggling to remember just what it was that you did last night.

Did you stay up most of the night drinking single malt and watching Braveheart? (go to **Section 016**)

or Maybe you overdosed on Earl Grey while watching recorded highlights of Last Night of the Proms and Downton Abbey. (go to **Section 126**)

or Were you one of those that went out clubbing and partying and didn't plan on giving the referendum a second thought? (go to **Section 183**)

or Did you spend the night re-reading all the referendum literature before debating the pros and cons of independence with a group of well-informed Scots? (go to **Section 207**)

or Were you so worried about Scotland's fate that you decided to end it all rather than face an uncertain future, and so took a slow acting poison that should kill you any minute now… (go to **Section 231**)

or Whilst trying to remember what you did last night, do you suddenly realise that you have an exam that you've not revised for today and race out of your home to get to the exam so quickly that halfway there you realised that you hadn't put any trousers on? (go to **Section 312**)

—— Section 060 ——

You get some funny looks on the way, but most people seem to accept that on such a momentous day some people might dress up and treat it like some sort of party. At least there's no trouble and eventually you get to the polling station, walk up to the doors and pause.

You always thought that polling stations are places full of wonder and promise for the future. The almost-mystical locations that can alter a nations fate. Each one a powerful nexus where all possible destinies of the country intersect, just waiting for the public will to select one single possibility and to transform it into reality. Places of truly amazing, almost miraculous, transformative power.

But really they are just local primary schools that have swapped the kids for a naff sign saying 'POLLING STATION'.

Finally you approach the doors and prepare yourself to step inside.

DEAD CAT TIME

Yes it's time to peek inside Schrödinger's box and see how well Jess is…

Hello Jess. Where's Pat? (go to **Section 013**)

or Hello Pat. Where's Jess gone? (go to **Section 311**)

or That's not a cat that's George Galloway! (go to **Section 177**)

or Jess is curled up asleep, blissfully unaware of their role in the future of Scotland. (go to **Section 110**)

or Postcat Jess. Postcat Jess. Postcat Jess has left a mess! (go to **Section 366**)

or OMG! Jess is dead! Pat will be upset. (go to **Section 288**)

—— Section 061 ——

You always thought that it was a shame that Giant Pandas had become completely extinct, but now, with your time travel machine, you can undo that. You could travel back to a time when Giant Pandas were still common, when they roamed every high street, and bring some back to the present. If you brought enough then they would breed and once more the world would know the magnificent creatures.

Stopping only to get a giant bear-sized butterfly net, a bale of bamboo shoots and a gun loaded with tranquilliser darts, you set the controls for 1984AD, reasoning that if they still existed in 2014 then they must have been everywhere 30 years earlier.

September 18th 1984

Arriving in the dim and distant past of mid-1980s Britain you're initially shocked at the complete total and utter lack of Giant Pandas. You search up and down the high streets and shopping centres and can't spot any.

But your persistence is eventually rewarded as just after dusk you spot what you think has got to be a breeding pair. Their distinctive white faces and black eyes standing out from a good distance away. You waste no time in creeping up on them and quickly capturing them in your net before taking them through a time portal back to 2027.

So that's two Pandas, but you need more. Where to find more?

Suddenly you have a brainwave. You can travel back to September 17th 1984, a whole day before you panda-napped the two you already have, and grab them from then.

Within half an hour (of your experienced time) you're standing back in your room with a sedated pair of pandas from September 18th and another identical pair from September 17th.

Not a bad start, but you still need more than just four…

Five hours (of your time) later your house is starting to get a bit crammed. You've got drugged Pandas from every day between September 18th 1984 and August 3rd 1984.

But you need more than just 58 pairs of pandas if you're to repopulate the world and this is taking too much time. If only there was a quicker way…

Then it hits you. If you do a small jump back in time, you can bring back the 58 pairs of pandas that were here 10 minutes ago and put them with the 58 pairs that are here now. You'll double the number that you currently have. And then you can wait a few minutes and repeat the process. It's genius and you're fairly sure it's not causing any sort of temporal paradox or you wouldn't be able to do it. You just need to remember to stop before you've got more pandas than there are atoms in the universe.

It's not long before your neighbourhood is filled with 59,392 breeding pairs of Giant Pandas and that's when they start to recover from the tranquilliser darts. Almost immediately you spot that something is very wrong - these Pandas talk, often quoting Poe, Lovecraft or Nietzsche, and for a species famed for it's lack of sex drive they seem quite interested in getting off with each other…

Of course! How stupid could you have been!

They're not pandas they're the only other long-extinct creature to share the distinctive white face with black eyes: Goths! The more depressing and serious, weaker relation of emos. That explains the overwhelming atmosphere of superiority, patchouli oil and nihilistic hopelessness.

No! It can't be. You've brought back the wrong species - now the modern world will be overrun by these people in black, depressing everyone with their moody introspection and songs by Nick Cave and The Cure. And it's all your fault - you've brought about the Gothocalypse!

It appears that the end is nigh. Civilisation wrecked. But then the sun rises and they all mysteriously disappear.

That's it, like vampires and Giger aliens, goths seek a nocturnal existence out of the public eye. Maybe people and goths can find a way to co-exist as long as normal people always remember to keep them supplied with hairspray and white foundation and that they mostly come at night... mostly.

The End

Should it actually happen in your reality, this ending is NOT covered by the 100% money back guarantee. If not getting your money back depresses you maybe you should start wearing black and listen to some Bauhaus...

—— Section 062 ——

On the way home you realise that that's now three times you've been to hospital with a blue face. You wonder how you'd been so silly to make the same mistake again.

DEAD CAT TIME
Thomas? Thomas? Are you okay in there?

Oh dear - that's not looking good (go to **Section 229**)
or Thomas has a stiffy - a little cat erection (go to **Section 304**)
or Thomas has a stiffy - rigor mortis has set in (go to **Section 129**)
or Thomas has eaten his own tail, but is otherwise fine (go to **Section 031**)
or Thomas has somehow regrown the tail he'd eaten. (go to **Section 118**)
or Thomas has used an infinitely improbable but still finitely possible quantum quirk to vanish. (go to **Section 266**)

—— Section 063 ——

You wake up...

You feel groggy, from a troubled night of strange dreams, made even stranger as you can't actually remember eating cheese before bed.

Oddly as you awake the world looks a little strange, not so much bleary through eyes still half-asleep but almost slightly pixellated with a slight lag as you move your head. This only lasts a few seconds before going though, as if someone had fine-tuned the settings of your world experience so that it felt more like reality normally does.

Whilst you were sleeping, someone has set up a highland games meet in your head and legions of Morris dancers have crashed it, starting a bloody battle of handkerchiefs versus cabers.

"Oh my head. What was I thinking last night? I'm not 18 anymore. I need more sleep... another 24 hours should do. What time is it anyway? Hell... What day is it?"

The bedside clock tells you it's only quarter to seven - far too early to be awake and feeling like this, especially on a Thursday. Just a second... Thursday? Isn't something happening today? No. Not the bin collection - that's tomorrow isn't it?

Thursday, Thursday, Thursday. Nope - nothing's materialising from your still-fogged memory.

Thursday... Thursday... Thursday?

Shit! THURSDAY!

It's Thursday September 18th! It's today. The day of destiny. The day of the referendum.

Whilst still not feeling 100 per cent, or even 54 per cent, you feel the weight of history on you and so somehow manage to leave your bed, still struggling to remember just what it was that you did last night.

Did you stay up most of the night drinking single malt and watching Braveheart? (go to **Section 016**)

or Maybe you overdosed on Earl Grey while watching recorded highlights of Last Night of the Proms and Downton Abbey. (go to **Section 126**)

or Were you one of those that went out clubbing and partying and didn't plan on giving the referendum a second thought? (go to **Section 183**)

or Did you spend the night re-reading all the referendum literature before debating the pros and cons of independence with a group of well-informed Scots? (go to **Section 207**)

—— Section 064 ——

On BizBites TV there's a look at Scotland's major businesses and it's global trade relations. It's no surprise to see the usual suspects featuring heavily: Whisky, shortbread and Argyle socks. What's slightly less expected is the impact that comedy has on the balance of trade, with the Edinburgh Festival bringing in thousands of visitors and Billy Connolly and other Scottish comedians being famous and in demand around the world.

These cash cows are always under virtual attack from other countries, especially Ireland which constantly tries to undermine Scotland's grip on Whisky and Gaelic humour. It makes you wonder if Scotland needs to get a bit more aggressive about protecting it's businesses and international trade.

You eventually decide to turn off the TV and start to think about your future and the future of Scotland, and where the priorities lie for both of you.

Vigorously defend Scottish business interests and keep Trident nuclear missiles as they'll always be useful as a fallback threat if Scotland needs them (go to **Section 247**)

or Allow rUK (rest of the UK) to base Trident in Scotland as long as Scotland has launch codes and veto on their use (go to **Section 155**)

or Get rid of Trident (go to **Section 048**)

or Keep Trident on the basis that the world is safer if you keep a veto over rUKs nukes (go to **Section 369**)

or I don't want to think about all this - just give me something random! (go to **Section 375**)

—— Section 065 ——

"Thanks but I think I'll pass this time. I'm enjoying the conversation here too much" you say to the punster.

"Nae probs - maybe next time" he says and he and his friend leave the bar.

You get back to chatting with Kelly, continuing the debate from earlier. As the night wears on you start to feel like there may be real chemistry between the two of you, and you think she feels the same.

Eventually the bar is closing for the night and so you walk Kelly home.

When you get to her front door, unexpectedly she asks if you'd like to come in for a coffee.

'Oh not again' you think.

What happens next is inevitable.

Sex. Hot sex. Hot sexy sex. Really hot sex. Really really hot sexy sexy sex. Sex so hot you're surprised that the flame-haired vixen's hair doesn't really spontaneously burst into flame. Really really really hot sexy sex so hot and sexy that it can't be described in any greater detail than just 'really really really really hot sexy sexy sexy sex' or this book would be banned under obscenity law.

You make love for what must be 3, 4, maybe even 5 minutes, and you're pleased to say you had no problems achieving orgasm. You showed Kelly what an accomplished gold-medal winning lover you were by impressively coming first both times. Though her performance wasn't as really really really hot as you hoped it'd be - you're not even certain that she completed the race.

As you walk home you fondly remember her really really hot sexy sultry voice when she turned to you after you'd finished and said "not really what I'd expected. Maybe you'd best leave. I'll finish the job off myself."

Thinking about last night brings a smile to your face this morning as you jump into the shower to 'remember in more detail' and freshen up. (go to **Section 120**)

—— Section 066 ——

Stopping only to grab a black leather jacket, black jeans and black sunglasses you head back in time to California 1971.

Your first stop is a telephone kiosk where you rip a page from a directory.

You start going to each house listed on the page you took, walking up to the front door, knocking and waiting for an answer. When one comes in your best Devon accent you say "Ello moi luvver. Oi be lookin' fur Sarah Connor oi be. Izzat you?" before turning and walking away.

It's almost worth doing just for the baffled look that most people give you but there's more at work. You keep doing it until, turning away from the latest doorway you've visited, you hear the woman who answered the door call to her son "James! It's one of your weirdo film making buddies for you."

It was worth going through a page full of Cameron households. You can return home now, happy that you've planted the seed of an idea in the young James Cameron's head. You can't wait for the next time you watch The Terminator - it's going to crack you up if the cyborg assassin from the future now sounds like a West Country yokel.

Yes you could have gone back in time to change something to help Scotland or the world, but whats the point of having both independence and time machines if you can't piss about a bit?

The End

Should it actually happen in your reality, this ending is <u>NOT</u> covered by the 100% money back guarantee. Unlike the Terminator your money isn't likely to say "Oi'll be bock, moi luvver".

—— Section 067 ——

You wake up...

You feel groggy, from a troubled night of strange dreams, made even stranger as you can't actually remember eating cheese before bed.

Whilst you were sleeping, someone has set up a highland games meet in your head and legions of Morris dancers have crashed it, starting a bloody battle of handkerchiefs versus cabers.

"Oh my head. What was I thinking last night? I'm not 18 anymore. I need more sleep... another 24 hours should do.[8] What time is it anyway? Hell... What day is it?"

The bedside clock tells you it's only quarter to seven - far too early to be awake and feeling like this, especially on a Thursday. Just a second... Thursday? Isn't something happening today? No. Not the bin collection - that's tomorrow isn't it?

Thursday, Thursday, Thursday. Nope - nothing's materialising from your still-fogged memory.

Thursday... Thursday... Thursday?

Shit! THURSDAY!

It's Thursday September 18th! It's today. The day of destiny. The day of the referendum.

Whilst still not feeling 100 per cent, or even 54 per cent, you feel the weight of history on you and so somehow manage to leave your bed, still struggling to remember just what it was that you did last night.

Did you stay up most of the night drinking single malt and watching Braveheart? (go to **Section 024**)

or Maybe you overdosed on Earl Grey while watching recorded highlights of Last Night of the Proms and Downton Abbey. (go to **Section 136**)

or Were you one of those that went out clubbing and partying and didn't plan on giving the referendum a second thought? (go to **Section 175**)

or Did you spend the night re-reading all the referendum literature before debating the pros and cons of independence with a group of well-informed Scots? (go to **Section 214**)

or Were you so worried about Scotland's fate that you decided to end it all rather than face an uncertain future, and so took a slow acting poison that should kill you any minute now... (go to **Section 239**)

or Whilst trying to remember what you did last night, do you suddenly realise that you have an exam that you've not revised for today and race out of your home to get to the exam so quickly that halfway there you realised that you hadn't put any trousers on? (go to **Section 327**)

—— Section 068 ——

September 18th 2019

Realising that the health of Scotland's people must come first, Holyrood decided to avoid giving incentives to video game companies and instead started a campaign to get people interested in real sports.

However it soon became apparent that most people who hadn't previously been interested in sports weren't very good at sports, since they'd spent their whole life fairly inactive and living a generally unhealthy lifestyle. Trying to push sports without spending money on programmes to improve healthy eating and lifestyle wasn't as productive as you'd have liked.

They tried though, bless them but there's only so many 'sports' that fat unhealthy people can do.

Before long you had world class players in the sports of darts and marbles. Providing that the sport involved either standing and drinking whilst throwing a small weapon or crawling about on the floor flicking glass spheres about then Scotland could produce any number of world class players!

So today saw the International Federation of Marble Players 2019 World Finals held in Scotland at Elgin. You're glad to say that a Scot took the title again, with another of your countrymen coming second. The highest position an Englishman made was fourth, after narrowly being beaten by a Greek player without any trace of irony.

It may not be particularly active sports, but it's still good to say that Scotland rules the world!

The End

Should it actually happen in your reality, this ending is NOT covered by the 100% money back guarantee. You'd only spend it on pies and pints. Not refunding your money is helping make you healthier. You should thank me.

—— Section 069 ——

The 'YES' vote won and so a new independent Scotland, free from English rule is soon created. It's an extremely exciting time to be Scottish and alive, and still exciting but not quite as much to be only one of those things.

There are still arguments over certain technical aspects of the split, but in many ways Scotland can forget the past that was imposed upon it and has a very rare opportunity: As a new country it has tabula rasa, a clean slate, a fresh pair of knickers to decide its priorities, create its laws and shape its future society, all without the skidmarks of history dirtying the picture.

In the weeks after the election, you saw some interesting TV programmes, just proving that even when a nation earns a fresh start it still gets fed the same old crap by the mass media. Though maybe that will change in time.

You especially remember, a few weeks after the poll, turning on the TV.

For some reason it'd been left on one of the 24hr news channels. (go to **Section 010**)

or It's tuned to independent terrestrial TV (STV) (go to **Section 344**)

or Oh you've no idea how that happened - it's on McBabeStation (go to **Section 190**)

or It's on SciTech TV - the science and technology channel (go to **Section 277**)

—— Section 070 ——

You think a little bit more...

It's really hard trying to make up your mind when you can't remember all the relevant information. Oh god what should you do...

Maybe you need even longer - but will that help at all? Don't panic.. Don't panic... don't panic... it's only the future of the country at stake.

Vote for 'Yes'. (go to **Section 374**)

or Vote 'No'. (go to **Section 144**)

or Wait and think about it a little longer. (go to **Section 035**)

or Flip a coin. That's the way to decide. (go to **Section 279**)

Flip a coin. But what sort of coin? (go to **Section 008**)

And is heads yes or heads no? (go to **Section 139**)

I suppose heads should be 'No' since it shows the queen of the United Kingdom, (go to **Section 212**)

but then she'd still be the queen of Scotland if the 'Yes' vote wins independence. (go to **Section 222**)

Oh this coin flipping is far too confusing, but it's the only way to decide. (go to **Section 328**)

Okay heads is 'Yes', tails 'No'. (go to **Section 354**)

Should it be the other way round? (go to **Section 092**)

or Oh god you can't decide - the stress is too much! (go to **Section 368**)

—— Section 071 ——

You wake up...

Feeling groggy as if you've barely slept at all. Last night you tossed and turned as terrible dreams filled your head. Dreams of cyclopean sunken cities where the geometry is skewed beyond known physics and something otherworldly stirs, dead but dreaming.

That'll teach you to eat a nice bit of cheese on toast just before bed.

Or at least you think it must have been the cheese affecting your dreams. The only other thing it could possibly be is that dusty old tome you read last week in the restricted stacks of Edinburgh University. Well that or the pagan rite you attended last Walpurgis Night. But you refuse to believe that the *Necronomicon* and blood sacrifices to Shub Niggurath could affect your dreams as much as a good thick slice of Red Leicester could.

"Oh my head. What was I thinking last night? I'm not 18 anymore. I need more sleep... another 24 hours should do. What time is it anyway? Hell... What day is it?"

The bedside clock tells you it's only quarter to seven - far too early to be awake and feeling like this, especially on a Thursday. Just a second... Thursday? Isn't something happening today? No. Not the bin collection - that's tomorrow isn't it?

Thursday, Thursday, Thursday. Nope - nothing's materialising from your still-fogged memory.

Thursday... Thursday... Thursday?

Shit! THURSDAY!

It's Thursday September 18th! It's today. The day of destiny. The day of the referendum.

Whilst still not feeling 100 per cent, or even 54 per cent, you feel the weight of history on you and so somehow manage to leave your bed, still struggling to remember just what it was that you did last night.

Did you stay up most of the night drinking single malt and watching Braveheart? (go to **Section 016**)

or Maybe you overdosed on Earl Grey while watching recorded highlights of Last Night of the Proms and Downton Abbey. (go to **Section 126**)

or Were you one of those that went out clubbing and partying and didn't plan on giving the referendum a second thought? (go to **Section 183**)

or Did you spend the night re-reading all the referendum literature and debating the pros and cons of independence with a group of well-informed Scots? (go to **Section 207**)

—— Section 072 ——

September 18th 2015

The studio lights dim and Ant or maybe Dec, it's certainly one of them, announces "The winner of The Rex Factor, Scotland's search for a new monarch is…"

Then they wait for dramatic tension.

Then they wait a bit more.

Then you start to wish you'd taped it so you could fast forward this wait.

Then they still haven't announced the winner.

"**Alex Salmond!**"

Alex jumps up and down on the stage "Yes! Yes! Quite right ya bastids. This is my country! My country!" then he seems to remember that he's on live TV and calms down adopting a much milder manner to say "Oh I'm touched. Really. How kind. I can't thank you all enough. This means so much to me."

Somehow he conjures up a tear from his eye. It looks like a tear of emotional disbelief at how lucky he is and thanks for the faith his people have in him, but it's funny that the tears only started after he appeared to put one hand in his trouser pocket and twisted.

Oh well - at least you know King Alex wanted to rule Scotland and that he'll probably do his best for the country. You're sure everything will turn out fine.

The End of the beginning

Should it actually happen in your reality, this ending is NOT covered by the 100% money back guarantee. You're not the king, I don't need to explain to you why it's not covered.

—— Section 073 ——

September 18th 2019

After switching off the TV set on that fateful day not long after the referendum, you raced outside to seek your fortune in the world of musicals. Outside a storm was blowing and whilst it didn't threaten to deliver a tornado it still reminded you slightly of the twister at the start of The Wizard of Oz. The wind was so strong that it blew down a large branch of a tree that clipped you slightly knocking you to the floor.

Luckily you were okay, and quickly picked yourself up, but it reminded you that you had to be careful out in such bad weather. And my! Look at how bad the weather actually was.

Despite your earlier thoughts that this Scottish storm wouldn't deliver a tornado, suddenly, over the rooftops of nearby houses, you see a massive whirlwind sweeping up debris, roof tiles and trees from the ground and whizzing it around and around and up higher and higher.

That's worrying - it seems to be coming your way and there's no way you can outrun it, given that you feel slightly dizzy from the branch that hit you and you don't even have a bike and a small yappy dog to help you. Despite this you turn and try to run. But it's pointless, as you thought it would be. In a few seconds the twister is upon you and you feel your feet leaving the ground as you're carried up, up and away. Soon consciousness leaves you.

You come around to find yourself surrounded by lots of happy, apparently-friendly midgets with orange faces.

"Welcome to Oz!" says a strange small man with an odd mix of Australian and Scottish accent.

"I'm in Australia?"

"No - Oz Oz not Oz. We're the umpa-lumpas!"

"But *you're* not in *The Wizard of Oz*!"

"We know, it's the author getting mixed up and not doing his research again. Anyway here - stick these on." He says handing you a pair of bright red 12-hole Doc Martens in just your size.

"Oh you really shouldn't have…" you say, accepting the boots and starting to put them on.

"Don't mention it - we grabbed them off the wicked witch of the South you killed when your book fell on her." He points over a short distance away where a steaming pair of striped stockings stick out from under a copy of the hefty pro-independence tome *Scotland's Future.*

Circling the book is a golden yellow road, that spirals out before heading off into the distance.

"It's great here, but I just want to get home to see how well Scotland does with it's new independence. How do I do that?" you ask.

All the umpa-lumpas start singing "Follow the road paved with gold! Follow the road paved with gold! Fuck off and see the Wizard, the Wonky Wizard. Fuck off!" Before making the repetition of the phrase "Fuck off!" more musical than you've ever heard it before.

"Isn't it meant to be a yellow brick road?" you ask the head umpa-lumpa.

"Yes - but we're already dangerously close to infringing intellectual property so this is the road paved with gold earned from North Sea Oil. Anyway it's still the right road to the Wonky Wizard, so fuck off."

You start walking along the road paved with gold, singing as you go and before too many scenes have passed, you've met 3 travelling companions, the Tinpot Man, the British Lion and the Scared Crown, all of whom seem to have serious issues…

The Tinpot Man is running a country but has no idea about what currency he'll use. He wants to see the Wizard and sings a great song called "*If I only had a coin*".

The British Lion keeps saying "Grrrowll, we're better together Grrrrowl." They have a very England-centric view and want to see the Wizard to get a better idea about how the UK outside of London sees his Westminster Rule. He sings a catchy song about "*If I only had a clue*".

The Scared Crown is a monarch who's worried about the disintegration of their Kingdom and the effort that monarchy takes as one gets older. They wish they had a decent successor so that they could retire. They want to see the Wizard as much as any of you, and so set off singing "*If I only had an heir (who wasn't a Charlie)*".

You slowly make your way towards the Wizard, despite being hounded by flying monkeys far too scary to be in any fun family musical.

Eventually you arrive at the gates of the Wizard's home, which looks suspiciously like a factory, and you knock and you wait. And you knock again and wait again.

Eventually Gene Wilder walks out wearing a top hat, a fine suit and walking with a cane. He greets you all with "Welcome to the Emerald City, my choco-dream factory situated in the Republic of Ireland for tax purposes."

"Ooooh the Wizard" whisper your 3 companions.

You spot the error straight away and say "That's not the Wizard, that's Willy Wonka. A totally different musical."

"It is the Wonka Wizard - a wizard of chocolate confectionary."

"Oh. I thought you'd been saying Wonky Wizard… my mistake."

The Wonka Wizard speaks up "No not really your mistake. It's shoddy research again and things getting confused in slightly damaged minds…."

"Anyway - how can I help you? Nothing as simple as an everlasting gobstopper is it?"

You speak up "No, Wonka Wizard, we're all missing something and you're the only one who can help us."

"Why what do you need?"

You point at the Tinpot Man. "He needs a currency or Scotland could be in real trouble."

"Easy to fix" says the Wizard pulling out a piece of paper and a pen from behind his back. "Just sign this contract, Alex, and I'll produce a near-endless supply of golden foil-covered chocolate coins for you."

You next point at the Scared Crown. "She's getting on a bit and needs a successor who isn't a right Charlie."

"Don't worry, Liz" says the Wizard, "Not all Charlies are bad. I'll let you borrow mine, he doesn't talk to plants, sell biscuits at extortionate prices or go to bed with horses. And he's good at finding golden tickets."

You point at the British Lion and say "He hasn't got a clue."

The Wizard laughs benignly, "Oh David, David, David. There's not much I can do about that, but not to worry - you'll be voted out before long and then it won't matter that you're clueless, you'll still be fine sitting on the boards of many FTSE100 companies."

"So that's everyone sorted, isn't it?" asks the Wizard.

"Err no, Mr Wonka Wizard, sir. I want to go home to Scotland and you're the only one who can help me."

"You've always been able to go home, just click your heels together and say there's no place like home."

You try it.

"There's no place like home. There's no place like home. There's no place like home."

Nothing happened. You click your ruby dockers together but still nothing happens.

You really slam your docker heels together shouting "Cut out this shite, I jus wanna go home."

But still nothing happens.

You look at the Wizard for words of wisdom and he thinks a moment before opening his mouth.

"Bugger - that's me out of ideas. Want some candy?".

Meanwhile back home, it is now today, September 18th 2019, and at your bedside Judy Garland finishes singing. After nearly 5 years in a coma with decreasing signs of brain activity, your family have finally decided to turn off your life support.

You never did recover from that tree branch hitting you not long after the referendum. Heaven knows why you were out and about in such a bad storm in the first place. But then again, throughout your life you had a tendency to do odd things almost like you believed you lived a charmed life in one of those musicals you always loved so much.

The End

Should it actually happen in your reality, this ending is <u>NOT</u> covered by the 100% money back guarantee. Maybe the wizard can change this and fix it for you to get a refund. Word to the wise though: Not all men offering to 'fix it' for you and asking if you want chocolate are Wizards.

—— Section 074 ——

You struggle to open the doors but they just won't move no matter how hard you push. God you must be deteriorating quicker than you thought, you may only have minutes before you're too weak to walk. Sure you've not lived a saintly life, but you're hardly the worst sinner. You certainly don't deserve to die here on the pavement, so close to help but what may as well be a thousand miles away if you can't get into the building.

Then you notice the small sign on the door that says 'pull'.

You feel an idiot for not noticing it earlier, but then you realise what this means: *Terminal Facial Cyanitis* must be affecting your mental capabilities, your eyesight or both! This is worse than just bleeding buckets of blue blood and bile, or any number of other alliterative phrases. Instead of just dying a dreadful death, the disease is going to make you look like a right dick first.

You pull the door and step inside, hoping that nobody noticed.

Finally, with salvation, or at least pain relief in your dying hours, so close, you give your details to the nurse on reception.

DEAD CAT TIME

You've not heard a noise out of that box for a while… wonder if Holly is still alive?

Shhh… you'll wake her up (go to **Section 006**)
or Oh so that's what a dead cat being eaten by maggots looks like! (go to **Section 093**)
or Does Dr Schrödinger expect you to clean up all that cat shit? (go to **Section 397**)
or The cat's dead and you can't be sure it's face isn't blue… (go to **Section 165**)
or Holly looks pleased to see you, but more pleased to be fed (go to **Section 112**)
or Holly ignores you, upset that her litter hasn't been cleaned (go to **Section 241**)
or Holly died after scratching "J'accuse" into the side of the box (go to **Section 324**)

—— Section 075 ——

September 18th 2016

Throughout the past two years you've been travelling all over Scotland seeing all the fine countryside and staying in many of the excellent hotels and B&Bs.

Near the start of your trip you decided to write a blog about it. The blog went down so well that you were asked to write a weekly column about your travels for a national newspaper. That was such a success that you're now releasing an eagerly awaited book about all the interesting and beautiful nooks and crannies that are there to visit in the new independent Scotland.

Seeing the stunning landscapes and attractions of your homeland seems set to provide you with an enjoyable lifestyle that will make you happy (and rich) for years to come. It's an added bonus that your writings help boost Scottish Tourism.

The End

What do you mean '*this ending is boring*'?

Well okay I admit it's not exactly high-adrenaline or filled with intrigue and surprise (unless you prefer sunny vacations in the med and are surprised that anyone can enjoy domestic holidays).

I had to include this as a balancing factor to all the other tourism endings that aren't quite so happy. I felt it only right to point out that some universes have a thriving Scottish tourist industry where people can have an enjoyable holiday *and live to tell the tale.*

But that isn't good enough for *you*, is it?
Okay I give in. In some universes it actually went like this…

September 18th 2016

Soon after *Yes-Day* you started travelling all over Scotland seeing all the fine countryside and staying in many of the excellent hotels and B&Bs. Part of you was angry at the fly-on-the-wall documentary being so obviously biased in its portrayal of Scottish tourism and so you set out to prove it wrong.

Near the start of your trip you decided to write a blog about it so that everyone else could read about the great places you went to. The blog went down so well that you were asked to write a weekly column about your travels for a national newspaper. That was such a success that you released a much-lauded book about all the interesting and beautiful nooks and crannies that are there to visit in the new independent Scotland.

Of course this new-found level of fame had it's downsides. Any level of fame can attract undesirable attention from odd 'fans'. The weirdoes. The cranks. The nutters.

And it's one of these self-proclaimed 'number one fans' who followed you to the furthest backwaters of the highlands. Followed is such a nicer word than stalked…

It was two weeks ago that they finally met you.

Two weeks ago that they told you they loved you. Two weeks ago that you told them to stop being silly. Two weeks ago that they insisted they weren't being silly. Two weeks ago that you told them to leave you alone. Two weeks ago that you threatened to call the police. Two weeks ago that you broke their heart. Two weeks ago that they broke your heart. Really broke it. Two weeks ago that they plunged the knife into your chest. Two weeks ago that they cut your heart in two. Two weeks ago that you died in their arms as they told you they still loved you.

It's still two weeks to go until someone taking their dog for a long walk in the countryside finds you. It's ironic that it was your description of hidden nooks and crannies that provided the ideal disposal spot for your physical remains.

The End

Should it actually happen in your reality, this ending is <u>NOT</u> covered by the 100% money back guarantee. There! Are you happy now? You could have had a nice continuing 'holiday' and been paid for writing about it, but no. You wanted something more exciting didn't you.

Well I hope you're as happy as the worms and flies and fungi feasting on your bloated corpse.

—— Section 076 ——

"No need to get angry... We all just want a pleasant debate" you say, putting your hands up in front of your chest to show your submission.

"Ah no worries man, I'm only joshin' wiv ya" says the drunk then he laughs and, with a look of slight embarrassment, his mate nervously follows.

"We'll sit down and we'll no be any trouble. Don't you worry. We're as keen to discuss what this vote means as you are."

You all sit down and you feel the room soon return to the pleasant debate it had been throughout most of the night. (go to **Section 365**)

—— Section 077 ——

Watching the EUSport TV channel you're treated to live coverage of the 2022 World Cup being re-awarded after Qatar was stripped of the tournament for being cheating, bribing unsportsmanlike shits. Which, apparently, isn't in the spirit of things for a sport where diving to get a penalty is pretty much okay.

You're only half watching as it's expected that the competition finals may go to England or somewhere decent and you'd quite like the chance for a holiday somewhere decent in 8 years time.

On TV, the president of FIFA, Septic Bladder, steps up to the podium to make the announcement.

"The final decision of the totally incorruptible FIFA committee is that the 2022 world cup be awarded to… Scotland."

You can't believe it. Scotland your homeland awarded the world cup. Take that England!

The TV shot switches to show the scene in the auditorium where the team representing the Scottish bid can't believe it either. Alex Salmond is jumping up and down whilst playing a celebratory round of keepy-uppy with a couple of world famous brilliant Scottish players (who have asked to remain nameless so that the author doesn't need to do research).

The shot then changes to a camera focussing on Seb Coe, Prince William and David Cameron as they rock back and forth, crying painful tears of disbelief.

It shows what a difference independence can make. Not long ago Scotland was nowhere near a winning bid, but suddenly all it took was independence and half the other countries to be found bribing FIFA officials and the cup is coming home.

Now all Scotland needs is to return to its former status as a top international football team and then win the cup on home turf. You imagine that winning the chance to host the tournament could be all that is needed to inspire your countrymen to greatness. It might even inspire you.

Maybe you should see what's on the other side.

Switch over to Early2Bed TV (go to **Section 290**)
or See what's on Frag! TV (go to **Section 081**)

—— Section 078 ——

You wake up...

For the umpteenth time and think "*Wow - this is obviously some sort of dream within a dream within a dream within a dream within a dream, just like that film Inception but in a dodgy indie-published book and even more confusing.*"

You vow to skip any self-indulgent crap that the author has written and jump straight to making a decision about what you did last night. Which is ironic as the author decided to keep the self-indulgent crap to a minimum this time around.

Did you stay up most of the night drinking single malt and watching Braveheart? (go to **Section 016**)

or Maybe you overdosed on Earl Grey while watching recorded highlights of Last Night of the Proms and Downton Abbey. (go to **Section 126**)

or Were you one of those that went out clubbing and partying and didn't plan on giving the referendum a second thought? (go to **Section 183**)

or Did you spend the night re-reading all the referendum literature and debating the pros and cons of independence with a group of well-informed Scots? (go to **Section 207**)

—— Section 079 ——

September 18th 2018

Soon after *Yes-Day* the government decided that the very best thing it could do for its people was to improve their health and lifespan. The very first job of any government except a tyrannical dictatorship (obviously) should be to keep its populace healthy and happy.

But at the same time, it was seen as important that Scottish businesses be given a boost.

The idea for a joint campaign was put out to various ad agencies, and before long the now-famous "***Bye England! Bye Early Death! Buy***

Scottish!" posters were plastered up all over the nation.

Initial reports suggested that the campaign was a huge success. The slogan was memorable, the image of a man in a kilt flicking the V-sign at a David Cameron look-alike was memorable, the idea of eating healthily and not deep-frying everything was memorable.

Sadly the list of Scottish food companies that the public knew was somewhat less than memorable.

Most people supported the idea of buying Scottish food but, because of the name, wrongly thought that Ronald McDonald ran a Scottish company. Sales of Big McBurgers and Happy-if-you-get-through-this-without-a-coronary Meals rocketed as people did their patriotic duty. The Golden Arches profits expanded as quickly as the Scottish people's waistlines did as the ad campaigns well-meaning message got totally scrambled.

Scotland was finished, no longer the once proud-nation of fit Celtic warriors that it had been. It had been reduced to a nation of chubbies who could walk 20 metres without getting short of breath.

The End

Should it actually happen in your reality, this ending is covered by the 100% money back guarantee. Just run over here and I'll give you the money in person. What do you mean forget it then? It's only 30 feet... oh if you're not really bothered then. I can't wait here all day for you, I've got to go and patent real-life heavy duty belly-wheels for the people as fat as you.

—— Section 080 ——

You wait...

You're already bored of waiting. The only thing to do is worry or watch the other people, but that's just annoying.

Take those two youths over by the blood donor poster for example.

"A pint! That's most of me arm innit!"

"No idea mate - I don't do that old pints and ounces shit. Ain't a pint just under half a litre?"

"No idea - it's just a quote from some old Alfred Hitchcock film me gran told me about once. Hitchcock's in hospital an' he sees a poster asking for blood donors to give a pint an' he says 'A pint! That's most of me arm innit?' Me gran thought it were proper funny."

"I s'pose people used to laugh at anything after the war."

Thankfully at this point your name is called by the nurse from reception and she leads you through to an examination cubicle.

DEAD CAT TIME
Has anyone fed Tiddles today? No? I'll see how he is then.

He's fine and ready to play! (go to **Section 188**)
or He's fine and ready for some food! (go to **Section 140**)
or He's fine… if you didn't want a living cat. (go to **Section 391**)

—— Section 081 ——

Frag! TV specialises in presenting "all the news and reviews if you don't want to lose!" In other words it's in-depth news, reviews, guides, tips and tournament-footage from the world of video-gaming.

Pwnage!!!! the weekly news show starts with a hype piece about the latest game in the *Call of Violence* first person shooter franchise that's due to launch soon. It shows in-game footage, that looks very realistic, of you getting chance to play as a Russian soldier rampaging through a Ukrainian town with orders to pretend that you're there accidentally. Another flashback sequence has you playing as UK special forces where you've got to covertly kill a member of the royal family in Paris. Put that with the chance to shoot Syrian jihadists and shoot down civilian airliners and it looks like another best seller for people who need to prove that they're real men, and not just unpopular adolescents trying to avoid doing their homework…

After the break, the middle section has a look at the current top 10 video games and you're pleased to see that *RockyStart* games from Edinburgh are still hanging in there at number 10 with their massive hit *Car Jacking Hooker Killer V*.

That game really shows how Scotland can compete on the world stage when it comes to video games. It's over a year since it was launched, racking up opening-weekend worldwide sales that any Hollywood movie would be envious of. To still be in the top 10 now shows what a popular game it is.

It even manages to stay popular despite the moral panic every time a new version comes that games affect the way people act and it's teaching people to be immoral, drug-running, ho-slapping, cap-in-ass-popping criminals who like rap music and have no thought for anyone but themselves.

What bull! Games can't really influence peoples behaviour, as you've played lots of Scot-developed apps on your phone and never once have you felt the urge to attack fruit with your karate chop, run a farm or protect your house from zombies through the careful planting of foliage.

Admittedly there was that one time that you threw a parrot at a pig sty, but that could have happened to anyone at anytime, the games had nothing to do with it.

You eventually decide to turn off the TV and start to think about your future and the future of Scotland, and where the priorities lie for both of you.

IT and video game businesses in Scotland are already respected around the world, maybe more financial help would make them undisputed world leaders (go to **Section 253**)

or Silicon Glen is already doing well - it doesn't need anymore help (go to **Section 350**)

or The government should give breaks to video game companies whilst advertising the benefits of a healthy, sporty lifestyle (go to **Section 012**)

or *Car Jacking Hooker Killer V* contributes so much to the treasury, give breaks for companies producing similar games (go to **Section 388**)

or Holyrood should give breaks to companies making non-violent games that are fun for everyone (go to **Section 125**)

or Games like *Car Jacking Hooker Killer V* may cause crime, so ban them but encourage development of non-violent games (go to **Section 325**)

or People should be encouraged to play real sports, not just lounge in front of TVs playing video games (go to **Section 068**)

or I don't want to think about all this - just give me something random! (go to **Section 375**)

—— Section 082 ——

You wake up...

You feel all flammerty, from a restless night of peculiar dreams, made even stranger as you can't actually remember eating any stilton before retiring to bed last night.

Whilst you were sleeping, someone has obviously commandeered your skull and organised a referendum drum-off between Evelyn Glennie and the chocolate-selling gorilla who thinks he's Phil Collins.

Just a second. This isn't right. You've already woken up today. What sort of cheap-ass-shittery is that Judgement Dave pulling just copying sections, changing the odd word and thinking that that counts as another x-hundred words written?!?!?!

Probably the same sort of cheap-ass-shittery that makes him invent words like 'flammerty'. The same sort that makes him think that repeating alternating question marks and exclamation marks is a good way to increase his character count. He's probably forgotten that he's being paid by the word and so punctuation doesn't earn him anything. What a dick.

If you can just ignore the author's oh-too-obvious failings maybe you can get on with making it through today and deciding the future of

Scotland. First you just have to remember what you did last night…

Did you stay up most of the night drinking single malt and watching Braveheart? (go to **Section 016**)

or Maybe you overdosed on Earl Grey while watching recorded highlights of Last Night of the Proms and Downton Abbey. (go to **Section 126**)

or Were you one of those that went out clubbing and partying and didn't plan on giving the referendum a second thought? (go to **Section 183**)

or Did you spend the night re-reading all the referendum literature and debating the pros and cons of independence with a group of well-informed Scots? (go to **Section 207**)

—— Section 083 ——

You really hope that you'll get some form of polling station this time.

DEAD CAT TIME

Yes it's time to peek inside Schrödinger's box and see how well Jess is…

Hello Jess. Where's Pat? (go to **Section 013**)

or That's not a cat that's George Galloway! (go to **Section 177**)

or Postcat Jess. Postcat Jess. Postcat Jess has left a mess! (go to **Section 366**)

or OMG! Jess is dead! Pat will be upset. (go to **Section 288**)

—— Section 084 ——

The punster's fist surprises you as it arcs towards your head before making solid contact. Really solid contact. So solid that you blank out and slump to the floor unconscious.

The next thing you're aware of is waking up in hospital attached to so many bleeping machines that you sound like mid-80s early techno. Within minutes of being awake a nurse notices that you've come round and attends to you.

You ask what happened and she says that you shouldn't worry, you've been in a little fight and you were unconscious for several hours.

You ask "how did I get here?" but ignoring the question, she just locks the door and starts to strip down to her cupless basque, calling you daddy and shoving her ample tits in your face.

'Oh not again' you think.

What happens next is inevitable.

Sex. Hot sex. Really hot sex. Really really hot sex. Sexy sex that's hotter than a British office without any opening windows or air con on the one muggy day in July when the temperature hits 30 degrees (or Summer as that day is also known). Sex that's hotter than an overpriced americano to go from an international coffee chain, one of the ones where the lid of the cardboard cup has warnings that the contents are hot. Sexy nursey sexy sex so hot it justifies the NHS budget all by itself. Sex so hot that it can't be described in any greater detail than just 'really hot sex' or this book would be banned under obscenity law. Suffice to say that you have really really really hot sexy sexy nursey sex.

The next thing you know is the nurse is dressed again and saying "did you hear that? It was your friend."

"What?" you ask.

"It was your friend brought you in. Well I thinks she's your friend. The redhead, Kelly something or other, I think. She brought you in anyway. Said you'd been attacked at a debate."

"What are you on about?"

"You asked how you got here. But I wasn't sure if you were drifting a bit when I told you it was your friend."

Oh… Maybe you didn't have hot sex, really hot sex, really really really hot nursey sex after all. You just imagined it.

Suddenly you remember the vote.

"How long do I have to stay here? I'll still get to vote won't I?"

The nurse carefully studies the medical notes at the end of your bed before replying.

"Obviously it's really up to the doctor. But going off similar cases I'd say after being unconscious for so long and the way that you're still drifting a bit we'd usually want to keep you in for observation for at least 24 hours - maybe even as long as a week."

No! After so much research, studying the arguments, debating the pros and cons, it looks like you won't even get the chance to vote… and all because of some drunk dickhead.

"As I say that's what usually happens, but we're aware that you're in the middle of a **You Decide!** adventure and the author spent a lot of time on the rest of the book and doesn't want you to miss it all because you're in hospital. So, if you're feeling up to it, you can be discharged immediately."

Something about the way that nurse Dean says you can be 'discharged immediately' is just soooooo sexy, in a really really sexy nursey kind of way.

"Oh I'm ***up*** to it alright, nurse Dean" you say, indicating your now-swollen member.

And just to dispel any confusion since this is a book cashing in on a political event, by *member* I don't mean your parliamentary representative, your member of parliament whether MP or SMP. No. I mean your penis. And by swollen I mean that it's swollen from horniness not from any sort of allergic reaction or injury.

Maybe it would have been easier if I just said you *pointed at your raging boner.*

Luckily the nurse doesn't need any disambiguatory explanation as she looks at you then goes to the door and locks it before turning, ripping open her top and saying 'Oh Daddy, call me Cindy".

'Oh not again' you think.

What happens next is inevitable.

Sex. Hot sex. Really hot sex. Really really hot sex. Sexy sex that's hotter than the previous sex that whilst really really really really hot did eventually turn out to be nothing but a figment of your semi-conscious imagination. This time this really really really hot sexy sexy sex is really really really real.

Though, once again, it can't really be described in detail for fear of becoming obscene.

After a couple of hours of really really hot wanton sex, when you've finished and got your breath back, you discharge yourself.

Then you wipe up the mess and leave the hospital for home.

You can't quite remember getting home, but you must have and then you fell asleep again. Not because you're very tired. It's just the head injury.

So that's how you came to be waking up again at quarter to seven. You just didn't realise that it's now nearly 7pm not 7am - you'd better get ready and go to vote before the polls close. You just need to freshen up first.

Stepping into the shower to get cleaned up you feel nauseous, which is probably still just concussion, but you manage to dispel all thoughts of vomiting by remembering your brief liaison with Nurse Cindy. (go to **Section 120**)

—— Section 085 ——

"I suppose I should take it more seriously."

"Sure you should" said Andy, "but let us get you another drink first."

When Andy returns with another round he tells you that there's a nearby public debate on tonight all about the referendum. It's only at the local debating hall and he'd considered popping over to it.

"What's the point in that? There's taking it seriously and there's being bored shitless. I don't mind one but this sounds more like the other."

"Maybe" he says "though it'd be okay wouldn't it if we have a few more drinks here first and then grabbed a few cans on the way over. You wouldn't take it over-serious then would you?"

"Aye that sounds like a plan" you say.

And 6 drinks later you're on your way to the debate. (go to **Section 265**)

—— Section 086 ——

Yeah!

Oh thank you, thank you, thank you! I knew you'd come around. I told you you were my favouritest, bestest, loveliest-ever reader. I did tell you didn't I? I meant to anyway.

You won't regret this - not at all.

Oh and this is what happens when you wake up… (go to **Section 071**)

PS - I lurrrvvvvve you.

PPS - And I mean that in a very physical, but consensual, kind of way.

—— Section 087 ——

September 18th 2019

The flood of rich Tory Hooray Henrys from the Home Counties came to Scotland but it was mainly limited to convenient distances from the cities and wherever was trendy this month.

This was somewhat irritating to Holyrood as it had hoped that the one benefit of an influx of rich Tories was that they'd bring their money up to spend in rural environments that needed the cash injection. But these areas were usually some way from the cities and not 'trendy', so they didn't get anything.

The government decided that they needed to improve the infrastructure and especially broadband access in the most rural of places so that they would attract the riches from the Southern neighbours.

Even though this was for the benefit of the local communities, the plan faced much criticism in it's initial form. Some minor changes were made and the plan was ready for rollout.

2018 saw the cabling up the rural areas started in earnest as the Scottish Highlands Information Technology Expansion was launched. The programme worked wonders in getting English people (especially rich Tory bankers and stockbrokers) to buy property in the less popular areas, especially as if a property was bought which didn't have fast broadband it was guaranteed to be installed within 48 hrs.

So now, 5 years after Yes-Day, the programme is regarded as a major success and everyone is happy.

The buyers are happy knowing that they have full connectivity to the internet services that they now rely on. The government is happy as it has won praise for the extra money that now flows into the rural areas. The existing locals are happy because of the minor changes the government agreed to make before launching the programme.

It had been agreed that every house receiving the super-fast cable broadband (or marked to receive it within 48hrs) would have a permanent brass plaque marking that the Scottish Highlands Information Technology Expansion had paid for the installation and for providing the service.

Those plaques simply read "English Tory S.H.I.T.E. here."

The dumb sassenachs never notice the alternate meaning and so the laughs, and their money, keep on coming.

The End

Should it actually happen in your reality, this ending is <u>NOT</u> covered by the 100% money back guarantee. Don't blame me - I don't make the rules.

Oh. Actually I do, don't I?

Oh well - no refunds and no reasons why. Suck it up.

—— Section 088 ——

You wake up...

From a troubled nights sleep of strange dreams that leave you feeling like you never slept at all, and makes you wonder if you absent-mindedly nibbled on a block of Emmental before bed.

It doesn't help that whilst you were sleeping, someone has decided to start rebuilding Hadrian's wall in your head and now it feels full of blokes called '*oi! Dave*' listening to what the DJ assures you are 'non-stop hits' on a loud radio, drinking sweet, milky tea and shouting 'phwoaaarrr' at anything in a skirt.

"Oh my head. What was I thinking last night? I'm not 18 anymore. Need. More. Sleep. What time is it anyway? Hell... What day is it?"

The bedside clock tells you it's only six O'Clock - far too early to be awake and feeling like this, especially today. Isn't today a special day? No, not Christmas day - that's still months away isn't it?

That's it - it's February the 2nd - Groundhog Day! How could you forget

- you need to get up as fast as you can or you'll never get to shag Andie MacDowell!

Just a second. That's not right. It's not February the 2nd and you're not Bill Murray. No it's September 18th 2014 - the day of destiny, day to decide etc etc yada yada

It may not be Groundhog Day, but you've definitely been here before. You know the drill. Just pick what you did last night and we can get on with things.

Did you stay up most of the night drinking single malt and watching Braveheart? (go to **Section 016**)

or Maybe you overdosed on Earl Grey while watching recorded highlights of Last Night of the Proms and Downton Abbey. (go to **Section 126**)

or Were you one of those that went out clubbing and partying and didn't plan on giving the referendum a second thought? (go to **Section 183**)

or Did you spend the night re-reading all the referendum literature and debating the pros and cons of independence with a group of well-informed Scots? (go to **Section 207**)

—— Section 089 ——

Arriving at the busy A&E department you hurry into the hospital and join a small queue waiting to see the nurse on reception.

After you've been waiting a couple of minutes someone else joins the queue behind you. Within seconds they're making a fuss calling "Excuse me, let me through, I think I'm dying."

You turn to look at the noisy new arrival and say "Aren't we all - that's why we're at A&E, you prick. Fuckin' wait your turn"

You know that you look bad with a beaten and bruised face, but it's nothing compared to the guy making a fuss. Whatever illness or injury he's got has made his face turn a nasty streaky blue. It crosses your mind to let him go ahead to the front of the queue just so he's not near you and you don't catch anything off him. But then you think "no, fuck him." He can wait his turn like everyone else.

You book in with the cute nurse on reception and after waiting for only twenty minutes or so you're seen by the doctor. For some reason he doesn't seem to totally believe you when you say you were jumped by 7 or 8 really big guys who you'd swear were trained by special forces, maybe even the SAS. He might have bought that if you hadn't said that you were winning the fight until they pulled their assault rifles out on you.

He checks you over and gives you a clean bill of health but tells you to call the hospital if, in the next 48 hours, you feel dizzy or your headaches get worse.

Feeling relieved that you got checked out, you go home and freshen up with a shower. (go to **Section 295**)

—— Section 090 ——

You wait...

Dum-de-dum. This is soooo boring.

Waiting for a doctor is worse than waiting for a bus, except you've never known 3 doctors turn up at once.

Dum-de-dum.

It's amazing how boring waiting rooms are. Almost as if they are designed to make waiting as bad as possible so as to deter people from bothering hospitals with their petty injuries, illnesses and other life-threatening conditions.

Dum-de-dum-de-dum.

DEAD CAT TIME

I'm too bored to even make up a cat name and some possible fates for the cat. Just pick one of the following three boring options.

Option One (go to **Section 236**)
or Option Two (go to **Section 246**)
or Option Three (go to **Section 317**)

—— Section 091 ——

You open the door and the sound of bagpipes greets you.

You know some people knock the drone of the pipes, but they really are far more versatile than many people give them credit, as beautifully demonstrated by the interesting song cover currently being played. It sounds vaguely familiar to you but you can't quite place it yet.

No wonder it took you a few moments to recognise it, it's not normally a pure instrumental, but just after you do it's confirmed as '*Bob the Builder*' when the officials manning the polling station all join in singing "**Yes we can!**"

You're sure that you must have heard of less-subtle attempts at subliminal programming, but if you have you certainly can't remember when. You try harder to think of an example, but all that comes to mind is the repetitive phrase "*buy all Judgement Dave's books buy all Judgement Dave's books buy all Judgement Dave's books*".

Of course it'll take more than subliminals to persuade you to change your mind. You're showing your support with the clothes you're wearing and everybody in the polling station can see where your loyalties lie.

There's something you don't like about the pipes trying to influence people so you ask the piper to change to a different song. Surprisingly he does.

It takes a minute or two for you to recognise the new tune as the 80s hit 'Owner of a Lonely Heart'. Interesting choice you think. It takes a little longer for you remember that it was a hit for the prog rock band 'Yes'...

As you're listening to the music, you take in the tartan decorations and numerous Scottish flags adorning every wall and flat surface other than the floor. Then you notice that the attendants have a table full of little glasses of special 'Independence whisky' and a selection of shortbread and haggis with a sign inviting you to enjoy some Scottish hospitality. You go over to the table and one of the attendants quickly tells you that all 47 glasses of whisky and the numerous foodstuffs have been reserved. You get the feeling that nobody here likes you and so decide that you need to get this over with as quickly as you can.

You try to exchange pleasantries with the lady (who is dressed in full traditional highland dress) sat behind the desk dealing with addresses including your home, but she obviously wants nothing to do with you. Once you've confirmed your identity, she says "you should be ashamed, laddy", gives you your ballot paper and points you in the direction of the small individual booths that you can go in to cast your vote in private.

As you walk across the room to the polling booth, it is with the weight of a country's destiny bearing down on your shoulders... (go to **Section 184**)

—— Section 092 ——

The coin flies up...

And then comes back down again landing decisively on 'Tails'.

That's interesting. You think you'd decided that tails is a YES vote, so you pick up the teeny tiny pencil and place a cross in the 'YES' box.

You fold the ballot paper and happily stroll out of the booth, walk across the floor and pop the folded ballot in the box. You exchange knowing nods with the station attendants. You know and they know that you have fulfilled your democratic duty.

It's surprisingly easy when you use a coin and don't worry too much about political arguments. You hardly know why people treat it as such a big deal.

Life is normal until the results are announced. (go to **Section 321**)

—— Section 093 ——

The nurse tries to remain professional, but seems distinctly worried by your appearance and description of what's happened to you. Working here, she's obviously no stranger to various exotic and deadly diseases, such as Ebola, Marburg virus, Dengue and Lassa Fever so it's particularly worrying that she seems to be finding it hard to suppress a shocked grimace at your condition. But she still tries, even though, if you were only a passerby and didn't know how serious your condition is you may have misinterpreted her look as merely trying to suppress a smile.

At the end of your description you say "Should I take a ticket and go and sit in the waiting room?"

She looks at you again, the pity and fear pulling her face into a wide smile.

"No need to. We're very quiet this morning. Only you in so far, so you'll probably have everybody looking after you. Just follow me."

She leads you through the empty waiting room and into the treatment area.

"Doctor Jones?" she says and an attractive young brunette lady doctor comes out from one of the examination rooms.

"A patient for you."

"Oh thank god for that, nurse Murray. I've been going mad here with nothing to do, it's so frustrating. Not good at all, especially when I have the students here today. You're fine with students being present aren't you?"

The last question is directed at you. You say that you're fine. You don't really think you care who is present as long as the hospital saves you.

"Good. Can you stay as well please nurse? Just in case I need a hand, the students are the new lot from St Augustine's Medical Nunnery and frankly I don't know how much help they'd be with a man."

Nurse Murray agrees and you all go into the room the doctor had emerged from. Waiting in there are 7 or 8 nuns, obviously the St Augustine students.

The doctor instructs you to remove your outer garments before giving you a thorough examination.

Eventually she says "Hmmm.... Well you'll be pleased to know that I don't think it's anything deadly. No. It looks like you have a bad case of paint or dye making your face blue. The best treatment is probably just to have a thorough wash to remove the discolouration."

The doctor presses a button on the wall and the floor of the room starts to slide away revealing some sort of pool.

"Luckily we can help you there" she says to you, before saying to the nuns "I'm sorry sisters you'll probably want to avert your eyes from a man being bathed."

"As it's for medical reasons, the lord will understand. We'll even try our best to help" says one of the sisters. "But we can't get our habits wet" she continues and the nuns start to strip each other as the doctor and nurse lower you into the pool and then remove their sodden clothes.

'Oh not again' you think.

What happens next is inevitable.

Sex. Hot sex. Really hot sex. Really really hot sexy sex. Really really really sexy sex so hot you wouldn't believe it if it was in a book. Sex so really really really hot that you wouldn't believe it at all if it wasn't actually, really happening to you. Sex so hot that it can't be described in any greater detail than just 'really hot sex' or this book would be banned under obscenity law.

All the really hot sex in the pool seemed to do the trick, both in making you feel better and in removing all traces of blue from your face.

The only problem is that after all that really really really hot sexy sex you feel dirty, so you head home to have a shower before getting ready to go out and vote. (go to **Section 240**)

—— Section 094 ——

You can't remember precisely what happened for the rest of the night, but you're pretty sure that at the end of the night you didn't have to go home alone and it wasn't your home you went to.

You try to think of the details. You remember that you'd fancied the hot redhead, Casey or whatever she was called, all night. She looked a right goer and had a great set of assets. You're sure that, with a body like hers, you could manage to look past her being a boring intellectual who likes to debate.

You try harder to remember the details and have a vague recollection of having a passionate kiss. You cast your mind back as best you can.

'Oh not again' you thought.

What happened next was inevitable.

Sex. Hot sex. Hot sexy sex. Really hot sex. Really really hot sexy sexy sex. Sex so hot it made your chilli laced chicken tikka tindaloo look like plain old gravy. Sexy sex so hot you're surprised Kristie's fiery-red hair didn't really set on fire. Really really really hot sexy sex so hot and sexy that it can't be described in any greater detail than just 'really really really really hot sexy sexy sexy sex' or this book would be banned under obscenity law.

You make really really hot sweaty sexy physical animal sex for ages until you fall back on the bed exhausted and gently tell Cassie "thanks for the shag - I'm off now".

Ten minutes later you were home and in your own bed.

You're a bastard, but at least, remembering this, you're a smiling bastard as you jump into the shower to freshen up before you go to vote. (go to **Section 295**)

—— Section 095 ——

You press on along what seems to be a well travelled path. You're glad you spotted it as, in no time at all, the undergrowth to either side becomes far too dense to easily traverse.

After a minute or so, from up ahead, you start to hear the sound of branches breaking and the dense foliage being crushed as if something impossibly big is lumbering through the jungle. Most worrying is that the sounds are getting louder, as if some wild juggernaut is coming towards you.

You turn away from whatever behemoth is approaching and start running along the jungle path. You hope to lose the beast, but after sprinting as best you can for 5 minutes you can still hear it following. The only saving grace is that you're fairly sure it hasn't noticed you yet - if it had you're sure it would have made the extra effort to catch up to you and you're equally certain that you wouldn't much like that.

Suddenly you hear a collection of strange semi-human grunts from up ahead on the path. You stop running, wondering what to do. Panic sets in as you realise that you're caught between the devil and the deep blue sea. Or, more accurately, caught between what sounds like a giant roaring monster and a group of several grunting primitive apemen.

Do you stop and hide? (go to **Section 329**)
or Retreat away from the grunting. (go to **Section 040**)
or Steel yourself and press on ahead. (go to **Section 296**)

—— Section 096 ——

"Only pulling your leg..."

"I've been looking forward to it - it's not often people get a democratic chance to change a country's future in such a significant way. I just never mentioned it because I thought you didn't care for it."

Andy laughs and says "naw - I think it's great that we get a proper say. I'm just no sure yet if independence is what I want or not. You know I love Scotland, but I dinnae know if which way's for the best."

You remember seeing something in the local paper yesterday.

"Tell you what Andy, I think there's a debate on near here tonight. It could help you decide."

"A debate? Like that Question Time? That's boring."

"Sure *that's* boring - but it's bound to be different in real life.

Everything's better live. And there's bound to be some fit students there an' we can get some lager on the way."

That persuades him - and after another couple of drinks you're heading off to the debate. (go to **Section 265**)

—— Section 097 ——

The punster's fist surprises you as it arcs towards your head but you soon recover to dodge out of it's path before countering with a punch to your opponents guts.

Putting into practice everything you ever learned in your misspent youth playing street fighter in the arcades, you follow up with a left jab, a right, an uppercut and then try to finish by throwing a blazing fireball, but it turns out that that's a lot harder to do in real life.

"Okay! Stop - please stop. We're going" cries the punster, trying to protect his head but not trying to counterattack. You let him run off with his mate out of the debating hall and suddenly worry what reaction you'll get from the other people here for the discussion.

You needn't have worried as, as soon as the drunks have gone, you're rewarded with a spontaneous round of applause.

You perform a deep bow in mock-appreciation before sitting back down and letting the debate continue. (go to **Section 108**)

—— Section 098 ——

You open the door...

Hoping that the hint was wrong and that this is really the normal polling station and not a weird room that you won't enjoy. Nope - the hint was correct.

Almost immediately you know that you've entered the wrong room because you are in a large arena that is packed full of thousands of people all in white boiler suits.

Everybody is looking straight ahead at the stage where a fairly-slight man with a beard is talking. You listen to what the man has to say but for some reason you can't remember what he said. You think you were following his talk quite well until he called you down to the stage and spoke with you.

Or did he? Probably not? You can't really remember.

All you know for sure is that he definitely definitely was not Derren Brown and he definitely definitely was not programming an army of human automatons to do his bidding whilst totally unaware that they've ever even met him.

Sorry what was that? Derren Brown? You've never even heard of him.

Certainly never been in the same room as him. You'd remember if you had.

You didn't exit a room as you can't even remember ever being in a room, certainly not one with any sort of famous mentalist in, and decide to look for the polling station behind a different door. (go to **Section 337**)

—— **Section 099** ——

No! Just No!

Have you not learnt anything from this book? Or if not from this book, did you never read *Even More Dragon Gold!* or any of the other books in the same series?

If you did then you would know that it is not a good idea to go seeking goblin-banshees because if you meet one then the very best that you can hope for is that you escape with a quick death after the monster has ripped you a new arsehole. And that's if you're very, very, *very* lucky.

Why don't you just go back and pick another option? One that will be far less painful for you…

Go on.

Still here?

Okay - if you insist. One arsehole obviously isn't enough for you. Let's go and grab you another.

Excited at the thought of going to Camelot you make up your mind to grab some armour and a sword so that you don't look out of place. Luckily you know that you can grab some LARP (Live-Action Role Playing) gear from *a friend*.

Of course it's from a friend. Who are you trying to kid? We all know that it's you who dresses up at weekends and pretends that you're a mighty barbarian warrior who's nothing like the reality of a 10 stone wimp who makes web-pages. That's why you're so keen to charge forward, full-steam ahead into the waiting jaws of goblin-banshee doom.

Anyway, since I couldn't dissuade you, you go into the spare bedroom and get into your best Barbarian LARP armour (complete with foam musculature to give you visible pecs and biceps). You grab your mighty battle axe and are ready to travel to the past in search of the dreaded goblin-banshee.

September 18th Days-of-Yore

You arrive in a great hall in a great castle surrounded by a great number of knights in great armour and carrying great swords who all look greatly pissed off at you.

It doesn't look great.

Suddenly one of the knights cries "What foul magicks are at work that the Ice Warriors of the North may just appear at will in Camelot?"

And he's answered by another brave chivalrous Knight saying "Don't know. Don't care. Just twat him."

At this point the great number of great knights take both great swords and great delight in putting great distance between various parts of your body that should be attached.

Now I, as the author, have got to say that that really does surprise me. I really thought that you'd die at the hands of a goblin-banshee but it turns out that you looked just like an invading barbarian from the Northern Wastes. They must also wear foam armour and have artificial muscles. It's no wonder that King Arthur and the Knights of the Round Table won many battles if all they ever fought were office workers covered in foam.

Anyway, enough of my musing, let's get back to your death.

With your final breath you just manage to weakly say "Goblin-Banshee?"

Hearing this the knights spin around shouting "Where?" and as you pass away you hear one say "The barbarous fool is pulling your leg, you know that Sir Lancelot killed the last goblin-banshee last week."

The End

Should it actually happen in your reality, this ending is NOT covered by the 100% money back guarantee. I wonder what annoys you the most: not getting a refund, being killed by your own stupidity at ignoring my advice or missing the last goblin-banshee by a week.

—— Section 100 ——

You suddenly find yourself back in the fancy dress shop, apparently safe from all dangers.

"Thanks for saving me - but no thanks. You can have this cursed costume back I'd rather wear my normal clothes than go through this voodoo doodoo."

The shopkeeper looks at you and says "Sorry, no can do. You've soiled the costume now, you've got to take it."

"It's only a drop of urine and that's your fault really - it's your weird magical costume that put me in mortal danger. If it wasn't for that I wouldn't have pissed meself!" you reason.

"That's as may be, but, for one, I've already taken the payment out of your wallet and, two, it's in the rules: look." He points to a sign behind the counter.

"Keep calm and dress up? What's that got to do with anything?" you ask.

He shakes his head and says "the other sign."

"No dogging?"

"The other other sign."

Oh - he must mean the one between the keep calm sign and the no dogging sign that clearly says in bold 5-inch high letters 'If you piss in it you buy it. No exceptions.'

You grudgingly accept that you have to buy the soiled costume and so leave the shop, occasionally shaking your leg in an attempt to dry it, heading off in the direction of the polling station. (go to **Section 189**)

—— Section 101 ——

The rats crawl forwards towards your face. You're almost ready to tell the man from the ministry everything. Hell you'd tell him anything he wants to hear if he just gets the rats away from your delicate fleshy lips, your nasal snack and oh-so-vulnerable eyes.

You still don't know how you got here.

Then it hits you. This is section 101 in the adventure and so the author dropped an Easter Egg here in the form of a reference to 1984 that is in a section that is not linked to anywhere else in the book. So to get here you have obviously made a mistake, the author ballsed up his links or you were looking for Easter Eggs. Well done!

—— Section 102 ——

Med TV is showing a roundup of the current state of medical science that reminds you how much good modern medicine has done but also how we can't afford to get complacent as new diseases develop.

It's the usual sensationalist docudrama looking at possible ways in which mankind could be wiped out by deadly bacteria, viruses and other assorted nasties. You suspect that the fall of man is just as likely to be brought on by a rash of suicides caused by the dreadful puns and stabs at attempted humour that the programme makers have used for each apocalyptic vignette.

One flu over the cuckoo's nest! Topic of Cancer! Beware the march of AIDS! The tale of antibiotic and uncle death of mankind! Old Age: the Age Old killer!

One of the worst was about the threat of death from dehydration striking disco dancers affected by dysentery which they called *Saturday Shite Fever!* With characteristic lack of taste the film illustrating this featured many dancers in white trousers succumbing to the disease on the dance floor. You could tell sufferers by the way they used their walk...

Just as bad is the way that the programme shows very little new - in fact some of the sections seem like rehashes of previous productions. You're so certain that the film about the possible resurgence of Black Death was ripped off from a documentary you saw a few years ago that you're surprised they didn't call that section "Bubonic Plaguerism!"

You eventually decide to turn off the TV and start to think about your future and the future of Scotland, and where the priorities lie for both of you.

Do you decide to devote your life to medical research, and hope that increased state-funding helps you make progress (go to **Section 367**)

or The shows you've just watched have convinced you that scientists and doctors have everything in hand, so there's nothing stopping you leading a hedonistic life inspired by the likes of Gayer TV (go to **Section 297**)

or You'd rather see more effort put into space exploration, but it's too costly for just the Scottish government to fund. If only you could find a way to make space exploration profitable (go to **Section 204**)

or Thinking of the SciTech TV show you watched, you dedicate your life to advanced scientific research (go to **Section 255**)

or I don't want to think about all this - just give me something random! (go to **Section 375**)

—— Section 103 ——

You wake up...

In agony, feeling some sort of liquid draining from around you and multiple cables, pipes and other connectors being ripped out of your body. Above you an electrical storm is raging in an angry sky on the other side of the clear dome just in front of your face.

The dome rises and you struggle to sit up and look around you. For as far as you can see theres some sort of gigantic array of man-sized pods, each one clearly containing a person connected up to wires, cables and pipes...

It looks vaguely familiar...

Oh that's it - *The Matrix!* It must have been a documentary: the matrix's last gamble to stop people realising they were being farmed by making a multi-million dollar film stating the truth... That explains a lot. You always thought that was a distinct possibility, because if you weren't living in a preset simulated world then you should have won the lottery by now. You've played it every week for 10 years, the odds against being a jackpot winner must be astronomical. Nearly as improbable as Keanu Reeves being a famous actor yet showing so little ability to act.

Suddenly you hear a synthetic voice say "fuck this isn't him. The *wrong one* maybe, but not ***The One***. Plug him back in."

Robotic arms grab you and plug cables, wires, pipes and drips back into you before forcing you to lie back down. As the dome closes above you and starts to fill with fluid, you start to drift off into a chemically-induced virtual sleep.

You wake up...

Again, but everything seems normal - not like that weird dream you know you had but can't quite remember.

"Oh my head. What was I thinking last night? I'm not 18 anymore. I need more sleep... another 24 hours should do. What time is it anyway? Hell... What day is it?"

The bedside clock tells you it's only quarter to seven - far too early to be awake and feeling like this, especially on a Thursday. Just a second... Thursday? Isn't something happening today? No. Not the bin collection - that's tomorrow isn't it?

Thursday, Thursday, Thursday. Nope - nothing's materialising from your still-fogged memory.

Thursday... Thursday... Thursday?

Shit! THURSDAY!

It's Thursday September 18th! It's today. The day of destiny. The day of the referendum.

Whilst still not feeling 100 per cent, or even 54 per cent, you feel the weight of history on you and so somehow manage to leave your bed, still struggling to remember just what it was that you did last night.

Did you stay up most of the night drinking single malt and watching Braveheart? (go to **Section 016**)

or Maybe you overdosed on Earl Grey while watching recorded highlights of Last Night of the Proms and Downton Abbey. (go to **Section 126**)

or Were you one of those that went out clubbing and partying and didn't plan on giving the referendum a second thought? (go to **Section 183**)

or Did you spend the night re-reading all the referendum literature and debating the pros and cons of independence with a group of well-informed Scots? (go to **Section 207**)

—— Section 104 ——

September 18th 2022

You're surprised that it's only 8 years since you decided to dedicate your life to paleontological genetics - trying to clone dinosaurs from their remains. The fact that we hadn't managed to clone much of any great size, never mind from millennia-old DNA, wasn't going to stand in your way.

So you began your search for a viable source of dinosaur genetic material and eventually found some in a 65-million year old mosquito trapped in amber. It's the type of thing you'd have only thought possible in books and films if it hadn't really happened to you.

You started work on extracting the DNA and, with the help of modern-day lizards and amphibians and gene-splicing techniques you finally created your first dinosaurs.

But what to do with them?

It would have been far too easy to become rich and famous by farming them to provide a solution to world hunger, but where would be the fun in that? How exactly would that solve mankind's incessant search for new forms of entertainment and spectator sports?

No! The only thing that feels right to you is to make lots of different types of dinosaur and train them to compete against each other in free-running races across urban landscapes.

You're sure that the world will be gripped at the sight of Tyrannosaurs leaping from building to building; velociraptors jumping up through windows in one-swift motion; Allosaurs leaping off skyscrapers to land in a perfect roll and Iguanodons running up walls as if they were some sort of prehistoric Jackie Chan.

The journey had been long and hard, and many free-running specialists had been eaten along the way, but now you were ready for the first professional race to be run across the Glasgow skyline and shown across the world.

It was the biggest sporting event of the century - billions of pounds changed hands in bets. The global interest was off the scale.

Finally you lined up the competitors and fired the starter pistol and off they ran, climbed, jumped, rolled and slid. The race was even better than you expected, with only a couple of buildings being accidentally demolished. The overall injury rate was lower than forecast, though there were a few more fatalities than planned including 7 people turned into mid-race snacks. In total it was nothing the emergency services couldn't handle.

Everyone thought it had been a great success.

At the end of the night you took the massive beasts back to their home and purpose-built training grounds in the backwaters of Scotland. After years of watching dodgy SciFi films, you had been worried that something would go wrong but the race had gone without hitch and now you could sleep easy. Tomorrow you'd start preparations for the next race. And the next race. And the race after that. You could happily roll out the races worldwide within weeks, as you'd already bred tens-of-thousands of dinosaurs anticipating such a rapid expansion of the sport.

As you slept the dinosaurs were unhappy. Of course they were. They'd felt the thrill of racing across a real city and now they were trapped again in their stables in the Scottish highlands.

But, of course, it's hard to keep a beast locked up once you've taught it to be a skilled free-runner…

The dinosaurs escaped that night. All of them.

They roamed wild from city to city, leaping majestically from tower block to skyscraper. From bungalow to terraced street. Stopping only to feast on helpless humans or to mate to increase their number.

Before 2 years had passed the dinosaurs had nearly wiped out mankind and returned to their position as rightful rulers of the planet.

The end of humanity had been brought about all because of your hubris in thinking you could create and control Jurassic Parkour.

The End (of humanity)

Should it actually happen in your reality, this ending is <u>NOT</u> covered by the 100% money back guarantee. But you can have a piece of paper with IOU written on it if you really want (and are prepared to make it yourself).

—— Section 105 ——

"I'm sorry mate… I dunno what I was thinking. Maybe I shouldn't drink so much. Still friends?" you say putting out your hand to shake.

What Andy does next surprises you. He gives you a slap across the face like a girl and then, as you stand there surprised, shakes your hand.

"Now we're good."

He starts grinning and you can't help but join him.

"Fancy going somewhere else?" you say.

"Well if you're up fer it, there's a political debate about the referendum on tonight. We could go there…"

You don't much fancy a debate, but you feel you ought to make up to Andy for being a dick. "I s'pose so, but can we get some cans on the way?"

"Sure - long as you don't start nothing."

You give him your assurance you won't be any trouble and set off to the debate. Surely you won't be trouble, not twice in one night... (go to **Section 265**)

—— Section 106 ——

You wake up...

In an embarrassingly damp patch of bed.

Damn - what was I dreaming about?

Guess you'll never know, but it must have been hot sex.

Really hot sex. Really really hot sex. Really really really hot sex. Sex so hot it would be worth mentioning it in the foreword of any book that dared to include scenes of such really really really really hot sex.

You stop wondering about the dreams of really hot sex that you've forgotten, and start to concentrate on a different sort of banging - namely the headache banging away behind your eyes.

"Oh my head. What was I thinking last night? I'm not 18 anymore. I need more sleep... another 24 hours should do. What time is it anyway? Hell... What day is it?"

The bedside clock tells you it's only quarter to seven - far too early to be awake and feeling like this, especially on a Thursday. Just a second... Thursday? Isn't something happening today? No. Not the bin collection - that's tomorrow isn't it?

Thursday, Thursday, Thursday. Nope - nothing's materialising from your still-fogged memory.

Thursday... Thursday... Thursday?

Shit! THURSDAY!

It's Thursday September 18th! It's today. The day of destiny. The day of the referendum.

Whilst still not feeling 100 per cent, or even 54 per cent, you feel the weight of history on you and so somehow manage to leave your bed, still struggling to remember just what it was that you did last night.

Did you stay up most of the night drinking single malt and watching Braveheart? (go to **Section 016**)

or Maybe you overdosed on Earl Grey while watching recorded highlights of Last Night of the Proms and Downton Abbey. (go to **Section 126**)

or Were you one of those that went out clubbing and partying and didn't plan on giving the referendum a second thought? (go to **Section 183**)

or Did you spend the night re-reading all the referendum literature and debating the pros and cons of independence with a group of well-informed Scots? (go to **Section 207**)

—— Section 107 ——

You wait...

Dum-de-dum. This is boring. You hate queues at the best of times but it's even worse when you're ill and waiting to be seen by a doctor.

Dum-de-dum.

It's amazing how boring waiting rooms are. Almost as if they are designed to make waiting as bad as possible so as to deter people from bothering hospitals with their petty injuries, illnesses and other life-threatening conditions.

Dum-de-dum-de-dum.

DEAD CAT TIME

I'm too bored to even make up a cat name and some possible fates for the cat. Just pick one of the following three boring options.

Option One (go to **Section 384**)
or Option Two (go to **Section 080**)
or Option Three (go to **Section 163**)

—— Section 108 ——

For the next few hours points were made by each side. Counter-points were made in answer to them. At times the independence campaigners made great arguments that seemed to beat the opposition to submission. But then, just when the Pro-independence supporters seemed to be beaten to submission they'd make a stunning counter-argument that left the 'Better Together' camp floundering.

So many great points were being made from all sides. You even made seven or eight yourself and for a while you got into a heated exchange with a young redhead who had a well-formed pair that were particular impressive.

You remember thinking though, that maybe you were being given an easy ride after the earlier altercation. Everyone seemed happy that you'd stood up to the drunks and so most were happy not to challenge you if you said that black was white or the moon at night was brighter than the sun in the day.

Despite your suspicion that no-one was challenging you, you had discovered how much fun it was to discuss serious matters with so many people. You decided that this may be the first but it wouldn't be the last time that you mass debate in public.

Back and forth it went. If it was a football match then it would have been close for all 3 chukkas, neither side scoring a field goal or try, either in open play or by penalty shot. It was too close to call with both teams equal on points after extra time. [*Note to editor - can you check this, I'm not really a big football fan so may have got some terminology slightly off.*]

By the time the debate was over, many issues had been discussed but you'd be surprised if floating voters had been convincingly converted to either side. You'd be even more surprised if the points raised had made anybody change their vote if they'd already decided which way they were going.

Ah well. It may not have really changed anything, but it was interesting and stimulating, and at the end of the debate some people were going to a local bar for a few drinks and asked you to join them.

Do you apologise and head straight back home (go to **Section 315**)
or Go to the bar for a drink or two. (go to **Section 154**)

—— Section 109 ——

September 18th 2024

After *Yes-Day* the fledgling nation had trouble deciding exactly where to prioritise its budget. After much to-ing and fro-ing it was decided to capitalise upon Scottish arts and cultural success.

Despite pouring money into popular music and the popularity of shows such as *The Voice* and *The X Factor*, by late 2017 there still weren't enough profitable singers making an impact on the world stage (and so bringing home government tax revenues). Something needed to be done to make sure that more people attempted to pursue career mirroring the most popular Scottish singers.

And so, in 2018, the government passed *Boyle's Law* linking volume and pressure. More precisely it stated that the volume of SuBo impersonators must be directly proportional to the pressure that the Scottish government was under to balance it's books. It also created incentives for people to become SuBo impersonators.

Overnight the number of Scots trying to make a living as Annie Lenox, Proclaimers or Deacon Blue impersonators fell as more and more people, young and old, male and female, talented and otherwise, all donned makeup, dodgy teeth and a dress and collectively dreamed a dream that could melt the cold hard heart of Simon Cowell.

The tsunami of SuBos spilled out across the globe. Within months impersonators had infested the Americas (North and South), Europe, Africa and Asia. Even Antarctica had a small colony of SuBos. The only place to escape was Australia, which refused to let SuBos into the country in case they upset the delicate ecosystem and ended up killing off kangaroos.

The government of Scotland became incredibly rich and powerful on the back of these singing oddities, but, as all other forms of singing were driven out of fashion, even many Scottish commentators asked if the cost had been too high.

The End (of culture)

Should it actually happen in your reality, this ending is NOT covered by the 100% money back guarantee. Let's face it you're hopefully okay with a little physics - the book happily mentioned quantum physics or Schrödinger's Cat in it's description and this ending references Boyle's Law, so you'll be fine with me describing your loss of the price of the book to me as a financial form of entropy. So to give a refund would violate the laws of Thermodynamics and we know that that can't happen.

—— Section 110 ——

You open the door...

And almost immediately know that you've entered the wrong room as someone says "Ah, Lord Vader, we've been awaiting your presence. The blueprints for the new deathstar are ready for your approval."

In the centre of the hi-tech room, the architects are sat with your lieutenants around a table upon which are the new blueprints.

"ARE YOU CERTAIN THAT THEY ARE INDESTRUCTIBLE THIS TIME?" you ask in your imposingly asthmatic voice.

"Oh yes, Lord Vader, we've learnt from our past mistakes we've hired some top architects this time."

"SO THERE ARE NO EXPOSED WEAK POINTS LIKE INSUFFICIENTLY PROTECTED VENTS LEADING TO CRITICAL WEAKNESSES?"

"Oh no, not at all, Lord Vader. As I say we've hired top architects who really know how to design a construct. They're very very good. They did the Pompidou Centre, you know."

"THE POMPIDOU CENTRE?"

"Yes, Lord Vader, the Pompidou Centre, in Paris."

"YOU MEAN THE ONE WITH ALL ITS INTERNAL PIPES AND WORKINGS ON THE OUTSIDE. ALL EXPOSED TO REBEL ASSAULT?"

"Oh fuck."

You exit the room and decide to look for the polling station behind a different door. (go to **Section 083**)

—— Section 111 ——

September 18th 2017

Ever after seeing David Icke on the TV you couldn't get his theory that humanity is ruled by a race of 8 feet tall shape-shifting lizards out of your head. You wondered what would make someone make such seemingly insane claims.

The only reason that you could think of was that the claims may not be quite as insane as everyone (except David Icke) seemed to think. Maybe he really did know the truth and was frantically trying Cassandra-like to warn mankind.

You decided to hunt down the evidence that only David Icke had seen for certain, but you knew must exist.

Most of the next 3 years is spent trying to get into parliamentary meetings, royal households, G20 meetings - anything and everything where people of power congregate. Anywhere that the cold blooded illuminati metamorphs may lurk and reveal their true selves.

You have some success, at getting into events and protected locations that is. You manage to get some compromising pictures and recordings of several illicit meetings and deals that help fund your research. But you never once see anything lizardy in a position of power.

This year you were on the verge of giving up, when you noticed that the G9 summit was taking place in Scotland (which had temporary membership of the elite country club). And so a month ago you applied to work in the venue and, somehow, passed the security checks and was accepted.

You didn't notice anything odd before or at the summit, which started yesterday, until you noticed that all the top ranking delegates from all countries had booked a 2 hour section of the morning for a private stroll in the highlands without camera crews observing them. That was odd enough, but what was really odd was when you followed at a discreet distance and saw them leave their security details not far into the walk.

You followed them further into the wilds and eventually saw them enter a small hole in a rock-face. You waited a couple of minutes and hurried over to the hole to discover a small tunnel leading downwards. After a couple of minutes navigating mainly by touch, the tunnel opened up into a strange bluish cavern illuminated by torchlight.

You looked around and couldn't spot the delegates, but what you did see was far more amazing.

The cavern was filled with over 100, maybe even 200, 8 feet tall saurians with strangely intelligent eyes. For some odd reason, they all seem to be talking English, although some have foreign accents and one even sounds just like Angela Merkel who you'd just followed. They're discussing a range of topics such as international banking, trade deficits and what to do about Camilla. As you covertly watch them you notice that some lizards are wearing medals, some crowns or chains of office.

Suddenly at the far end of the cavern, there's movement on a small rocky ledge about 15 feet off the cavern floor, as 3 figures enter from a tunnel you hadn't noticed before now.

The creatures at the front and back are more of the giant lizards, armed with deadly-looking swords and some form of bizarre firearm, but the figure in the middle is unmistakably human. More than that it is David Icke.

No!

Not only was David telling the truth about the lizards, but they've obviously caught him and have brought him here, under close guard, for who knows what foul purpose: Judgement? Torture? Execution?

You fear that you are about to find out.

The guards to either side of the captive human lower their weapons.

David Icke starts to speak in a loud voice "Brothers and Sisters, thank you all for coming, but, please, were all among friends here. Feel free to change into the natural form."

Before you started your search for the truth, you wondered what would make someone make such seemingly insane claims. You didn't realise that one reason would be to cover up a real conspiracy that seemed even more insane.

There are some secrets that mankind was never meant to know. Secrets that the human mind is too frail to comprehend without fracturing into madness.

A race of ungodly creatures that secretly rule mankind is such a secret. And seeing the hundreds of 8-feet tall lizards turn into their natural form of normal-sized David Ickes shatters your sanity and sends you running from the cavern, gibbering to a life with no hope of escaping the asylum.

But you don't want to escape. Not to the outside; to the normal world; to the world of the Ickes.

The End

Should it actually happen in your reality, this ending is covered by the 100% money back guarantee. But I don't think they allow you money in the asylum - you could sharpen the edges of coins to use as weapons or fold notes into paper planes that could easily take someone's eye out (according to parents and teachers everywhere although I've never seen it happen).

Instead I'll donate it on your behalf to a struggling author with his own obvious mental problems… Sorry.

—— Section 112 ——

The nurse looks at you and says "You've got to be joking… another one. Take a ticket and sit down in the waiting room. No complaining and don't be any trouble or I'll get security to kick you out. Right?"

You're too fragile to put up much resistance, so you agree weakly and take a ticket from the machine the nurse indicated on the wall.

Hmmm - number 42. That's not great. Oh well they probably keep it running day after day, for all you know you might only be the third or fourth person to come in today. You go over to the entrance to the waiting room and walk in… "Bloody hell"

You were right that they must keep the tickets just cycling day after day, but it obviously clicked around again this morning as there must be 50 or 60 people waiting here. All with the tell-tale blue faces of *Acute Facial Azuritis*.

You wait for ages. Nobody seems to be going through to be examined or treated and there's a steady stream of new arrivals coming in, each one with the now familiar diseased blue face of certain death.

Eventually, after 2 or 3 hours waiting, it looks like the stream of new arrivals has dried up but you've still not seen anyone leave to be attended to. The number of people in the waiting room has numbered somewhere around 130 for half an hour or more.

Then the nurse from reception comes through the waiting room and opens the door to the treatment areas.

"I think they're all here now doctor" you hear her call, before turning and heading back to reception. The room becomes alive with murmurs as people turn to their neighbours and wonder aloud about what is happening.

Within a minute or so a doctor steps into the room from the treatment areas. He coughs for your attention and, almost immediately, the murmuring stops.

"Good morning everyone. I'm Doctor Morgan and I'd like to thank you all for your patience. I'd also like to ask if you could all go back home and have a good wash. I'll be very very surprised if any of you are actually ill and frankly, my colleagues and I are sick of this happening every time there's some sort of political, national or sporting event. We're the National Health Service not the national school of makeup removal. Now piss off the lot of you."

As the doctor turns and starts to go back through the door he came from, you hear someone call out for a second opinion. As Doctor Morgan disappears another, younger doctor pokes her head through the doorway.

"Doctor Morgan's right - fuck off will you. Someone really ill might need us" she says before ducking back, closing the door and, going off the sound, locks and bolts it.

The voice that called for a second opinion says "fair enough I suppose" and people start to leave. Obviously the doctors are used to this and know that none of you really have any kind of disease, never mind some sort of deadly tropical hemorrhagic disease.

But maybe you should walk over to the A&E department, just to be sure. (go to **Section 389**)

or Screw that! I'm obviously saved. I'm going back home to get cleaned up. (go to **Section 294**)

—— Section 113 ——

Channel 4 is showing a fly on the wall programme set at a small hotel on the shores of Loch Ness.

It's surprising that already, in just a few weeks of independence, there's been an increase in tourism to the country and the bookings for 2015 are far higher than usual.

Of course the Channel 4 programme doesn't show this, so much as show a hotel that is so efficiently well run that it could be relocated to 1970s Torquay and run by Basil Fawlty and nobody would notice much difference. It's the typical fly-on-the-wall format, pick a few well-meaning people just trying to make a living, film them for a few weeks and then edit the film in such a way to show every single little disaster that makes them look like incompetent fools.

It doesn't actually help matters that it looks like this hotel actually is managed (if you can call it that) by a pair of fantasists who honestly think that the 12 bedroom '*Hotel Paradise*' is the start of a globe-spanning empire. The fact that they've been going for 20 years and still only have the first small hotel is immaterial to them. At least they aren't shown as total losers by the editors making sure one of them says "*I've seen Nessie, you know*" every 10 minutes…

It's annoying that TV choses to show this as an example of a Scottish Hotel, as you know that there are thousands of great hotels and B&Bs in the stunning countryside of your homeland. The tourism trade is doing well, but you're sure it could do even better if shows like this gave a more positive image.

You eventually decide to turn off the TV and start to think about your future and the future of Scotland, and where the priorities lie for both of you.

Should the government do its best to boost tourism (go to **Section 224**)

or Do you go on holiday in Scotland to help the domestic tourist industry (go to **Section 332**)

or You could travel all over Scotland and write about it (go to **Section 075**)

or Go on holiday to the hotel from the TV show, just to see how biased the programme was (go to **Section 128**)

or I don't want to think about all this - just give me something random! (go to **Section 375**)

—— Section 114 ——

At the Cafe you decide to order a meal of your own devising: *The Union Special.* A meal you only have occasionally because, whilst you like the way it celebrates all of the UK, it does cost quite a bit to do that.

You order, and pay, and ten minutes later your feast arrives.

A good thick oaty porridge with just a dash of whisky in it, to represent Scotland. A full English breakfast, oddly enough that's for England. Wales is represented by Welsh Rarebit and Ireland by a pint or two of Guinness[9]. Finally, to show that the Union is greater than the sum of it's parts, it's all topped off with a selection of British Lamb, British Beef and British Pork.

Most fittingly for such a meal, you face the Herculean task of trying to eat it all with the true British blitz spirit.

When you've finished, you can barely move and have to rest for an hour or so. But after that you head home and jump in the shower to freshen up. (go to **Section 258**)

—— Section 115 ——

You really hope that you'll get some form of polling station this time.

DEAD CAT TIME
Yes it's time to peek inside Schrödinger's box and see how well Jess is…

Hello Jess. Where's Pat? (go to **Section 003**)
or That's not a cat that's a shaved dog! (go to **Section 091**)
or Postcat Jess. Postcat Jess. Postcat Jess has left a mess! (go to **Section 254**)
or OMG! Jess is dead! Pat will be upset. (go to **Section 377**)

—— Section 116 ——

You rush back to the changing room but when you get there you can't spot your normal clothes or your phone, your money, your credit cards. How odd…

You go out to ask the shopkeeper if he knows where your belongings have gone, but when you exit the changing room you're back in the correct building but there's no sign of the shopkeeper. Or the shop fittings, shop stock, shop signs. Basically the shop and all signs of it have vanished in the few minutes you've been in the changing room.

Oh fuck.

You know what's happened. You've been scammed. You've seen all the shows on TV warning about the rise in fake fancy-dress shop cons and you thought '*It'll never happen to me*'. But it has happened to you. You got suckered in by the fact that you'd lived next door to the 'shop' for the past two years, you'd seen it's adverts in the local paper, read the flyers it pushed through your door.

You didn't realise that the con artist 'shopkeeper' was playing the long game, slowly winning your confidence over a period of years so that they could eventually escape with your sweatpants, tee-shirt, 5-year old iPhone, debit card (with bugger all left on the account overdraft) and about £12.80 in change. But that's how these tricksters make their living, knowing who's worth the sting and working towards trapping them, no matter how long or difficult it is. You know. You've seen Hustle.

You give up all hope of ever seeing the counterfeit shopkeeper again. No. He'll be halfway to Monte Carlo by now, ready to live the high life on his ill-gotten gains.

Feeling like a right mug, you leave the fake shop and head to the polling station. (go to **Section 189**)

—— Section 117 ——

On BBC2 there's a documentary looking at the future role of Scotland in Great Britain, Europe and the world at large.

While you're only a fairly small nation in terms of geographic area, in socio-economic terms you can play an important and highly influential role. You can become what the UK could have been if it didn't have the colonial baggage and spend so much time trying to culture a 'special relationship' with the USA.

Though in fairness the UK *does* have a special relationship with America; 'special' just like the special friendship 'friends with benefits' have, and it's clear which friend is getting shafted. Often you'd see an international crisis developing and the UK would stand firm beside America, like a loyal wife standing beside an adulterous criminal MP, and you'd follow the situation until…

'Oh not again' you think.

What happens next is inevitable.

Sex. Hot sex. Really hot sex. Really really hot international sex. Really really hot sexy sex so diplomatically hot you're surprised the UK Prime Minister doesn't die from exhaustion at the shafting he, and his country, are usually getting. Sex so hot that it can't be described in any greater detail than just 'really hot sex' or this book would be banned under obscenity law.

Yes - the UK has a 'special relationship' alright.

Scotland may not have that, but it has most of the international influence of the UK without the sucky, brown-nosing and hated history. Playing things right it can become the country that others want to be.

It can be the English speaking nation of choice for international trade and tourism: not as arrogant as the US, not an American lapdog like England, not racist like Australia, not insignificant like Canada and New Zealand. No - Scotland can beat all of those if it handles things right. Or even if it handles things wrongly but never gets caught out…

You eventually decide to turn off the TV and start to think about your future and the future of Scotland, and where the priorities lie for both of you.

Invest heavily on whatever it takes to beat England in trade and industry to prove that independence was the right thing for Scotland (go to **Section 147**) or Keep a close eye on your supposed allies South of the border, but don't spend too much money (go to **Section 007**)

or A new country needs a new ruler - let's get rid of Queen Elizabeth and find a new monarch (go to **Section 237**)

or Monarchies are so yester-century, let's elect a president! (go to **Section 330**)

or I don't want to think about all this - just give me something random! (go to **Section 375**)

—— Section 118 ——

You arrive home...

Without any further adventures and decide that after everything that's happened to you, you could do with a shower and a change of clothes before going out to vote.

Hopefully a good shower will let you get rid of all remaining traces of blue colouring on your face.

Soon you're jumping in the shower and scrubbing away. (go to **Section 240**)

—— Section 119 ——

You enter the polling booth, close the little privacy curtain and look at the ballot paper. It's such a small piece of paper. Almost too small and unassuming for the role it plays in this historic day.

You turn your attention to the single question on the ballot paper.

Should Scotland be an independent country?

Such a small sentence. Almost too small and unassuming for the massive decision it represents, with all its implications and knock-on effects. Whichever way the vote goes, those six little words play an important role in making history.

Okay - it's time to make a decision and make your mark, so you pick up the pencil ready. It's such a small pencil, almost too small and unassuming for the vital part it plays in this most momentous of days. It's a pencil that would look small in a betting shop and would be dwarfed by the pens in Argos.

It's taking the piss.

If everything today was sized appropriately for the important role they play, then the question should be printed on sheets of A0 paper in letters 6-inch high. You should have to make your mark with a paint roller in black paint. A big bold black cross would be more appropriate for the significance of this vote.

It's too late to change the ballot conditions, so, doing your best to ignore how small and insignificant everything seems, you prepare to cast your vote.

Vote for 'Yes'. (go to **Section 374**)
or Vote 'No'. (go to **Section 144**)
or Wait and think about it a little longer. (go to **Section 180**)
or Flip a coin. That's the way to decide. (go to **Section 279**)
Flip a coin. But what sort of coin? (go to **Section 008**)
And is heads yes or heads no? (go to **Section 139**)
I suppose heads should be 'No' since it shows the queen of the United Kingdom, (go to **Section 212**)
but then she'd still be the queen of Scotland if the 'Yes' vote wins independence. (go to **Section 222**)
Oh this coin flipping is far too confusing, but it's the only way to decide. (go to **Section 328**)
Okay heads is 'Yes', tails 'No'. (go to **Section 354**)
Should it be the other way round? (go to **Section 092**)
or Oh god you can't decide - the stress is too much! (go to **Section 368**)

—— Section 120 ——

Stepping out of the shower...

You dry off and try to decide what to wear today. Maybe you should wear something special. Then again, maybe not.

Do you decide to wear an outfit showing support for all the union? (go to **Section 148**)
or Do you think it's better to show your support for independence? (go to **Section 215**)
or Maybe you should just wear what you'd usually wear. (go to **Section 403**)
or Is today the day to make an impact wearing something weird? (go to **Section 234**)

—— Section 121 ——

"I need time to think" you say to the good doctor, who replies "of course you do - it must be hard for you, thinking that is."

"Why don't you go home and just let it sink in over the next few days. Or weeks. Months even. You should be fine if you don't come back here for four or five years while you think about it."

The doctor sees you out of the cubicle and, half in a daze, you wander out of the hospital and start walking home, your mind mulling over your future, or lack of one, with both *cerebral faeces syndrome* and *acute cubital anal disambiguation failure*. If you were more alert you'd notice that passers by are avoiding you more than usual and not just because of the blue face, but also due to the slumbering zombie-like shamble and crazy, thousand-yard stare you've adopted whilst so deep in thought.

It takes you over an hour to get home.

You're not sure why as it's usually only a 30 minute walk. You were wandering about only semi-conscious and you're not quite sure you remember the route you took or anything that happened to you. You've a vague recollection of having an argument after stepping in dog dirt, and for some reason there are brown flecks all over you and your oddly-brown hands stink of dog shit. But a vague recollection is all you can summon up.

Opening your front door you realise that there's only two options available to you.

You can either mope about, fearful for your diseased future and probably die a bitter young man or you can try to snap yourself out of it, forget about the diagnosis, get cleaned up, get dressed and go out to vote, to help Scotland's future, to make your mark on the world.

Ten minutes later you're stepping into the shower and trying to get rid of all remaining traces of blue colouring on your face and dog shit on your hands.

You pretty much manage to get cleaned up okay. (go to **Section 240**)

— Section 122 —

On ScottishLivingTV there's the new programme *Tomorrows Scotland* looking at the short to medium possibilities for the now independent nation.

The episode currently on screen takes a look at the future political structure and whether Scotland needs it's own monarch or president. Since winning independence there's been much talk of unrest at keeping the Queen as Scottish monarch when she spends so much time living in London. The likes of Canada, Australia and New Zealand have talked about becoming republics before, but for Scotland it's a real possibility whilst the wind of change is blowing through the nation.

The only real downside you can see is that you're not sure you'd like King Alex or President Salmond. He's already been quite full of himself since winning at *Yes-Day*. If he were to become King or President he'd be more insufferable than Tony Blair was as UK Prime Minister.

Mind you, if Scotland got rid of Queen Elizabeth, it wouldn't necessarily be Alex Salmond that replaced her…

You eventually decide to change the channel.

Change to BizBites TV (go to **Section 349**)
or Do you watch BBC2 (go to **Section 117**)

—— Section 123 ——

The Odds and Sods

Wow! Thomas decided to send you here to the collection of endings that never got written up. This isn't a normal ending, but the best ones of those are usually in the individual TV channels, rather than in the DEAD CAT TIME random ending selector.

I initially thought that this book would take a couple of weeks to write, since it wasn't bound to our single reality. It actually took over 2 months to do and, due to the looming referendum, had to be published before some of the possible endings that had been thought up were written up.

So here are a few of them in brief.

After much hard negotiating with a hard-nosed Westminster, you accidentally stumble upon the shocking truth that David Cameron is actually.... A normal human being with feelings and stuff. It's probably best that that one didn't make it in - the shock could kill people.

Like the above, but you find out that he's actually a radio controlled robot controlled by Nick Clegg. Who'd've thunked?

Like the above but in addition to that, Nick Clegg is actually a robot being controlled by Angela Merkel. What an efficient way to takeover a country without needing to fire a shot... Those cunning Germans!

Like the above, but Angela Merkel is a robot controlled by China or Japan or Taiwan. Of course she is - who did you think was making such technologically advanced robots? It's partly because these were all so so obvious that I didn't write them up earlier.

After a 'NO' vote win, Alex Salmond starts applying to be the leader of any country that will have him. He eventually becomes the muslim leader of a North African Caliphate or the President of the USA (as Republicans get convinced that he's just as American as Obama and preferable to Sarah Palin).

I had something involving the film Avatar and eblula, and it was really good, but I've forgotten exactly what it was. I think it was along the lines of the aliens from Avatar coming to earth after the disease has killed nearly everyone and thinking that we're just like them as the surviving humans are all blue.

There was bound to be something involving the phrases 'muffled flange' and 'fox felching' but I've not developed this any further. If you chose to develop it further, don't get caught. I can't be your defence.

You wake up on the 19th September 2014 after a night celebrating to find that everyone is talking like a pirate. You wonder what's going on before remembering that September 19th is International Talk Like a Pirate Day (it really is). But then you realise that people aren't talking in Robert Newton's piratical West Country accent but are talking French and all seem to be of African descent and carrying automatic weapons. Whilst the country was hungover, Scotland has been hijacked by Somali pirates using International Talk Like a Pirate Day as a source of cover-puns to get them into the country without anyone noticing.

And that's probably all I have chance to put here. Still it's a minor look behind the scenes at what could have been…

There were several more surreal ideas I'd been kicking about, but to explain them in enough detail that you get what I'm talking about would basically mean writing them up in full.

I'd do anything for love but I won't do that.

Or Nigel Farage covered in whipped cream.

Or out of it for that matter.

The Stop (well it's not really an 'end' is it?)

—— Section 124 ——

You make your excuses and head off towards home. You've had quite enough excitement for one night.

Now, stood here in your bathroom in the cold light of day, last night's events don't really seem to be the stuff that legend's are made of. But at the time it all felt incredibly thrilling and the debate gave you serious food for thought even though it didn't decide how you'll vote today.

You take a moment to think back to some of the highlights of the debate, but the excitement could easily become too much for you and distract you from getting ready to vote.

You hadn't realised just how exciting you found the debate and so now absent-mindedly wonder if it's normal for memories of political discussion to give grown men erections. Maybe it's not so much the debate as remembering the fiery redhead you spent so much time arguing with.

Still thinking about the nice, well-formed pair of salient points she had you jump into the shower to freshen up. (go to **Section 120**)

—— Section 125 ——

September 18th 2025

After *Yes-Day*, the Scottish government knew that the big-bucks triple A titles like *Car Jacking Hooker Killer V* didn't really need much help to conquer the world - they were already doing it. Which was good, because whilst the tax income is always welcomed, actively supporting such violent games can be a volatile position to be in if the voters find out.

The companies that could do with breaks and assistance were those creating nice non-violent games that anyone can play and enjoy. Games for mobile phones. Games like *Samurai Veg Chopper* - where people have to sweep their fingers across the screen to chop up flying veg to prepare a tasty meal.

The Scottish government gave these companies tax breaks and incentives and before long everyone was happy.

The public got a range of affordable veg-chopping games that were easy to learn, fun to play and hard to master.

The developers found it easier to make and sell games, even having so much success that before long people were able to chop-up vegetables on the popular games consoles as well as mobile devices.

The Scottish coffers got increased income and sales tax from the developers.

Everyone was happy.

Everyone.

Today, on the 11th anniversary of *Yes-Day*, the population of Earth awoke to the unexplained appearance of mile-wide flying saucers moving into position to hover above the world's 219 most populous cities.

The planet held it's breath for an hour while nothing seemed to happen. No communication came from the ships and they didn't appear to respond to any attempts to make contact with them. 154 minutes after the saucers had arrived the extraterrestrial invaders made themselves known in an audio broadcast apparently taking over all TV, radio and internet feeds and transmitted in every language used by mankind.

"People of Earth" said the English version "For too long you have subjugated, tortured and executed my people. Now it is time to teach you a lesson: Payback's a bitch."

You, like many others, wondered who the invaders were. Mankind hadn't ever had contact with aliens, unless rumours about Roswell and Area 51 were true.

The worldwide attacks that followed were sudden, vicious and brutal. No quarter was spared. One by one they hunted you down, slicing you apart with their high-powered laser grid weapons and blades that the Predator from the films would be proud of.

The sentient cucumbers of Saturn had been watching our video feeds for years. They had seen the untold pain inflicted upon their terrestrial cousins. They had been appalled and horrified. So horrified that they called a truce with the race of intelligent Tomatoes they'd been fighting for years. Before long they'd also signed truces with the Carrot and Broccoli Alliance and the Mighty Empire of the Radish.

They pooled resources and soon had a fleet of invasion craft en route to the offending 3rd planet, where no quarter was to be given.

As you are finally confronted by a pair of well-armed infantry Peppers you suddenly regret having been a vegetarian for most of your life. Thinking of the words the Supreme Over-Gherkin said in his broadcast you realise that you agree with him: Payback *is* a bitch.

The End

Should it actually happen in your reality, this ending is NOT covered by the 100% money back guarantee. Instead of trying to apply for a refund you should really be prioritising visiting a doctor or other health professional to check that this really did happen in your reality and that you're not having some sort of breakdown.

—— Section 126 ——

You remember tears welling up in your eyes...

As you put down your cup of Earl Grey, started to wave your miniature union flag and sang Land of Hope and Glory at the top of your voice.

England. Scotland. Walesland. What did it matter?

It's all one proud island. Whatever we call it, this is our land. Our home. Our nation.

Sure; we've not always got on together as well as we could, but, like any slightly dysfunctional family, deep down we love each other and, despite the gentle ribbing, we're there for each other. Heck we even quite like the strange cousins across the Irish Sea, even though they're not part of the mainland and occasional cause us all sorts of trouble.

England. Scotland. Welshland. This land. Our land. Yes - **Our Land**.

Was there any real point in separating part of the great union, just so it could have it's own name?

Does a rose by any other name not smell as sweet?

Does a rose by any other name not grow beauty from horse shit?

Does a rose by any other name not make you feel a prick every now and then (unless you've asked the florist to de-thorn it)?

The bard of Avon was right. When he wrote those words, Shakespeare could almost have been thinking about Scottish devolution plans. He knew that all the decades that Scotland and England had flourished together had been the most prosperous of their entire histories and shouldn't be thrown away in haste.

No. Like any marriage, the countries had occasional differences but they had to work through it. You don't throw away a good marriage and head for the divorce lawyers just because of a coalition government that no-one voted for.

England. Scotland. Welshwalesland.
Ireland. Holland. New Zealand.
Switzerland. Swaziland. Old Zealand.
My land. Your land. Our land.
It was all one single glorious land.
Our land.

You begin to choke up, emotion getting the better of you, and down the rest of your tea in one go. You're not normally so reckless but that's the sort of mood you're in. It just felt right - and to hell with the consequences.

You remember having another Earl Grey, then another, then... oh who knows how many you had before passing out on your bed, still fully clothed, both in your union flag suit and in despair that the nightmare of the union being broken up could perhaps become a reality.

But that was last night. You can't dwell on that all day. Even though you can't wait to get ready and go out to vote there's the everyday matters to see to first. Knowing that your dogs won't take themselves for a walk, you throw on some scruffs and grab their leads.

Do you take them out for walkies straight away (go to **Section 170**)
or Check your email first. (go to **Section 373**)

—— Section 127 ——

You open the door and you're greeted by the sound of a music system blasting out 90s pop music. You recognise the track as the biggest hit that *2 Unlimited* had - you think it was called *No Limits*.

It only takes a few moments for you to realise that something's wrong: the CD or record seems to be stuck in a loop. It just keeps repeating part of the chorus.

No no. No no no no. kzt No no. No no no no. kzt No no. No no no no. kzt No no. No no no no. kzt No no. No no no no. kzt No no…

Oh! Suddenly you realise what it is - it's not a broken music player but an intentional loop acting as a slightly less than subliminal hint about how to vote.

You look around the room and see it's adorned with union flags and graphical reminders of the long and great history that Scotland has shared with the rest of the UK.

You're really beginning to get the idea that this polling station may be slightly biased towards the 'NO' vote.

You go to exchange pleasantries with the lady (dressed in an equal mix of red, white and blue) behind the desk dealing with addresses including your home, but she smiles widely at your attire and greets you like a long-lost brother. Once you've confirmed your identity, she says "You know what's the right thing to do, laddy", gives you your ballot paper and points you in the direction of the small individual booths that you can go in to cast your vote in private.

As you walk across the room to the polling booth, it is with the weight of a country's destiny bearing down on your shoulders… (go to **Section 119**)

—— Section 128 ——

September 18th 2015

Just one year after *Yes-Day* you decide to do your bit to help Scottish tourism and take advantage of the warm summer to holiday in the wild expanses of your own country.

You choose to go to *Hotel Paradise* on the shores of Loch Ness, the same hotel that was cruelly misrepresented in the fly-on-the-wall documentary you watched all those months earlier.

Even checking in, after the process takes well over 10 minutes as they seem to have no idea that you'd booked online, you start to wonder if the TV show was unduly unkind. You certainly wouldn't be trusting the owners to organise any brewery-based alcohol-centred parties anytime soon.

Finally you're booked in and as one of the owners hands you the key she finally says her catch phrase from the TV show.

"I've seen Nessie, you know."

"Really?" You say, humouring her as it's no doubt all of the experience of staying here though you're fairly certain that the conversation is about to move onto Nessie memorabilia you can purchase from the hotel.

"Aye - she's always oot an aboot. If you wanna see her yerself, you're best chance is probbly just before dusk - she likes to do a few lengths before bed."

That evening you take an early meal before setting off for a stroll along the loch before sundown, camera ready just in case you see any floating debris that looks slightly like the distinctive neck of a Plesiosaur. You know that the whole Nessie myth is bunkum, but there's no harm in bunkum if you get a photo out of it that you can sell to a gullible paper or go viral with on twatter.

You've been walking for nearly 20 minutes and haven't seen any length-swimming dinosaurs or mythic dragons. You have seen some gorgeous scenery though as you appreciate the almost magical atmosphere around the lake. It's easy to imagine creatures of myth and legend here, and the loch is absolutely enormous. You can understand how once cryptozoologists get the idea of Nessie into their heads they can spend decades searching for her and still not lose heart when they find no trace. The lake's *that* big.

You could hide a million large dinosaurs in it and still be lucky if you managed to see one.

You're just about to turn back towards the hotel when you hear a disturbance in the water, and, looking carefully, notice a lot of ripples about 100 metres from the shore. It looks as if something large disturbed the surface of the loch. You tell yourself that it's probably just a large bird diving under to fish… but still you get your camera ready for when the creature resurfaces.

You can barely believe your eyes when it does.

Rushing into the hotel entrance, you see that the male owner is manning the lobby. You bound over to him, excited to share your stunning photos.

"I've seen her. Nessie - look!" you exclaim shoving the screen of your camera under his face.

He looks closely for a few seconds before announcing "Auch - that's no Nessie."

What?! After all the times you've seen him and his wife going on about the creature he's not going to say that you're imagining it is he? You decide to challenge him on his assertion that it's not Nessie.

"I'm sorry I know what that is. You can't seriously be trying to tell me that it's just a log?"

"Naw - that's nae a log, it's got a heid for starters. But it's definitely no Nessie. That's Eliot, that is."

"Eliot? Eliot Nessie? Come off it I wasn't born yesterday and I know what I saw, what this is!" In agitation you've raised your voice a little bringing the co-owner to the lobby.

"What's all this commotion?" she asks.

"Look" you shove the camera under her nose.

"I've seen Nessie. I've got proof, but your husband's trying to tell me it's another Plesiosaur called 'Eliot'."

"Naw. That's ridiculous." She says.

"I know."

"He don't know what he's talking aboot. Eliot'll be on holiday this time of year. Tha's Una, that is."

They go on to tell you about how Nessie isn't a lone oddity - of course she isn't, how would she survive alone for thousands of years? That just wouldn't make sense. No, if they're to be believed, there's at least 59 Plesiosaurs living in the loch (counting Eliot who always goes on holiday in September so isn't here at the moment).

You retire to bed not sure exactly what is going on. You know that you saw something. The photos are proof that you saw something, and you were sure it was Nessie. But talking to the owners just makes it all seem too crazy to possibly be true.

Are you in some sort of hidden camera show? Is Derren Brown hiding in a nearby van? Or are the owners just pulling your leg, sincere but deluded or proper headcases who really believe in a whole family of Loch Ness monsters?

Whatever the truth of the matter, you decide that they're pretty much harmless 'characters' that add some colour to both the hotel and the local area.

Of course you rethink this opinion later that evening when they kill you at the stroke of midnight and skin you before dancing, completely naked, around a bonfire. Actually it's wrong to call them both completely naked, as the man is now wearing your face like a mask. Just like the Loch Ness god-beasts told him to do to make them happy.

The End

Should it actually happen in your reality, this ending is NOT covered by the 100% money back guarantee. Because I'm hedging my bets by pandering to the saurian god-monsters of Loch Ness.

—— Section 129 ——

Thirty minutes later as you walk up to your front door, you're feeling wonderful. Of course you weren't going to die - it's just the daft way you painted your face. How could you have been so stupid?

Again.

You're feeling quite happy to be alive. On the way home you even let on to a complete stranger in the street, which is something you never normally do. Mind you you had to say something to stop yourself from laughing at the sight of the idiot struggling with 5 dogs that were taking him for a walk.

Soon you are in the shower, freshening up and removing all traces of blue from your face. (go to **Section 240**)

—— Section 130 ——

"I know who I'm voting for"

Andy doesn't look surprised at all. "I knew you would. So I don't need to ask which way yer voting, do I? Scotland the brave. Scotland the free, eh?"

You look at Andy and snap at him "How I'm voting's between me an the ballot box. None of your fuckin' business."

"Alright just asking, mate. No need to be a prick."

Maybe you've had more to drink than you realise because you know Andy's your mate and isn't trying to be nasty, but being called a prick immediately makes you furious.

You give him a shove and warn him "Callin' me a prick? Watch what yer saying fuckface."

But as he doesn't immediately apologise profusely the drink gets the better of you and you start shoving him more and before long things have escalated. (go to **Section 197**)

—— Section 131 ——

You look around the shop and soon spot the perfect costume: A bright green, adult-sized Godzilla outfit.

You've always fancied being a giant fire breathing, laser-eyed lizard. No-one will stand in your way as you smash skyscrapers underfoot, terrorise whole cities and place a little cross in a box on a ballot paper.

Oh yes - Godzilla it is. As you hand over the money to the shopkeeper you just hope that that annoying little shit Godzooky isn't anywhere close.

Proudly you walk out of the shop, exaggerating your steps and making deep 'boom' noises with every footfall.

It's great to be Godzilla on the way to the polling station. (go to **Section 004**)

—— Section 132 ——

September 18th 2022

Despite bad weather delaying many of the tournaments games, the World Cup Final is here at last and it just happens to be on the 8th anniversary of *Yes-day*. What a great omen for Scotland, who have a real chance to win a historic victory on home soil. All they're got to do is beat the United Arab Emirates and that shouldn't be too hard as they've only made it this far by fluke.

Late in the second half and it's still a goal-less game when, in the 3rd minute of stoppage time, McAdam sends a perfect pass straight to your feet at the halfway line. You turn and start running the ball downfield. You beat one man on the turn, a second with sheer pace before flicking the ball up and over the last defender in your way. Racing around him you get to the ball just in time to volley it with a stunning overhead scissor-kick from just inside the penalty spot.

The shot looks good but the UAE keeper's diving towards it. The next couple of seconds seem to last an eternity as the keeper closes in on the ball that is slowly curling away from him. Finally the keeper gets to the ball, but only manages to get the very tips of his fingers on it… which is just enough to push it onto the top left corner of the goalposts.

The ball rebounds before being cleared away by a defender scrambling back.

You can't believe that you missed that. It was a difficult shot, but you're used to making difficult shots. For anyone else that was nearly impossible but for you it might have well been an open goal, and still you didn't score.

Still in disbelief, you stand up and look towards your goal and are shocked to see that a series of quick passes has moved the ball the length of the field. It's now at the feet of the Arabs star forward who is charging onwards just inside your own penalty box.

As the referee looks at his watch and starts to raise the game-ending whistle to his lips, the Arab player shoots - a last ditch attempt to end the game in regular time. Your keeper dives at the ball rocketing towards him and…

GOOOAALLL YOUUUUU-NITED ARAB EMIRATES!!!!!

You can't believe it. That's all it takes to win the cup.

"Cheating piece of shit" you mutter, throwing the game controller at the floor in disgust.

You're still glad that you took up football after Scotland was awarded the World Cup Finals back in 2014. That would never have happened without an Independent Scotland.

But despite getting the cup, sports and health funding was never the priority it should have been in Scotland. And that's why the real Scottish football team never made it to the world cup finals and your cup final defeat was only in a game of *Fuckin' Soccer 2022* against the Playstation 6's computer-controlled UAE opponents.

Of course it's not really called Fuckin' Soccer. Officially it's ProCreation Soccer 2022, the football game developed in Italy by the Catholic Church to directly compete with the Pro Evolution Soccer franchise. Because it's not only soccer that Italians do better than Scotland, apparently it's video games as well.

A shame, as you really believe that Scotland could have been inspired to become the top of the world in soccer or video games if only the new government had invested correctly after *Yes-Day.*

The end of the beginning

Should it actually happen in your reality, this ending is <u>NOT</u> covered by the 100% money back guarantee. Looks like lucks not looking up for you. Oh well. Maybe next time.

—— Section 133 ——

You enter the examination cubicle and hear the waiting doctor say "Oh I thought I recognised the name. It's you."

You're pleased to see that it's Doctor Cook - the same doctor who treated you the last two times you ended up blue-faced in A&E. At least he's familiar with you and he's stopped you from dying on your previous visits.

"So what exactly is the problem?"

"L-look at my face… I'm blue. I'm leaking. I'm dying."

"Really."

The doctor looks closely at your face whilst pulling on a pair of latex gloves and picking up a cotton wool swab.

"Hold still this won't hurt."

He daubs at the outside of your cheek then looks at the blue residue.

"How long have you been displaying these symptoms? Since waking up this morning, the day of the referendum?"

You confirm that and reflect on how good he is. He probably recognises the disease and he's such an expert he can tell how long you've been suffering just by a swab.

The way he says "thought as much" makes you realise just how bad your situation is. You'd think that he'd be pleased at making a quick diagnosis, but no - he seems annoyed and irritated, obviously at the severity of the disease you have as the only other thing that could be causing it is you, and he's got far too good a bedside manner to show irritation at a patient.

"Well I'm afraid that we're going to have to do some more tests and we'll have to do them immediately. I'm really concerned this time."

Within seconds, before you have chance to question him, you're rushed away to be prepped.

Soon you find yourself in what looks like an operating theatre.

Before you know it Dr Cook is telling you that you may feel some discomfort and shoving an endoscope up your bum. May feel some discomfort? No shit Sherlock.

After what feels like ages but is probably only 10 minutes or so he withdraws the camera and gives you a clean bill of health.

"I can't see anything that may be causing a blue face, so I can only conclude that you've probably got a slight residue on your face from painting it blue again. The best thing to do is probably to get dressed, go home and wash it off. Unless you want me to have a deeper look with the endoscope just to be sure… do you?"

You agree to do that and quickly get dressed.

He's such a nice doctor that as you pass him on the way out he even apologises for forgetting to lube the endoscope.

It's not long before you're home and jumping in the shower to freshen up. (go to **Section 240**)

—— Section 134 ——

You open the door and almost immediately know that you've entered the wrong room because you seem to be in a broom cupboard. Hmm that's not right.

You exit the room and decide to look for the polling station behind a different door. (go to **Section 083**)

—— **Section 135** ——

September 18th 2021

After *Yes-Day* you start doing your best to find a solution to the world's hunger problems.

Your early experiments and culinary explorations show that a viable foodstuff that provides a nutritionally healthy mix can be made from mixing a special blend of Soya with just a little bit of other additives to create a little flavour and textural variation. Testing your product on fasting Christians before Easter, it's soon obvious that Soyalent could really be the answer to the world's starving millions.

Soon your product is hitting the shelves of global supermarkets. It sells almost faster than it can be made. Before long it's a household name and you're being invited onto talkshows to be interviewed about your wonder food. Like tonight when you're on the BBC1 early-evening magazine show.

"So tell us about your Soyalent range - there are quite a few flavours available aren't there?" asks the interviewer.

"Oh yes - and more being developed all the time. We started off with Soyalent Brown 3 years ago. That's made from the core mix with haggis added. Soyalent Red contains tomatoes. Soyalent yellow is sweetcorn. Soyalent Green is… err…"

"What… what is it? It's people isn't it?"

"No - don't be ridiculous - Soyalent Green is Broccoli."

"Oh that surprised me."

"Then there's Soyalent white - that's neeps and tatties. And last but not least, Soyalent Tartan with a Piper on the Box."

"So *Soyalent Tartan with a Piper on the Box* is ***people!***"

"No, silly, it's shortbread - we thought it good to have a sweet option."

The rest of the interview goes without hitch and your product continues it's climb to becoming the staple diet of over 85% of all people on Earth. Before the decade is out you've managed to solve famine and give future food security, making the world a better place for all.

The End

Should it actually happen in your reality, this ending is <u>NOT</u> covered by the 100% money back guarantee. What is it with you wanting a refund every time a reality leaves you rich, famous and happy?

—— Section 136 ——

You remember tears welling up in your eyes...

As you put down your cup of Earl Grey, started to wave your miniature union flag and sang Land of Hope and Glory at the top of your voice.

England. Scotland. Walesland. What did it matter?

It's all one proud island. Whatever we call it, this is our land. Our home. Our nation.

Sure; we've not always got on together as well as we could, but, like any slightly dysfunctional family, deep down we love each other and, despite the gentle ribbing, we're there for each other. Heck we even quite like the strange cousins - *ktheaaaarrrrrr*

What the hell was that?

You could have sworn there was a strange noise behind you. It sounded like... no it couldn't be.... it's not possible...

You turn around slowly, scared to see what made the whiny rasping sound but even more scared to stay looking ahead with god-knows-what behind you.

"Cunty Knobends!"

Did you really think you could outwit the goblin-banshee that easily? Did you really think it would let you escape? Did you? Did you? Did you?

Because the goblin-banshee didn't think that. No. The goblin-banshee thought it would hunt you down, rip you a new arsehole and use you like a glove puppet. And that is what it is doing.

Your last thought, as the final strands of consciousness and life slip away, is "I don't mind being used as a glove puppet, but I do wish it'd stop making me say *'gottle of geer'*."

The End

Should it actually happen in your reality, this ending is <u>NOT</u> covered by the 100% money back guarantee. The publishers are terrified of goblin-banshees and we're not going to risk annoying one by giving a refund to one of their victims. That's way to risky. We'd rather call Pinhead a big girl's blouse, go to Hannibal Lecter's for dinner and be fisted by Freddy Krueger.

—— Section 137 ——

It's highly likely that your best bet for finding proof that the Loch Ness Monster really exists is to go back a few thousand years and look for it then, when it may not be as wary of people.

Jumping back and forth in time, you play the stock market to amass a fortune and then design and pay for a special Nessie-shaped submarine to use in your hunt for the creature. When you have the finished sub, you jump back in time to begin your search.

September 18th 2000 BC

Arriving at Loch Ness over 4,000 years ago, you enter the lake in your cunningly disguised submersible and start your search.

Your hunch about Nessie not being as wary of people in the past appears to have been correct, because you soon spot her and manage to get up quite close to the inquisitive creature.

You can hardly believe your luck and it's remarkable that you have the presence of mind to start the video cameras recording. Nessie is a stunning creature, though you're glad to see that you guessed correctly that she'd be similar to a prehistoric Plesiosaur and so you managed to design a sub very similar to the actual creature.

In fact it's so similar you can hardly tell the difference. You just look a little stiff or false, but certainly more realistic than a human sex doll looks compared to a real human.

Just as you think this, Nessie looks straight at you and you swear that she winks.

'Oh not again' you think.

What happens next is inevitable.

Sex. Hot sex. Really hot sex. Really really hot sea monster sex. Sex so hot you're surprised your SONAR boom doesn't fall off. Sex so hot that it can't be described in any greater detail than just 'really hot sex' or this book would be banned under obscenity law. Sex so hot that if it was any hotter Loch Ness would boil away in a cloud of sexy sexy steam.

You knew you shouldn't have made the submarine with realistic genitalia, but it was the only place to put the large SONAR boom without it looking out of place. Although you do suppose that you didn't need to paint it quite so accurately - although part of you thinks you'd rather be shagged by a sea monster than have people laughing at your unrealistic SONAR cock.

You sit tight, thinking all that you need to do is wait and you'll be free again. You have 6 hours of air until you need to surface again and this shouldn't take more than 10 or 20 minutes. Maybe 30 minutes. An hour at most.

You'd think that would be so, but after two hours you're really panicking. Nessie is probably the most considerate lover you've ever had. She's not going to let you go until you're well and truly spent, and that's going to take a while for your metal SONAR boom…

After ten hours of vigorous underwater sex, Nessie finally gives up and swims off with a large smile on her face. Of course you don't see the smile as you died some 4 hours earlier.

It's a good job that, over the next few hundred years, sediment covers your submarine. It'll be hard for scientists to explain it's presence if ever anyone spots your sub. It'll be even harder for them to explain and understand the video recording you made.

The End

Should it actually happen in your reality, this ending is NOT covered by the 100% money back guarantee. It should be, but, to be honest, I'm laughing too much that someone smart enough to invent time travel is dumb enough to get bonked to death by the Loch Ness Monster.

—— Section 138 ——

You really hope that you'll get some form of polling station this time.

DEAD CAT TIME

Yes it's time to peek inside Schrödinger's box and see how well Jess is…

Hello Jess. Where's Pat? (go to **Section 395**)

or That's not a cat that's a shaved dog! (go to **Section 161**)

or Postcat Jess. Postcat Jess. Postcat Jess has left a mess! (go to **Section 039**)

or OMG! Jess is dead! Pat will be upset. (go to **Section 209**)

—— Section 139 ——

The coin flies up…

Arcing upwards and upwards. You watch it slow then you watch it falling back down, picking up speed, coming nearer and faster and faster and nearer until…

"Owwww!"

Watching the coin you have somehow managed to cut yourself with it just above your left eye. It's only a small cut but it's bleeding quite a bit.

You try to ignore it and cast your vote, but as you look at the ballot paper you drip blood over both boxes, 'YES' and 'NO'.

Hmmmm… I suppose that counts as a spoilt paper.

You fold the ballot paper and, without making eye contact with anybody, walk across the floor and pop the folded ballot in the box. You ignore the station attendants and walk out quickly, embarrassed that they somehow know what you did.

With everything you have to worry about whenever there's a poll it's really annoying that even coin-tosses are out to complicate things. No wonder people treat votes as a big deal.

You go home and carry on as normal until the results are announced. (go to **Section 321**)

—— Section 140 ——

You enter the examination cubicle and hear the waiting doctor say "Oh… You again."

You're pleased to see that it's Doctor Cook - the same doctor who treated you the last two times you ended up blue-faced in A&E. At least he's familiar with you and he's stopped you from dying on your previous visits.

"So what exactly is the problem? As if I can't tell."

"L-look at my face… I'm blue. I'm leaking. I'm dying."

"Really."

The doctor looks closely at your face whilst pulling on a pair of latex gloves and picking up a cotton wool swab.

"Hold still this won't hurt."

He daubs at the outside of your cheek then looks at the blue residue.

"How long have you been displaying these symptoms? Since waking up this morning, the day of the referendum?"

You confirm that and reflect on how good he is. He probably recognises the disease and he's such an expert he can tell how long you've been suffering just by a swab.

The way he says "Well… Whaddya know" makes you realise that you've done it again.

"Oh… let me guess. Nothing wrong with me except a slight residue from painting my face, so I should go home and wash it off and let you deal with sick people who actually need your help?"

"Got it in one. And here was I not realising that you were medically trained."

"I should go before you get upset with me, shouldn't I?"

"Best do."

You exit the examination cubicle before he changes his mind and decides to do more tests of a painful nature. As you leave the area you hear him let off a badly-muffled stream of expletives.

You rush home and have a shower to freshen up and remove all signs of a blue face. (go to **Section 240**)

—— Section 141 ——

You get some funny looks on the way, but most people seem to accept that on such a momentous day some people might dress up and treat it like some sort of party. At least there's no trouble and eventually you get to the polling station, walk up to the doors and pause.

You always thought that polling stations are places full of wonder and promise for the future. The almost-mystical locations that can alter a nations fate. Each one a powerful nexus where all possible destinies of the country intersect, just waiting for the public will to select one single possibility and to transform it into reality. Places of truly amazing, almost miraculous, transformative power.

But really they are just local primary schools that have swapped the kids for a naff sign saying 'POLLING STATION'.

Finally you approach the doors and prepare yourself to step inside.

DEAD CAT TIME

Yes it's time to peek inside Schrödinger's box and see how well Jess is…

Hello Jess. Where's Pat? (go to **Section 013**)

or Hello Pat. Where's Jess gone? (go to **Section 018**)

or That's not a cat that's George Galloway! (go to **Section 177**)

or Jess is curled up asleep, blissfully unaware of their role in the future of Scotland. (go to **Section 287**)

or Postcat Jess. Postcat Jess. Postcat Jess has left a mess! (go to **Section 366**)

or OMG! Jess is dead! Pat will be upset. (go to **Section 288**)

—— Section 142 ——

Your fist travels in a perfect arc in the direction of the bloke's head. You place your weight behind it perfectly. You apply the correct force to accelerate perfectly.

And you put all this together to somehow execute a perfect miss by a good half inch or more.

Reacting as quickly as some video game fighter, your opponent sidesteps before bringing his knee up forcibly, obviously aiming to drive your testicles into your stomach.

Well you say obviously - to be honest it's somewhat less than obvious as he completely misses and instead knees a perfectly good chair.

"Oww shit!" he cries and for some reason it's the funniest thing you've seen all year.

You double up almost as if you'd been kneed in the goolies, but it's actually laughter that's having this effect on you.

"Aw mate - that is the fuckin' funniest thing I've ever seen. You're no fighter are you? Well tell you what we'll be good an jus' siddown over there. We'll be no more trouble."

You and Andy stick to your word and sit down to 'enjoy' the debate. (go to **Section 251**)

—— Section 143 ——

You race to the left feeling good that by heeding the lessons taught by *'Even More Dragon Gold!'* you've probably escaped a hideous twin-arsed death at the hands of a goblin-banshee.

But sadly you soon realise that the passage you've taken is a dead end. You're not sure why there's a dead end in the castle, but you know from various adventure games and other non-linear books from childhood that, inexplicably, castles and dungeons always have dead ends in the most annoying places. It's almost as if they're put there by sadistic game designers and authors just to make life awkward.

You've no time to muse any more about the dead end, as you can hear the angry knights closing on your position. You look around for somewhere to hide and immediately spot three large barrels.

Hiding in barrels always worked for Scooby and Shaggy, so, given that the alternative is to face the bloodthirsty mob, it's worth a shot.

You jump into a barrel just before the mob arrives at the dead end.

Now if you remember correctly, the way it worked for Scooby was that whenever the mask-wearing caretaker would look into a barrel, he'd move to a different barrel. Hmmm... you seem to have a set of faulty barrels as you can't spot the magic passageway to get from one barrel to another...

That's really bad news as the mob look into all three barrels and spot you immediately before showing you how sharp their swords are.

Thanks in part to the lies spread by children's cartoons, you are dead.

The End

This ending is <u>NOT</u> covered by the 100% money back guarantee should it actually happen in your reality. You really ran into a dead end, yes a **<u>dead</u>** end, and then tried to hide by copying a cartoon dog? No refund for you, dickhead.

—— Section 144 ——

You pick up the teeny tiny pencil...

And make a cross in the 'NO' box.

You fold the ballot paper and, trying not to make eye contact with anybody, walk across the floor and pop the folded ballot in the box. You exchange knowing nods with the station attendants. You know and they know that you have fulfilled your democratic duty.

For such a momentous historic vote it all seems like an anticlimax now.

All you can do is go home and carry on as normal until the results are announced. (go to **Section 321**)

—— Section 145 ——

Your fist flies in a perfect trajectory before making solid contact with the bloke's face. From the sound and feel of the hit you're sure you've broken his nose and he drops to the floor as if he's blacked out for a second or two.

Seeing how easily he went down, you feel like a total and utter bully. He had no hope against you.

Hoping you've not actually done him a serious injury or killed him, you and Andy quickly flee from the debating hall.

Just in case the authorities are called you race home earlier than you planned.

Admittedly that's not a great storyline for a **You Decide!** story, but to be fair it was **you** who **decided** to hit him. If you hadn't done that you'd probably have had a much better adventure.

As the author I'm a little concerned that you may have barely suppressed anger-management issues. Sure you may not really attack people in real life, but you did it so quickly in this book... Fictional people have feelings too. They can be hurt and injured just like flesh and blood.

Are you seeing a psychiatrist or other mental health specialist about your violent tendencies? Don't you think you should?

What do you mean I'd better shut up or you'll hit me? I'm the bloody author, you can't threaten me, well not now you've presumably bought the book anyway.

What did you just say?

Well if that's your attitude just get in that bloody shower on the morning of Thursday 18th September and get cleaned up. You've got voting to do. (go to **Section 295**)

—— Section 146 ——

At the bar there are still lots of people talking about the referendum, but now with you all having a couple of drinks inside you it's a little less formal, a little noisier and there's a lot more bollocks being said.

The two drunks who intruded on the debate are there. They say they were only having a laugh and apologise for any disrespect by buying you a drink. They claim that they actually found the debate interesting once they sat down and listened.

"Aye - was good, but I was gaggin' for a drink by the end, wasn't I Andy?" says the punster to you and his mate before apologising yet again and buying another round.

You can tell how drunk they are by the way they keep forgetting that they've apologised and go on to repeat themselves. So far they've apologised 4 or 5 times, buying you a drink each time…

It's good that they do, as eventually it helps you build up the courage to go over and speak to the redhead you'd debated with.

You soon find out her name is Kelly and she's as concerned and confused about the referendum as you are. She enjoyed the debate and says she thought you made a great point about future currency and the share of UK debt in the event of independence. In return you compliment her on her amazing pair of points and as you do you suddenly realise that she's not got a bad pair of tits either. She's really quite attractive and you seem to be getting on pretty well.

After an hour or so the drunks come over to say they're off for a curry and you can join them. Forgetting your earlier conversation, they say that they'll even buy yours as they have to find some way to apologise for being dicks earlier.

Do you join them for a curry? (go to **Section 015**)

or Decline with the hope of getting to know Kelly better? (go to **Section 022**)

or Wait to see what Kelly wants to do and do the same. (go to **Section 333**)

or Decline as it's late and you're happy just chatting with Kelly. (go to **Section 065**)

—— Section 147 ——

September 18th 2018

Despite knowing that Holyrood will hang you out to dry if you get caught, you're remarkably relaxed as you bypass the electronic door locks and gain entry to the small nondescript regional office of *Britannic Mass*

Haulage in Newcastle on Tyne.

It might seem odd for a Scottish state security operative (or spy, if you prefer) to break into a trucking company in England, but you know that the company is just a front for one of the MI6 operations that you suspect of industrial espionage North of the border.

You quickly locate the office you want. It looks normal but you know it actually contains a range of high-tech anti-intrusion measures to rival the vault room of any Hollywood heist movie.

Switching your goggles to UV you can see the invisible high-frequency laser beams zigzagging the floor. You carefully avoid them, ignoring the heat sensors in the corners of the room since they can't spot you in your thermal-neutral bodysuit. You quickly make your way to the wall where you know the safe is located.

You move the picture covering the concealed safety box - you think it's a nice touch that it's a framed photograph of the Gringott's set from the Harry Potter films. At last - the safe itself.

It's funny how with all the high tech anti-intrusion systems the safe itself is an old multi-tumbler device. Maybe MI6 were hoping that anyone who could beat the hi-tech would fail at the lo-tech safe, and anyone who was a skilled lo-tech safe cracker couldn't beat the hi-tech security.

Of course they never counted on someone like you - skilled with the hi-tech and crafty enough to use some human-engineering to beat the lo-tech. All it took was a call to one of the secretaries whilst pretending to work for the safe manufacturer. She gave out the combination quite happily after you'd 'proved' you were legitimate and had paid her a couple of compliments.

As you open the safe lock, almost on autopilot, you remember back to that afternoon not long after *Yes-Day* when you switched on the television and watched the programme about your newly independent homelands place in the world, and how it might be bettered.

It was clear to you that England, your old friend, was now perhaps your closest rival. It would do anything to beat Scotland and prove that voting 'Yes' in the referendum had been a gross mistake.

You always believed in the truth behind the phrase '*keep your friends close, but keep your enemies closer*' and so you knew what you had to do to help your country flourish.

The very next day you'd applied to join the newly formed *Scottish Intelligence Service*. Weeks of background checks and tests followed and luckily you somehow passed with flying colours (despite whatever you did in the early parts of this book). Soon you were being trained up as an SI6 field operative to be tasked with industrial espionage, non-industrial espionage and counter-espionage against your old allies in England.

It was great! Just like all the episodes of Spooks you'd watched and nearly as good as the Bourne and Bond films, but with a sexier lead man (in your opinion).

A voice in your ear rips you back to the present by asking "Have you got the shecret documentsh yet, double-ohh shixtynine?"

It's your tech backup, Special Agent 0087 sat in the white plumbers van parked across the road from the office you're in.

"Yes, Sean, I have. Didn't you see? Did you fall asleep again?" You ask, knowing the answer.

Holyrood saw it as a massive PR coup getting Sean Connery to return to Scotland from his self-imposed tax exile, but age isn't being kind to him and he's now convinced that he really was a super secret agent called James McBond. The upshot of this is that he only returned if he was allowed to play an active role in Scottish Intelligence, and you've ended up being lumped with the nearly 90-year old actor. It's not so bad, as you're probably SI6's top agent and you seldom need active support mid-mission, so having 0087 sat sleeping in the van keeps him out of trouble and usually there's no great problem.

No answer from Sean. You ask again "Did you fall asleep?" and are answered by a gentle snore in your earpiece.

Oh well - he's not doing any harm by kipping and you'll be out of here in another couple of minutes.

And that's how smoothly most of your jobs go, as time and time again you do the behind the scenes work that lets Scotland become the 2nd biggest economy in Europe. You knew what you were doing when you chose 'Yes'.

The End of the beginning

Should it actually happen in your reality, this ending is <u>NOT</u> covered by the 100% money back guarantee. You've had your fun, don't push it.

—— Section 148 ——

You show your support for the whole of the United Kingdom. It's not easy trying to decide the best way to do this, but eventually you settle on an ensemble using various pieces of clothing from all over the union.

You've a fine traditional Scottish kilt featuring the tartan and golden arches of the clan McDonald which you've proudly owned ever since getting it in a happy meal last year.

You've a rugby shirt from the Welsh national team, featuring traditional coal dust and velcro on the arms.

You've an English Morris dancer's poncey shoes and effeminate socks.

And from Northern Ireland you've got something that really, really, really sums up the idea of Northern Ireland, possibly white gloves and a sash of some form[10].

And to top it all off, a city gent's bowler hat adorned with a rose, a thistle, a leek and a shamrock.

You pin a 'Better Together' campaign badge onto the rugby shirt and look at yourself in the mirror.

Damn! You've done a bloody good job.

If the very sight of you doesn't persuade people to vote 'NO' then there's no sense of fairness or justice in the world.

Humming 'God Save the Queen' you leave for the polling station. (go to **Section 271**)

—— Section 149 ——

September 18th 2014

Yes-Day was when it started.

Nobody realised it then of course. The United Kingdom and most of Europe had been watching the Scottish referendum. Further away people had been busy fighting ebola that had spent months spreading out of Western Africa.

People were definitely interested in the referendum or ebola, nobody was interested in both. Which is why it took a long time for anyone to notice that a new hemorrhagic fever, a mutated form of ebola, had taken hold in Scotland.

Patient Zero was admitted to hospital on the 18th September itself. He showed signs of a blue face and seemed to be leaking blue fluid as his organs turned blue and bled out. He died a week later by which time there were already another 276 identified cases in Scotland and another 34 confirmed cases around the rest of the world (mainly in the UK and EU). He was the first death from *St Andrew's Cross Disease*.

Within a month all of those cases had died and there were over 120,000 known cases in 48 countries. So far the disease was killing nearly 100% of all those infected. The media had dubbed the disease 'eblula' but many called it the Blue Death, which was probably the most accurate name.

Nobody could cure the disease despite trying a range of approaches. A Dr Cook famously thought that the entire disease was made up by time wasters and tried to 'cure' it by a mix of rectal endoscopy and sarcasm. He failed. Other failed attempts involved prayer, expressive dance and homeopathy. Nothing seemed to work - and homeopathy worked even less well than Dr Cook's sarcasm and anal intrusion by camera.

Within 6 months there were over quarter of a million fatalities and 10 million known cases. It was well on it's way to becoming a pandemic, aided partly by the authorities slow reactions to the emerging plague.

Without serious additional funding the best efforts of the NHS, WHO and America's CDC could not halt the diseases rapid growth.

Eventually the world took the killer as seriously as it had needed to from the very start. Petty regional and religious rivalries were put aside as finding a cure became the number one aim of all the worlds nations. After all, there's no point fighting your neighbour if you're both dead from disease in a year or two.

But despite humanity's combined efforts, the search for a cure had come too late. St Andrew's Cross Disease continued spreading exponentially and within 3 years everybody was dead.

The End

Should it actually happen in your reality, this ending is <u>NOT</u> covered by the 100% money back guarantee. If this happened to your reality then I'm not giving you a refund as I want absolutely zero contact with you. I'm not even running the risk that I might somehow catch eblula from you just by reading an email from you. Go away. Get a bell around your neck, keep calling "unclean" and live a life of solitude well away from me.

—— Section 150 ——

September 18th 2015

Following the referendum, Scotland started to devote a good deal of money to pure science and technology research. This allowed many more researchers to do work which would put Scotland at the forefront of science.

You knew that devoting your life to science would eventually pay off big-time - and today's the day it all becomes worthwhile. Because today's the day that you finally become the first person to use the working time travel portal generator you've invented.

You actually thought it would take a lot longer to invent a working machine. You weren't even certain that it was actually possible. You knew it was theoretically possible, especially if you just ignored any theories that precluded it. The good thing was that all the gubbins that Einstein and co wrote were just theories, and so unproven. So in your eyes it was just as valid to decide that they were wrong and time travel was possible. But still the going was hard.

But then, just 10 minutes ago, you had a breakthrough.

You awoke to find an odd looking machine on your desk along with a user manual and a note.

The note read as follows:

Hi,

I've done it! You've done it! We've done it! Maybe I/you/we need to rethink personal pronouns with respect to time travel and multiple-universe selves... ***Iouwe****'ve done it! Hmmm...* ***Iouwe****'ll have to work on that, it feels clumsy but it'll have to do for this letter to me, to you, to us... err... to* ***meyous****.*

Anyway, Iouwe've done it! Iouwe've finally created viable time travel.

It took meyous 42 years of research, but Iouwe got there. Of course Iouwe missed out on ***myour*** *life, which really pissed meyous off so that's why Iouwe've decided to come back to 2015 when Iouwe're only a year into research to drop off a spare machine and the instruction manual. Now you can have fun for the rest of your life and Iouwe've still got a working time machine. Genius hey? Pretty sure it's not a paradox or Iouwe couldn't have done it.*

Iouwe can forget most of what Iouwe've seen in scifi about time travel and the manual's mainly filler, the most important rule of time travel is: Always keep a spare pack of AA batteries on you and never ever put them into the portal-generator the wrong way round.

Have fun,

Meyous

It's then that you notice that you have thoughtfully left yourself a pack of 4 new AA batteries next to the portal generator.

You may be a scientist, but you're far too excited to bother with reading manuals. You feel like you're a 7 year old on Christmas morning. Time Travelling Santa has been and now you want to play with your new toy. You're quite sure you'll figure out how to use it as you go along. After all it can't be too hard because according to the note, your future self invented this so it must be laid out in a way that makes sense and seems intuitive to you.

Now, picking up the portal generator and turning it on, you have the chance to see another time. The chance to change the past. To undo some great injustice or mistake. Or just to have a fun outing for shits 'n' giggles.

But when to travel to? That's the big question.

It'd be great to see dinosaurs, so 65 million years ago (go to **Section 032**)

or Wonder what the future holds... let's go to, oh lets say 802, 701 AD (go to **Section 014**)

or Exactly 30 seconds before you bought this book will be fine. You can't think of any bigger mistake that needs undoing. (go to **Section 392**)

or Just 2 seconds before you bought this book. The mistake needs undoing but you could do something else with those extra 28 seconds you save by not going back to 30 seconds before you buy. (go to **Section 023**)

—— Section 151 ——

You enter the examination cubicle and hear the waiting doctor say "Not you again."

You're pleased to see that it's Doctor Cook - the same doctor who treated you the last two times you ended up blue-faced in A&E. At least he's familiar with you and he's stopped you from dying on your previous visits.

"So what exactly is the problem?"

"L-look at my face… I'm blue. I'm leaking. I'm dying."

"Really."

The doctor looks closely at your face whilst pulling on a pair of latex gloves and picking up a cotton wool swab.

"Hold still this won't hurt."

He daubs at the outside of your cheek then looks at the blue residue. "How long have you been displaying these symptoms? Since waking up this morning, the day of the referendum?"

You confirm that and reflect on how good he is. He probably recognises the disease and he's such an expert he can tell how long you've been suffering just by a swab.

The way he says "thought as much" makes you realise just how bad your situation is. You'd think that he'd be pleased at making a quick diagnosis, but no - he seems annoyed and irritated, obviously at the severity of the disease you have as the only other thing that could be causing it is you, and he's got far too good a bedside manner to show irritation at a patient.

"Well I'm afraid that we're going to have to do some more tests and we'll have to do them immediately. I'm really very very concerned this time."

Within seconds, before you have chance to question him, you're rushed away to be prepped.

Soon you find yourself in what looks like an operating theatre. You're half prepared for Dr Cook to perform another rectal endoscopy like he has when you've been in before. What you aren't prepared for is when he comes up to you and explains that he's going to try some new equipment.

"You see I've now performed two rectal endoscopies on you when you've previously come to the hospital presenting with a blue face and so far neither of them has found a reason for your face nor for why you keep coming back. So I've decided that we may need to perform an internal examination with a much more powerful camera than this old thing." He waves the snake-like cable of the endoscope in front of you.

"So I've called in a favour and a friend at the BBC has kindly lent me some top-notch HD video equipment." He indicates over past the far end of the gurney and you follow his direction to see a full studio camera setup, including a large camera on a mobile floor-based stand complete with a cameraman seated on it. As if that isn't enough the sound man has a 3 feet long shotgun mic on a 10 feet long boom.

You look back at Dr Cook terrified. He just smiles and nods "Yes they are..."

The following 60 minutes of agony are too terrible to describe in this book for fear a lady, minor or gentleman of delicate disposition should ever mistakenly read it. Luckily if any such person really wants to know what happened it should be airing on BBC2 next autumn.

BBC
YOU MAY FEEL JUST A
LITTLE DISCOMFORT AS
THE CAMERA GOES IN

At the end of the ordeal, Dr Cook comes up to you and gives you a clean bill of health.

"Wow that HD camera really does give a great picture but I can't see anything that may be causing a blue face. I can only conclude that you've probably got a slight residue on your face from painting it blue again. The best thing to do is probably to get dressed, go home and wash it off. Unless you want me to have a bring the crew up here and have a good look through your mouth just to be sure... do you?"

You agree to do that and quickly get dressed.

He's such a nice doctor that as you pass him on the way out he even apologises that the camera crew hadn't been lubed but "to be honest it wouldn't really have helped much, would it?" He also promises to get hold of an even bigger 3D-HD camera for next time, if there is a next time.

It's not long before you're home and jumping in the shower to freshen up. (go to **Section 240**)

—— Section 152 ——

"There's a vote tomorrow?"

"Course there is, yer great numpty. Referendum day, ain't it. The day we decide the future direction of our great nation."

You'd forgotten about that, but you're not going to admit it, so you look straight at Andy and laugh "Ha ha. How could I forget? Of course I'm voting." (go to **Section 202**)

or "Only pulling your leg mate - I couldn't forget that" and that's the truth. (go to **Section 096**)

or "Oh that vote. I'm really not that interested in it." (go to **Section 166**)

—— Section 153 ——

The 'NO' vote won...

Really? You really thought that the most interesting and exciting outcomes would come from staying together and maintaining the status quo?

Heck that'd be boring even if the band Status Quo got involved and learnt a 4th chord especially for the occasion.

The whole point of this critically acclaimed (in some universes) work of literature (Yes! Literature!) was to let you explore the myriad ways in which full devolution would change the world. Some ways were good. Some ways were bad. Some ways were so bad they were just asking to be spanked. Some ways were so good that if they asked to be spanked you couldn't really say no as they were too good to let them down by not indulging in their sadomasochistic urges. But you've turned your back on all those possibilities and chosen to go with what's safe.

Just in case you were wondering, what happens next is that:

- ECONOMY - stays pretty much the same and maybe gets a bit better as some further powers are devolved to Scotland.
- SPORTS - stays pretty much the same as Scotland enjoys the same poor sports funding that the rest of the UK gets, except for any additional spending that happens as a result of the extra devolved

powers.

- EDUCATION - stays pretty much the same as Scotland…
- HEALTH - stays pretty much…
- ARTS - stays…

I think you get the idea. Not saying that a 'NO' vote is good or bad for Scotland or the rest of the UK and the world, but it is pretty boring in the context of this book.

Your lack of imagination and ambition in changing the world makes me wonder if you're actually some sort of politician. Are you?

The End

Unless you want to reconsider and see what happens when the YES vote wins… (go to **Section 069**)

This ending is NOT covered by the 100% money back guarantee should it actually happen in your reality. Seriously - you've reached the end. You've hopefully already got your moneys-worth out of the book. If you've not yet just try reading it again and pick different options. It'll be like a whole new book (except for the bits that are the same, that is).

—— Section 154 ——

At the bar there are still lots of people talking about the referendum, but now with you all having a couple of drinks inside you it's a little less formal, a little noisier and there's a lot more bollocks being said.

Everybody keeps thanking you for dealing with the punning drunks and backs up their thanks by buying you a drink.

It's good that they do, as eventually it helps you build up the courage to go over and speak to the redhead you'd debated with.

You soon find out her name is Kelly and she's as concerned and confused about the referendum as you are. She enjoyed the debate and says she thought you made a great point about future currency and the share of UK debt in the event of independence. In return you compliment her on her amazing pair of points and as you do you suddenly realise that she's not got a bad pair of tits either. She's really quite attractive and you seem to be getting on pretty well.

Eventually the bar is closing for the night and so you walk Kelly home.

When you get to her front door, unexpectedly she asks if you'd like to come in for a coffee.

'Oh not again' you think.

What happens next is inevitable.

Sex. Hot sex. Hot sexy sex. Really hot sex. Really really hot sexy sexy sex. Sex so hot you're surprised that the fiery-haired minx's hair doesn't really spontaneously burst into flame. Really really really hot sexy sex so hot and sexy that it can't be described in any greater detail than just 'really really really really hot sexy sexy sexy sex' or this book would be banned under obscenity law.

You make love for what must be 3, 4, maybe even 5 hours, and you're pleased to say that neither of you had any problems achieving orgasm, time after time. You showed Kelly what an accomplished gold-medal winning lover you were, acting the perfect gent and making sure she was fully spent before you allowed yourself your sweet release.

As you walk home you fondly remember her really really hot sexy sultry voice when she turned to you after you'd both finally finished and promised to see you again. Soon.

Thinking about last night brings a smile to your face this morning as you jump into the shower to 'remember in more detail' and freshen up. (go to **Section 120**)

—— Section 155 ——

September 18th 2015

"There's really nothing we can do, Mr President" said the Scottish home secretary to President Salmond, all the time wondering if the situation really warranted an emergency meeting of the Scottish Security Council.

"But you've seen the broadcast - there must be something" said the Scottish premier.

"We don't think it was serious."

"Not serious?"

"No, Mr President, we're pretty sure it's not serious. As I'm sure you know, Ronnie Corbett *is* a well known comedian. He was just making a joke when he suggested you were incompetent."

"But that's treason - he's meant to be Scottish. Fucka was born in Edinburgh." Slurred Mr President before downing his whisky and pouring himself another tumbler full. "He can't go down to those wee bastids at the BBC an' broadcast a speech attacking me like that. I've got ma pride an I got Trident - ah'm no to be fucked with."

The home secretary realises he needs to defuse the situation.

"It was just the usual type of shaggy dog story he's always done. It wasn't meant to cause offence, even if it was in the *Yes-Day* anniversary show."

At this point Field General Murray steps in.

"With respect Mr President, as much as I love conflict, I'm not sure that nuclear weapons are the answer to a comedians TV routine. Why don't you try to calm down, maybe ease up on the drink and go watch the Alien films again. You know you like them and there really is nothing, no bold gesture, no action, no stuff whatsoever that you can do about this tonight."

"Auch! Bollox to all that - I say we do stuff an' nuke wee shite, Ron Corbett. It's the only way to be sure."

As soon as President Salmond said that phrase two distinct lines of consequence were simultaneously thrown into action.

The first saw the President, certain that an aggressive approach was the right way to handle the situation, down his tumbler of fine single malt, and, resisting all attempts to dissuade him, he retrieved the nuclear launch codes. Within 10 minutes he had launched a pre-emptive thermonuclear strike on the English home of Ronnie Corbett.

The second line of consequence saw the author of **You Decide! The Future of Scotland** suddenly wonder if most people would get the really bad Aliens-based pun that had been crowbarred into the book. His only consolation was the thought that at least he hadn't made the bad pun - it was a drunk and angry Alex Salmond that had done it.

In the grand scheme of things the first line of consequence was the most significant, leading as it did to both USA and Russia believing that the other side had launched a nuclear strike and launching their own nukes before it was too late. The cold wars Mutually Assured Destruction had finally come about because of a small man with a black chair upsetting a big man with a whisky.

Compared to that the author didn't feel too bad about the pun.

The End (of everything)

Should it actually happen in your reality, this ending is covered by the 100% money back guarantee. Just provide proof of purchase and sworn testimonies from Ronnie Corbett and the leaders of Scotland, the US and Russia, each stating that Ronnie Corbett was directly responsible for the death of all mankind and the reduction of Earth to a barren radioactive wasteland.

—— Section 156 ——

That's odd...

You've walked straight into some kind of stone-built castle, but not a ruined one like all the castles you've ever been to. This one seems to still be a proper building.

You wonder what happened to the shop keeper and all the fancy-dress costumes? You've heard of pop-up shops but never of pop-up castles or pop-down shops.

You hear footsteps approaching from around the bend in the corridor. You think that maybe it's the shopkeeper returning, but when the person making the noise appears it's not him. Instead it's some sort of pike carrying guard in medieval blue and gold livery and leather armour. As they pass you they salute.

Hmmm… something about that seems odd but you can't quite put your finger on it.

The costume looked perfect - another great outfit from Mr Ben's Megastore. Then you realise that the guard must have been about 5 feet tall - a lot shorter than any police, soldiers, guards or security men you've ever seen. It really ruins the illusion that the costume creates, which is ironic as centuries ago people were shorter on average, so he was probably a realistic size for a medieval guard.

By the time you've thought about what was odd about the guard, he's walked off, which is annoying as you could have asked him if he knew where the shopkeeper is.

He must be around here somewhere.

Do you carry on into the castle looking for the shopkeeper? (go to **Section 302**)

or Head back into the changing rooms. (go to **Section 116**)

—— Section 157 ——

You open the door and almost immediately know that you've entered the wrong room because in front of you there's what appears to be a meeting of the Womens' Institute (or some similar organisation) as the room is full of middle- to old-aged women sat around talking about jam and knitting.

They turn to look at you, shock on some of there faces.

"What is the meaning of this?" asks the group leader.

You're lost for words and know it must be apparent. How exactly can you explain why you've barged in on a WI meeting dressed in your finest BDSM gear? Luckily you're not left floundering for long.

"You know that you were meant to be here half an hour ago" says the leader.

All the seated ladies move their chairs to form a big ring around you and from somewhere some raunchy music starts.

'Oh not again' you think.

What happens next is inevitable.

Sex. Hot sex. Really hot sex. Really really hot sex. Really really really hot sexy sex. Sex that's hotter than the meals on wheels dinners that some of these ladies ate last night. Sex so hot that it can't be described in any greater detail than just '*really* hot sex' or this book would be banned under obscenity law.

Talk about hot - there's nothing that some of these experienced octogenarians won't do. They've seen it all before and, given the chance, they'll do it all again. Who ever knew that homemade blackberry jam acted as such a good lubricant?

Two hours later, you are a thoroughly exhausted shadow of your former self as you finally leave.

You exit the room and decide to look for the polling station behind a different door. (go to **Section 083**)

—— Section 158 ——

You pull on the sword for a few moments more, but it's blatantly stuck fast and isn't going to shift even a single millimetre. You could strain and strain until something goes pop and your knightly name is changed to Sir Tenninjury. You're pretty sure that you want to avoid giving yourself a hernia in the dark ages, even if Merlin is on hand to treat it.

There's only one thing for it.

You point and stare into the corner of the room and, remembering to sound like you belong in the distant past, shout "Fucketh me sidewards if mine eyes deceiveth me not, verily it be a goblin-banshee!"

You hear one voice ask "why are you talking strangely? Can you smell toast?" But the question is almost drowned out as most people gasp, several ladies faint, the men draw their weapons and everybody turns to look into the corner you indicated… Giving you a chance to run out the hall as fast as you can.

As you leave the hall you hear voices shouting behind you.

"There's nothing there."

"What are you talking ab- eh where's he gone?"

"He's not the rightful King, he's an imposter kill him!"

"I thought it was funny that he's wearing plastic armour made in Taiwan."

Just as you get to a T-junction in the corridor, you hear the clanking of real armour as the assembled knights and guards start chasing after you, no doubt intent on ending your life.

Do you turn left? (go to **Section 216**)
or Turn right? (go to **Section 291**)

—— Section 159 ——

September 18th 2030

Immediately following *Yes-Day*, President Salmond decided that he wasn't interested in building massive empires or even expanding past the existing borders of Scotland.

What he really wanted was to get rid of nuclear weapons (as he'd said he would) and create a stable/neutral state with a high standard of living for his people. He also wanted Scotland to become an internationally respected independent state that could be trusted as a centre for technical excellence, scientific research and financial security.

Thinking about it, he realised that he wanted his country to become Switzerland. Yes Switzerland! But without talking foreign languages and hiding Nazi gold, and with some of the chocolate being deep-fried.

But the world already has one Switzerland and so Scotland needed something to set it apart, and hopefully something to help it make money and attract tourists.

It was obvious - McBabes and gambling. President Salmond made a plan to turn Scotland into an internationally renowned mix of Switzerland, Monaco and Las Vegas.

For some reason this turns out to be very popular and before long Scotland is *the* destination for playboys, millionaires, films about accidentally killing hookers and tuxedo-wearing secret agents.

The End

Should it actually happen in your reality, this ending is <u>NOT</u> covered by the 100% money back guarantee. It would have been but I put it all on black and the ball said red...

—— Section 160 ——

The taxi drops you off at the School of Tropical Diseases.

Sometimes something happens that reaffirms your faith in humanity. That makes you realise we're not all selfish misanthropists, but that many people are caring and all too willing to help another soul in need. You can never tell when something like that will happen. They always surprise you.

Just as the taxi driver surprised you with his altruism this morning.

He must have known that you were sick and in need, because even though his meter showed nearly 25 pounds by the time you pulled up outside the School of Tropical Diseases, he flat out refused to accept any money off you. You tried to pay but he just wouldn't have it.

"Keep yer money. Keep it to yerself. I don't need it" he insisted.

Not only that, but realising that you may be very sick, he placed a handkerchief over his nose and mouth as he turned down the fare. Obviously acknowledging the load your immune system was already be under and not wanting to place it under any more stress from his assorted germs and diseases. Not many would be so sensitive to your plight.

If you manage to survive this, you're going to make sure that you thank the man properly, the only way that's fitting, the only way you can... by mentioning him anecdotally in every single media interview you get asked to do. Little does he know but by virtue of his kindness that taxi driver may be about to become a particularly minor footnote in medical history.

But first you have to beat this disease - and to do that you walk towards the entrance to the School of Tropical Diseases.

DEAD CAT TIME

It's time to peek inside Schrödinger's box and see how Treeno's doing...

Hello Treeno. Would you like a nice tin of - oh you've eaten it already. (go to **Section 074**)

or Treeno! How are you managing to cause trouble in what's essentially an empty box? (go to **Section 284**)

or Well she looks just like you feel. (go to **Section 376**)

or Awwwww look at da cutsie ickle puddy tat all asleep! Oh wait - she's dead. (go to **Section 358**)

—— Section 161 ——

You open the door and the sound of bagpipes greets you.

You think you're gonna be at home here.

You know some people knock the drone of the pipes, but they're just ignorant bastards as far as you're concerned. The pipes are a glorious instrument and they really are far more versatile than the idiots give them credit, as beautifully demonstrated by the interesting song cover currently being played. It sounds vaguely familiar to you but you can't quite place it yet.

No wonder it took you a few moments to recognise it, it's not normally a pure instrumental, but just after you do it's confirmed as '*Bob the Builder*' when the officials manning the polling station all join in singing "**Yes we can!**"

You're sure that you must have heard of less-subtle attempts at subliminal programming, but if you have you certainly can't remember when. You try harder to think of an example, but all that comes to mind is the repetitive phrase "*buy all Judgement Dave's books buy all Judgement Dave's books buy all Judgement Dave's books*".

Of course there's no subliminals needed for you. You're showing your support with the clothes you're wearing and everybody in the polling station can see where your loyalties lie.

You stop a moment to listen to the pipes and appreciate the tartan decorations and numerous Scottish flags adorning every wall and flat surface other than the floor. As you stand there the attendants offer you a wee dram of special 'Independence whisky' and a selection of shortbread and haggis. This is as close to heaven as a polling station could be.

You're greeted by the lady (in full traditional highland dress) behind the desk dealing with addresses including your home as if you are a long-lost family member. Once you've confirmed your identity, she says "we're all proud of you, laddy", gives you your ballot paper and points you in the direction of the small individual booths that you can go in to cast your vote in private.

As you walk across the room to the polling booth, it is with the weight of a country's destiny bearing down on your shoulders… (go to **Section 393**)

—— Section 162 ——

You and Andy start shoving each other again and before long you're beating the living crap out of each other.

You can't really understand how things escalated to this so quickly. It must be the drink. You can be bit of a dick when you've had a few and you've been thinking for a while that you should maybe cut back a bit.

"Yes you should cut back" says an oddly-familiar voice to the side of you.

Still fighting you quickly get Andy in a headlock and turn to see who told you to cut back. Oh its… what's you're old headmaster doing here? You thought that he'd died a couple of years ago. Oh well, you must be mistaken, he's obviously alive. "Stay out of this" you tell him.

"Stay out of this, *SIR*. I'm not surprised by this, drunken fighting in the street. You were always trouble, boy."

"Yes, you *were* always trouble" says Andy strangely - it must be the headlock making him sound odd, as he sounds more like…

Turning back to Andy you see that now it's somehow your dad that you have in a headlock and you're suddenly aware that you've wet your pants.

Oh not *this* dream again… (go to **Section 082**)

—— Section 163 ——

You wait...

You're already bored of waiting. The only thing to do is worry or watch the other people, but that's just annoying.

Take those two youths over by the blood donor poster for example.

"A pint! That's most of me arm innit!"

"No idea mate - I don't do that old pints and ounces shit. Ain't a pint just under half a litre?"

"No idea - it's just a quote from some old Alfred Hitchcock film me gran told me about once. Hitchcock's in hospital an' he sees a poster asking for blood donors to give a pint an' he says 'A pint! That's most of me arm innit?' Me gran thought it were proper funny."

"I s'pose people used to laugh at anything after the war."

Thankfully at this point your name is called by the nurse from reception and she leads you through to an examination cubicle.

DEAD CAT TIME

Has anyone fed Tiddles today? No? I'll see how he is then.

He's fine and ready to play! (go to **Section 320**)
Or He's fine and ready for some food! (go to **Section 133**)
Or He's fine... if you didn't want a living cat. (go to **Section 188**)

—— Section 164 ——

"Alright mate... We dinnae want no trouble - we'll be off" you say. Then you and Andy head off leaving them to their political debate.

You don't fancy going back to the club and it's still a little early to go home, so you turn to Andy and ask him "Fancy a curry? Could go to the Raj."

"Nah mate I'm fine - I ate before coming out. To be honest I was quite up for that debate. Bit of a letdown getting kicked out. I might just go home."

You were up for staying out longer, but you know when Andy's in a mood like this there's no point arguing with him and you never like going for a curry or drink by yourself. You think that looks a bit sad.

You say your byes and both head home, you've had a good time out, but it's ended much earlier than you'd planned.

Thinking how bad your head is this morning as you get into the shower to freshen up, maybe it was for the best that you didn't stay out drinking til even later. (go to **Section 295**)

—— Section 165 ——

The nurse barely lets you get started describing your symptoms once she's seen your face. She blanches at the sight of you and hits a button under the front desk.

An alarm starts blaring out and emergency strobe lights start to strobe. Within seconds you're surrounded by people in full biohazard protective suits who strap you to a gurney and rush you through several corridors until you finally pass through decontamination showers and enter some sort of isolation tent.

You're not sure why they've got a tent set up inside a brick building, but you're not complaining because it makes you feel like you're in an American film or TV show when a deadly disease strikes and the CDC go into full emergency mode. And that's really exciting…

…Until you realise that in those shows lots of people that get strapped to gurneys don't survive for much longer.

The next few weeks are like a montage from one of those same films or TV shows. Doctors race back and forth working around the clock. Test after test after test is performed, but still the docs seem no closer to a cure. Medical staff look increasingly worried as each day without a cure, maybe even without hope, passes.

Then, finally, the mildest glimmer of hope. By a stroke of luck, one of the doctors makes a breakthrough. The last few montage-like scenes see you being treated and, slowly but surely, recovering. The last traces of blue leaving your face.

Finally, having fully recovered, you are discharged from hospital.

As you leave you wonder what happened with the referendum. You've been in hospital for so long but you were in such a dire state that you never gave the vote a single thought. Now that you return to the normal world you feel you ought to find out who won and so you decide to ask a nurse.

"Excuse me, nurse Dean, can I ask who won the referendum?"

"How should I know - the polls haven't even closed yet."

You're confused by this. "But I came in here on the day of the referendum and I've been here for weeks. Surely you must know who won."

"You're forgetting that we treated you in montage - your treatment may have taken weeks but we fit it in to only a few minutes. It's not even lunch time yet."

That explains it.

You thank the nurse and race home to freshen up in the shower before you go to vote. (go to **Section 240**)

—— Section 166 ——

"Oh... that vote..."

"You see, Andy, my take on it is that all votes are like that *Aliens versus Predator* film."

Andy looks slightly puzzled before saying "You mean they're utter shite and after them you wonder why you ever bothered?"

"Naw - well yeah, but what I was meaning was that they're like the AvP strap line, y'know 'whoever wins we lose'. See, all politicians are lying self-serving shites aren't they. So why would I want to spend my life voting when I could spend my life living?"

Andy looks almost horrified. "You don't really mean that do you? Even if that's usually true, *this* vote means something. We have a chance to *really* change the future."

You remember saying "Yeah I'm serious as a heart attack." (go to **Section 174**)

or Was it "Well I suppose there's always one exception." (go to **Section 206**)

—— Section 167 ——

That's odd...

You've walked straight into some kind of tropical jungle. What happened to the shop keeper and all the fancy-dress costumes? Maybe it's some kind of hidden camera prank show.

You look around but you can't spot the hidden cameras, but maybe that's because a hidden camera show uses cameras that are hidden. The clue was in the name.

As you keep on looking for any not-quite-as-hidden-as-the-producers-would-like-cameras it strikes you that the jungle flora doesn't just look like fake plants. It doesn't even look like plants you've seen before in Scotland. Or plants as exotic as those from other parts of the United Kingdom.

You're pretty sure that you've never seen plants this odd or this big on David Attenborough shows from the Amazon.

No - these plants look ginormous, almost prehistoric.

You must remember when Beadle, or Riley or whoever it is presenting the candid camera show, jumps out to ask them what fertiliser they've used to grow the plants. You've no real interest in knowing for yourself, but your mum would probably want to know and if you forget to ask then Christmas dinner at her place will be tortuous.

"Why didn't you ask what they used? Eh? Eh? Was it just horse shit and Baby Bio or something special?"

You don't need that going on in your ear all through dinner, the Queen's speech and whatever 4 year old film the BBC have splashed out on to follow Liz.

Do you carry on into the jungle looking for the shopkeeper? (go to **Section 095**)
or Head back into the changing rooms. (go to **Section 116**)

—— Section 168 ——

You open the door and almost immediately know that you've entered the wrong room because in front of you there's what appears to be a boardroom with a long table in the middle of it and annotated several maps of the world on clipboards and walls around the room.

All very odd when you're expecting to enter a polling station, but what astonishes you most are the 'people' sat around the table having a meeting, as each one appears to be a 7-feet tall lizard. Of course you say that that astonishes you most, but it really pales into insignificance when compared to the fact that they are all speaking excellent English. And that seems fairly minor when you consider that upon seeing you the chairlizard says "About time, Nigel, we've been waiting for you."

For the next 2 hours you're in a constant panic dreading that you'll be spotted as an imposter in a Godzilla costume. You barely take in the discussion that's taking place deciding the fates of entire nations over the next decade or so.

You slowly realise that you're at a meeting of the secret cabal of shapeshifting lizards that rule the world. The lizard illuminati or lilaruminati, if you will.

Eventually, when there's a break called for insects and basking, you seize your chance to escape and leave as inconspicuously as you can.

You exit the room and decide to look for the polling station behind a different door. (go to **Section 083**)

—— Section 169 ——

On Gayer TV when you switch over, onscreen there is a scantily-clad bubbly trio of young men; a ginger-haired, blond and brown crewcut all sat on a sofa in their tartan underwear and talking to you. Yes - you.

It's good to know that you're watching 100% Scottish laddies, the sort of people you might bump into in a bar and that, here on TV, they are showing interest in *you*. Not just any viewer. No - you.

One of the McBlokes says "Mmmmm we know what you're thinking" and they begin to undress each other further whilst applying liberal amounts of baby oil to their friends toned bodies.

'Oh not again' you think.

What happens next is inevitable.

Sex. Hot sex. Really hot sex. Really really hot solo sex. Sex so hot you're surprised your hand doesn't fall off. Sex so hot that it can't be described in any greater detail than just 'really hot sex' or this book would be banned under obscenity law. Sex so hot that if it was any hotter you'd have to wear an oven glove. Sex so really really hot that partway through you think it'd be a bit of a kinky change to wear an oven glove so you go and grab them from the kitchen before continuing your self-loving.

Eventually after a couple of minutes you reach for the tissues and the remote and turn over the TV, making a mental note to put the oven gloves in the wash.

You turn over to Muzikal+ TV (go to **Section 313**)

or Maybe you watch Med TV (go to **Section 102**)

—— Section 170 ——

"Walkies!"

As soon as you shout it, Hamish your Scottish Terrier comes bounding up to you excitedly wagging his tail. Behind him, just as excited is Tommy your Old English Sheepdog.

"Good boys" you say, wondering where the others are.

"Walkies!" you call again and Paddy, Gwen and Britannia all come running in.

You thought it only right that you had dogs to celebrate all the Union. Obviously Hamish and Tommy are Scotland and England. Paddy's your Irish Setter, but obviously only for Northern Ireland. Britannia is a British Bulldog, she represents the whole.

Last but not least, little Gwen represents Wales. You don't know what breed she is, some sort of loveable mongrel in all likelihood, but you thought that she embodied the Welsh nation perfectly since she's incontinent and likes to take a leak everywhere she goes.

Now that you have them all on leads, it's time to set off.

Do you decide to take your dogs out for a long walk in the park so you can maybe grab breakfast at a cafe you like (go to **Section 034**)

or Just take them for a quick stroll around the block then you'll have time to breakfast at home or go out (go to **Section 339**)

—— Section 171 ——

You get into the shower and let the hot water wash over you. You can feel all the aches, pains and bruises slowly wash away.

Okay the bruises may not wash away, but the pain does.

A few bruises will make you look really tough. You just hope nobody finds out what really happened, but you're sure that Andy won't tell anyone.

After a good half hour you feel a lot better. (go to **Section 295**)

—— Section 172 ——

Oh sod you then!

The End

Should it actually happen in your reality, this ending is NOT covered by the 100% money back guarantee. Really, what sort of mugs do you think the publishers are? Instead, why don't you try to recover something from the book by starting it again and picking different options? Pretend not to care quite so much, have some fun - it's probably all make believe unless it actually happens to your reality.

—— Section 173 ——

The new government realises the importance of spending on science and technology. Some might argue that problems with the economy or education or housing or defence or anything else take priority, but the government was certain that solutions can be found to problems in all those areas if only enough effort is put into R&D.

And so it came to pass that government funding and tax breaks soon made Scotland a hotbed of groundbreaking research, the envy of the rest of the world.

Science advanced at an unprecedented rate and before long the inventions and concrete benefits were filtering down to the ordinary person in the street. Soon Scots were living in a Halcyon age not unlike that predicted by the most-optimistic 20th Century science fictions. It was an age of peace. An age of plenty. An age where disease had been conquered. An age where ageing had been vanquished. An age where war and disharmony had been dispelled as there was more than enough for all.

Since technological advances mean that food and goods are plentiful and nobody needs to perform what 20th century man would recognise as 'work' to survive, more people turn to exploring the arts and crafts. There is a boom in exciting new artists, playwrights, writers and musicians as people freed from the shackles of the 9-to-5 use the creativity they'd always yearned to set free.

It truly was the golden age of man.

Okay it's not really humorous, but you're happy and you can't have everything. Maybe since your every need is provided for you can make your own comedy now you're living in your perfect society.

The End

Should it actually happen in your reality, this ending is NOT covered by the 100% money back guarantee. You're living in a technological utopia - don't get greedy!

—— Section 174 ——

"You really believe we can change things?"

"Bollocks we can - if voting changed anything it'd be illegal and that's why I couldn't care less about tomorrow."

As you say these words to Andy you realise that the very last thing that you want to do in the whole world is to read a book about all the possible outcomes of the referendum. Actually that's not quite true - the last thing you'd want to do is read a book about all the possible outcomes of the referendum whilst being George Osborne's gimpy sex slave. Actually even that could get worse, you could be reading a book about all the possible outcomes of the referendum whilst being George Osborne's gimpy sex slave and somehow get cramp.

And a paper cut. There's nothing worse than a paper cut.

But if you can avoid paper cuts, cramp and being forcibly enslaved in George's dungeon then the last thing you want to do is read a book about all possible outcomes of the referendum.

So you decide to stop reading.

The End

Should it actually happen in your reality, this ending is NOT covered by the 100% money back guarantee. Though in all probability, even if it were covered, you're too apathetic to try reclaiming your money back. Instead, why don't you try to get more from the book by starting it again and picking different options?

—— Section 175 ——

Oh what a night!

Late September back in '63… Or was it mid September in 2014? You're always getting those two mixed up.

You had fun drinking, dancing, loving.

You had more fun juggling, lion taming and fire eating.

Then you had even more fun cross-stitching, pill-popping and badger-baiting.

But the most fun you had was when you started bullshitting about everything you'd been doing earlier in the night. Still the drinking, dancing and loving was good, old-fashioned harmless fun[11].

The only serious bit of the night was when the DJ started playing Mike Oldfield's *Tubular Bells*. Your mate Andy said "That's weird it's not like it's Halloween or anything so why's he playing the Exorcist tune?"

You turned to Andy saying "I've no idea" but when you faced him he had gone. Not just moved away, but completely vanished. Just like everybody else. All of a sudden you seemed to be the only person anywhere in the club.

"What the? This just isn't possible" you thought. Nor was it possible that the temperature had just plummeted in an instant to what felt like subzero temperatures. But that *had* happened too. Looking at the air in front of your face, you could barely tell what were the last remaining wisps of dry ice and what was your breath made visible by the chill.

You look around the dance floor - trying to scan for any other person. None there. Turn. None there. Turn. None… wait you're sure you caught a movement out of the corner of your eye.

"Shitting Fuckknuckles!"

Is all you manage to exclaim as, appearing from literally nowhere, the goblin-banshee eviscerates you before ripping you a new arsehole.

Your dying thought is that you really should have paid more attention to those *pick-your-own-dodgy-adventure* books when you were a child, they'd have warned you about this kind of thing. Which is somewhat better than your next-to-dying thought which was that a second arsehole would have been really handy on the mornings after twenty pints and a vindaloo. But alas, you realise this simple fact of life too late…

The End

Should it actually happen in your reality, this ending is <u>NOT</u> covered by the 100% money back guarantee. There's probably a good reason why it's not covered, but if we told you what it was you'd only start complaining and looking for a loophole to still claim. It's simpler for everyone if we just don't tell you the reason why.

—— Section 176 ——

As usual Suds is showing a British feel-good soap opera designed to make everybody happy because their existence isn't quite as dreadful as the characters lives are.

Feeling down at work? Well don't worry as Phil has it worse, he's down at work and about to lose his job.

Feeling down at work and about to lose your job? It could be worse - Phil's just found out his missus has been having an affair and is leaving him.

Feeling down at work, about to lose your job and found out that your wife's having an affair? Well at least you're not Phil - that poor bugger has just been told he has arse cancer and only 2 months to live unless he has the arsectomy that would give him a 50-50 chance of living for 6 months.

And *if* you have cancer and still want to compete further… All this is happening to Phil only days after he found out that he was pregnant, lost his left leg in an industrial accident and was gang raped by midgets as he lay bleeding out by the wood chipper. Then the paramedic who came when he called 999 was actually an incontinent conman who cleaned out his wallet and dirtied up his face. All this just days after a local newspaper had a front-page splash wrongly revealing him to be a kiddy-fiddler, his ex-wife turned out to be two Bulgarian men in disguise and the laundrette washing machine had a non-colourfast red sock in it when he did a white wash (which seemed to complicate the nonce allegations).

And on top of all that, he's only got frozen lasagne in for tea and he bloody hates that.

He'd top himself if it wasn't for a nice cuppa tea at the cafe.

Of course he'll probably try and commit suicide tomorrow anyway as you're sure he's bipolar and about to receive a massive unexpected tax bill that'll push him over the edge. It's almost a dead cert as there's not been a suicide attempt in this show for at least 17 episodes so one is due anytime now.

No matter how terrible your life is, an omnibus edition of *your* week wouldn't look quite as bad as Phil's.

And that's the idea behind Coronationdale, EmmerEnders, Brookstreet and all the other grimly joyous UK soaps and the soaps disguised as dramas, like Doctors, Holby and Today in Westminster. They're all little slices of other people's lives that are so realistically depressing they make our own lives seem positively blessed.

You eventually decide to turn off the TV, make yourself a cuppa and start to think about your future and the future of Scotland, and where the priorities lie for both of you.

The SciTech show really convinced you that Scotland try to reach out to the stars, and you should get personally involved (go to **Section 033**)

or Space looks interesting, but people need entertainment (go to **Section 345**)

or Space exploration is too costly for just the Scottish government to fund. If only you could find a way to make space exploration profitable (go to **Section 338**)

or There's no need to keep staring into space surely, there's enough to be going on with on Earth (go to **Section 316**)

or I don't want to think about all this - just give me something random! (go to **Section 375**)

—— Section 177 ——

You open the door and the sound of bagpipes greets you.

You know some people knock the drone of the pipes, but they really are far more versatile than many people give them credit, as beautifully demonstrated by the interesting song cover currently being played. It sounds vaguely familiar to you but you can't quite place it yet.

No wonder it took you a few moments to recognise it, it's not normally a pure instrumental, but just after you do it's confirmed as '*Bob the Builder*' when the officials manning the polling station all join in singing "**Yes we can!**"

You're sure that you must have heard of less-subtle attempts at subliminal programming, but if you have you certainly can't remember when. You try harder to think of an example, but all that comes to mind is the repetitive phrase "*buy all Judgement Dave's books buy all Judgement Dave's books buy all Judgement Dave's books*".

You stop a moment to listen to the pipes and appreciate the tartan decorations and numerous Scottish flags adorning every wall and flat surface other than the floor. As you stand there the attendants offer you a wee dram of special 'Independence whisky' and a selection of shortbread and haggis.

You're really beginning to get the idea that this polling station may be slightly biased towards the 'YES' vote.

You're greeted by the lady (in full traditional highland dress) behind the desk dealing with addresses including your home. She looks you up and down in disbelief, shakes her head and says "Well it takes all sorts I suppose". Once you've confirmed your identity, she says "you know what you should do, laddy", gives you your ballot paper and points you in the direction of the small individual booths that you can go in to cast your vote in private.

As you walk across the room to the polling booth, it is with the weight of a country's destiny bearing down on your shoulders... (go to **Section 119**)

—— Section 178 ——

You look around the shop and soon spot the perfect costume: Boris Johnson complete with blue suit, wig of crazy blonde hair, cycle helmet and air of likeable posh-idiot. He's the next best outrageous comedy character after Ali G, Rab C Nesbitt and George W Bush.

You quickly pay the shopkeeper and get changed into the outfit. You can almost feel yourself becoming more and more unbelievable and wacky as you slowly get into character.

By the time you've finished it's all you can do to stop yourself having a game of wiff waff or hanging from a zipline before you leave the shop.

Now where's that polling station? You need to vote to stop the state-educated oiks getting their way. (go to **Section 225**)

—— Section 179 ——

September 18th 2017

Following *Yes-Day*, the Scottish government funnelled a sizeable amount of it's budget to pure science and technology research. This allowed many more researchers to do work which would put Scotland at the forefront of science.

You knew that devoting your life to science would eventually pay off big-time - but you never realised just how long a struggle it would be. Three years it's taken but finally today's the day it all becomes worthwhile. Because today's the day that you finally become the first person to use the working time travel portal generator you've invented.

You actually thought it would take a little longer to invent a working machine. You weren't even certain that it was actually possible. You knew it was theoretically possible, especially if you just ignored any theories that precluded it. The good thing was that all the gubbins that Einstein and co wrote were just theories, and so unproven. So in your eyes it was just as valid to decide that they were wrong and time travel was possible. But still the going was hard.

But then, just 10 minutes ago, you had a breakthrough.

You awoke to find an odd looking machine on your desk along with a user manual and a note.

The note read as follows:

Hi,

I've done it! You've done it! We've done it! Maybe I/you/we need to rethink personal pronouns with respect to time travel and multiple-universe selves… ***Weiyou****'ve done it! Hmmm…* ***weiyou****'ll have to work on that, it feels clumsy but it'll have to do for this letter to me, to you, to us… err… to* ***usmeyou****.*

Anyway, weiyou've done it! Weiyou've finally created viable time travel.

It took usmeyou 42 years of research, but weiyou got there. Of course weiyou missed out on ***yourmyour*** *life, which really pissed usmeyou off so that's why weiyou've decided to come back to 2027 when weiyou're only 3 years into research to drop off a spare machine and the instruction manual. Now you can have fun for the rest of your life and weiyou've still got a working time machine. Genius hey? Pretty sure it's not a paradox or weiyou couldn't have done it.*

Weiyou can forget most of what weiyou've seen in scifi about time travel and the manual's mainly filler, the most important rule of time travel is: Always keep a spare pack of AA batteries on you and never ever put them into the portal-generator the wrong way round.

Have fun,

Usmeyou

PS - Just realised that weiyou could have gone back to anytime and so could have given usmeyou this machine back in 2014 and then weiyou wouldn't have had to waste anytime on research. Pissflaps.

What a numpty you've been. You could have saved yourself years of work. You'll never forgive yourself. Then you notice that you have thoughtfully left yourself a pack of 4 new AA batteries next to the portal generator. All is forgiven - you're back in your good books now.

You may be a scientist, but you're far too excited to bother with reading manuals. You feel like you're a man with a new barbecue. There's no time to plan things or consider safety, you just want to play with the new toys you've got. You're quite sure you'll figure out how to use the time machine as you go along. After all it can't be too hard because according to the note, your future self invented this so it must be laid out in a way that makes sense and seems intuitive to you.

Now, picking up the portal generator and turning it on, you have the chance to see another time. The chance to change the past. To undo some great injustice or mistake. Or just to have a fun outing for shits 'n' giggles.

But when to travel to? That's the big question.

It'd be great to see the conception of little Indy-Pendy, the last panda that meant so much to Scotland after *Yes-Day*, and if you take some photos you could pay for all the research you did (go to **Section 301**)

or It's a shame that pandas all died out, maybe you could use the time machine to save them by travelling back to when the Edinburgh Pandas were still alive (go to **Section 336**)

or Maybe you should save them by travelling back a bit further in time, say the mid-1980s when there were probably loads of Pandas (go to **Section 061**)

or Maybe you should ignore the pandas and go to the start of the universe (go to **Section 357**)

or What a ridiculous idea going to the mid-80s to save Pandas - you need a time period much earlier than that (go to **Section 380**)

or Travel to exactly 30 seconds before you bought this book. You can't think of any bigger mistake that needs undoing. (go to **Section 392**)

or Go to just 2 seconds before you bought this book. The mistake needs undoing but you could do something else with those extra 28 seconds you save by not going back to 30 seconds before you buy. (go to **Section 023**)

—— Section 180 ——

You think a bit longer...

It's fair enough trying to weigh up the pros and cons when you can remember them all. But you can't remember any...

Maybe you need a bit longer.

Vote for 'Yes'. (go to **Section 374**)

or Vote 'No'. (go to **Section 144**)

or Wait and think about it a little longer. (go to **Section 201**)

or Flip a coin. That's the way to decide. (go to **Section 279**)

Flip a coin. But what sort of coin? (go to **Section 008**)

And is heads yes or heads no? (go to **Section 139**)

I suppose heads should be 'No' since it shows the queen of the United Kingdom, (go to **Section 212**)

but then she'd still be the queen of Scotland if the 'Yes' vote wins independence. (go to **Section 222**)

Oh this coin flipping is far too confusing, but it's the only way to decide. (go to **Section 328**)

Okay heads is 'Yes', tails 'No'. (go to **Section 354**)

Should it be the other way round? (go to **Section 092**)

or Oh god you can't decide - the stress is too much! (go to **Section 368**)

—— Section 181 ——

September 18th 2015

The studio lights dim and Dec or maybe Ant, it's certainly one of them, announces "The winner of The Rex Factor, Scotland's search for a new monarch is…"

Then they wait for dramatic tension.

Then they wait a bit more.

Then you start to wish you'd taped it so you could fast forward this wait.

Then they're still waiting to announce the winner.

"**Holly McPhearson!**"

Of course it is. Holly steps forward and is crowned by Ant or maybe Dec, it's certainly one of them.

You don't think it was really the right thing to do letting Holly enter the competition. She was a depressed, ex-heroin addict who never knew her dad and had suffered domestic abuse for years from a string of boyfriends who pimped her out. All this time her only real friend in the entire world had been her maternal grandmother who died a week before The Rex Factor started.

In other words she'd had all the good breaks in life for someone wanting to win a talent show. It just wasn't fair to the other contestants to let her compete.

You're not sure how good a queen she'll make. She's no prior experience running a country and if she relapses she may just demand that parliament blows the entire budget on heroin for her, but you guess you'll find out and if she does get the country into serious debt she can always reduce the deficit by turning tricks. Probably be able to charge premium prices as the Queen.

The End of the beginning

Should it actually happen in your reality, this ending is NOT covered by the 100% money back guarantee. You're not the king, I don't need to explain to you why it's not covered.

—— Section 182 ——

September 18th 69 million years BC

Arriving in the past you start looking for recognisable dinosaurs and you are not disappointed.

Within an hour you've seen diplodocus grazing from treetops, tiny archaeopteryx flitting through the trees, mighty pteranodons flying up above the trees and tyrannosaurs crashing through the trees. Did I mention that you appeared in the past near some trees? No? Well you did.

Then you see some type of enormous dinosaur that you don't recognise. Some unknown type of gigantic monster. The huge creature truly is the most vast thunder lizard you can imagine.

The immense sauropod must have detected your presence, for it turns towards you, rotating it's body and re-orientating itself as if to run at you. Which is what it now does - it crashes towards you, sprinting in your direction, charging your way. Nothing will stop it as it crushes flora underfoot, the plant-life flattened by it's mass so that no vegetation is left untouched as it presses the undergrowth into the ground.

Locked still in fear and paralysed by terror, you get a good look at the monstrosity. Gazing intently at it's unusual body as hurls itself towards your scared-stiff form.

It wasn't an allosaurus, a tyrannosaurus, a stegosaurus, or any-other-saurus you knew of. No, this was a discovery unknown to science. A new found creature outside man's knowledge. Something previously hidden from human intellectual endeavours.

As the person to find it it would be down to you to name the race. To give the species a unique linguistic identifier. To establish the accepted label for the creatures.

But what to use for this mad behemoth, this insane juggernaut, this crazy giant, this lunatic land-based leviathan charging at you?

As it ploughs into you killing you, ripping the life from your body, extinguishing your flame, destroying your essence, you realise that there could only be one name for such a fantastic beast, such a mythical life form, this animal of nightmares.

That name is...

THE SAURUS.

The End

Should it actually happen in your reality, this ending is <u>NOT</u> covered by the 100% money back guarantee. There'll be no renumeration, refund nor recompense in any form of coin, currency or monetary tokens. I hope, wish and intend that that is clear, crystal and fully apparent.

—— Section 183 ——

Oh what a night!

Late September back in '63… Or was it mid September in 2014? You're always getting those two mixed up.

You had fun drinking, dancing, loving.

You had more fun juggling, lion taming and fire eating.

Then you had even more fun cross-stitching, pill-popping and badger-baiting.

But the most fun you had was when you started bullshitting about everything you'd been doing earlier in the night. Still the drinking, dancing and loving was good, old-fashioned harmless fun[12].

The only problem was things got a bit serious when you were already a little bit pissed and the DJ started playing a selection of songs by The Proclaimers and Deacon Blue. A load of people cheered and your mate Andy asked whether you'd decided how you were going to vote in the referendum.

You clearly remember saying to him "Who cares, mate - I'm havin' fun". (go to **Section 282**)

or Was it "There's a vote tomorrow?" (go to **Section 152**)

or No - You remember now it was "I know who I'm voting for, but it's between me and the ballot box." (go to **Section 130**)

—— Section 184 ——

You enter the polling booth, close the little privacy curtain and look at the ballot paper. It's such a small piece of paper. Almost too small and unassuming for the role it plays in this historic day.

You turn your attention to the single question on the ballot paper.

Should Scotland be an independent country?

Such a small sentence. Almost too small and unassuming for the massive decision it represents, with all its implications and knock-on effects. Whichever way the vote goes, those six little words play an important role in making history.

Okay - it's time to make a decision and make your mark, so you pick up the pencil ready. It's such a small pencil, almost too small and unassuming for the vital part it plays in this most momentous of days. It's a pencil that would look small in a betting shop and would be dwarfed by the pens in Argos.

It's taking the piss.

If everything today was sized appropriately for the important role they play, then the question should be printed on sheets of A0 paper in letters 6-inch high. You should have to make your mark with a paint roller and the option of just using ridiculous lime green paint for voting 'YES' or a mix of red, white and blue paint to create a great union-loving cross in the 'NO' box.

It's too late to change the ballot conditions, so, doing your best to ignore how small and insignificant everything seems, you prepare to cast your vote.

Vote for 'Yes'. (go to **Section 017**)
or Vote 'No'. (go to **Section 025**)
or Wait and think about it a little longer. (go to **Section 180**)
or Flip a coin. That's the way to decide. (go to **Section 279**)
Flip a coin. But what sort of coin? (go to **Section 008**)
And is heads yes or heads no? (go to **Section 139**)
I suppose heads should be 'No' since it shows the queen of the United Kingdom, (go to **Section 212**)
but then she'd still be the queen of Scotland if the 'Yes' vote wins independence. (go to **Section 222**)
Oh this coin flipping is far too confusing, but it's the only way to decide. (go to **Section 328**)
Okay heads is 'Yes', tails 'No'. (go to **Section 354**)
Should it be the other way round? (go to **Section 092**)
or Oh god you can't decide - the stress is too much! (go to **Section 275**)

—— Section 185 ——

The start room melts away...

As the world you have been experiencing is replaced by the full edutainment experience. (go to **Section 063**)

—— Section 186 ——

The punster's fist surprises you as it arcs towards your head before making solid contact. You blank out for a few seconds and come-to just in time to see the drunken pair race out of the debating hall.

There's shocked silence in the room which breaks into applause as, unsteadily, you slowly get to your feet. Your nose hurts like hell, it feels swollen and tender to touch and it's obvious, when you pull your hand away, that it's bleeding profusely.

"Owww I dink dey might have boken my dose" you say, your unusual speech impediment providing more evidence that indeed they might have broken your nose.

Refusing to go to hospital for anything as minor as a broken nose, you sit back down and the debate continues. (go to **Section 108**)

—— Section 187 ——

September 18th 2015

Watching the programme about Scottish creatures of myth and legend, you realised that people love that type of thing. Maybe that's partly why fantasy books and films do so well.

People love the idea of being a sword-wielding hero and escaping from everyday life.

The sort of sad cases who rave on and on about Game of Thrones.

The sort of saddoes who play demons and dragons, fighting armies of orcs armed with nothing but 3d20 dice.

The sort of losers who dress up as dwarves for fantasy conventions (although not the sort of sexy saddoes who dress as buxom elves - you think that they're probably alright).

The sort of saddoes who are so into fantasy life that they even read those books that pretend to be adventures allowing you to make decisions and choose your own way through the story.

'*What complete losers*', you think, '*you'll never be caught dead reading one of those.*'

Saddoes they may be. But they are saddoes with money to spend on programmes and books and films and games and dressing up at conventions and… an idea starts to form.

Six months later your 'Game of Scottish Dragons' fantasy-adventure park opens in the highlands.

By cashing in on Scottish nationalism following independence you've somehow already managed to get nearly 500 bookings for the next 3 months. 500 bookings at £250 per day to sleep in a tent and wave a foam sword and if they don't manage to slay the Giant Haggis of Auld Dundee then you don't even feed them.

You wish your countrymen weren't so dumb, but as long as they are you may as well cash in. Next year you should be pulling in the Americans as well - they love anything connected to the Auld Country and don't know jack about real history…

All in all, independence could be good for you.

The End

Should it actually happen in your reality, this ending is NOT covered by the 100% money back guarantee. I would consider paying you back 7 DragonGroats but you don't have a DragonGroat account to pay it into. Too bad.

—— Section 188 ——

You enter the examination cubicle and are happy to be welcomed by a doctor of obvious foreign heritage. You're not racist but you know that foreign doctors really know their stuff. Only the best foreign doctors get to come and work in the UK and the ones who were born here but of foreign heritage are even better, as they've worked so hard to escape their immigrant roots. Yes - foreign doctors and foreign-looking doctors are definitely the best and are just what you want to see when you obviously have a deadly disease turning you into blue mush.

Doctor Nassir will have you diagnosed and on the way back to good health in no time. It's a sign of his pure professionalism that he doesn't waste time on small talk but cuts straight to the chase.

"So what is wrong with you?"

"L-look at my face… I'm blue. I'm leaking. I'm dying."

The doctor looks closely at your face whilst pulling on a pair of latex gloves and picking up a cotton wool swab.

"Hold still this won't hurt."

He dabs at the outside of your cheek then looks at the blue residue.

"Hmmm.. How long have you been displaying these symptoms?"

You tell him since waking this morning.

"And have you been doing anything unusual recently? Maybe a trip to Africa, unprotected sex with prostitutes, eaten any seafood that tasted odd or even… just painted your face because you're a patriot and it's the Referendum today?"

Wow he's good. Maybe the Liberian ebola outbreak has put the health service on high alert looking out for similar diseases here. You can't remember where the blue dye was made - could it have been Africa?

"Yes doctor - the last one. What does it mean? Is it serious?"

The doctor looks deadly serious. "I'm afraid there's not much we can do for you, I just hope I don't catch it."

"Why what is it? How long have I got?"

"Potentially years - you've got an acute case of *neural faeces syndrome.* Otherwise known as shit-for-brains. You've painted your face blue and need to go home and wash it off instead of fucking about here wasting my time. Now piss off."

You've never seen anyone pull off latex gloves and throw them into a bin in such an annoyed manner as this 'so-called-doctor' Nassir. Stupid foreign idiot - what does he know? You knew you should have had a good Scottish doctor. Someone who knows what's normal over here.

Since Dr Nassir says you're ok, you go straight home and jump in the shower to freshen up before going to vote. (go to **Section 240**)

—— Section 189 ——

You get some funny looks on the way, but most people seem to accept that on such a momentous day some people might dress up and treat it like some sort of party. At least there's no trouble and eventually you get to the polling station, walk up to the doors and pause.

You always thought that polling stations are places full of wonder and promise for the future. The almost-mystical locations that can alter a nations fate. Each one a powerful nexus where all possible destinies of the country intersect, just waiting for the public will to select one single possibility and to transform it into reality. Places of truly amazing, almost miraculous, transformative power.

But really they are just local primary schools that have swapped the kids for a naff sign saying 'POLLING STATION'.

Finally you approach the doors and prepare yourself to step inside.

DEAD CAT TIME

Yes it's time to peek inside Schrödinger's box and see how well Jess is...

Hello Jess. Where's Pat? (go to **Section 013**)

or Hello Pat. Where's Jess gone? (go to **Section 400**)

or That's not a cat that's George Galloway! (go to **Section 177**)

or Jess is curled up asleep, blissfully unaware of their role in the future of Scotland. (go to **Section 220**)

or Postcat Jess. Postcat Jess. Postcat Jess has left a mess! (go to **Section 366**)

or OMG! Jess is dead! Pat will be upset. (go to **Section 288**)

—— Section 190 ——

McBabeStation is on TV when you switch on with a scantily-clad bubbly trio of young women; a redhead, blonde and brunette all sat on a sofa in their tartan underwear and talking to you. Yes - you.

It's good to know that you're watching 100% Scottish lassies, the sort of people you might bump into in a bar and that, here on TV, they are showing interest in *you*. Not just any viewer. No - you.

One of the McBabes says "Mmmmm we know what you're thinking" and they begin to undress each other further whilst applying liberal amounts of baby oil to their friends toned bodies.

'Oh not again' you think.

What happens next is inevitable.

Sex. Hot sex. Really hot sex. Really really hot solo sex. Sex so hot you're surprised your hand doesn't fall off. Sex so hot that it can't be described in any greater detail than just 'really hot sex' or this book would be banned under obscenity law. Sex so hot that if it was any hotter you'd have to wear an oven glove. Sex so really really hot that partway through you think it'd be a bit of a kinky change to wear an oven glove so you go and grab them from the kitchen before continuing your self-loving.

Eventually after a couple of minutes you reach for the tissues and the remote and turn over the TV, making a mental note to put the oven gloves in the wash.

You turn over to ScotParli TV (go to **Section 050**)
or Maybe you watch SciTech TV (go to **Section 362**)

—— Section 191 ——

I thought you'd gone!

What do you mean *you* thought *I'd* gone?

I wrote this just for you, no-one else. Sure some other people may read this, but they mean nothing to me… Not like you do.

You're my favourite reader. My one true reader. I'm not stopping writing it just because you're still a little undecided about whether it's worth your time or not. What sort of ~~an author~~ a serious pioneering multiverse explorer/researcher would that make me?

A very shitty one. That's what.

No - I'm here for the long run. I'll never leave you. Never give up on you.

In my heart of hearts I know that one day, maybe not today, maybe not tomorrow, but one day, you'll reconsider and come back to me, asking just what really happens after you wake up on the 18th of September 2014. And when you do, I'll still be here for you. Patiently waiting, for you, for as long as it takes.

Bet that Alex Salmond wouldn't do that. Alistair Darling wouldn't do that. J K Rowling wouldn't care if you read about *Hairy Putter and the Toilet of Fiery Doom* or not. Once they've got your vote or your money they all leave you.

But I won't.

I'm here for you, whenever you come back.

Just take your time and come back when you are ready. I won't rush you.

So have you reconsidered and want to find out what happens when you wake up? (go to **Section 086**)

or Are you really off for now? (go to **Section 172**)

—— Section 192 ——

Generic Ending Template

Lucky you - thanks to Thomas the cat you've hit upon the special generic ending. Just use this formula to make up any number of new endings whenever you want. Here goes…

September 18th 2014 or later

At some point after *Yes-Day* some sort of generic situation of your choosing developed or was desired.

The government and or yourself tried to do something to bring about or possibly to halt the generic situation. But there were some unintended side effects involving bad puns and/or some 4th wall breaking and possibly some sort of surreality.

Either none of this made sense so you panic and break the 4th wall, or it all makes perfect sense and so you plough on regardless (stopping only briefly to break the 4th wall).

Getting back on track, keeping on track or possibly flying wildly off course, you see/show that everything was far worse than it appeared or possibly that it was the exact opposite of what was thought or you realise that you were the teacher after all.

The End

Should it actually happen in your reality, this ending is <u>NOT</u> covered by the 100% money back guarantee. For some reason or another that makes no sense.

—— Section 193 ——

He obviously tries to make himself look bigger but it's laughable.

"Aye I'll make you leave if I have to. But it's better for you if you and your friend just walk out that door now."

Then he starts to try guiding you and Andy out the door.

Do you walk out quietly? (go to **Section 164**)

or Are you gonna deck the twat? (go to **Section 299**)

—— Section 194 ——

As soon as you say that you realise it may have been a mistake.

The nurse calmly and coldly says "Some of these 'dodgy accident claims' are in real pain rather than just some sort of idiot who's painted their face and then panicked. Now sit down and wait."

As it's probably not wise to further upset the person who controls the waiting queue you do as you are told. (go to **Section 055**)

—— Section 195 ——

You call the dogs and race off as fast as Gwen's bladder will let you before the odd blue-faced zombie gets too close to you.

"Phew! That was close" you think later as you finally close your front door on the world. You're not 100% certain if you want to risk going back out to the cafe, but their breakfasts are so nice.

Do you make yourself a breakfast feast at home (go to **Section 257**)

or Go out to a local cafe for breakfast (go to **Section 114**)

or Are you so excited you skip breakfast, keen to jump in the shower, freshen up and get ready to go out and vote as quickly as you can. (go to **Section 258**)

—— **Section 196** ——

You can't remember quite what happened for the rest of the night, but you're pretty sure that at the end of the night you didn't have to go home alone and it wasn't your home you went to.

You try to think of the details. You remember that you'd fancied the hot redhead, Cally or whatever she was called, all night. She looked a right goer and had a great pair. You're sure that, with a body like hers, you could manage to look past her being a boring intellectual who likes to debate.

You try harder to remember the details and have a vague recollection of having a passionate cuddle before your partner headed down to your groin and starting caressing your balls with their tongue. You cast your mind back as best you can.

'Oh not again' you thought.

What happened next was inevitable.

Sex. Hot sex. Hot sexy sex. Really hot sex. Really really hot sexy sexy sex. Sex so hot it made your chilli laced beef tindaloo look like plain old gravy. Really really really hot sexy sex so hot and sexy that it can't be described in any greater detail than just 'really really really really hot sexy sexy sexy sex' or this book would be banned under obscenity law.

You make really really hot sweaty sexy physical animal sex for ages until you fall back on the bed exhausted and gently take your partner's golden hair in your hands.

Yes what a ni- just a second. Golden hair? Carly's a redhead, a sexy redhead with really hot sexy long red hair. So how come you remember golden hair?

Lovely thick luscious golden hair - so thick it was almost like fur. And golden like next doors retrieve-

Oh shit.

Not again.

Exactly how pissed were you?

Feeling dirty beyond belief, and in a dirty way not a sexy way, you jump into the shower to freshen up and wash away all traces of pedigree chum before you go to vote. (go to **Section 295**)

—— **Section 197** ——

Suddenly you're surrounded on all sides by solid walls of muscle stretching up above you. The eagle-eyed bouncers have noticed that things may be about to get out of hand and have decided to throw you both out before they do.

"C'mon you two - outside now."

He asks so politely really, considering you don't have any say in the matter - the firm grip on your neck indicates as much. You're both taken to the club door and unceremoniously thrown out on the street.

You pick yourselves up and square up to each other again.

Do you continue your fight out here (go to **Section 162**)
or Apologise and maybe go somewhere else (go to **Section 105**)
or Laugh it off. (go to **Section 238**)

—— Section 198 ——

You're not going to A&E just because you took a bit of a beating.

No. You'll get cleaned up and if you look really bad you think you still have a bit of spot concealer around that some ex left at your place. You can dig that out and cover up the worst of the damage - or, being referendum day, you could even get a fancy dress costume so your face is covered.

Of course that's only really necessary if you still look a bad mess after you've showered and cleaned yourself up. You won't need to cover it up if there's just a few bruises. Instead you'll just tell everyone that you got jumped by 4 or 5 big blokes and you should see the state that you left them in. Yeah. That's what you'll do.

But first to get cleaned up.

DEAD CAT TIME
Hey Pickle! Are you still alive in there?

Miaowww (which is living cat speak for 'yes') (go to **Section 213**)
or Silence (which is dead cat speak for 'no') (go to **Section 171**)

—— Section 199 ——

It's all very expensive and maybe a bit too expensive for a one-off just for referendum day. If only they had something a bit cheaper.

That's when you spot the clothes rack next to the shop counter. '*Bargain Rack: Everything £5 or less*' claims the sign. Well that's more like it. You start rummaging through the selection of costumes on the rack and are quickly disgusted at the range of shockingly inappropriate options available.

A comedy Fred West… Who'd want that? It might only be a quid but even so, you'd have to be sick to think that's funny.

Maggie Thatcher? Double-You Tee Eff. Even if you wanted to wear that you'd get lynched before you'd made it half a mile from the shop. You'd be more popular in a Hitler costume - which is a fitting thought as you come across the next costume of everyone's favourite 3rd Reich Fuhrer.

No - it's no use. None of these will do they're all a load of bol- wait a minute... What's that one?

You missed it a minute ago, but now you spot it. There is one single costume that might just work. The garish yellow baggy-panted tracksuit, fake gold jewellery, big cigar, glasses and wig of long white hair. Yes it's perfect, and for some reason it's only 50p. What a steal! You've got to have it.

It's you who takes the costume to the till. It's you who pays the shopkeeper. You who takes the costume and enters the changing room. You who undresses from your sweatpants and tee.

Yes it's you who does all those things. But it's everybody's favourite radio 1 DJ, TV personality and charity worker, Jimmy Savile OBE,who leaves the shop heading off to the polling station. (go to **Section 399**)

—— Section 200 ——

You open the door hoping that the hint was wrong and that this is really the normal polling station and not a weird room that you won't enjoy. Nope - the hint was correct.

Almost immediately know that you're entered the wrong room as it appears to be a domestic kitchen. Sat, with his back to you, is a man with a hairstyle two decades too-young for his age. He's tapping away at a MacBook keyboard, apparently working on some document or another.

He hasn't noticed you yet so you move in closer to see what he's typing. What you see on the screen horrifies you as he is typing "What you see on the screen horrifies you as he is typing "What you see on the screen horrifies you as...

The implications of this chill your soul as much as they would the man typing at the MacBook, if only he was smart enough to fully consider them.

You exit the kitchen and decide to look for the polling station behind a different door. (go to **Section 337**)

—— Section 201 ——

You think just a little bit longer...

Oh there was something about currency, but you can't remember if it was good or bad. The bits you remember about EU and NATO membership and national debt are similarly sketchy...

You're starting to get a bit stressed about this...

Maybe you need a bit longer to remember in better detail.

Vote for 'Yes'. (go to **Section 374**)

or Vote 'No'. (go to **Section 144**)

or Wait and think about it a little longer. (go to **Section 070**)
or Flip a coin. That's the way to decide. (go to **Section 279**)
Flip a coin. But what sort of coin? (go to **Section 008**)
And is heads yes or heads no? (go to **Section 139**)
I suppose heads should be 'No' since it shows the queen of the United Kingdom, (go to **Section 212**)
but then she'd still be the queen of Scotland if the 'Yes' vote wins independence. (go to **Section 222**)
Oh this coin flipping is far too confusing, but it's the only way to decide. (go to **Section 328**)
Okay heads is 'Yes', tails 'No'. (go to **Section 354**)
Should it be the other way round? (go to **Section 092**)
or Oh god you can't decide - the stress is too much! (go to **Section 368**)

—— Section 202 ——

Of course I'm voting...

"You know me, I wouldn't miss it for the world"

From the way Andy looks at you it's clear he knows that you're bullshitting him.

"So which way are you planning to vote?"

"The right way. I was gonna go down to the school and see the polling people and get the paper and put a tick in a little box. Why how are you planning to vote?"

"No you numpty. I mean are you gonna vote aye or naw?"

"Oh - I haven't decided yet. Still trying to make my mind up."

"Are you? Well there's a debate about the referendum on nearby, we could go. If you're undecided it could really help you make your mind up."

Unwilling to admit you were lying about planning to vote, you agree and after another couple of rounds you're on you way to the debate. (go to **Section 265**)

—— Section 203 ——

September 18th 2032

You stand on top of a small hillock in the glorious sun and cast your eyes over this part of your land. You're so glad that you decided to become a farmer back in 2014.

You started small, with just 10 acres and a herd of 20 beasts that you yourself had rounded up from the wild, but you'd soon grown to become one of the largest land owners in the Scottish Highlands. Your meat was shipped internationally and reported to feed anything up to a quarter of the entire human race. Not bad for the young lad who had little but a dream.

You look out now at one of your herds of free-range haggi. Nearly 500 of the strange beasties moving as one, almost looking like a ground-based flock of birds.

Of course your path to major haggis farmer hadn't been entirely without problems. The early days were particularly difficult. You had a lot to learn about haggis-husbandry - their diet, mating habits, natural predators, diseases and well-being. You dreaded being struck by the foot and mouth epidemic of 2019, especially as it's far harder to protect haggi on account of their each having 17 legs. But, where other farmers fell, you were lucky.

Yes you were lucky, but through your luck the world had reaped great dividends and hopefully will for many years to come.

The End

Should it actually happen in your reality, this ending is <u>NOT</u> covered by the 100% money back guarantee. You're rich from selling haggis around the world. Is it even worth bothering wasting your time trying to get back a handful of coins?

—— Section 204 ——

September 18th 2028

You cast your mind back to that fateful morning soon after *Yes-Day* when you turned on the TV and saw a programme about scientific discoveries and the future of space exploration before having a quick one-off-the-wrist to the McBlokes on Gayer TV. It was that that made you realise that sex is always the way forward for new technology.

You can create a machine that does all housework, composes great works of art, makes you money and reverses global warming, even price it at £100 and you'd only sell a handful.

But if you stick a couple of vibrating self-lubricating holes and a multi-speed 10" butt plug on it and raise the price to a grand then they'll sell like hot cakes. They'll even sell like hot cakes would if *they* had sex toys attached (*note to self: patent vibrating Buttenburg cake and Anal Angel Cake*). They'll sell so well that you'll be set for life.

You were convinced that the way to make space exploration financially viable, self-sustaining or even profitable was to find a way to meld sex and space into one single venture, and who better to target than homosexuals? Many of them seem to have more disposable income (partly due to few having children) so selling the idea of space sex to them was obvious.

Before long the business plan for the first McBlokeSpaceStation had been approved.

By the end of 2019 the first small station opened it's airlock doors for business in orbit around the Earth. It became a roaring success, and was soon expanding to many times it's initial size. It really helped that initial traffic from millionaires keen to be amongst the first people to experience zero-G sex provided enough income to drive down prices and start regular orbital flights to and from the station. Business boomed and space exploration boomed with it.

By 2023 the next few stations had been planned and soon station modules were on course for Mars and Venus. In 2026 your business empire successfully placed a pair of sex-addicts in Saturn's orbit for two whole run throughs of the Karma Sutra before safely returning them to Earth. As more McBlokeSpaceStations come online, demand is through the ceiling and keeps rising, especially now that it's affordable to virtually everyone.

Of course you get a lot of PWUSFWEVAEs, *people with unusual and specific fetishes which are equally valid as anybody else's*, if we're using the language of 21st Century politically correctness. Though it's a lot easier to use old English and just call them perverts.

A lot of these pervs come just for zero-G sex with the Ian Krankie sexbots. You're not sure which is worse, that they may be into schoolboys' dads, into the dads of women dressed as schoolboys or into robots that look like the dads of robot women dressed as schoolboys. Or they could just come for the zero-G and end up up Ian whilst Wee Jimmy Kranky watched because it's '*the thing to do*', in much the same way as how a trip to Las Vegas just isn't a trip to Las Vegas unless you've accidentally killed a hooker.

You think back over all this as you sit back in your executive office on McBlokeSpaceStation Mars-69. Your business is still expanding and you don't intend to ever stop exploring all over the whole fucking universe. And you won't have to as long as people don't stop paying you for the chance to keep fucking all over the whole explored universe.

It's all both moving faster than you expected and taking an age, and so, happy that you're ready to move to the further reaches of the solar system, you gaze out to your next destination you say to your P.A. the words that you never thought you would ever live to say:

"Next stop, Uranus!"

"I thought you'd never ask, sir" he says bending over and dropping his shorts.

"No Marcus" you say "I meant the planet. I even pronounced it your-ann-us rather than your-anus."

"Oh. Sorry sir - the pronunciation didn't come through in the text" apologises Marcus before starting to pull up his clothing.

You stop his hand. "Oh there's no need to rush…"

The End

Should it actually happen in your reality, this ending is <u>NOT</u> covered by the 100% money back guarantee. You liked that obvious Uranus pun, didn't you. Admit it, you did. That's worth more than any refund ever could be.

— Section 205 —

The winner of Scotland's first Presidential election is announced as William Wallace, a true Scottish hero.

Of course it can't really be *the* William Wallace, the 13th Century Scottish Warrior, can it?

Your doubt is soon dispelled when President Wallace steps up to the podium to give his victory speech. It must be him - it is him. He looks just like he did in the Hollywood documentary *Braveheart,* although instead of a sword he's carrying a can of lager and staggering slightly. He wobbles up to the podium.

"G'day cobbers, Sheilas, fellow Scots… but, strewth, I don't mean the evil Christ-killing Jewish ones, no way, mate. With so many Scottish men in skirts I thought I had Buckley's chance in this election but, thanks to all you good straight Christians, I creamed it."

Oh no! As the new President goes on to talk about the massive list of people he has to thank, pausing only to point out how gay Jews have ruined the world, the realisation hits you that you and your countrymen have only gone and elected famous antipodean actor and drunk Mad Mel as the first President of Scotland. You've taken him straight from Hollywood to Holyrood (via a quick unsuccessful breather in the Priory).

He finally seems to be winding up his acceptance speech.

"All this talking's got me throat as dry as a nun's nasty, so cheers again mates, and I hope you'll join me in a tinny of the amber before we really hit the turps."

With that he raises his can of beer in a lager salute, before downing it.

"Anyone need a lift - I'm driving" he manages to say before appearing to pass out and fall over, completely inebriated.

Still - it could be worse, you reason. If you were mistakenly electing a dodgy character from down under you could have ended up with Rolf Harris and his wandering peg-leg. Lucky escape really.

The End

Should it actually happen in your reality, this ending is <u>NOT</u> covered by the 100% money back guarantee. Whatever.

—— Section 206 ——

"Well I suppose there's always one exception."

"And this is it, mate! You've got to believe our votes will make a difference."

"Really?"

"Yeah, really."

"Are you several drinks ahead of me tonight or something, mate?"

"Ha. No - I just have little bit of a head-start to feeling good from natural optimism. I assume the political system works for the good of everyone."

"Well you know what they say about assuming don't you: Don't assume because it makes an 'assu' out of 'me'."

"They say that?"

"Yeah - read it on mugs and everything."

"Anyway I heard there was this debate on about the referendum tonight, over at the debating hall. You fancy it?"

"Christ no - a debate like question time? That'd bore me shitless."

"Wasn't it you said that quote there's always one exception?"

"Well yeah, but…"

"An' debates always get their fair share of fit students who think they're clever but are just gagging for a real man."

"Drink up then - we'll get some cans on the way" you say before downing your 7th drink of the night and heading to the door. (go to **Section 265**)

—— Section 207 ——

Oh what a night!

Late September back in '63… Or was it mid September in 2014? You're always getting those two mixed up.

You had fun reading, watching, studying.
You had more fun analysing, interpolating and scrutinising.
Then you had even more fun querying, philosophising and debating.

Oh the reports and the books and the agendas and… and… oh just everything about the night was marvellous. You watched and listened to hours of debates, documentaries and interviews before leaving home to join about 80 other like-minded souls for a public debate that went on into the early hours.

The debating hall was appropriately dressed for the occasion - with a good mix of union flags and St Andrew's saltires and loads of large cuddly thistles with faces, arms and legs - some sort of promotional item from the Glasgow Commonwealth Games you think.

God this was the life for you. The thrill of verbally sparring with intellectual equals, ripping apart each others arguments for and against independence as rhetoric, points of view and the occasional insult get thrown back and forth across the room.

People who look upon debates (especially political debates) as boring just don't know what they were missing. At times the debate got so heated you were worried that it might really kick off big-time, with several people talking out of turn, interrupting each other (without making points of order) and the chairman completely losing control of the situation.

But luckily it never *quite* reached that level of unadulterated anarchy.

No. It stopped just short of that chaos because even though emotions were running high, everyone there was passionate that the future of Scotland and the Union be debated to everybody's satisfaction. No political stone would be left unturned, no avenue unexplored, no dilemma unaddressed, no woman no cry.

Now, as you go about your morning ablutions, you remember your reaction when someone, who you fear had misjudged the meeting and turned up with their mate, both having had more than enough drinks, tried making a joke about how he liked his pizzas with thin crusts and so he'd never agree to a Scotland that was in-deep-pan-dent.

As he said it, the atmosphere in the room suddenly changed.

That was a bad pun, delivered poorly, but there's nothing so serious you can't laugh about it. (go to **Section 250**)

or You remember that it was a crap pun, but what angered you more was how he dared joke about the most serious political decision that the Scottish people would have to answer in decades. Perhaps ever. (go to **Section 044**)

or The pun doesn't anger you as much as they way it's been made by some drunken idiot interrupting a serious debate. You're going to throw them out before they really disrupt the meeting. (go to **Section 278**)

—— Section 208 ——

Your fist flies in a perfect trajectory before making solid contact with the bloke's face. You're sure that this is going to be an easy win - the little guy certainly isn't a fighter.

But then he surprises you by shouting "You'll regret that, shithead!" and unleashes a blazing flurry of blows on your head. This catches you totally off-guard and in seconds you're on the floor. That's a terrible position to be in, so you've no real option but to shout at him to stop.

It must have worked, there blows stop coming. Then you notice why. The psycho's grabbed one of the cuddly 3-feet long Commonwealth Games thistle mascots off a nearby table and raises it above his head.

Slamming it down into you he screams "You" then he raises it up and swings again shouting "can't". He continues to scream beating you with the thistle to punctuate each word.

"Treat. People. That. Way. You. Bully. Think. It's. Fine. Just. Because. You're. Bigger. Than. Me. Do. You? Do. You? Well. It's."

He continues for a good 30 seconds or more, but by now you've almost zoned out under the constant barrage and the realisation that you may be being beaten to death with a cuddly toy. That's not the way you thought your life would end.

You're certainly not really hearing his words, just an angry scream of pent-up aggression that's obviously been brewing for years if not decades.

As suddenly as the beating started, it ends.

You're in no state to do anything but start crawling away as best you can until Andy helps you to your feet and you quickly leave the building.

When you're clear you turn your anger and disappointment towards Andy.

"Well thanks a lot mate - why didn't you help me?"

"Two against one's no fair. Besides he was half your size and you started it. I'm not gonna be accused of bullying some wimpy debater."

He may have a point, you should have won that fight easily. But in your current mood, pointing that out isn't winning Andy any points.

"Besides turned out he's a fucking psychopath, ain't he? If I'd joined in he'd have killed us both. You needed me to stay outta it so I could tell the police who'd killed you. Get you justice."

You turn to Andy and tell him to just fuck off. You're going home.

That's what happened last night and why you have such a bad head this morning. An excess of alcohol and a fight can leave you a bit achey in the morning. Then you see yourself in the mirror.

Ouch. No wonder you feel bad. You took a right beating. It would maybe be a good idea to get checked over at the local hospital Accident and Emergency department.

Do you go to A&E? (go to **Section 089**)

or Ignore it and get cleaned up and ready to go out and vote. (go to **Section 198**)

—— Section 209 ——

You open the door and you are suddenly hit by an almost physical underwhelming tsunami of ordinariness. The polling station looks like every other polling station that's ever existed in the past 50 or 60 years in the UK.

But then what did you really expect?

It looks like a normal polling station because it is a normal polling station. Nobody's going to dress primary schools up in union flags and saltires just because the subject of the vote is Scottish independence.

You exchange the briefest of pleasantries with the normal lady behind the desk dealing with addresses including your home. Once you've confirmed your identity, she gives you your ballot paper and points you in the direction of the small individual booths that you can go in to cast your vote in private.

As you walk across the room to the polling booth, it is with the weight of a country's destiny bearing down on your shoulders… (go to **Section 393**)

—— Section 210 ——

September 18th 2015

A year of very tough negotiations and uncertainty for business and it seems that Scotland is still no closer to solving the currency question.

Westminster and the Bank of England had flat out refused to let you use the British Pound Sterling, and the Scottish people didn't much want the Euro, but without adopting the Euro Brussels didn't want to let them gain automatic EU-membership.

Alex Salmond had started to wonder if maybe a new currency was the way forward. But no. A brand new currency would cost a fortune to implement. It was just too risky, there's no way he'd inflict that on Scotland. A new currency is absolutely, totally, utterly, unquestioningly not an option.

Worrying about the currency, he'd been losing sleep recently, and so last night his wife Moira suggested he take a night off. Maybe play a game and get an early night, for today he had a full schedule of *Yes-Day* anniversary celebrations to attend.

Reluctantly Alex agreed. Winning referenda and running a new country were both hard tasks, and he hadn't had a night off in nearly 400 days.

Before long Moira had got out Alex's favourite board game - Scrabble. "This will help you forget about currency problems", she said. Sure enough it did. Alex was worried about the terrible letters he kept getting and soon Moira was winning by nearly 100 points.

Ironically several of her words were money-based like 'dollar', 'pound' and 'fiscal', so the Scottish PMs mind kept jumping from his awful letters to currency issues and back again. Much like the currency issue, when he looked at his letter rack, Alex was at a loss at what to do.

Then it hit him - an answer. He picked his terrible letters off his rack one-by-one, placing them on the board. Z - L - O - T - Y.

"Well done, Zloty! The Polish currency" said Moira. "That's 17 points plus 10 for making MINTY."

"Not so fast" said Alex as he picked up his last two letter tiles and placed them on the board.

"MCZLOTY? That's not a word" said Moira.

"It is now, it's our new currency the Scottish McZloty. 50 point bonus for using all 7 letters and it's on a triple word score." replied Alex.

Mr Salmond announced the new currency to the nation during today's anniversary celebrations. He didn't say how he came up with it and he doesn't know if it's the currency to make Scotland a winner, but it's certainly the currency to make him a winner at Scrabble.

That's a good enough result for now.

The End

Should it actually happen in your reality, this ending is covered by the 100% money back guarantee. But I can only pay it straight into your McZloty account - is that okay?

—— Section 211 ——

You try to explain that the referendum is the most important day for Scotland in decades, if not centuries, and you're all there to help you decide which way to vote. That it's very serious and it's hardly fitting joking about it all the time, but that anybody and everybody is welcome if they're happy to sit and listen to, and maybe even join in, the debate.

"Ah no worries, , I was jus havin' a laugh" says the punster.

You all sit down and you feel the room soon return to the pleasant debate it had been throughout most of the night. (go to **Section 365**)

—— Section 212 ——

The coin flies up...

And then comes back down again landing on the floor and balancing perfectly on it's edge. You wait a minute to see if it wobbles over onto one of the faces, but it doesn't budge.

That's very interesting. That must be the universe telling you that both YES and NO are equally valid votes, so you pick up the teeny tiny pencil and place a cross in the 'YES' box and another cross in the 'NO' box.

You fold the ballot paper and happily stroll out of the booth, walk across the floor and pop the folded ballot in the box. You exchange knowing nods with the station attendants. You know and they know that you have fulfilled your democratic duty.

It's surprisingly easy when you use a coin and don't worry too much about political arguments. You hardly know why people treat it as such a big deal.

You go home and carry on as normal until the results are announced. (go to **Section 321**)

—— Section 213 ——

You get into the shower and let the water wash away all the aches and pains.

You hadn't realised until now that you have got a cracking headache from the beating you took. Maybe you shouldn't have swung at the little guy, but it just annoyed you that someone smaller than you was making you leave.

You're more used to being the one who tells other people what to do.

God your head is bad. Maybe you should take some paracetamol when you get out of the shower, but for now you just close your eyes and let the water wash over you.

That was a big mistake.

You suddenly feel very dizzy and the next thing you now you've slipped in the bath and as you fall down you crack your temple on the hot water top.

Luckily the impact makes you lose consciousness and so you're not in pain as your life ebbs away, your blood flowing down the plughole with the warm water that still washes over you.

The End

This ending is NOT covered by the 100% money back guarantee should it actually happen in your reality. The psycho was right as he thrashed you: you were trying to be a bully. And we think it'd be wrong for us to give money to a bully, especially as a reward for dying due to their physical intimidation backfiring. So there.

—— Section 214 ——

Oh what a night!

Late September back in '63… Or was it mid September in 2014? You're always getting those two mixed up.

You had fun reading, watching, studying.

You had more fun analysing, interpolating and scrutinising.

Then you had even more fun querying, philosophising and debating.

Oh the reports and the books and the agendas and… and… oh just everything about the night was marvellous. You watched and listened to hours of debates, documentaries and interviews before noticing something very strange about one of the programmes.

The commentary was talking about devolution whilst the images showed the Scottish Highlands, but for just one or two seconds there was an old well in the background and you're sure you saw… no you must be mistaken… but you'd swear you saw it.

You rewind the programme on your TiVo and pause on the shot with the well in it.

"No way… that's not possible"

Even though the programme is paused, something is moving on the screen. Something dark and indistinct is crawling out of the well. Dragging itself up. Clawing it's way forward towards the screen.

You can't tear your eyes away from it, as it slowly approaches. Seeing it's sallow, sickly grey skin, you're thankful that it's long black hair hides whatever blasphemous excuse it has for a face.

Just a second that looks like… no it can't be…

"Pissy Quimburgers!"

Is all you can exclaim as the goblin-banshee raises it's head to stare straight at you before leaping, talon-like hands first, through the TV screen and into your reality.

"Wow I'm in agony, but not too much that I can't appreciate how realistic these modern 3D TVs are" you think as the goblin-banshee rips you a new arsehole.

Your final dying thought is how ironic it is that the goblin-banshee choses to roll your disembodied testicles around in its hand as if they were nothing more than Chinese meditation balls, when, in life, you used to roll them around in your own hand whilst 'meditating' upon images of Chinese women…

The End

Should it actually happen in your reality, this ending is NOT covered by the 100% money back guarantee. Well you're already dead so can't claim the money back in person. #Yolo as buddhists often say. Or are they the ones that say #Yolamtaittrasoeatbaowtu (You only live as many times as it takes to reach a state of enlightenment and to be at one with the universe)?

—— Section 215 ——

You show your support for Scottish independence, dressing in full traditional national dress.

White shirt, black tie, black jacket, a good tartan waistcoat, matching kilt, a modest day sporran, white stockings, sgian dubh and ghillies. Which just leaves your head to dress correctly.

No traditional dress is complete without the appropriate headwear, so you finish off the outfit with your big tartan hat complete with masses of fake ginger hair spilling out from under it.

You look in the mirror and think "Aye - you've done well. Traditional Scottish dress for a momentous day."

There's just one thing missing, so before leaving home you stop to pin a

'Yes Scotland' campaign badge to your jacket.

Damn! You've done a bloody good job. If the very sight of you doesn't persuade people to vote 'YES' then there's no sense of fairness or justice in the world. Humming 'Scotland the Brave' you leave for the polling station. (go to **Section 326**)

—— Section 216 ——

You think for a second hoping for divine guidance, but none is coming. You can hear the other knights coming after you, baying for your blood. Oh which way…

Suddenly, searching your memory for anything that might help you, you remember reading the book '*Even More Dragon Gold!*' and that in that book turning left was the best thing to do.

Well it's as good a way as any to decide which way to go, so you quickly race to the left.

The corridor quickly bends to the right, and partway along the bend you stop and look back. It seems that you may have lost your pursuers and so you turn back to continue along the path and are surprised to see that, as if by magic, the shopkeeper has appeared and is stood there in front of you.

He looks at you disapprovingly, shakes his head and says "Oh I don't know what's up with people these days. You're nowhere near as good at fancy dress escapades as they were in the 1970s. Back then a city gent in a suit and bowler hat could put on a suit of armour and within ten minutes he'd have slain the dragonkin, won a fair maidens hand in a joust and saved the entire kingdom. Whereas all you've managed to do is totally ruin Arthurian legend. Now people through the ages will only know him as a coward who wets himself at the first sign of trouble."

"I do not!"

The shopkeeper points to a trail of liquid drops on the floor leading back to where you've come from.

"Well maybe a little - but it was scary. They want to bloody kill me."

The shopkeeper looks at you disappointedly and says "I know how they feel."

"For fucks sake take me back to the shop" you shout.

"Manners really. They were better in the 70s as well."

And with a wave of the shopkeeper's hand you're back in the shop. (go to **Section 100**)

—— Section 217 ——

You open the door and almost immediately know that you've entered the wrong room because you stumble into a large laboratory where 20 or 30 children in school uniform are working hard at stoves and bunsen burners. An unhappy looking man with a dodgy moustache that singles him out as a chemistry teacher is walking around hitting the children with a riding crop.

"C'mon make me meth, you little shits. I can't wait until I get Cancer, I want it now." he shouts.

Then, out of the corner of his eye, he sees you and comes running over.

"Oh hello can I help you? Parents aren't allowed in here whilst the class is in session, you know."

"I'm not a parent."

"Police?" he says seeming panicked.

"No, I'm just looking for the polling station."

"Oh in that case: Fuck off and one word to the head and you're dead."

You exit the room and decide to look for the polling station behind a different door. (go to **Section 115**)

—— Section 218 ——

As soon as you say that you realise it may have been a really bad mistake.

The nurse puts on a false smile that wouldn't be too out of place on a shark and then calmly and coldly says "You're quite right I'm not a doctor. I'm just the person who decides just how long you'll be waiting until you're seen by a doctor. I really do hope you're a patient patient. Now sit down and wait."

You do as she says and sit in the waiting room, wishing you'd brought a book to read. (go to **Section 236**)

—— Section 219 ——

Bad luck...

As usual for a weekday, BBC1 is showing some sort of property porn. You think this one has just come on but you can't stand this sort of show so you're set on quickly changing channels again.

Just as you pick up the TV controller again, you hear the female presenter say, in an attractive Scottish lilt, "Welcome to the very first edition of *Escape for the Cuntery*."

What did she just say? You must have misheard her surely. You pause before changing channels, wanting to know exactly what sort of show this is.

"If you're rich and looking to move north or maybe buy a holiday home in Scotland, then *Escape for the Cuntery* may be the show for you" she continues until her male co-presenter interrupts.

"I'm sorry Kirsty, but I think we'll have to change the name of the show."

"And why's that Dougal?"

"Well in your accent it's a bit ambiguous what the title is. It sounds like it could be either *Escape for the Country* or *Escape for the Cuntery*."

"Oh it doesn't, does it? How embarrassing. We'll have to change that then."

"Aye we will - it'll be a lot clearer if we just call it *Escape for the Tory Cunts*."

Well you're hooked now and there's no way you're changing channel.

When the show ends you check the programme guide and think that calling the show *Escape for the Cunt Tories* was pretty much spot on as it was showing Scottish country houses with a minimum asking price of £1.25 million. The sort of places only affordable to English Home Counties Hoorays who could happily pay an assistant to find them a second home rather than inflict a TV show on the 99% of the nation who can't afford anything like the prices asked.

You eventually decide to turn off the TV and start to think about your future and the future of Scotland, and where the priorities lie for both of you.

Try to improve broadband access to rural areas to help attract English money to the areas (go to **Section 087**)

or Spotting a chance to make some money, do you start investing in Scottish property (go to **Section 371**)

or You should try to help the planet, but you can do that whilst enjoying city life in your home that continues rising in value (go to **Section 235**)

or Who cares about the planet? (go to **Section 383**)

or You don't mind the English coming to Scotland as long as they aren't a drain on the state (go to **Section 043**)

or I don't want to think about all this - just give me something random! (go to **Section 375**)

—— Section 220 ——

You open the door and almost immediately know that you've entered the wrong room because this certainly doesn't look like any polling station that you've ever seen.

Instead it's a white oval room with the walls filled of video monitors each one showing a dove at various stages of decomposition.

You don't know why anyone would create a room like this, but you know that you don't much like it.

You exit the room and decide to look for the polling station behind a different door. (go to **Section 083**)

— Section 221 —

You wait...

You're already bored of waiting. The only thing to do is worry or watch the other people, but that's just annoying.

Take those two youths over by the blood donor poster for example.

"A pint! That's most of me arm innit!"

"No idea mate - I don't do that old pints and ounces shit. Ain't a pint just under half a litre?"

"No idea - it's just a quote from some old Alfred Hitchcock film me gran told me about once. Hitchcock's in hospital an' he sees a poster asking for blood donors to give a pint an' he says 'A pint! That's most of me arm innit?' Me gran thought it were proper funny."

"I s'pose people used to laugh at anything after the war."

Thankfully at this point your name is called by the nurse from reception and she leads you through to an examination cubicle.

DEAD CAT TIME

Has anyone fed Tiddles today? No? I'll see how he is then.

He's fine and ready to play! (go to **Section 320**)
or He's fine and ready for some food! (go to **Section 140**)
or He's fine... if you didn't want a living cat. (go to **Section 391**)

— Section 222 —

The coin flies up...

Arcing upwards and upwards, slowing it's ascent until...

It just stops and hangs there. Stubbornly remaining at the peak of it's trajectory. You wait a minute to see if it decides to descend again, but it doesn't budge.

That's very interesting. That must be the universe telling you that neither YES nor NO are good votes, so you pick up the teeny tiny pencil and scrawl 'NONE OF THE ABOVE' in big letters across your ballot paper.

You fold the ballot paper and happily stroll out of the booth, walk across the floor and pop the folded ballot in the box. You exchange knowing nods with the station attendants. You know and they know that you have fulfilled your democratic duty.

It's surprisingly easy when you use a coin and don't worry too much about political arguments. You hardly know why people treat it as such a big deal.

You go home and carry on as normal until the results are announced. (go to **Section 321**)

— Section 223 —

You ask for ice and you're lucky that either the castle has a well-stocked ice house or is the only medieval castle with a working ice machine.

Either way as you use the ice to cool off and look at the sword in the stone you have an idea.

Quickly you pack ice around the sword and then you wait a few minutes, trying to ignore the murmurs of the crowd and only answering questions about what you are doing by saying "just wait and see."

Eventually you decide it is time to try again. Planting your feet firmly on either side of the stone, you take a strong two handed grip on the hilt of the sword and start to pull as hard as you can.

Almost immediately the sword starts to move, having contracted due to the cold, and moments later you stand before the crowd proudly brandishing Excalibur.

They don't appreciate that it was simple physics that let you retrieve the sword. Instead they are all happy in their belief that you are the real king, destined to rule over Albion for evermore.

Yours is a happy reign. After defeating the dragonkin that afternoon you lead Camelot to years of harmony.

Yours is a happy reign. The lands of Britain prosper with only the odd case of black-magic-induced plague or invading spectral warriors, and you soon deal with those.

Yours is a happy reign. As you introduce the people of Camelot to a new form of entertainment where they each pay a groat to pick six numbers that provide several days of hope, before they then watch totally different numbers being drawn out of a magic machine.

Yours is a happy reign. You establish the Round Table, insisting that the knights of the Round Table better themselves, raise money for charity and dress up as Santa at Christmas. Traditions that you are sure will last up to 21st Century Britain.

Yours is a happy reign, as much for you as for your loyal subjects. You live out your days in comparative luxury and barely ever stop to wonder what happened to your modern Scotland as you're too busy bonking Guinevere, Morgana and Sharon (as those on intimate terms with the Lady of the Lake call her).

It's a good job that Merlin managed to make up *Bull Gules*, a magical potion of energy, or you'd never have it in you for all the hot sex, really hot sex and really really hot sex they demand.

Of course it's not all hot sex, really hot sex or really really hot sex. You're teaching the peasants how to cook authentic Scottish Indian takeaways and how to brew lager.

Well, even kings have got to have hobbies.

The End

This ending is <u>NOT</u> covered by the 100% money back guarantee should it actually happen in your reality. This is purely because the author has seen 'Merlin' and considers you jammy enough if you're shagging Guinevere, Morgana and Sharon. It'd be taking the piss if you get to do that and get your money back as well.

—— Section 224 ——

September 18th 2015

The government realise what a great asset the country and history of Scotland is and so pour money into boosting tourism and it's national and international profile as am holiday destination.

It's partly due to this that just one year after *Yes Day* you decide to take advantage of a warm Scottish summer and holiday in the wilds of your own country.

So today you find yourself out enjoying the sunshine and hiking along what is either a large stream or a small river. As you walk along you're amazed to spot a large man in a suit with his back to you and his head down, stood facing the water and frantically moving his right hand up and down. It's obvious what he's doing.

Yuck - you don't need to see some pervert masturbating.

It may be miles away from the towns, and he may think he's got solitude but, in your opinion, it's still disgusting doing it in public like that. What if an innocent child was to come across him. Or worse: what if he was to come across an innocent child? Rather than ignore him you decide to challenge him about it.

"Oi! You. Stop wanking" you call as you get closer.

But he seems impervious to your shouts. You realise that this is because he appears to have reached the climax of his self-abuse, as he lets out a loud groan and sends cables of semen arcing out over the water.

"That's fuckin' disgusting - are you a perv or something?"

The man finally takes notice of you and turns to face you, raising his head.

God! How you wish you'd let him be. For it is no normal human face that gazes at you with fury in it's eyes. No it is some kind of half-human half-fish face, almost as if it's owner was sickened by the fictional Innsmouth taint.

But worse than that is the way that the face looks oddly familiar. Almost like a piscine version of- no! NO! It can't be! That's pure madness. It can't possibly be…

But it *is*.

Standing before you is Alex Salmond! Or should that be Alex Salmon?

As the angry 7 feet tall fishman charges forward you turn to try escaping but instead find yourself face to face with some strange fishwoman.

"Just stay there laddie" commands the unmistakeable voice of Alex Salmonds deputy, Nicola the Sturgeon.

Within seconds she's restrained you and Alex Salmon(d) is raining down punches upon your helpless body. As the pair beat you to a pulp, you realise that David Ickes new book was correct. Alex just wanted an independent Scotland so he could rule it and control his ancient spawning grounds in the highland streams.

Your dying thought is that it's truly amazing that nobody ever realised Salmond was anything but entirely human, though not quite as amazing as the fact that this means David Icke wasn't *quite* as full of shit as everyone always thought…

The End

Should it actually happen in your reality, this ending is NOT covered by the 100% money back guarantee. You've reached this ending and now want your money back? Something fishy about that if you ask me.

—— Section 225 ——

You get some funny looks on the way, but most people seem to accept that on such a momentous day some people might dress up and treat it like some sort of party. At least there's no trouble and eventually you get to the polling station, walk up to the doors and pause.

You always thought that polling stations are places full of wonder and promise for the future. The almost-mystical locations that can alter a nations fate. Each one a powerful nexus where all possible destinies of the country intersect, just waiting for the public will to select one single possibility and to transform it into reality. Places of truly amazing, almost miraculous, transformative power.

But really they are just local primary schools that have swapped the kids for a naff sign saying 'POLLING STATION'.

Finally you approach the doors and prepare yourself to step inside.

DEAD CAT TIME

Yes it's time to peek inside Schrödinger's box and see how well Jess is…

Hello Jess. Where's Pat? (go to **Section 013**)

or Hello Pat. Where's Jess gone? (go to **Section 045**)

or That's not a cat that's George Galloway! (go to **Section 177**)

or Jess is curled up asleep, blissfully unaware of their role in the future of Scotland. (go to **Section 340**)

or Postcat Jess. Postcat Jess. Postcat Jess has left a mess! (go to **Section 366**)

or OMG! Jess is dead! Pat will be upset. (go to **Section 288**)

—— Section 226 ——

You turn back to the nurse and say "You don't understand - I'm dying."

"Dying, eh? Just like the last two times you turned up at A&E with a blue face?"

"No - this time I'm really really dying. I could be dead any moment now. I need to see a doctor."

"Do you really think you're more important than anyone else waiting here?"

Do you reply "No I'm sorry, I'll sit down and be quiet" (go to **Section 055**)

or "Yes. I could be dying not just pretending to have an injury for a dodgy accident claim" (go to **Section 194**)

or "I could be dying as far as you know. I mean, you're not even a doctor are you?" (go to **Section 218**)

—— Section 227 ——

September 18th 2015

Finally after a year of very tough negotiations and uncertainty for Scottish business, today sees the currency question solved as Scotland turns its back on rUK (the rest of the UK) and signs an agreement that should help guarantee a prosperous future.

Westminster and the Bank of England had flat out refused to let you use the British Pound Sterling, and, immediately after the referendum, the Scottish people didn't much want the Euro, but without adopting the Euro Brussels didn't want to let Scotland gain automatic EU-membership.

The Scottish government knew that EU-membership was important. Most of your international trade is with Europe. So a campaign was launched to persuade the nation that it was for the best.

It was whilst working upon this campaign that you came to work for Prime Minister Salmond's office and so end up assisting him at today's historic meeting in Brussels.

As Salmond and Merkel and the other EU country leaders (with the noticeable exception of the rUK who claims to be washing their hair tonight) sign the historic document accepting Scotland into the EU and the Eurozone, you think that you're not really surprised that an agreement was reached. Though you are surprised that an agreement was reached so quickly. You're more surprised by how little time it took after the papers were signed before Angela Merkel and Francois Hollande are telling their best Cameron and Clegg jokes.

You're shocked at how graphic some of the jokes are. You're shocked that Merkel, a German, has a sense of humour. But you're most shocked that they still take the piss out of Cameron and Clegg and they don't even run rUK since the May elections.

Of course, Salmond manages to return with equally blue jokes about the pair of clowns and before long you're all getting on like a house on fire. You think that adopting the Euro was definitely the right thing to do.

The End

Should it actually happen in your reality, this ending is <u>NOT</u> covered by the 100% money back guarantee. Because I don't have a Euro cheque account. I can do you monopoly money if that's any good. No? Sorry.

—— Section 228 ——

SciTech TV is showing a programme about the great history of scientists and inventors that Scotland has produced.

You never realised how influential your homeland had been in virtually all areas of modern technology and pure science. The show gives potted biographies of Alexander Graham Bell, John Logie Baird, John Dunlop, James Watt, John McAdam, Alexander Fleming, Mungo Ponton, John Napier and William McWhirter to name but a few.

All those greats of the past and it doesn't even get around to mentioning the inventors of Chicken Tikka Masala or deep fried confectionary.

There's then a section upon current research and inventors in Scotland, mentioning the excellent work being done in genetics and cloning, Artificial Intelligence, robotics and computing and hi-tech fabrics for 21st century smart-kilts.

The show goes on to ponder how an independent Scotland could affect science, maybe increased government aid would raise Scotland back to the forefront of research in even more areas. Then again, who knows? And governments only have so much money to spread around...

You eventually decide to turn off the TV and start to think about your future and the future of Scotland, and where the priorities lie for both of you.

Are you inspired to personally become a scientist on the theoretical boundaries of science (go to **Section 150**)

or Forget science! Something must be done about the impending food crisis and you're the person to do it (go to **Section 203**)

or Does the government invest heavily in science and technology (go to **Section 173**)

or Maybe science can help avert the impending food crisis (go to **Section 268**)

or Invest heavily in Science, but don't neglect the arts (go to **Section 322**)

or Science is all well and good, but what about fun - we need some sort of entertainment (go to **Section 248**)

or Science is all well and good, but what about fun - we need spectator sports (go to **Section 104**)

or I don't want to think about all this - just give me something random! (go to **Section 375**)

—— Section 229 ——

Thirty minutes later as you walk up to your front door, you're feeling wonderful. Of course you weren't going to die - it's just the daft way you painted your face. How could you have been so stupid?

Again.

You enter your home vowing never, ever, ever, ever to make that same mistake again. Deep down, though, you know that you will do it again sometime.

Soon you are in the shower, freshening up and removing all traces of blue from your face. (go to **Section 240**)

—— Section 230 ——

Getting Dressed

Hi folks! You're here because you didn't want to read all about what you did last night/this morning and thought you'd jump straight to when you get out of the shower and get dressed ready to go out and vote.

So just one question, what was your general attitude up to now?

You already support Scottish Independence - Yes Scotland! (go to **Section 240**)

or You already support the continued union and NO vote - Better Together! (go to **Section 258**)

or You're still undecided, but take it seriously so studied all the literature and arguments (go to **Section 120**)

or Referendum? Today you say? I'm not that bothered I partied all night. (go to **Section 295**)

—— Section 231 ——

No wonder you feel bad...

It's all that [*deadly slow-acting poison that can't be mentioned as some already-suicidal arse will kill themselves with it and then the parents will blame this book*[13]] that you took last night. You can almost feel the poison pumping through your veins as your body starts to slowly go numb.

Maybe it was an overreaction, but what have you ever achieved in your life? Nothing worth mentioning - that's what. So why should you think it could get any better when the future of your homeland is in the balance? Uncertain times like this are not good for losers who have never, ever, ever achieved anything of note.

As consciousness slips away, your dying thought is the realisation that, in a world of infinite possibility you somehow found what could be the shortest ever ending to any non-linear *create-your-own-story-by-making-choices-about-what-to-do* book. Now *that's* an achievement.

That final thought lets you die with a smile on your face.

The End

This ending is covered by the 100% money back guarantee should it actually happen in your reality. To reclaim the cost of your book please personally present the publishers with proof of purchase and irrefutable proof of your suicide using the exact drug that the author was thinking of but kept being redacted and assurance that this book can be linked to your death for unethical marketing purposes whilst not being responsible for your demise in any legal way. This offer is rendered void by your return to life in any way shape or form, including but not limited to physical, spiritual or metaphorical.

—— Section 232 ——

Oh no! It's a total disaster!

You're partway through cooking your 8th pack of bacon when you somehow manage to set the kitchen on fire. You bash at the flames trying to put the fire out but all you manage to do is spread the fire about.

Fighting a fire whilst under the influence of bacon-narcosis isn't a smart idea and common sense says you should get out of the house and call the fire brigade, but the delicious salty pigmeat has inebriated you beyond common sense.

You try to hit the flames with a dish towel, but maybe you should have wet it first, as all you do is set the towel on fire. And then you set your trousers on fire. You realise that things are out of your control as you spank at the fire in your crotch.

'Oh not again' you think.

What happens next is inevitable.

Fire. Hot fire. Really hot fire. Really really hot fire. Really really really hot fiery fiery fire. Fire that's so hot that if it was sex it couldn't be described in any greater detail than just 'really hot' or this book would be banned under obscenity law.

But it's not sex. It's a house fire. A house fire that burns you to death.

Your dying thought is pleasure that at least your dogs probably got out, as they've always been good in a crisis, and also the thought that the fire is probably cooking the many packs of bacon to perfection. At least you won't be hungry in the afterlife.

The End

This ending is covered by the 100% money back guarantee should it actually happen in your reality. It's the least that the author can do since he also loves bacon and with you dead there's more of it for him. Just make sure that you provide proof of purchase (for the book, not the bacon) and proof of your own death. Offer void on a whim.

—— Section 233 ——

September 18th 2016

It took you over 19 months to track down the author. Not because he had taken steps to remain off the grid, but just because you really couldn't be arsed spending all your time on the hunt. It was almost as if, after writing numerous ways for you and mankind to die out, the author didn't want to write his own personal impending doom any quicker than necessary.

Finally, two years after Yes-Day you break into the author's home and creep up upon him whilst he sits typing away in the kitchen at a small MacBook.

You cough to get his attention and he nearly jumps out of his chair.

"Who, who the fuck are you?"

"I'm the protagonist" you say.

"You'll have to be more specific."

"What do you mean 'more specific'. I'm your protagonist. From your book."

"Which one?"

"You've only written one - **You Decide! The Future of Scotland**." you say.

"Oh.. Of course. You're the one who's been hunting me, aren't you? I've written a few more books since you. Kept my protagonists happier. I learnt from my mistakes with you."

"I don't care. It's time for you to pay for your crude stereotyping" you tell him.

"What crude stereotyping?" asked the author in what must surely be mock-innocence.

"After I watched Gayer TV you made me watch a musical on Muzikal+ TV. A musical! Just like a stereotyped fairy, and you know which musical it was don't you?"

"Yes - it was the Wizard of Oz. I well remember writing that section, after all it was only 5 or 6 hours ago and not nearly 2 years like you think."

"The Wizard of Oz! The Wizard of fucking Oz! Just because I'm a friend of Dorothy."

"Oh are you?" said the author. "I never realised. I never really mentioned your friends other than Andy or Kelly, and they only appear in some paths through the book. I don't *think* I mentioned anyone called Dorothy…"

"No I mean I'm gay. As well you know."

"Oh so you are… I never really paid that much attention to your sexuality. I tried to treat you pretty much the same as all the straight, bi and asexual protagonists. Sure there were probably more really hot sex scenes with women, but that's purely to help with sales. There were gay, group, solo and bestial scenes as well - or haven't you read them yet? You should - they're all really really really hot."

"So why did you make me watch The Wizard of Oz then?"

"To be honest I didn't make you - it's what was on when you chose to change channels. If you'd been two hours later it was *Sweeney Todd* then *Repo! The Genetic Opera*. And just before Wizard it'd been *The Pirates of Penzance*. You should have turned over then if you were bothered: there's nothing gay about singing pirates."

"Are you saying it's all my fault?"

"I'm not saying anything… But it *was* you who decided which parts to read and how to interpret them. If you'd chosen only slightly differently you could have been the person to cure all illness and get rid of homophobia and other bigotry along the way."

"I've had enough of this - you're going to pay" you say raising a heavy paperweight above your head ready to bring it down with deadly force.

"You can't kill me. Kill me and your story ends here. You'll be killing yourself." said the author, defiant to the end.

"Maybe that's a price worth paying" you say before arcing the paperweight down into the top of the author's head. You then raise the weight and bring it down again. And again.

And the author's life slipped away before he'd even had chance to finish the sentence he was busy typi

The End

Should it actually happen in your reality, this ending is <u>NOT</u> covered by the 100% money back guarantee. Both I and you and you and I are dead, at least we're dead if we ever existed at all.

—— Section 234 ——

An extra-special day demands an extra-special outfit as far as you're concerned.

You know that wearing fancy dress or something outlandish might get you all sorts of unwanted attention from idiots, thugs and weirdos but you just can't pass up this great opportunity to do something a bit different. Heck - the referendum is a once-in-a-lifetime event, it deserves a once-in-a-lifetime outfit.

Bearing that in mind you take a good look at your wardrobe.

Hmmm… not much there that immediately grabs you by the metaphoricals. You really could do with something more special than your usual collection of work suits, t-shirts, Star Wars outfits, drag artiste dress (just for parties, really) and leather bondage gear.

You wonder if there's any time left to get to a fancy-dress shop. But that could take hours and hours, surely you don't have time. And it's no use looking online - sure there's a wide range of shops selling every sort of fancy-dress outfit you could possibly think of[14] but they'll never manage to get them to you in the next twenty or thirty minutes. The whole idea of dressing up is obviously a non-starter. If only you'd thought of it a few days ago, then you could have arranged something.

Then you have that face-palming moment that everybody gets from time to time, when you suddenly remember that you live next door to the largest fancy dress shop in the whole of Scotland.

Phew - that's a stroke of luck!

Pulling on some sweatpants and a tee and grabbing your phone and wallet, you head out the door and within 30 seconds you're walking into *Mr Ben's Fancy-dress Megastore* and already looking at the myriad outfits available.

Oh what to be?

Maybe a musician or singer? They seem to have a good supply of them, each available in several variations. You could be Michael Jackson (at a variety of skin tones), Elvis (at a variety of weights) or even Justin Bieber (at a variety of twattish criminality).

No - none of those feel quite right. If only there was an assistant to help you decide what would work best.

Just as you think this; as if by magic, the shopkeeper appeared.

Then, as you hear a door swing shut, you realise it wasn't magic at all; he'd just walked out of the staff-only back room where he'd been enjoying a cuppa.

You spend a few minutes explaining your need to find the perfect costume for the referendum and discussing possible options with the shopkeeper. You appreciate that business is hard for companies that specialise in helping people to look like tits, but even you're surprised by the hard sell he's giving you. It's almost as if he's not had anyone try a costume on in his changing room for years.

Eventually you come to a decision about what you'll wear today.

You decide to wear a giant haggis costume. (go to **Section 005**)

or You decide to wear a caveman costume. (go to **Section 334**)

or You decide to wear a Godzilla lizard costume. (go to **Section 131**)

or Nothing could be more relevant to the Scottish referendum than a comedy Boris Johnson outfit, could it? (go to **Section 178**)

or Why not try a medieval knight, complete with broadsword and shield. (go to **Section 263**)

or What about dressing as the Loch Ness monster? (go to **Section 244**)

or Maybe you should just dress up as the biggest, dorkiest IT nerd in the whole of Scotland. (go to **Section 370**)

or Is three years too soon to dress as a deceased star of TV and radio? Because they've got some costumes going really, really cheap. (go to **Section 199**)

or After all that you decide to go back home and put on your Darth Vader outfit. (go to **Section 298**)

or Maybe you'll save your money and wear what you usually put on for weekend parties. (go to **Section 057**)

—— Section 235 ——

September 18th 2035

After the historic win on *Yes-Day*, you and many of your countrymen weren't too concerned about the planet and instead concentrated on building the best Scotland that you could.

Everybody knew that there is little that governments can do to persuade people to be environmentally friendly outside of punitive measures, and the new government didn't want to impose any of them that might have people doubting that the Yes vote was a good thing.

Instead it was expected that people could go on living much as they always had done and enough people were already becoming environmentally aware enough to have an impact through the personal measures that each took.

However it turns out that in the great scheme of things hanging a dreamcatcher above your bed, burning incense and recycling glass-and-plastic-when-you-can-be-arsed-to-and-there-is-nothing-too-icky-to-dirty-your-hands wasn't *quite* enough.

Nor was doing all that *and* using second-hand toilet paper, buying some energy-saving low-power lightbulbs (but not too many as you like to be able to see things) and only using the car if the destination is over 2 minutes walk away.

No - it turns out that saving the planet is quite a big task that needed to be taken seriously at governmental and international levels.

And so it was that the next decades saw the ice caps melt and the sea level rise. Slowly, but surely the plains of Southern England were flooded and rendered uninhabitable. Despite this, it wasn't all good news for you as the displaced people crowded into Scotland.

Still, at least people's personal efforts had delayed the inevitable by anything up to 2 weeks.

The End

Should it actually happen in your reality, this ending is covered by the 100% money back guarantee. Okay since you were one of the ones that tried to save the planet (however futile the gesture) you can have a refund. I can't actually give you the money directly, but I have negotiated a discount on swimming lessons for you so that you're prepared when sea-level rises. You don't need to do anything, just go to your local baths and be aware that the price you pay is lower than it would have been if it had been higher.

—— Section 236 ——

You wait...

Dum-de-dum.

This is so boring. Why oh why do you have to wait so long to be seen by a doctor? Would it be any quicker to die and hope that you get reincarnated? At least you'd probably see a doctor in about 9 months time if you did that.

Dum-de-dum.

It's amazing how boring waiting rooms are. Almost as if they are designed to make waiting as bad as possible so as to deter people from bothering hospitals with their petty injuries, illnesses and other life-threatening conditions.

Dum-de-dum-de-dum.

DEAD CAT TIME

I'm too bored to even make up a cat name and some possible fates for the cat. Just pick one of the following three boring options.

Option One (go to **Section 317**)

or Option Two (go to **Section 090**)
or Option Three (go to **Section 055**)

—— **Section 237** ——

The Scottish people decide that they want a fresh start without the Windsors ruling them. If they're going to have a monarch then they'd rather have a good Scottish royal family than a mixture of Germans and Greeks.

But who to pick? The choice is put out to the popular vote over a 10-week TV show called *The Rex Factor* and presented by Ant and Dec, because no matter how hard you try, the new Scotland can't get rid of them.

So finally tonight, on the anniversary of Yes-Day and at the end of the series, the new King or Queen of Scotland, by popular telephone vote, is found to be...

The person who wanted it most (go to **Section 072**)
or A natural King (go to **Section 027**)
or A complete outsider (go to **Section 181**)
or A surprise to you (go to **Section 292**)
or A surprise to everyone (go to **Section 245**)

—— **Section 238** ——

Andy adopts the stance of a 19th century boxer and you're sure he's about to blether on about Queensbury rules.

You can't help but burst out laughing.

"Oh Andy mate, you're no fighter, are youse."

He stops, looks comically hurt and joins you laughing. "I don't normally need to be - I'm your mate aren't I?"

"Aye - we're mates. Sorry about that before."

"No worries. I'll get ya back sometime."

"Fancy going somewhere else?" you say.

"Well if you're up fer it, there's a political debate about the referendum on tonight. We could go there..."

You don't much fancy a debate, but you feel you ought to make up to Andy for being a dick.

"I s'pose so, but can we get some cans on the way?"

"Sure - long as you don't start nothing."

You give him your assurance you won't be any trouble and set off to the debate. Surely you won't be trouble, not twice in one night... (go to **Section 265**)

—— Section 239 ——

No wonder you feel bad...

It's all that [*deadly slow-acting poison that can't be mentioned as some already-suicidal arse will kill themselves with it and then the parents will blame this book*[15]] that you took last night. You can almost feel the poison pumping through your veins as your body starts to slowly go numb.

Maybe it was an overreaction, but what have you ever achieved in your life? Nothing worth mentioning - that's what. So why should you think it could get any better when the future of your homeland is in the balance? Uncertain times like this are not good for losers who have never, ever, ever achieved anything of note.

As consciousness starts slipping away, you think you hear a strange noise... *Ktheaaaarrrrrr...* That sounds like... oh it can't be! Just then a fleeting shadow catches your eye.

"Cheesy Felchlips!"

Is all you manage to weakly say as, appearing from literally nowhere, the goblin-banshee eviscerates you before ripping you a new arsehole.

As the combined effects of the poison, blood-loss and shock conspire to end your wretched life, your last thought is that maybe a quicker-acting poison would have saved you from this painful twin-arsed demise. Don't worry about it - it wouldn't have. The goblin-banshee always gets its way.

The End

Should it actually happen in your reality, this ending is <u>NOT</u> covered by the 100% money back guarantee. Partly because you deserved your fate, partly because we don't want to upset the goblin-banshee but mainly because we can't process any refund at the moment as we're too busy laughing at you, you deceased twin-arsed freak.

—— Section 240 ——

Stepping out of the shower you dry off and try to decide what to wear today. Maybe you should wear something special. Then again, maybe not.

Do you show your support for independent Scotland? (go to **Section 215**)

or Maybe you should just wear what you'd usually wear. (go to **Section 403**)

or Is today the day to make an impact wearing something weird? (go to **Section 234**)

—— Section 241 ——

The nurse looks at you and says "Yeah, yeah, another one. Take a ticket and go through to the waiting room. Don't be any trouble or I won't bother to get security, I'll kick you out myself. Right?"

You're too fragile to put up much resistance, so you agree weakly and take a ticket from the machine the nurse indicated on the wall.

Hmmm - number 13. You hope that's not unlucky. Oh well, at least it means there won't be many people ahead of you.

You go over to the entrance to the waiting room and walk in…

"Bloody Hell!"

The ticket machine must have recently ticked over from 99 to zero again, as there must be 30 or more people here and each one has the distinct blue face of *Cyanitic Fever*.

Luckily it doesn't look like you'll have to wait too long as the doctors seem to be processing people quite quickly. In just 10 minutes you've seen 6 or 7 people be called through to the examination and treatment rooms.

Before an hour has passed, you're called through and a nurse leads you to a room where a doctor is waiting, filling a syringe from a small bottle.

You're sat down and the nurse starts to wipe your upper arm with a sterile swab and disinfectant.

"What are you doing? Don't you need to examine me?"

"It's okay we've seen a lot of people with your symptoms this morning" the doctor reassures you before indicating the bottle of liquid he's just used to fill the syringe.

"A quick shot of this and you'll be able to return home. Then just make sure you have a good shower, drink plenty of fluids and take a couple of paracetamol if you need to."

"What is that?" you ask about the miracle cure you're about to be injected with.

"Oh this? It's a super new drug specially formulated for your disease."

You read it's name off the bottle's label "$P_{14}C_{3}BO$ - that sounds very science-y. It must be good."

The doctor says "you'll just feel bit of a prick" and injects you.

As he does you realise that the chemical compound looks familiar. You tell the doctor.

"You ever seen leet speak doc?"

"Errr, no, I don't think so. What is it?"

"It's a computer gaming nerd way of writing - you swap number for letters, like a 4 for an A or a 3 for an E."

"Oh - why are you telling me this?"

"Well I've just noticed that $P_{14}C_{3}BO$ looks like the leet speak version of 'placebo'."

The doctor seems almost slightly panicked for some reason.

"Oh does it? Complete coincidence, I'm sure. This is a proper medicine. Real, proper, working medicine. Not just weak saline solution."

"Oh it's okay doc, I know it's medicine. I trust you. You're a highly trained professional. You wouldn't waste your time injecting people with something like weak saline solution, would you?"

"No. Of course not. Off you go now. Remember fluids, paracetamol and have a shower. That's very important. A good shower, so the real medicine really works."

You say thank you and leave, already feeling a lot better as the $P_{14}C_3BO$ starts to work. On the way home you keep singing Placebo's *Nancy Boy* to yourself. You still can't work out why the name of the band seemed to panic the doctor.

As soon as you get back you make sure you jump in the shower and have a good scrub to make sure the medicine works properly. (go to **Section 240**)

—— Section 242 ——

Somehow you sense that you aren't supposed to be here. You're still not sure how the hell you got to this section. Was it a mistake on your part? Were you just picking pages at random? Or did the incompetent author fuck up and get the links wrong when he manually created them?

The last one sounds most likely - he's a prick. He deserves to be taken out, hunted down and punished.

You decide here and now that, no matter what it takes, *you* are going to look for the author. You're going to find him and make him pay for his substandard linkages. You're sure that many others must feel the same, so maybe once you're done with him you'll sell him to other men. You imagine you'd get a good price for him - ten times what it costs you. At least.

You just need to figure out how to get him. Maybe if you find him, you can lock onto him and trick him into capture. You just need to find the right bait to put on the hook at the end of your metaphorical fishing line, to draw him in so you can catch him in your net.

Hopefully he won't find out about your plans and make a run for it - it'd really piss you off if he made a break for the Arctic. You hate the cold, and if he makes you freeze you'd be tempted to just shoot to kill.

But don't think about that.

Instead just think about hunting him down, capturing him and maybe, just maybe, one day making an electronic dance or EBM song about the whole experience.

—— Section 243 ——

You pick up the teeny tiny pencil...

And you're not sure exactly why, given you'd been supporting independence up until now, but you make a cross in the 'NO' box.

Immediately you wonder if you have done the right thing... It doesn't really matter if you have or not. You've done it - and that is that.

You fold the ballot paper and, trying not to make eye contact with anybody, walk across the floor and pop the folded ballot in the box. You exchange knowing nods with the station attendants. You know and they know that you have fulfilled your democratic duty.

For such a momentous historic vote it all seems like an anticlimax now. You just hope that you chose correctly.

All you can do is go home and carry on as normal until the results are announced. (go to **Section 321**)

—— Section 244 ——

You look around the shop and the costume that leaps out at you is a big green Nessie. Not only does it appear to be just your size but it's also an absolute bargain as it shows some wear and tear. The Nessie is always popular as students like to hire it out and go up to Loch Ness for the weekend to see if they can make it onto YouTube courtesy of gullible English and American tourists.

You know this because you used to do that when you were a student.

You don't think you'll fool any tourists today, but it's still going to be fun dressing as Nessie to vote on Scottish independence.

Despite the lack of water, Nessie is off to the polling station. (go to **Section 141**)

—— Section 245 ——

September 18th 2015

The studio lights dim and Ant or maybe Dec, it's certainly one of them, announces "The winner of The Rex Factor, Scotland's search for a new monarch is..."

Then they wait for dramatic tension.

Then they wait a bit more.

Then you start to wish you'd taped it so you could fast forward this wait.

Then they still haven't announced the winner.

Then, together, they both read out a name that stuns you.

"**Aslan the lion.**"

Wow! That came from your blindside. You could have handled Alex Salmond, Billy Conolly or Sean Connery becoming king, at least they're real people. You could maybe even understand the manager of the Inverness branch of Burger King being made monarch, not least because his whoppers are tasty and he makes sure that his branch has the cleanest toilets in town. But somehow a fictional talking lion who just happens to be some sort of king in Narnia has won.

You now suspect that the author is taking the piss big time. Which is a shame as he isn't, this really really happened, and it turns out that, in the realities where Aslan becomes the new monarch, he makes a very wise and noble King of Scotland who sits on the throne for the next 56 years of peace and prosperity.

The End of the beginning

Should it actually happen in your reality, this ending is NOT covered by the 100% money back guarantee. You're not the king, I don't need to explain to you why it's not covered.

—— Section 246 ——

You wait…

Dum-de-dum. This is still boring. Why oh why do you have to wait so long to be seen by a doctor?

Dum-de-dum.

It's amazing how boring waiting rooms are. Almost as if they are designed to make waiting as bad as possible so as to deter people from bothering hospitals with their petty injuries, illnesses and other life-threatening conditions.

Dum-de-dum-de-dum.

DEAD CAT TIME

I'm too bored to even make up a cat name and some possible fates for the cat. Just pick one of the following three boring options.

Option One (go to **Section 307**)
or Option Two (go to **Section 289**)
or Option Three (go to **Section 331**)

—— Section 247 ——

September 18th 2016

It didn't take long for Alex Salmond to become President promising a strong Scotland that would aggressively protect it's exports.

The first country in line to feel the might of Scotland was Ireland. President Salmond insisted that they stop calling their drink 'whiskey' and instead call it something like 'Leprechaun Juice'.

It didn't matter to the new leader that Whisky was protected to whiskies of Scottish origin and non-Scotch whiskies could be called whiskey. In his book a strong Scotland had to make it clear that whisky could never be spelled with an 'E' and any so-called whisky from outside Scotland was effectively a fake drink trying to illegally capitalise on centuries of Scots know-how.

Ireland didn't respond at first. The Irish leadership thought it was just a bit of friendly banter between Gaelic buddies. Until President Salmond repeated the demands and gave Ireland a deadline to respond of 09:30 on the second anniversary of *Yes-Day* or Scotland would "kick ya fuckin' heids in".

09:30 on September 18th 2016 came and went.

In the absence of an acceptable response from Ireland, it was at 09:32 that The Whisk(e)y War officially broke out.

The world held it's breath, knowing only that President Salmond was good friends with Kim Jong-Un and Vladimir Putin, but not knowing what lessons they'd taught him nor how far he would go.

By 09:40 the worst became apparent. President Salmond issued the launch code authorisation for strategic nuclear first strikes on Dublin, Cork and Tipperary (the latter because he'd never liked the song and wanted to make it an even longer way away).

By 10:00 it was all over. Ireland surrendered and Scotland faced international condemnation - especially from American Bourbon and Rye whiskey manufacturers.

It took 20 years for the Irish spirits industry to recover, but in a way Scotland's pre-emptive strike had done it a long term favour. The radioactive materials in 'Leprechaun Juice' had a tendency to turn urine into bright glowing colours for 48 hrs after drinking any. That was a powerful marketing tool, especially when coupled with the ability of Guinness to turn many a shit to pure black.

Before long Ireland came to totally dominate the booming odd-coloured bodily waste drinks market and both Scotland and Ireland were happy and prospered.

Nobody ever spoke about the gangs of hideous radioactive mutants roaming the barrens of Tipperary - luckily it was such a long way from so many people it was easy to forget about them.

The End

Should it actually happen in your reality, this ending is <u>NOT</u> covered by the 100% money back guarantee. I'm keeping hold of the money to buy a fallout shelter just in case President Salmond discovers that I still have a bottle of bourbon that someone bought me back in 2010…

—— Section 248 ——

September 18th 2022

You're surprised that it's only 8 years since you decided to dedicate your life to paleontological genetics - trying to clone dinosaurs from their remains. The fact that we hadn't managed to clone much of any great size, never mind from millennia-old DNA, wasn't going to stand in your way.

So you began your search for a viable source of dinosaur genetic material and eventually found some in a 65-million year old mosquito trapped in amber. It's the type of thing you'd have only thought possible in books and films if it hadn't really happened to you.

You started work on extracting the DNA and, with the help of modern-day lizards and amphibians and gene-splicing techniques you finally created your first dinosaurs.

But what to do with them?

Maybe you could start farming them to help provide a solution to world hunger, but where would be the fun in that? No - the only thing that feels right to you is to make lots of different types of dinosaur and put them all together in a theme park for people to stare at. A sort of dinosaur zoo.

Obviously the best place to do this would be on some sort of remote island, but as they cost a fortune to buy you decided to do the next best thing and buy up 200 acres of Scottish highland.

It's been a long hard slog, but today you're ready to open to the public.

At 9am you fling open the front gates. The park is open!

But for how long? Stood in front of you is an officious looking man in a 3-piece suit. He forces an A4 envelope into your hand.

"I'm Maurice Shytehawk from Shytehawk, Moorcock and Balls. We're representing the author Michael Crichton and film director Steven Spielberg and this is an order forcing you to immediately close *Jurassic Park* as it infringes the intellectual property of our clients."

You're amazed. Amazed not that they took umbrage at your business venture, but amazed that they don't seem to be able to get anything right.

"Unlike you and your idiot clients, I know my history and how to read" you say and point up at the sign above the gates. The sign reading, correctly and non-IP-infringingly, '*Cretaceous Park*'.

Needless to say, Cretaceous Park is a runaway success.

Until the dinosaurs escape and kill lots of people.

The End (of boring theme parks)

Should it actually happen in your reality, this ending is <u>NOT</u> covered by the 100% money back guarantee. Unless I'm allowed a trio of pet velociraptors to help me deal with chuggers.

—— Section 249 ——

September 18th 2027

After *Yes-Day*, the Scottish government funnelled a sizeable amount of it's budget to pure science and technology research. This allowed many more researchers to do work which would put Scotland at the forefront of science.

You knew that devoting your life to science would eventually pay off big-time - but you never realised just how long a struggle it would be. Thirteen years it's taken but finally today's the day it all becomes worthwhile. Because today's the day that you finally become the first person to use the working time travel portal generator you've invented.

You actually thought it would take a little longer to invent a working machine. You weren't even certain that it was actually possible. You knew it was theoretically possible, especially if you just ignored any theories that precluded it. The good thing was that all the gubbins that Einstein and co wrote were just theories, and so unproven. So in your eyes it was just as valid to decide that they were wrong and time travel was possible. But still the going was hard.

But then, just 10 minutes ago, you had a breakthrough.

You awoke to find an odd looking machine on your desk along with a user manual and a note.

The note read as follows:

Hi,

I've done it! You've done it! We've done it! Maybe I/you/we need to rethink personal pronouns with respect to time travel and multiple-universe selves... ***Iouwe****'ve done it! Hmmm...* ***Iouwe****'ll have to work on that, it feels clumsy but it'll have to do for this letter to me, to you, to us... err... to* ***meyous****.*

Anyway, Iouwe've done it! Iouwe've finally created viable time travel.

It took meyous 42 years of research, but Iouwe got there. Of course Iouwe missed out on ***myour*** *life, which really pissed meyous off so that's why Iouwe've decided to come back to 2027 when Iouwe're only 13 years into research to drop off a spare machine and the instruction manual. Now you can have fun for the rest of your life and Iouwe've still got a working time machine. Genius hey? Pretty sure it's not a paradox or Iouwe couldn't have done it.*

Iouwe can forget most of what Iouwe've seen in scifi about time travel and the manual's mainly filler, the most important rule of time travel is: Always keep a spare pack of AA batteries on you and never ever put them into the portal-generator the wrong way round.

Have fun,

Meyous

PS - Just realised that Iouwe could have gone back to anytime and so could have given meyous this machine back in 2014 and then Iouwe wouldn't have had to waste anytime on research. Bugger.

What a numpty you've been. You could have saved yourself years of work. You'll never forgive yourself. Then you notice that you have thoughtfully left yourself a pack of 4 new AA batteries next to the portal generator. All is forgiven - you're back in your good books now.

You may be a scientist, but you're far too excited to bother with reading manuals. You feel like you're a 78 year old on an all expenses-paid trip to a brothel. The Time Travelling Madam has been and now you want to play with the new playthings she's left you. You're quite sure you'll figure out how to use it as you go along. After all it can't be too hard because according to the note, your future self invented this so it must be laid out in a way that makes sense and seems intuitive to you.

Now, picking up the portal generator and turning it on, you have the chance to see another time. The chance to change the past. To undo some great injustice or mistake. Or just to have a fun outing for shits 'n' giggles.

But when to travel to? That's the big question.

Travel to the past to try spotting Nessie (go to **Section 137**)

or Travel to Arthurian times chasing the fabled goblin-banshee (go to **Section 099**)

or It'd be great to travel to prehistory and see dinosaurs (go to **Section 262**)

or Travel to exactly 30 seconds before you bought this book. You can't think of any bigger mistake that needs undoing. (go to **Section 392**)

or Go to just 2 seconds before you bought this book. The mistake needs undoing but you could do something else with those extra 28 seconds you save by not going back to 30 seconds before you buy. (go to **Section 023**)

—— Section 250 ——

Surely that was some sort of pun-ishment!

The whole room tensed up after he said it. Maybe that was the straw that broke the back of the camel of peaceful discussion. The one that shattered the spine of the dromedary of civilised argument.

Things could get bloody any second now…

Someone had to act. And fast.

Whilst it would never normally make you laugh, especially not with the drunk's slurred delivery, you do occasionally like the odd bad pun (and let's face it there's no other sort) and you know that puns don't kill people, people who are forced to endure puns kill people. So, thinking quickly, you leapt into action and loudly let out an audible groan.

Within seconds other speakers joined in the groan, and the drunk grinned from ear to ear. In his mind he had got a physical response from his audience and was now a stand-up hero. But in your mind you knew that you were the real hero here. It was your heroic groan that had defused a particularly volatile situation that was rapidly heading towards a repeat of the 2009 Inverness Women's Institute Bring and Buy Massacre.

And we all know how that played out…

It also added a welcome touch of levity to the otherwise deadly-serious debate, acting as a much needed pressure release to stop the debate careering out of the chair's control.

Now, accepting that he's the star, the drunk and his friend sit down, each crack open a can of lager and listen to the rest of the debate.

You're happy enough that they won't be disruptive and quickly settle back into the debate. (go to **Section 365**)

—— Section 251 ——

For the next few hours loads of gobshites who obviously think they're smarter than the rest of you talk complete and utter bollocks. They never get to agree on anything. One side says that their approach is better for some reason or another and then the other side just says that's wrong and that their own side is better for exactly the same sort of convoluted reason. You never realised that debates could be so mind-numbingly dull.

It's worse than that time you got home from the club early and accidentally switched the TV from Babe Station to Question Time just as you were getting a little over-excited.

It's no wonder that politicians are all cocks if they do this for a living.

At least at the end of the night several of them are going to a nearby bar for drinks, including some pretty redhead girl and the guy who asked you to leave. As you fancy one and feel like you maybe should apologise to the other, you and Andy join them. The fact that it means more drinking has nothing to do with the decision.

At the bar you keep meaning to apologise to the bloke but, as far as you can remember this morning, you never quite got around to it. But you're not too worried as the drinks are flowing and you're past caring.

Eventually it hits that time when you feel like something to eat, so you and Andy decide to go for a curry. Since you've still not apologised to that bloke yet, and he's talking to the redhead, you invite them to join you for a trip to The Raj Tandoori Curry House.

You and Andy keep making lots of really funny jokes and you can see that the bloke (who you think might be called Will or Bill or was it Tim) and the redhead (Kylie or Carlie or something) seem to love your witty banter even though they both keep mentioning politics. You think they're only doing that for appearances or maybe they're a bit overawed as neither of them is as funny as you are.

You keep the drinks coming and before too long you all order some food. You go for your usual arse-burning Tindaloo - and you can't help but smile inside that Will (or Bill or Tom) orders a Bhuna. The big girl - no wonder he pretty much shat himself when he asked you to leave.

The conversation slows as you all tuck in to the food and the ever-flowing drink means that things got a bit hazy after that.

DEAD CAT TIME

You can just about remember looking in on Blue to see how he's doing.

Was he curled up sleeping? (go to **Section 341**)
or Busy licking his arse? (go to **Section 094**)
or Chasing his own tail? (go to **Section 196**)

—— Section 252 ——

You turn back to Nurse Dean and say "Can I ask how long the wait is, please?"

She looks up from the computer and says that it's probably anywhere between about 20 and 30 minutes.

You look concerned at that.

"I do have some control over the queue, so seeing as you asked so politely I'll see if I can fit you in any quicker."

You thank her and sit down to wait. (go to **Section 323**)

—— Section 253 ——

September 18th 2020

With tax breaks for technology and entertainment companies, the Scottish video game industry in Silicon Glenn becomes *the* world leader. One of the most popular forms of entertainment (aside from the internationally best-selling Krankies real-feel robosex dolls '*They're Fanny-dabidozi*') to emerge from the area is the development of Verses - the VRS Virtual Reality Simulations.

These provided computer-generated worlds, populated by Artificial Intelligences and other people, that look and feel entirely realistic to the people 'playing' (or more correctly 'experiencing') them. They had Verses for everything - romantic dramas, action thrillers, sci-fis, high fantasy, mundane soap operas and, of course, porn (which helped popularise the technology).

They even have a brand new historical edutainment Verse allowing the young Scots of today to relive the excitement of *Yes-Day* as if they were actually there and able to vote. You know this because your 13 year old nephew, with the VRSim player add-on for the Playstation 6, asks you try it out so you can tell him whether it really is realistic.

As you put on the VR headset, the world you can see and feel morphs into the start 'room' of the '*How Scotland Said Yes*' Verse as the equipment overrides your senses, interacting directly with your brain via direct electrical stimulation.

From the middle of the room, a bonny pair of computer generated customer service avatars walk towards you. The male avatar is in full highland dress and playing the bagpipes, the female is also in traditional dress with long blonde hair.

The piper keeps playing as the blonde greets you.

"Welcome to *How Scotland Said Yes*. We hope you enjoy your historic voting experience. Please be aware that some users may notice slight audio or visual aberrations, motion sickness or some mild agony as the system fine tunes your brain interface. These symptoms should pass within a couple of minutes. If you experience persistent agony, or any tell-tale signs of epilepsy, unusual bleeding or death, please consult a medically-trained professional."

"Would you like the full Verse or just a taster?"

Do you take a quick look at it? (go to **Section 272**)

Or Maybe you'd rather play it through properly? (go to **Section 185**)

—— Section 254 ——

You open the door and the first thing that you notice is that you can hear what sounds like a cold war numbers station playing from a nearby radio. There are bursts of some classical music interrupted every minute or so by a child's voice reading out a series of 27 numbers and colours. Every minute it is the same sequence that the child says.

Sat behind the desk waiting to hand out ballot papers is a gorilla in a traditional male Greek dress. You walk over to it and once you have confirmed your identity, the gorilla gives you your ballot paper, points to the individual polling booths and says "You can vote over there, then put the folded ballot paper in this box when you've finished" in perfect Swahili.

Of course that's not the weird bit.

It's not weird that there are 10 pairs of ballroom dancers dancing to the numbers station, each with a number on their back and a man-sized fly judging them. It's not weird that the obviously female gorilla is in male dress and is wearing different colour eye liner on each eye. It's not weird that neither shade matches her skin tone. It's not even weird that the dancers are dancing in 4/4 time but the classical music is clearly a waltz.

The weird bit is that you understood the gorilla perfectly well and you don't even speak Swahili.

As you walk across the room to the polling booth, it is with the weight of a country's destiny bearing down on your shoulders… (go to **Section 393**)

—— Section 255 ——

September 18th 2056

Finally after 42 years of research you've done it! You've invented a working time travel machine.

People said you couldn't do it, but you knew you could and eventually you've proved them wrong. Just like you did when they said you couldn't eat a whole bass guitar in one sitting, couldn't get rid of used engine oil in the drinking water reservoir or that you couldn't kill 10 hitch-hikers over the space of a year and get away with it. But you proved them wrong every single time. Of course they also said you couldn't call Piers Morgan talented and keep a straight face, but you never claimed you could do everything.

But here you are with the first two copies of working time travel portal generators. Why 2 copies, you ask? Because whilst overjoyed that you've finally invented it, it has taken up your entire life. 42 years. 42 years of nothing but scribbling on blackboards in the lab, making weird machines in the lab and driving around looking for hitch-hikers not in the lab.

You don't want to have to have done that for ever so you just need to pop back in time to leave the spare machine with yourself in the past so you don't need to continue developing it.

You pop back and leave the machine, a manual and a spare set of AA batteries. Jumping back to 2056 you Hop that the past you will use the time travel device wisely.

Now you've got that out of the way, it's time for some fun… Where to?

Go to 69 million years BC and see the dinosaurs (go to **Section 182**)

or You can't miss this opportunity to mess with people's heads - try around the early 1970s (go to **Section 066**)

or Exactly 30 seconds before you bought this book will be fine. You can't think of any bigger mistake that needs undoing. (go to **Section 392**)

or Just 2 seconds before you bought this book. The mistake needs undoing but you could do something else with those extra 28 seconds you save by not going back to 30 seconds before you buy. (go to **Section 023**)

—— Section 256 ——

Aaaaaaargh!

The stress is too much. How are you meant to decide the future of an entire nation? It's not fair - you're only human. What if you make a mistake? What if you end up wrecking Scotland's future. What if you do that and the press finds out it was all your fault? You'll be hounded in the street. People will throw things at you. You'll probably be regarded lower than Fred Talbot or Dave Lee Travis. OH GOD!

You can't take it...

You pick up the teeny tiny pencil and go to put a cross in a box to get it over with, but instead a sudden panic makes you accidentally scribble "SCOTLAND THE BRAVE FOREVER" in large letters across your ballot paper.

Hmmmm... I suppose that counts as a spoilt paper.

You fold the ballot paper and, without making eye contact with anybody, walk across the floor and pop the folded ballot in the box. The station attendants say something, but you ignore them and walk out quickly, embarrassed that they somehow know what you did.

For such a momentous historic vote it all seems like an anticlimax now.

All you can do is go home and carry on as normal until the results are announced. (go to **Section 321**)

—— Section 257 ——

You make yourself a breakfast that celebrates the union.

You use fine English bacon to represent England. The best Scottish bacon to represent Scotland. Superb Welsh bacon for Wales and a fine Northern Irish bacon to finish the set. All topped off with a good helping of Great British bacon to represent how bacony the Union can be when it all pulls together.

Okay you don't mind admitting it. You're not a great cook but you can do bacon, which is good because you bloody love bacon.

You wolf down the bacon feast in double-quick time. There's something about the political process that makes you hungry, both with anticipation and actual hunger, so you decide to make round two of your United Bacondom breakfast.

DEAD CAT TIME

You've not heard any noise from the box for a while, which is odd because Patch was miaowwwwwing constantly for hours before that. You wonder how he is...

He's just sleeping. You think… (go to **Section 054**)
or Can cats sleep without breathing? (go to **Section 232**)
or Oh poor Patch… (go to **Section 283**)
or Still… that's a nice new pair of cat-skin gloves for you! (go to **Section 346**)

—— Section 258 ——

Stepping out of the shower you dry off and try to decide what to wear today. Maybe you should wear something special. Then again, maybe not.

Do you decide to wear an outfit showing support for all the union? (go to **Section 148**)
or Maybe you should just wear what you'd usually wear. (go to **Section 403**)
or Is today the day to make an impact wearing something weird? (go to **Section 234**)

—— Section 259 ——

You get some funny looks on the way, but most people seem to accept that on such a momentous day some people might dress up and treat it like some sort of party. At least there's no trouble and eventually you get to the polling station, walk up to the doors and pause.

You always thought that polling stations are places full of wonder and promise for the future. The almost-mystical locations that can alter a nations fate. Each one a powerful nexus where all possible destinies of the country intersect, just waiting for the public will to select one single possibility and to transform it into reality. Places of truly amazing, almost miraculous, transformative power.

But really they are just local primary schools that have swapped the kids for a naff sign saying 'POLLING STATION'.

Finally you approach the doors and prepare yourself to step inside.

DEAD CAT TIME

Yes it's time to peek inside Schrödinger's box and see how well Jess is…

Hello Jess. Where's Pat? (go to **Section 013**)
or Hello Pat. Where's Jess gone? (go to **Section 348**)
or That's not a cat that's George Galloway! (go to **Section 177**)
or Jess is curled up asleep, blissfully unaware of their role in the future of

Scotland. (go to **Section 134**)

or Postcat Jess. Postcat Jess. Postcat Jess has left a mess! (go to **Section 366**)

or OMG! Jess is dead! Pat will be upset. (go to **Section 288**)

—— Section 260 ——

September 18th 2023

In the years following *Yes-Day* the Scottish government poured money into encouraging scientific and technological research and development.

This had benefits across the board, with big advances being made relatively quickly in transport, theoretical particle physics, food manufacturing, IT, geological analysis and nuclear fission. The public, as a whole, barely noticed any of these advances.

It also had advances in creating *SuperBuck* - an especially strong cider that was cheaper to make and "*Gets you pissed! Fast!*" as the award winning advertising campaign claimed. The public noticed this one alright.

As did you.

And it intrigued you. You had spent years trying to invent a time machine after reading an odd book several years ago that claimed to be researched using time travel and dimension hopping. Despite making some theoretical progress you found that it's not as easy as Hollywood scriptwriters make out, partly because DeLoreans are really rare these days.

Maybe the reports of SuperBuck helping jog people's creativity would help… The book's author had certainly claimed that it had helped them.

You started to experiment.

Before long you had discovered that just 2 pints could make you incredibly drunk. So drunk that, with the aid of a shoebox you were able to travel anywhere in time and space and even into other parallel surrealities.

Of course it wasn't just any shoebox. No! That would be mad! It was a shoebox that you'd gaffer-taped shut and upon which you'd used a biro to hastily scribble '*Time Travelling Dimension Hopper*',

With the aid of the box, you started journeying back and forth, here and there, nowhere and everywhere, past and future - all the time writing full notes about the realities and times that you visited. One day this would make an excellent book you thought.

Then that 'one day' came, and you realised that, when sober, your extensive notes about your travels seemed to be an illegible scrawl half covered in kebab-sauce and vomit. You didn't recall writing them all in Enchluzian technoscript…

My god! It's not technoscript. Obviously the Lords of Time, offended by your lax regard of temporal paradoxes, had attempted to sabotage your attempt to write a book showing possible futures so that anyone could read them. You were buggered if you were going to let them scupper your plans so easily. Your only hope was to drink another pint of SuperBuck and try to write your book in one go.

Two days later you had finished your work. Now all that was left to do was to travel back to 2014 and publish ***You Decide! The Future of Scotland*** so that people could explore the possible futures after the Scottish Referendum.

With this last task completed, you raise another bottle of SuperBuck and wonder if you managed to remember it correctly - after all it has been about 9 years since you first read the odd book.

The End

Should it actually happen in your reality, this ending is covered by the 100% money back guarantee. I don't even need any proof of purchase as you are I and I am you and we trust us implicitly. To get your refund just go to your wallet and give yourself the money. I'll do the same just in case we got ourselves mixed up.

—— Section 261 ——

This is all you need, some inebriated numpty causing trouble. You square up to him, trying to make yourself look big and threatening.

"Aye I'll make you if I have to. But it's better for you if you and your friend just walk out that door now."

You start to 'guide' the two interlopers towards the door but they obviously aren't going to go quietly.

Suddenly the one who called you a wee man, and still hasn't made clear what he meant by it, tries to pull away, turns and throws a punch at you.

DEAD CAT TIME

Let's collapse a probability wave and have a peep at how Purrcy is doing in the box!

Purrcy is alive and well, happily curled up in the corner (go to **Section 309**)

or You'd like some catnip, wouldn't you Purrcy? It's like pussy crack. (go to **Section 186**)

or No you can't have more catnip, not less you pay first (go to **Section 097**)

or Poor Purrcy, turning tricks for his catnip fix (go to **Section 394**) or OMG he's dead - with a catnip syringe stuck in his paw. (go to **Section 084**)

—— Section 262 ——

Setting the controls...

For 68 million years BC, you open the portal and make the jump, but something is wrong. Something is very wrong.

Feeling just like Peter Capaldi with an ever defective time machine you appear to have jumped to only about 6,000 BC. Odd.

You try to jump to 68 million years BC again. But you don't move. It's almost as if you can't go back any further for some odd reason. Maybe there's a temporal anomaly in the area. Speaking of the area, you have a look at where you've ended up.

You're in a gorgeous park or wild garden. There's beautiful flowers and animals everywhere.

You look around but think that you're probably alone so you have a stroll appreciating the fantastic range of flora and fauna on show. It's like nowhere you've ever been and you have a look at the sky to make sure you're not in some sort of tropical garden at a zoo or the Eden project.

Then you hear what sounds like an old man give a short exclamation of 'bugger!' You go towards the voice to see what's up and soon stumble across a very, very old wizened man in white robes trying to dig a hole with a spade. He seems to be having a right job as he's picked a spot where there's a mass of plant roots and he's certainly no spring chicken.

"Are you okay there?" you ask.

He jumps, "Oh for my... What are you doing here? Oh wait I know - you're a time traveller aren't you. Well no time to chat, work to do."

He's obviously a bit mad.

"What are you doing? And do you need any help?" you ask.

"I'm ok - I'm not an invalid you know. Just burying these bones - bit of a practical joke" he says, indicating what looks like some dinosaur bones and fossils. "I should really have placed them before putting the last 10 metres of top soil down but my memory..."

Yes he's totally mad.

"Actually you can help me. I'm on bit of a tight schedule, I've only got a few days to get all this finished. Say, what's your name?"

You tell him your name. "What?" he says, so you repeat your name.

"No no that's not a good name. I'll call you Adam. Now be a good, err, what shall I call you? Man that's it. Be a good man and pop off your clothes."

"I'm sorry get undressed? why?"

"To procreate of course. Oh sorry I forgot, Adam, meet Eve."

He waves behind you and you turn to see a gorgeous naked woman.

"Now get begatting an' don't piss me off or I'll make you begat off out of this paradise. So, whatever you do, don't go scrumpin' my fucking apples." Says the old man as he gets back to digging.

You look at Eve and she smiles. You take off your clothes as the old man wanted and Eve smiles more and winks at you.

"Oh not again" you think.

What happens next is inevitable.

The Beginning

Should it actually happen in your reality, this ending is <u>NOT</u> covered by the 100% money back guarantee. I don't pay out refunds to relatives, and that includes distant ancestors, sorry.

—— Section 263 ——

You enter the dressing room to try on the chivalrous knight costume. It's hard to get into, as it's made up of separate pieces of fake plate mail, each one nice and shiny and looking like proper metal rather than the flimsy, cheap plastic it really is. It's the attention to detail that really makes it work - things like the red feather duster attachment on top of the helmet, just like a real knight would have. You're not sure what the insignia is on your shield, but the azure background and the contrasting small gold crowns all looks very impressive.

You put on all the plastic armour and your helmet before picking up your trusty sword and shield before looking at yourself in the changing room mirror.

You think you look damn impressive. You almost can't believe that you aren't really Sir Lancesgirlsalot from the fabled days of yore. All you need now is a sexy damsel in distress who's particularly grateful when you save her.

You think you'd better just have a walk around in the costume to make sure it's comfy enough.

With this in mind, you leave the dressing room. (go to **Section 156**)

—— Section 264 ——

You open the door and the sound of bagpipes greets you.

You know some people knock the drone of the pipes, but they really are far more versatile than many people give them credit, as aptly demonstrated by the interesting song cover currently being played. It sounds vaguely familiar to you but you can't quite place it yet.

No wonder it took you a few moments to recognise it, it's not normally a pure instrumental, but just after you do it's confirmed as '*Bob the Builder*' when the officials manning the polling station all join in singing "**Yes we can!**"

You're sure that you must have heard of less-subtle attempts at subliminal programming, but if you have you certainly can't remember when. You try harder to think of an example, but all that comes to mind is the repetitive phrase "*buy all Judgement Dave's books buy all Judgement Dave's books buy all Judgement Dave's books*".

You stop a moment to listen to the pipes and appreciate the tartan decorations and numerous Scottish flags adorning every wall and flat surface other than the floor. As you stand there the attendants offer you a wee dram of special 'Independence whisky' and a selection of shortbread and haggis.

You're really beginning to get the idea that this polling station may be slightly biased towards the 'YES' vote.

You're greeted by the lady (in full traditional highland dress) behind the desk dealing with addresses including your home. Once you've confirmed your identity, she says "you know what you should do, laddy", gives you your ballot paper and points you in the direction of the small individual booths that you can go in to cast your vote in private.

As you walk across the room to the polling booth, it is with the weight of a country's destiny bearing down on your shoulders… (go to **Section 119**)

—— Section 265 ——

It's only a few minute's away so you've stopped off to buy some cans of lager and then got to the right venue in no time, especially as the strange time-warping effects of alcohol have already kicked in.

Entering the debating hall you wonder if maybe you've already had too much to drink. But then you realise that the 3 feet tall, cuddly thistles with faces, arms and legs are just decorations. You think you vaguely recognise them as copies of the mascot from the Commonwealth Games in Glasgow earlier this summer.

You listen to a few minutes of the debate and god, is it boring. So boring that you can't resist the urge when the chair asks for another speaker, you stick up your hand.

"Whaddya doing?" asks Andy.

"Jus' you wait, bit of fun. Tha'sall."

You don't get picked by the chair the first time you put your hand up. Or the second time. But the third time you're picked to speak.

"Am sorry but I'm Scottish thru and thru and I'll never agree to the Yes vote. I'd rather vote better together or spoil me paper with a great big hairy cock an balls."

"Would you like to explain why?" asks the chair.

"Aye I would an all. I'd never agree to it because I likes me pizza I do. And I like it thin crust. So I's never gonna like being forced to accept in-deep-pan-dance."

You laugh like it's the funniest pun in the world. You can tell that Andy thinks it's ball-achingly funny too. But for some reason no-one else seems to be laughing. They're not even smiling. What a bunch of serious tossers.

Suddenly one of the humourless little wankers comes over to you and says "I think it's best for everybody if you leave now."

You look him straight in the eye and say "an whaddifa don't? You gon' make me wee man?" almost spitting the words out at him.

He pauses a second, you're sure he's weighing up whether it's worth taking a beating or just letting you be.

Do you laugh it off? (go to **Section 281**)
or Stand your ground? (go to **Section 193**)

—— Section 266 ——

You arrive home without any further adventures and decide that after everything that's happened to you, you could do with a shower and a change of clothes before going out to vote.

Hopefully a good shower will let you get rid of all remaining traces of blue colouring on your face. You almost feel sick at how stupid you've been.

You jump in the shower and scrub away for ages, this should return your face to normal. It's odd though that you really do feel a bit ill. You wouldn't have thought that realising the extremes of your own stupidity would be so draining or make you want to vomit, but suddenly it does.

Stepping out of the shower to vomit you check your face in the mirror.

It's worse than before. It's turned a darker blue and what looks like blue blood seems to be coming out of your eyes…

Within hours you have become the first fatality of a new hemorrhagic disease that will wipe out mankind in the coming months.

That's bad, but what's even worse is that the medical experts don't even name it after you but call it St Andrew's Cross disease after the way it started in Scotland with people who had painted their faces. And what's worse is that the world's media don't name it after you, or use the doctors name. Instead they finally decide to call it Eblula.

In a way it's good that you died first. You'd have hated to know that what was killing you was a disease with a wordplay-derived popular name. That would be the ultimate punishment.

The End

This ending is covered by the 100% money back guarantee should it actually happen in your reality. To claim please present proof of purchase as well as proof of your own personal death before eblula kills the book's author, its publishers and distributors.

—— Section 267 ——

You come to, as you're slapped about and dragged out of the van.

You think that you're in the middle of the woods and it's late at night though you have no way of being sure about either of these things. All that you know is that it is very dark and you're in woods. For all you know you could easily be near the edge of the woods or slightly right of the centre of the woods or anywhere else in the woods that isn't necessarily the exact middle.

"Get up" commands a gruff, manly voice from behind you. You struggle to your feet and make to look around at the voices owner, but feel a heavy weight hit you across the back of the head. "Keep your eyes ahead or I'll shoot you, and move it" says your captor, poking what you presume must be a gun into your back.

Shoot you? Wow! The day's suddenly turned very exciting. Maybe the heavy weight that hit you was you being pistol-whipped. That's just like what happens in action films and crime dramas, and you like those sort of films.

You get walked over to where a spade lies next to a shallow hole in the ground and forced to kneel.

Oh it is *just* like the films you like, but in those films it's normally a very bad thing to be kidnapped and forced at gunpoint to kneel by a shallow grave in the woods. Oh well - you suppose it's better than dying a slow painful death from *hemorrhagic facial cyanitis* and this way there might be a film made about your murder. You wonder who will play you. Hopefully Mel Gibson so that you're just like Braveheart…

In the far distance you hear a town hall clock strike the hour.

"Doctor McNulty's got a message for you toe-rag. Don't ever question a doctor or waste their fuckin' time. Course…*you* won't."

The gunshot goes off almost simultaneously with the 10th chime of the clock and as the bullet tears apart your corpus callosum, ending your life, you're amazed that you aren't angry at being killed. Not if there's a chance Mel Gibson will play you. But you are bloody livid at realising it's 10pm and the polling stations have now closed without you having a say in the future of Scotland...

The End

Should it actually happen in your reality, this ending is <u>NOT</u> covered by the 100% money back guarantee. The publishers are terrified of Big Jim McNally and we owe him money. He said he'd let us off a couple of grand if we include him in the book and describe him as 'an imposing man with rugged good looks' and a 'gruff, manly voice' but asked us not to let "any shitbags wot I 'ave to kill" get a refund. We're not going to upset Mr McNally as he can be very persuasively violent at times.

—— Section 268 ——

September 18th 2022

You stand on top of a small hillock in the glorious sun and cast your eyes over this part of the farm. You're so glad that you decided to become a scientist dedicated to finding some way to solve mankind's hunger.

Eight years of work in archeological genetics and finally on this day you are ready to show the world your creation.

You gaze at the herd of docile Styracosaurs before you. Each one a miracle of genetic engineering to bring back a long extinct creature. A long extinct creature that is quite easy to farm and can each provide meat for many hundreds of people.

And all this is because of you. Because you realised that farming dinosaurs was a possible solution to man's increasing desire for meat.

It had been a long, difficult journey though. Finding some viable DNA was incredibly hard, certainly not quite as easy as Richard Attenborough made out on film, but that was nowhere near as difficult as keeping their development under wraps until today when you are ready to announce them to the world.

There were so many difficulties and up until recently you weren't even sure if the end product would be very tasty or even if it would be edible. Luckily it turns out that it is edible and tasty - the processed meat tasting a lot like pig, which helped with finding a name for the new wonder meat.

You turn away from the farm. It's time to get moving if you're to make the announcement. It's time for the press meeting. Time to show the world the answer to it's rapacious hunger.

Time to reveal Jurassic Pork.

The End

Should it actually happen in your reality, this ending is NOT covered by the 100% money back guarantee. You really think someone who writes bad puns would give you a refund?

—— Section 269 ——

On Channel 5 there's a trashy documentary about the 10 most successful bloodthirsty expansionist empires in history.

It's the usual sort of disposable rubbish that contains little real value, but watching the show you do realise that the most successful empires in history had several things in common. They started small, had strong leaders and expanded quickly through violent conquest, not giving the rest of the world a chance to counter them until it was too late.

It almost makes you think that one day Scotland could forge it's own empire, much like Genghis Khan, Alexander the Great, Hitler, the Romans or the British Empire.

Maybe that's crazy talk… maybe not.

You eventually decide to turn off the TV and start to think about your future and the future of Scotland, and where the priorities lie for both of you.

Try to forge a new Scottish Empire and use Trident if you must (go to **Section 038**)

or Get rid of Trident as soon as you can (go to **Section 048**)

or It may take a lot longer, but make an empire that people want to join through peace, fairness and opportunity for all (go to **Section 386**)

or Empire schmempire! Thinking over the TV you've seen, you believe that Scotland should just set a good example as a smallish independent state. With no nukes but plenty of McBabes (go to **Section 159**)

or I don't want to think about all this - just give me something random! (go to **Section 375**)

—— Section 270 ——

September 18th 2035

It took years to save the pandas, but it was thought a worthwhile effort to aid in protecting the future of life on Earth through biodiversity.

Geneticists worked hard to manipulate the panda genome until they'd created a new panda that was interested in sex and had a taste for wider foods than just bamboo shoots. A panda that could survive.

It worked so well that before the end of the 2020's, pandas were plentiful. There were so many pandas that they started being used for scientific testing and some were mistreated.

Yes! Science had helped pandas to return from the brink of extinction. But in doing so, the pandas that thrived were somehow different. They were more intelligent than the old pandas.

Scientists looked at the pandas to try finding out why they were smarter and soon realised that they could extract a serum from the pandas that could be used to boost intelligence and memory in any mammal. It could even be used to make already intelligent pandas even smarter.

In a move that is no doubt obvious to some readers, the scientists decided to call this wonder serum ALZ-113…

The author could go into great detail about what happens next as the pandas become more and more intelligent before revolting against their historic (and continuing) mistreatment by humans and then forming their own civilisation as humanity crumbles from disease, but to be honest it's probably a lot easier for everyone if you just go and watch the new Planet of the Apes movies and imagine that every ape is a panda.

You can maybe even throw in some of the old films by imagining Charlton Heston saying "*Take your stinking paws off me, you damn dirty panda!*"

Just remember that this ending isn't a lack of imagination on the author's part because the whole book is devoid of imagination: it's all stuff that really happened/happens/will happen somewhere and somewhen in the multiverse.

It really shouldn't be listed as fiction at all.

The End

Should it actually happen in your reality, this ending is NOT covered by the 100% money back guarantee. I could give you a refund if there was a fixed currency conversion rate from pounds sterling to bamboo shoots, but there isn't.

—— Section 271 ——

On the way to the polling station you get a few passing cars and vans honking their horns. Some seem pleased and beam their smiling support to you, others not so pleased and (wrongly and unkindly) calling you a '*fuckin' sassenach*' or (possibly less wrongly but just as unkind) '*unionist wanker*'.

You walk up to the doors and pause.

You've always held the belief that polling stations are places full of wonder and promise for the future. That they're almost-mystical locations that can alter a nations fate. Each one a powerful nexus where all possible destinies of the country intersect, just waiting for the public will to select one single possibility and to transform it into reality. Places of truly amazing, almost miraculous, transformative power.

But really they are just local primary schools that have swapped the kids for a naff sign saying 'POLLING STATION'.

Finally you approach the doors and prepare yourself to step inside.

DEAD CAT TIME

Yes it's time to peek inside Schrödinger's box and see how well Jess is...

Hello Jess. Where's Pat? (go to **Section 003**)

or Hello Pat. Where's Jess gone? (go to **Section 382**)

or That's not a cat that's a shaved dog! (go to **Section 091**)

or Jess is curled up asleep, blissfully unaware of their role in the future of Scotland. (go to **Section 217**)

or Postcat Jess. Postcat Jess. Postcat Jess has left a mess! (go to **Section 254**)

or OMG! Jess is dead! Pat will be upset. (go to **Section 377**)

—— Section 272 ——

The start room melts away as the world you have been experiencing is replaced by the start of the computer-generated edutainment experience.

You wake up...

You feel groggy, from a troubled night of strange dreams, made even stranger as you can't actually remember eating cheese before bed.

Oddly as you awake the world looks a little strange, not so much bleary through eyes still half-asleep but almost slightly pixellated with a slight lag as you move your head. This only lasts a few seconds before going though, as if someone had fine-tuned the settings of your world experience so that it felt more like reality normally does.

Whilst you were sleeping, someone has set up a highland games meet in your head and legions of Morris dancers have crashed it, starting a bloody battle of handkerchiefs versus cabers.

"Oh my head. What was I thinking last night? I'm not 18 anymore. I need more sleep... another 24 hours should do. What time is it anyway? Hell... What day is it?"

The bedside clock tells you it's only quarter to seven - far too early to be awake and feeling like this, especially on a Thursday. Just a second... Thursday? Isn't something happening today? No. Not the bin collection - that's tomorrow isn't it?

Thursday, Thursday, Thursday. Nope - nothing's materialising from your still-fogged memory.

Thursday... Thursday... Thursday?

Shit! THURSDAY!

It's Thursday September 18th! It's today. The day of destiny. The day of the referendum.

Whilst still not feeling 100 per cent, or even 54 per cent, you feel the weight of history on you and so somehow manage to leave your bed, still struggling to remember just what it was that you did last night.

Your bedroom starts to pixellate and melt away and you remember that you're in an edutainment Verse.

You soon re-enter the sim's start room and shutdown the VRS.

Removing the headset you tell your nephew "Yeah - that's pretty realistic."

You know that this is the end of your current adventure, but surely with advancing technology like VRS and a new independent, optimistic Scotland the future is bright. Really bright.

The end of the beginning

Should it actually happen in your reality, this ending is NOT covered by the 100% money back guarantee. It's just not - you've got a bright future ahead of you. That's a happy ending.

—— Section 273 ——

You open the door and almost immediately know that you've entered the wrong room because in front of you rolling about naked in an absolutely massive mound of 20 and 50 pound notes are two men.

You know that this isn't the polling station but it takes you a few seconds to recognise the two ginger-haired men, mainly because you've never seen The Proclaimers naked before!

In fact you don't really twig who they are until you hear them boasting to each other in almost Machiavellian voices.

"HA ha haaaa - I would burn 500 pounds, and I would burn 500 more, just to be the person who spends a grand lighting a barbecue even though it's raining and it'll go out again immediately!"

"Ha ha ha haaaaaa!" they both laugh together.

"Aye an I'd fly to Los Angeles but I wouldna even fly first class, naw, I'd hire an entire airliner just to fly there just sos I could send a letter from America complaining about how much it costs to go to America."

"Ha ha ha haaaaaa!" they both laugh together and roll about some more.

Suddenly they spot you.

"Auch what the hell are you doin' here? You knowse we shouldna all be seen in the same place" says one of them.

"Aye if any fans get wind that we're quads they'll soon realise that we never walk a thousand miles at all. Naw they'll know that two of us hide at the start line and the other two appear at the finish, a thousand miles away" says the other one who looks more or less the same.

"An then the gravy boat'll be over - we'll be finished. A disgraced laughing stock."

You make to leave before they realise that you aren't the 3rd or 4th Proclaimer, but then they say "Oh don't go so fast. You may as well have a roll with us in all the fans money before youse go."

You strip off down to just the wig and glasses, praying that they don't realise you're just in fancy dress, and join them for a roll in the massive pile of cash.

After 5 minutes of laughing at how incredibly rich you all are (or are pretending to be) you decide to leave before they identify you as a fake ginger-haired musician.

You exit the room and decide to look for the polling station behind a different door. (go to **Section 083**)

—— Section 274 ——

"I don't want to die" you say, "I demand a second second opinion."

"You mean a third opinion? Mine and Doctor Nassir's aren't good enough. You really do like wasting our time, don't you. Doctor Cook was right about you."

You insist on a third opinion and eventually Dr McNulty acquiesces to your demands.

"Let me just make a quick phone call" says the good doctor before popping out of the room.

He returns after a few minutes and says "all sorted - just follow me" before leading you through the hospital.

Before long he's taken you to a loading bay at the rear of the building.

"Why are we here doctor?"

"Don't worry - I just had to call an outside specialist to deal with you. He'll be here in a minute."

Just then a white Ford transit van, driven by an imposing man with rugged good looks, pulls up to the loading bay beside you. It's odd that the specialist will be coming here, when it's obviously used for the delivery of medical supplies.

The van's driver gets out and opens the back doors and you can't help but notice that the van is empty - maybe it's making a pickup.

As he turns around, the driver says "This the one?" and you hear Dr McNulty reply "aye, Big Jim" at the same instant you feel him prick a hypodermic into your neck.

Within seconds everything goes dark and you slump to the floor unconscious... (go to **Section 267**)

—— Section 275 ——

Aaaaaaargh!

The stress is too much. How are you meant to decide the future of an entire nation? It's not fair - you're only human. What if you make a mistake? What if you end up wrecking Scotland's future. What if you do that and the press finds out it was all your fault? You'll be hounded in the street. People will throw things at you. You'll probably be regarded lower than Jimmy Savile or Chris Langham. OH GOD!

You can't take it...

You pick up the teeny tiny pencil and go to put a cross in a box to get it over with, but instead a sudden panic makes you accidentally scribble "BETTER TOGETHER FOREVER" in large letters across your ballot paper.

Hmmmm... I suppose that counts as a spoilt paper.

You fold the ballot paper and, without making eye contact with anybody, walk across the floor and pop the folded ballot in the box. The station attendants say something, but you ignore them and walk out quickly, embarrassed that they somehow know what you did.

For such a momentous historic vote it all seems like an anticlimax now.

All you can do is go home and carry on as normal until the results are announced. (go to **Section 321**)

—— Section 276 ——

You open the door and almost immediately know that you've entered the wrong room because in front of you rolling about naked in an absolutely massive mound of 20 and 50 pound notes are two ginger-haired men.

You know that this isn't the polling station but you've no idea what it is.

Suddenly the men stop rolling about and stare straight at you.

"Get him!" screams one and both men leap to their feet and start running at you.

You exit the room as quick as you can and decide to look for the polling station behind a different door. (go to **Section 138**)

— Section 277 —

SciTech TV is showing a look back at the scientific and technological breakthroughs of the past few decades. It's amazing to think just how much life has changed in that time.

Just 50 years ago most people had never left their country of birth or eaten instant mash and they walked everywhere as cars were too expensive and horses hadn't yet been invented.

Just 20 years ago practically nobody had heard of the internet, few people had mobile phones (partly because they were still the size of house-bricks and just as heavy) and only 1 in 40 people could afford an indoor toilet and a middle name.

Even just 10 years ago people still connected to the internet with dial-up modems, nobody in Scotland had ever got wasted on Jägerbombs and if you wanted to search the internet you had to Ask Jeeves (because only upper class butlers were trained to use google).

The most remarkable thing that the show points out is that the pace of scientific progress is constantly increasing and the next 20 years will see life change far more than the past 100 years.

You can't wait to see what the future holds with all the possibilities emerging in the fields of space travel, Artificial Intelligence, energy generation, quantum computing, wormhole generation, ice cream flavours and sexual deviancy. It truly is an exciting time to be alive.

Eventually the show ends and so you decide to switch channels.

You switch to watching Gaia TV (go to **Section 058**)
or You switch over to Gayer TV (go to **Section 169**)

— Section 278 —

You felt the atmosphere in the room change and so you stood up and walked over to the drunken interloper and his friend.

Trying your best to look imposing and serious, but not overly threatening, you say "I think it's best for everybody if you leave now."

He gives you a stern look and says "an whaddifa don't? You gon' make me wee man?"

You're not 100% certain if he's calling you a small man, questioning your post-urination cleanliness or asking if you're going to make him wet himself. Whichever it is, it's probably not good if you want a relatively peaceful night of debating where the only injuries are the egos of speakers losing their arguments.

Do you back down and let him be (go to **Section 076**)
or Try to remove him physically (go to **Section 261**)
or Try to reason with him. (go to **Section 211**)

—— Section 279 ——

The coin flies up...

And then comes back down again landing decisively on 'Heads'.

That's interesting. Heads is a YES vote, so you pick up the teeny tiny pencil and place a cross in the 'YES' box.

You fold the ballot paper and happily stroll out of the booth, walk across the floor and pop the folded ballot in the box. You exchange knowing nods with the station attendants. You know and they know that you have fulfilled your democratic duty.

It's surprisingly easy when you use a coin and don't worry too much about political arguments. You hardly know why people treat it as such a big deal.

You go home and carry on as normal until the results are announced. (go to **Section 321**)

—— Section 280 ——

September 18th 2016

The first 2 years since *Yes-Day* had been going fantastically well for Scotland. The power of independence-driven positivity lead Scots to great success in the arts, trade, sport and bagpipe concertos. It's many achievements made it the envy of the world.

This was why Alex Salmond had been invited down to England to appear on a chat show talking about how he'd done it.

Alex waited in the green room, still unsure exactly which show it was, but knowing that he could handle any interviewer. Eventually an assistant came to take him onto the set at last.

Walking on stage Alex was surprised to hear a mix of cheers and boos and to see David Cameron sat in one of two comfy chairs set a distance apart on stage. In front of him, holding a microphone, was the show's host.

Damn! He realised that he'd been tricked into appearing on the Jeremy McKyle Show. That explained the lie detector test and DNA swab that he'd been given earlier.

Jeremy explained that Alex was here because the rest of the UK (rUK) missed Scotland and wanted her back. RUK said that many of the big issues were caused by Scotland's problems with drink and drugs, though rUK did concede that that was probably just Scotland's way of trying to cope with the abusive relationship she felt trapped in…

Some progress was made but not much.

It was a real blow when the lie detector results came out and it turned out that rUK lied about whether he'd had diplomatic relations with another country while Scotland had been part of the UK. In the end he admitted being a right tart with the US and Germany… Much of the few minutes after that revelation had to be bleeped out for language and the bouncers had to step in between you both.

The show didn't reach any conclusions, but you will be following it up with help from McKyle's counsellors, and it looks likely that you'll at least be able to agree joint custody terms for Berwick-Upon-Tweed.

The End

Should it actually happen in your reality, this ending is NOT covered by the 100% money back guarantee. If you have a problem with that then you'll just have to go on Jeremy Kyle with me.

—— Section 281 ——

"Dinnae look so worried… I'm only joshin' wiv youse" you say.

"We'll sit down here we'll no be any trouble. Don't you worry. We're as keen to discuss what this vote means as you are."

The wee shite who challenged you looks relieved, although you can't be sure that he didn't cack his pants before you laughed it off.

So you do sit down, crack open a can of lager and listen to the debate. (go to **Section 251**)

—— Section 282 ——

"Leave it mate… I don't care about that right now. I'm bound to make my mind up sometime in the next couple of weeks."

He looks at you and says "You can't do that - the vote's tomorrow. Which way do you reckon you'll go?"

"Who cares? I'm havin' fun!"

"I can see that" said Andy, "but surely you are voting tomorrow, aren't ya? It's an important day whichever way you look at it."

Did you say "Oh stop going on an' get us another drink, will ya mate"? (go to **Section 049**)

or Was it "Yeah I suppose so - I really should take it more seriously." (go to **Section 085**)

—— Section 283 ——

Oh no! It's a total disaster!

You go to the fridge and realise that you only have one pack of bacon left. That's a mere 8 rashers. It's barely worth it…

Though '*barely worth it*' is still worth it, so you open the bacon and cook it up. Within minutes it's cooked, eaten and all that is left is a vague salty memory.

You decide it's time to freshen up in the shower and then get ready to vote! (go to **Section 258**)

—— Section 284 ——

You struggle to open the doors but they just won't move no matter how hard you push. God you must be deteriorating quicker than you thought, you may only have minutes before you're too weak to walk. Sure you've not lived a saintly life, but you're hardly the worst sinner. You certainly don't deserve to die here on the pavement, so close to help but what may as well be a thousand miles away if you can't get into the building.

Then you notice the small sign on the door that says 'closed'.

Looking around you see that the School of Tropical Diseases is only open Monday to Wednesday. You should be annoyed but instead you're reassured by the obvious realisation that the school would only be closed if deadly tropical diseases never strike between Thursday and Sunday. You're saved.

But maybe you should walk over to the A&E department, just to be sure. (go to **Section 389**)

or Screw that! I'm obviously saved. I'm going back home to get cleaned up. (go to **Section 062**)

—— Section 285 ——

September 18th 2015

Finally after a year of very tough negotiations and uncertainty for Scottish business, today sees the currency question solved as Scotland turns its back on rUK (the rest of the UK) and signs an agreement that you know will piss off the English government.

Westminster and the Bank of England had flat out refused to let you use the British Pound Sterling, and the Scottish people didn't much want the Euro, but without adopting the Euro Brussels didn't want to let them gain automatic EU-membership.

It looked dire - Scotland isn't really big enough to stand alone without any allies, so Alex Salmond and Holyrood looked further afield for a possible solution. And after a while one was found…

Today, one year after Yes-Day, Scotland signs the papers to become the 51st State of the United States of America, allowing it to officially use the US Dollar.

The deal was brokered by Donald Trump in return for a golf course and unlimited free boarding for rusty, his obedient toupee dog.

The people of Scotland are overjoyed at this result. It turns out that independence wasn't actually anywhere near as important as getting rid of the rule by posh English wankers who've never left the home counties. Joining the USA is doubly good as it'll really, really piss off the Tories in Westminster who bang on about the special relationship between the US and England.

Like much of the rest of Scotland, tonight you celebrate your bright new future by setting off some fireworks and drinking a good single malt to the sound of a lone piper playing The Star-Spangled Banner.

The End

Should it actually happen in your reality, this ending is <u>NOT</u> covered by the 100% money back guarantee. Because I don't have a US dollar cheque account. Sorry.

—— Section 286 ——

You wait…

Dum-de-dum. This is boring. You hate queues at the best of times but it's even worse when you're ill and waiting to be seen by a doctor.

Dum-de-dum.

It's amazing how boring waiting rooms are. Almost as if they are designed to make waiting as bad as possible so as to deter people from bothering hospitals with their petty injuries, illnesses and other life-threatening conditions.

Dum-de-dum-de-dum.

DEAD CAT TIME

I'm too bored to even make up a cat name and some possible fates for the cat. Just pick one of the following three boring options.

Option One (go to **Section 323**)
or Option Two (go to **Section 107**)
or Option Three (go to **Section 331**)

— Section 287 —

You open the door and almost immediately know that you're entered the wrong room because in front of you there's what appears to be a boardroom with a long table in the middle of it and annotated several maps of the world on clipboards and walls around the room.

All very odd when you're expecting to enter a polling station, but what astonishes you most are the 'people' sat around the table having a meeting, as each one appears to be a 7-feet tall lizard. Of course you say that that astonishes you most, but it really pales into insignificance when compared to the fact that they are all speaking excellent English. And that seems fairly minor when you consider that upon seeing you the chairlizard says "About time, Megan, we've been waiting for you."

For the next 3 hours you're in a constant panic dreading that you'll be spotted as an imposter in a Nessie costume.

You barely take in the discussion that's taking place deciding the fates of entire nations over the next decade or so.

You slowly realise that you're at a meeting of the secret cabal of shapeshifting lizards and other assorted cold-blooded creatures that rule the world. The lizard illuminati or lizuminati, if you will.

Eventually, when there's a break called for insects and basking, you seize your chance to escape and leave as inconspicuously as you can.

You exit the room and decide to look for the polling station behind a different door. (go to **Section 083**)

— Section 288 —

You open the door and you are suddenly hit by an almost physical underwhelming tsunami of ordinariness. The polling station looks like every other polling station that's ever existed in the past 50 or 60 years in the UK.

But then what did you really expect?

The most interesting thing ever to happen here is probably you walking in dressed as you are. Which is probably why, as you walk up to receive your ballot paper you get funny looks from the people behind the paste table they're using as a desk.

If truth be told, you do feel bit of a tit now. Which is good because it shows that the fancy-dress has done what it's supposed to do.

You exchange the briefest of pleasantries with the lady behind the desk dealing with addresses including your home. She looks you up and down in disbelief, shakes her head and says "Well it takes all sorts I suppose". Once you've confirmed your identity, she gives you your ballot paper and points you in the direction of the small individual booths that you can go in to cast your vote in private.

As you walk across the room to the polling booth, it is with the weight of a country's destiny bearing down on your shoulders… (go to **Section 119**)

—— Section 289 ——

You wait…

Dum-de-dum. This is boring. You hate queues at the best of times but it's even worse when you're ill and waiting to be seen by a doctor.

Dum-de-dum.

It's amazing how boring waiting rooms are. Almost as if they are designed to make waiting as bad as possible so as to deter people from bothering hospitals with their petty injuries, illnesses and other life-threatening conditions.

Dum-de-dum-de-dum.

DEAD CAT TIME

I'm too bored to even make up a cat name and some possible fates for the cat. Just pick one of the following three boring options.

Option One (go to **Section 384**)
or Option Two (go to **Section 011**)
or Option Three (go to **Section 163**)

—— Section 290 ——

Early2Bed TV promises all the information you need to make you *healthy, wealthy and wise* and regularly shows a strange mix of exercise and diet programmes, investment advice, household tips and philosophy. The programme that is currently on air is talking about exercise and its effect on wellbeing and longevity.

In the middle of the programme an onscreen table of figures and a series of info-graphics remind you that, for a rich, first world country, Scotland has a frankly appalling expected life span. Obesity and other avoidable bad habits continue to take a terrible toll on your nations populace. No matter how much money is poured into the health service it will never be enough unless peoples attitudes to health and exercise can be changed.

You're still mulling this over as you decide it's time to switch off the TV and go out for a bite to eat. You really fancy a nice deep-fried haggis supper so you decide to go to the local chippy. It's only 5 minutes away, but you don't feel much like walking today. Maybe watching all that exercise on TV has worn you out.

As you wait for a taxi to arrive you try to ignore your rumbling tum and instead start to think about your future and the future of Scotland, and where the priorities lie for both of you.

Should the government seize the opportunity to stop Scotland being seen as an unhealthy nation, capitalise on the recent Commonwealth Games and independence and prioritise health and sports (go to **Section 352**)

or The government should pour money into health and medical research to get Scotland healthy (go to **Section 396**)

or People will put on weight whatever the government does, so it's better to accept that and work on helping them to feel happy about themselves (go to **Section 021**)

or Don't worry about health and sport, Scotland will manage alright - it always does (go to **Section 132**)

or I don't want to think about all this - just give me something random! (go to **Section 375**)

—— Section 291 ——

You think for a second hoping for divine guidance, but none is coming. You can hear the other knights coming after you, baying for your blood. Oh which way…

"I'm in a right pickle" you think. "Just a second - right pickle, right. That'll do".

Well it's as good a way as any to decide which way to go, so you quickly race to the right.

Suddenly, searching your memory for anything that might help you, you remember reading the book '*Even More Dragon Gold!*' and that in that book turning right was the path to certain death. Still you can't go back, it sounds like the angry mob is hot on your heels and going forward there's another T-junction.

Do you race down the left passage? (go to **Section 143**)
or Dash into the right corridor? (go to **Section 387**)

—— Section 292 ——

September 18th 2015

The studio lights dim and Ant or maybe Dec, it's certainly one of them, announces "The winner of The Rex Factor, Scotland's search for a new monarch is…"

Then they wait for dramatic tension.

Then they wait a bit more.

Then you start to wish you'd taped it so you could fast forward this wait.

Then they still haven't announced the winner.

Then, together, they both read out a name that stuns you.

It's your name.

The End of the beginning

Should it actually happen in your reality, this ending is <u>NOT</u> covered by the 100% money back guarantee. You're not the king, I don't need to explain to you why it's not covered. Oh - you are the king. Err sorry your highness, but I can't do a refund at this very point in time as I left the refund monies in my other reality.

—— Section 293 ——

You open the door hoping that the hint was wrong and that this is a really normal polling station. But the hint did not lie.

The first thing that you notice is that you can hear what sounds like a cold war numbers station playing from a nearby radio. There are bursts of some classical music interrupted every minute or so by a child's voice reading out a series of 27 numbers and colours. Every minute it is the same sequence that the child says.

Sat behind the desk waiting to hand out ballot papers is a gorilla in a traditional male Greek dress. You walk over to it and once you have confirmed your identity, the gorilla gives you your ballot paper, points to the individual polling booths and says "You can vote over there, then put the folded ballot paper in this box when you've finished" in perfect Swahili.

Of course that's not the weird bit.

It's not weird that there are 10 pairs of ballroom dancers dancing to the numbers station, each with a number on their back and a man-sized fly judging them. It's not weird that the obviously female gorilla is in male dress and is wearing different colour eye liner on each eye. It's not weird that neither shade matches her skin tone. It's not even weird that the dancers are dancing in 4/4 time but the classical music is clearly a waltz.

The weird bit is that you understood the gorilla perfectly well and you don't even speak Swahili.

As you walk across the room to the polling booth, it is with the weight of a country's destiny bearing down on your shoulders… (go to **Section 119**)

—— Section 294 ——

You leave the hospital and start heading home.

DEAD CAT TIME

C'mon Macavity, let's see if you're still alive.

Oh dear - you really don't want to know… (go to **Section 229**)

or He's alive, but won't be if he tries to bite you again (go to **Section 266**)

or There's 2 cats - one alive and the other dead… (go to **Section 129**)

or Yuck - decomp stinks. (go to **Section 118**)

—— Section 295 ——

Stepping out of the shower you dry off and try to decide what to wear today. Maybe you should wear something special. Then again, maybe not.

Do you decide to wear an outfit showing support for all the union? (go to **Section 148**)

or Do you think it's better to show your support for independence? (go to **Section 215**)

or Maybe you should just wear what you'd usually wear. (go to **Section 403**)

or Is today the day to make an impact wearing something weird? (go to **Section 234**)

—— Section 296 ——

The noise behind you is getting closer so without much more than a second thought you press onwards. You soon stumble into a small clearing occupied by a group of seven or eight primitive tribal people dressed in animal skins and carrying spears. Each of their powerful-looking bodies is covered with masses of black hair and each has an overlarge forehead and brow.

Remembering the old posters showing the evolution of man, they look almost half-ape half-neanderthal and surprisingly similar to people you've seen on The Jeremy Kyle show.

Almost as one, they turn to face you and raise their spears.

Suddenly, without warning one throws his spear at you but luckily it whizzes by above your head! Then the other throw their spears each amazingly far too high to hit you.

That's when you hear the roar behind you and realise that they weren't trying to hit you but were aiming at whatever beast was crashing through the jungle.

Your turn to see an unmistakeable shape, one that you thought you'd never see in the flesh.

"Shit! A fuckin' Tyrannofuckinsaurus Rex!"

The long-extinct dinosaur is almost upon you and you vaguely register panicked grunts from the primitive hunting party as it surges forward, dipping down as it tries to grab you in it's mouthful of razor sharp teeth.

You have to think quick.

Sidestepping the giant maw you spot your chance to land a decisive strike. Jumping up you place all your weight and force behind a massive two-handed punch to the T-Rex's prehistoric groin.

Immediately the beast lets out a strangely high-pitched yelp and keels over on it's side. You feel almost bad for what you've done. Partly because you know how much being hit in the nads hurts but mainly because you've reduced a majestic apex predator to a laughing stock as it writhes about, trying in vain to cup it's bollocks with it's 'hands' and being foiled by it's inadequately tiny forelimbs.

You have to put it out of its misery.

Picking up one of the tribesman's spears from the ground you let out the traditional Scottish war-cry of "Get to fuck!" as you drive the weapon through the creature's eye socket, killing it instantly.

Oh well - that's one threat gone, but you can't rest on your laurels. The apemen behind you are making loud grunts and you still don't know if they are friendly or not.

You turn to face them, and are surprised that they all drop to their knees and start bowing down repeating what sounds like "Ugga manna gettathuck!

Gettathuck!"

You wonder what they are doing, then it hits you.

"Naw - I said: Get. To. Fuck. Get to fuck."

They try to repeat what you said, whilst still bowing to you, and after a minute or so you've managed to get them to say "getta fuck" with a vaguely Scottish accent.

This is going to be interesting…

Several hours later you're back at the tribal village enjoying their hospitality and feasting on T-Rex. It's not that nice raw, but if you can just show these people how to make fire, skewers and piri piri sauce then you could be onto a winner.

Sadly there's no time for that. You're eager to get back home to Scotland before the polling stations close. But that's slightly problematic as it becomes clear from the way they are treating you that they think you are some sort of god. Not only that but a mighty god called "Getta Fuck".

You're trying to explain that you need to go home and vote when a young female is lead up to you and presented to you. It only takes a few seconds to realise what is going on.

The tribe are desperate to avoid the wrath of Getta Fuck, and so are offering you this woman to do with as you please.

"Oh not again" you think before looking her over.

Saying she's a bit hairy (and not just down below but all over) is a mild understatement to say the least. Though she does have a great figure if you ignore the fuzz, and she's certainly no worse than that woman from Rotherham you shagged last New Years Eve when pissed off your face.

You suppose that, with a thorough shave and liberal use of your imagination, she could look remarkably like Raquel Welch in One Million Years BC.

"Oh well" you think, "I suppose there's no great rush in getting back to Scotland to vote in the referendum." You just need to find some flint to make a jurassic ladyshave.

If you must stay in prehistory, be worshipped as a god and teach primitive man the secrets of fire, speech and personal grooming, well, you'll just have to grit your teeth and find a way to cope.

It might help that, as a god, you'll have to have wild monkey sex with whichever women get offered to you. Just so as not to offend their primitive customs, obviously. It's the polite thing to do. And teaching good manners is an important part of being the *Father of Civilisation*. It's not like you'll enjoy it. No. Not really.

You bravely force a smile on your face as you regrettably accept your fate. Getta Fuck has gotta fuck. To endure constant offerings of hot sex.

Really hot sex. Really really hot sex.

The End

This ending is covered by the 100% money back guarantee should it actually happen in your reality. To reclaim the cost of your book please present the publishers with irrefutable evidence of your being the prehistoric father or mother of civilisation alongside your receipt for purchasing the book and an adult brontosaurus femur. Journeying back to the present from prehistory renders this offer void.

You've got to admit that that's a great deal, you jammy git. You get to have tons of really really really hot sex and your money back. It's a lot better deal than all the people who try to reclaim after dying. Some of them *really* suffered.

—— Section 297 ——

September 18th 2020

By the end of 2018 scientists and doctors had cures for most forms of work that needing doing and most forms of disease and illness that needed curing.

All work was done between robots, AIs and Chinese children (kept a decent distance away so no-one had to think about them). All diseases were cured by new super-antibiotics and anti-virals and all mental illnesses were cured by the application of a new generation of antidepressants, alcohol and sex.

Between sex robots and the complete eradication of sexually transmitted diseases, people who never needed to work managed to avoid work by screwing anything they could.

No man, woman, inanimate object or household pet was immune to either being shoved into an orifice or having things shoved into them - often both at the same time.

From the start, this worried some religious people (or killjoys as they were known) but they started to get even more preachy that it was against God's will when elephants, aardvarks and octopuses started to become common household pets…

Starting a year ago, there was a massive public backlash against these preachy God-botherers who wouldn't stop bothering the normal nihilistic hedonists and really could put a damper on any orgiastic party just by being in the same postal area.

The bible bashers responded by saying that God wouldn't stand for the way mankind was behaving, the bestiality and straight orgies were fine, but sodomy was banging out of order. If mankind didn't change his ways then the rapture and following apocalypse would surely be upon the earth.

Every sane rational person thought that this was pure madness. The old testament storm god Jehovah didn't exist. And since He didn't exist, He wasn't going to bring plagues or floods or famine or anything upon the earth, no matter how much adultery, ass-coveting and anal-fisting of aardvarks went on.

Some even questioned a hypothetical supreme being's sexuality if homosexuality bothered him so much.

But then…

The summer of 2020 saw floods across much of the Earth like it hadn't known in millennia…

Surely this was God's wrath.

Several UKIP councillors certainly thought it must be gay marriage causing the extreme weather.

Actually it turned out to be only slightly worse than the floods the world had seen every year for the past decade. Not so much God's wrath as Global Warming… So the indiscriminate fucking went on.

But then…

Today at the stroke of noon (Edinburgh Mean Time) all the righteous, straight, God-fearing people rose into the air and ascended to heaven… Before long the remaining population of the world was being visited by death, famine, war, pestilence and pay-day loans the five horsemen of the Fuckopalypse. Whole nations were turned to pillars of salt. The air burned and the seas boiled. Every sinner paid…

Out of all the weird possible futures, who'd have thought that the weirdest would be that an omnipotent god existed and despite being omniscient they were actually an ignorant homophobe? It's almost as if all those clergy men in dresses with a fondness for altar boys were right all this time…

The End

Should it actually happen in your reality, this ending is <u>NOT</u> covered by the 100% money back guarantee. Since God exists in your reality it's not unreasonable to presume He exists in mine too and that maybe He really is omniscient, omnipotent, omnipresent and Omni Consumer Products - and I don't fuck with deities like that. They have ED-209 robots, for Their sake!

—— **Section 298** ——

Nothing at the shop grabbed you so you go home and get into your custom-made Darth Vader outfit. You don't know why you didn't think of wearing this earlier - it's the perfect costume for any occasion. It's doubly perfect for the day of poll-based battle between the Holyrood independence rebels and the Westminster Empire.

Every detail of the costume is perfect. The black leather of the main body. The sturdy bootiness of the boots. The flowing black evility of the cape. The pretty-superfluous but pretty-none-the-less lights on the chest panel. The glowing rod of your light-sabre. The imperial coldness of your shiny helmet.

Looking in the mirror you feel an almost sexual thrill at how good you look. You think it looks almost perfect. Almost… But could you look better?

Wondering that you feel the overwhelming urge to spend a couple of minutes polishing your helmet.

When you've finished you decide that 'no - you couldn't look better', and so you leave for the polling station. (go to **Section 060**)

—— **Section 299** ——

You're not being forced to leave by some jumped up little shit so you suddenly stop and spin around swinging your fist towards the blokes head.

DEAD CAT TIME

What's Treeno up to? Let's collapse that wave function and find out - or alternatively open the lid of the box.

She's eaten all the food and moaning for more. (go to **Section 145**)

or She's eaten all the food and half the box and is moaning for more. (go to **Section 208**)

or She's eaten all the food, half the box and her own legs before bleeding to death. (go to **Section 142**)

—— **Section 300** ——

You get some very very funny looks on the way. You get a real mix of people from those that seem horrified (and try to avert their eyes whilst shielding children, the elderly and pets from you) to those that grin wildly and shout their approval. You think that most people seem to accept that on such a momentous day some people might dress up strangely and treat it like some sort of party.

At least there's no trouble and eventually you get to the polling station, walk up to the doors and pause.

You always thought that polling stations are places full of wonder and promise for the future. The almost-mystical locations that can alter a nations fate. Each one a powerful nexus where all possible destinies of the country intersect, just waiting for the public will to select one single possibility and to transform it into reality. Places of truly amazing, almost miraculous, transformative power.

But really they are just local primary schools that have swapped the kids for a naff sign saying 'POLLING STATION'.

Finally you approach the doors and prepare yourself to step inside.

DEAD CAT TIME

Yes it's time to peek inside Schrödinger's box and see how well Jess is…

Hello Jess. Where's Pat? (go to **Section 013**)

or Hello Pat. Where's Jess gone? (go to **Section 398**)

or That's not a cat that's George Galloway! (go to **Section 177**)

or Jess is curled up asleep, blissfully unaware of their role in the future of Scotland. (go to **Section 157**)

or Postcat Jess. Postcat Jess. Postcat Jess has left a mess! (go to **Section 366**)

or OMG! Jess is dead! Pat will be upset. (go to **Section 288**)

—— Section 301 ——

Stopping only long-enough to grab a camera and put on a panda costume (hired from *Mr Ben's Fancy-dress Megastore*), you're soon racing back through time to the Edinburgh Zoo early 2014.

Hidden behind some tall bamboo you watch as the male panda, wrong-dong, shows absolutely no real interest or ability at shagging Tian-Tian. You watch for an hour before giving up. Maybe Wrong-Dong is gay. You do get gay animals…

You decide to give him another chance and leap 23 hrs into the future, to witness another attempt at mating between the pair. Once again, Tian-Tian is left unimpregnated as the male shows more interest in nibbling bamboo shoots.

One more attempt you think, going forward another 23 hrs.

Another 5 jumps and you're starting to think nothing will ever happen. It doesn't matter if the zoo keepers show panda porn films, dress Tian-Tian in sexy underwear or give Wrong-Dong viagra, you've seen them try all sorts of things and nothing works.

You've finally given up and are just about to open a portal back to 2027 when, losing all interest in Wrong-Dong, Tian-Tian comes bounding over to you with a funny look in her eye and a wiggle in her powerful hips.

'Oh not again' you think.

What happens next is inevitable.

Sex. Hot sex. Really hot sex. Really really hot sexy animalistic sex. Really really really hot sexy sexy monochrome bear sex. Sex so hot you're not surprised Giant Pandas rarely have sex - it's just too hot for the male bears to cope with. Sex so hot that it can't be described in any greater detail than just 'really hot sex' or this book would be banned under obscenity law. Sex so hot you're surprised the synthetic panda suit you're wearing doesn't just burst into flames. Really, really, really hot sexy, sexy sex.

Eventually Tian-Tian has had her fun and leaves you alone, used and abused, a broken shell of the man in a panda suit you used to be. Without even exchanging phone numbers, you set a portal back to 2027 and do the inevitable time jump of shame.

Arriving back in the present, you tenderly pull off the panda suit and look at yourself in the mirror. Tian-Tian's bestial lovemaking has left you mauled, battered and bruised. No part of you isn't sore and marked. You even have two big black eyes where she - just a second. Look at your face... With the black eyes don't you look just like Indy-Pendy?

And the dates match...

You look into the mirror remembering how much hope Indy Pendy gave Scotland, how it helped the nation feel optimistic enough to vote 'Yes'. You think about that as you look yourself in the black eyes and, in your best Ray Winstone impersonation, say "Who's the daddy?"

You never got any photos, but you got something infinitely more valuable; the knowledge that you are the real Panda Poppa.

The End

Should it actually happen in your reality, this ending is <u>NOT</u> covered by the 100% money back guarantee. I may write many things that are juvenile or disgusting and you may think I have no standards, but even I don't give money to people who shag wild animals. Well not unless I can watch.

—— Section 302 ——

You continue on into the castle following the corridor and exploring side corridors almost at random. Your first impression of the castle was correct. It's not a ruin but a working castle that seems to be in good condition. Before long you're not sure you could find your way back to the changing room very easily.

After a while as you walk along you can hear several voices in the distance. One of them might be the shopkeeper, so you try to make your way towards them.

Eventually you come to a great hall, where the voices originate. There's a large group of knights, noblemen, fair ladies and assorted guards and attendants.

As you walk a guard in they all turn to you and bow, curtesy or snap to attention as a herald blows a fanfare.

"Errr… is that for me?"

You'll say this for the shopkeeper: he really goes the extra mile to make your costume experience feel authentic. You're just surprised it only cost a tenner for a days hire, but, you suppose, he probably gets student actors to play the parts for nothing but experience.

One of the knights addresses you "My king, I have grave news. The realm of Camelot suffers dire threat from the bewitched dragonkin, my lord. We must ride at once and face the threat."

That ruins the illusion somewhat. Why do you need to help out Camelot? You've never been there. It's a long way from Scotland and you're not really a massive fan of theme parks.

"Ahh… do I? I mean of course I doth! Well - let's get going then."

"But sire, first you must bear your sword if we are to vanquish our enemies."

You play along and raise your plastic sword high. "And here it is! Let's go get us some dragonkin."

The knight says "But sire, you need your mighty sword Excalibur, the scourge of wickedness and injustice" and indicates to the back of the room. The crowd parts and you can see the hilt of a sword emerging from the top of a large rock.

"Oh that sword. I wondered where I left it."

MEDIEVAL ROCK, PAPER, SCISSORS WAS A LOT HARDER BEFORE THE INVENTION OF SCISSORS
JD 14/9

You feel everyone staring at you. It's obvious that they expect you to pull the sword out of the stone, so, not wanting to disappoint so many drama students, you walk over to the rock.

Up close you appreciate the attention to detail that the shopkeeper pays. The sword and stone are probably plastic or maybe papier mache, but you can't tell that from a cursory inspection. The hilt looks like solid metal and the rock looks like, well, rock.

You place down your costume sword and shield and step up to the prop thinking that maybe you ought to improvise a speech to play along.

You grab the sword handle and start to pull, saying "For justice! For honour! For Camelot!"

Pull as you might the sword doesn't move at all. Maybe the shopkeeper doesn't pay proper attention to detail or he would have oiled this prop earlier.

You decide to try again and so take a better position and start to heave.

"For justice! For honour! For Camelot! For fucks sake it won't budge…"

You suddenly feel very hot as everyone stares at you and you hear the odd murmur of disbelief. The dawning realisation that you really are in medieval times and these people think you are King Arthur brings a wave of panic over you.

And foremost in your panic is the thought "What will they do when they realise I'm just me?"

Do you ask for some ice to cool off? (go to **Section 223**)
or Pull on the sword as hard as you can. (go to **Section 028**)
or Distract the onlookers and try to run away. (go to **Section 158**)

—— Section 303 ——

September 18th 2024

After Yes-Day Scotland put a lot of money into space technology, both in pressing forward towards the moon and other planets and in the form of scanning the skies for NEOs - Near Earth Objects that may be on a collision course for our world. A lot of this was paid for by the money from North Sea Oil, whilst the rest came from private backers and an undisclosed sum paid by the rest of the UK to Scotland in order that Trident missiles can still be housed in Scottish docks.

It's lucky that this configuration of factors was in place in Scotland, because it placed the country in a unique position to save the planet when disaster nearly struck.

17 days ago a Scottish NEO scanning station started tracking a large asteroid that appeared to be on a collision course. That was bad news, this asteroid was big enough to be a planet killer - it's collision would end all life on Earth. Even the cockroaches were shitting themselves.

Knowing that time was of the essence if the asteroid was to be deflected or destroyed before it was too close to matter, Holyrood sprang into action. The government commandeered several Trident nuclear warheads with the intention to transport them to the asteroid on a Scottish Space Programme rocket and then to detonate them there. The resulting explosion should deflect the asteroid from it's current path so that it narrowly misses a collision.

But if disaster was to be avoided they needed someone to perform the suicide mission of going with the warheads and detonating them. Luckily Alex Salmond had once seen the film Armageddon and knew the particular skills that were needed: The bravery of a North Sea Oil worker, the drilling expertise of a North Sea Oil worker and the all-out true American hero-ness of a North Sea Oil worker.

But where would the government find such a person, let alone a whole team of them? After two weeks of asking recruitment agencies they decided to ask on a North Sea Oil oil-rig. Luck was with them at last.

The team that agreed to the one way trip had also seen Armageddon, which saved time having to train them as they'd already seen the montage sequences. They agreed to save the planet on the sole condition that Bruce Willis was to be allowed nowhere near the film of their story.

This was agreed and the mission went lifted off 2 hours later, a mere 8 hours ago.

You don't need to know the details, but now you look at the sky and see the nuclear explosion that saves mankind.

The whole world is so grateful to Scotland that it agrees to increase trade in shortbread and kilts, and before long Scotland is a rich country due to these tokens of gratitude.

The only downside to the whole story, other than the deaths of a team of oil workers, is that Bruce Willis is already in talks to play the main role in the team's biopic.

The End

Should it actually happen in your reality, this ending is NOT covered by the 100% money back guarantee. Yeah it's brief but it's a sort of DEAD CAT additional ending, so don't stress it.

—— Section 304 ——

Thirty minutes later as you walk up to your front door, you're feeling wonderful. Of course you weren't going to die - it's just the daft way you painted your face. How could you have been so stupid?

Again.

No, you're not dying. You're a healthy man with decades ahead of you. You're in the peak of physical fitness. You're doing fine and so is the country you love. Today's going to work out well and you and Scotland are going to have a long and prosperous future together. It's fate, and you can't avoid fate. As you place your key in your front door you're feeling the most optimistic you've felt in a long time. Of course you are - you're fated to be.

You're also fated to be opening your front door just as a small meteorite is fated to smash into your home, exploding it apart as effectively as a purpose-built bomb. You are well and truly dead and virtually vaporised.

Hopefully your beloved Scotland will fare better from mistress fate. But there's no guarantees - never mind her fickle fingers, fate's a completely fickle bitch like that.

The End

This ending is covered by the 100% money back guarantee should it actually happen in your reality. To reclaim the cost of your book please personally present the publishers with irrefutable evidence of your death by high kinetic energy meteorite impact alongside the remains of the meteorite and proof of purchase. This offer is voided should you be brought back to life by any means, possible or otherwise, or should you be hit and killed by anything other than a naturally occurring meteorite exceptions to which include but are not limited to frozen lumps of excrement and/or urine ejected from the international space station and/or other manmade orbital mission, wayward extra-terrestrial alien anal probes (lubricated or otherwise), high-velocity Tulisas, Near-Earth-Minogues or any form of Simon Cowell. Any form of collision or other interaction with any judges of the X-factor, UK or otherwise, past or present will automatically void this offer.

—— Section 305 ——

You open the door and almost immediately know that you've entered the wrong room because you almost fall over a bloke in his 50s reading The Sun whilst sat on the toilet.

"Oi! Fuck off!" he shouts.

You quickly exit the room and decide to look for the polling station behind a different door. (go to **Section 138**)

—— Section 306 ——

September 18th 2017

The shows you watched not long after *Yes-Day* persuaded you that modern city living isn't the best way to treat the planet. A more natural lifestyle must be possible - is possible. You know that some of the Western isles are living in harmony with the planet, nurturing it and helping the plants and animals to thrive, and in return the planet looks after them: feeds them, clothes them and makes them well if they get ill.

Two months later you've moved most of your belongings into storage, sold some and arranged to move the rest to a village on a small island off the Western coast of Scotland.

Working in the fields and orchards, and drinking in the towns one tavern, you're soon accepted as an islander despite being the first new blood to move from the mainland in nearly 40 years. It probably helps that you join in with the old traditions - the bonfires and dances and songs to please the land and Gaia and keep the island safe and bountiful.

So now you find yourself on the morning of another harvest procession to give thanks for the years harvest to help ensure a good year of growing next year. Preparations for this years harvest procession have been especially vigorous as the summer's crops were disastrous. Other farming islands may put it down to the gulf stream and global warming, but the locals can't help but feel that maybe the old gods are upset at the island. So the procession and celebrations are to be taken especially serious today.

You get dressed for the parade and set off to the meeting point.

On the way you see, Old Ned, one of the islanders looking about as if searching for something.

"I've lost ma wee doggy - can you help me look fer him?"

Of course you can. You say so and ask the dogs name and what they look like.

"Oh it's Ronan," he looks at a piece of paper in his hand, "Ah mean Rowan and he's a err a err he's a normal dog. A normal dog-shaped dog."

Something about the man's description sets off an almost sixth sense tingling feeling that something isn't quite right. Then it hits you.

"Rowan? You mean like the missing girl in *The Wicker Man*?"

"Och I knew something would give me away. I thought it would be that I don't have a lead. Or a dog." And to be fair that should have probably tipped you off that something was up. In nearly 3 years you've never seen him with a dog. He's even told you on numerous occasions that he'd love a dog but he's got a terrible allergy to them.

"Now! Grab im!" shouts Old Ned and suddenly you're being restrained by 4 men who must have been hiding just out of sight.

You're subdued and forcibly taken away, not towards the meeting point of the procession but to the end, where the annual bonfire is held.

Before long you hear, and then see the procession approaching with Lord Paganisle at it's head, dressed as a woman as is usual. Not because of any symbolic meaning but just because he always feels more like himself in a dress.

Lord Paganisle looks you up and down and addresses you.

"There you are a man who comes to us with the authority of the king" he says. "A man who comes to us willingly. A man who comes to us a virgin."

"Sorry what was that?" you ask.

"A man who comes to us with the authority of the king. That's you. A policeman with the authority of the monarch of the mainland."

"I'm not a policeman."

"Maybe the king is Jesus - are you a Christian?" he asks.

"No."

"Elvis impersonator?"

"No. But I quite like Jailhouse Rock."

"That'll do. You come to us with a favourite song by the king. You come to us willingly. You-"

"Sorry, but willingly? Really? You had 4 goons drag me up here."

"My mistake. But we agree that you do come to us with a favourite song by the king. You come to us under duress and you come to us as a virgin."

"Actua-"

"Shut up - I don't care. We haven't got time to find another sacrifice to the old gods. Put him in the wicker man!"

Your captors turn you and lead you to an enormous hollow wicker effigy that must be 30feet high and stood on a large bonfire.

Your lead up a ladder into the torso of the man and the belly-door is firmly shut. You notice that the rest of the humanoid sacrifice is full of stuffed toys: sheep and pigs and ducks and teddy bears and even a toy giraffe.

Of course, these primitive islanders may be about to sacrifice you, a human, but they're not going to risk being prosecuted for cruelty to animals. That could really mess up their farming plans.

The islanders light the bonfire at the giant's feet and in seconds you can feel the rising heat on your skin.

"Oh God! Does this mean I'm Nicholas Cage?" you cry.

"Who?" replies Lord Paganisle. You forgot that since the island has no TVs, computers or cinema the islanders wouldn't be aware that a remake had already been made.

"Oh Good! I'm Edward Woodward" you cry. "Is this a remake? Is it in 3D?"

"Shut up! 3D, 2D who cares. It's no D as far as you're concerned."

Desperation hits you as the flames grow ever higher. As the wicker giant turns into an inferno, you plead "But Edward Woodward with no D is Ewar Woowar… I can't die an Ewar Woowar!"

But you do die. You die horribly. Burnt to death whilst young boys and girls toast marshmallows at your toes and you're choking on the poisonous fumes from all the stuffed toys burning around you.

On the plus side, the crops of 2018 really are superb.

The End

Should it actually happen in your reality, this ending is NOT covered by the 100% money back guarantee. No point really. I'd probably send you a cheque and it'd only go up in flames in the sacrificial fire.

—— Section 307 ——

You wait…

Dum-de-dum. This is boring. You hate queues at the best of times but it's even worse when you're ill and waiting to be seen by a doctor.

Dum-de-dum.

It's amazing how boring waiting rooms are. Almost as if they are designed to make waiting as bad as possible so as to deter people from bothering hospitals with their petty injuries, illnesses and other life-threatening conditions.

Dum-de-dum-de-dum.

DEAD CAT TIME

I'm too bored to even make up a cat name and some possible fates for the cat. Just pick one of the following three boring options.

Option One (go to **Section 037**)
or Option Two (go to **Section 011**)
or Option Three (go to **Section 163**)

—— Section 308 ——

The winner of Scotland's first Presidential election is announced as Alex Salmond - the man who has maybe done more than anyone else to earn independence for Scotland.

Sensing that he now has a public mandate to do whatever the hell he wants to do, President Salmond soon designs himself a new quasi-military uniform and awards himself honours, titles and pay for being Chief of Scottish Admiralty, Air Commander in Chief, Top Dog Soldierman and Head Curler for both Scotland's Mens and Womens Olympic teams. He also makes himself president for life and dissolves the democratically elected government.

Shortly after that, the Scottish press report that President Salmond may be moving to become slightly right wing. A report that was remarkable because all reporters involved in the story mysteriously disappeared the night after it was published. As did their families, their pets and their houses.

Scotland's new currency, the Salmond, is created with el Presidente's image (sporting a nice new pencil moustache) on both sides of each note and every coin.

Next he's making Conservative voters wear blue stars and banning them from running businesses or owning property. Before long they're being rounded up and shipped off to Haggis farms in the highlands.

There is outrage around the world, but, as so often happens when a crisis unfurls before us, too little is done too late.

One year into his rule, President Salmond declares that Newcastle and Tyneside have always historically been part of Scotland before annexing them. Journalists speculate that this may be the start of something much worse, but he continues to claim that he just wanted control of all branches of The Stand comedy club.

Things go downhill quickly from there until Europe is in the grip of continent-wide war that costs millions of lives.

And to think that the bloody war may have been avoided if only there'd been some sort of similar event in history that people could have learnt from and spotted the warning signs…

The End of the beginning

Should it actually happen in your reality, this ending is NOT covered by the 100% money back guarantee. I might have paid up if you'd taken steps to stop Herr Salmond, but you just stood by and watched, didn't you? Well - you stood or sat by and read the above, but it's more or less the same thing. You Scottish Nationalist sympathiser, you.

—— Section 309 ——

The punster's fist surprises you as it arcs towards your head, before surprising you even more as it falls short of it's target by at least half an inch.

You've never been much of a street fighter - the nearest you came to that was playing Tekken on the playstation, but you're not 100% certain that an ability to press buttons marked with square, triangle and cross all at the same time is any practical use in a real fight.

Acting on gut instinct, adrenalin triggering a fight or flight response like any wild animal in a life or death struggle, you dodge to the side and firmly bring your knee up into your assailant's crotch.

Or at least that's what you try to do. You actually miss your attacker's genitals as you slam your knee into a chair.

"Oww shit!" you exclaim, knowing that not only have you just really hurt yourself, but that you've passed the initiative back to the aggressive drunk. The question is can he take advantage of it?

And the answer is no.

The pissed up pugilistic punster bends over in half, as if your knee had found it's mark, and starts laughing.

"Aw mate - that is the fuckin' funniest thing I've ever seen. You're no fighter are you? Well tell you what we'll be good an jus' siddown over there. We'll be no more trouble."

They sit down to an uneasy silence. Nobody else in the room dares to question them and they don't want to be seen making a fuss over you.

You walk back to your chair, rubbing your painful knee, and before long the debate continues. (go to **Section 365**)

—— Section 310 ——

You suddenly find yourself back in the fancy dress shop, apparently safe from all dangers.

"Thanks for saving me - but no thanks. You can have this cursed costume back I'd rather wear my normal clothes than go through this voodoo doodoo."

The shopkeeper looks at you and says "Sorry, no can do. You've soiled the costume now, you've got to take it."

"Soiled it? I have not. I've only had it on for a few minutes, it's hardly dirty."

The shopkeeper sniffs the air and invites you to do the same. The unmistakable aroma of human faeces is wafting up from your southern regions.

"Oh. Well it's your fault - it's your weird magical costume that put me in mortal danger. If it wasn't for that I wouldn't have crapped meself!" you reason.

"That's as may be, but, for one, I've already taken the payment out of your wallet and, two, it's in the rules: look." He points to a sign behind the counter.

"No more than 5 children in the shop at once? What's that got to do with anything?" you ask.

He shakes his head and says "the other sign."

"No smoking?"

"The other other sign."

Oh - he must mean the one between the 5 child limit sign and the no smoking sign that clearly says in bold 5-inch high letters 'If you shit in it you buy it. No exceptions.'

You grudgingly accept that you have to buy the soiled costume and so leave the shop, in an odd waddle, heading off in the direction of the polling station. (go to **Section 189**)

—— Section 311 ——

You open the door and almost immediately know that you've entered the wrong room as someone says "Ah, Lord Vader, we've been awaiting your presence."

You look around and you seem to be in a boardroom with Kim Jong-Un, Rupert Murdoch, Alex Salmond and Piers Morgan.

Piers Morgan who spoke only moments earlier continues.

"As you know, we're expecting Alex here to become a very important world leader any day now. So we're busy trying to bring him up to speed on how to be a manipulative, lying, cheating, evil bastard. Basically how to use the darkside. And we thought that you are perfect to give him a masterclass."

At that moment the door opens and Vladimir Putin enters, bare-chested with a grizzly bear in a headlock.

"ASK HIM" you say with your evil asthma-voice "HE TAUGHT ME EVERYTHING I KNOW."

You exit the room and decide to look for the polling station behind a different door. (go to **Section 083**)

—— Section 312 ——

"I'm half-fuckin' naked..."

You scream as you realise your error.

What will people think of you leaving home with your cock on show? You'll be on a register for sure. People will point and whisper about you behind their hands. You'll spend every night and all weekend removing graffiti from your front door just so people don't think you've accepted the accusations of 'perv' and 'paedo scum'...

Just a second. There's no way you'd go out without trousers on... this is obviously a stress dream. Maybe you'll wake up soon... (go to **Section 088**)

—— Section 313 ——

Muzikal+ is showing The Wizard of Oz.

Of course it is.

This annoys you immensely. How dare the author clumsily apply stereotypes just because you chose to watch Gayer TV? It's disgusting that he thinks he can get away with that sort of thing in this day and age. You're just as individual as any other man, whether they're heterosexual or not is immaterial.

You can't just be lazily characterised as someone who likes camp musicals, flamboyant dress and anal sex. No - the author wouldn't do that to a straight man. He'd give them interests and thoughts that made them a rounded individual.

You should be a rounded individual as well. Just like other men you have interests and hobbies that make you uniquely you. You happen to like football, motor sports, boxing, curries and rock music. You do your own DIY and car maintenance, cook a mean chilli and can sew on sequins like a pro. And yes, you do like dance music but you have virtually no sense of rhythm and can't dance for toffee. No - you really don't know who the author thinks she is portraying you as a lazy stereotype. The bitch. If Judgement Dave turns up anywhere near you, you'll scratch her eyes out.

Your thoughts of the disservice the author has done to you are immediately cast out of your mind as Dorothy starts to sing 'Somewhere over the rainbow'. You can't be angry when Judy sings. She's just *that* fabulous.

You eventually turn off the TV after Dorothy is safely returned home and start to think about your future and the future of Scotland, and where the priorities lie for both of you.

Do you decide to hunt down the author and make them pay for the stereotyping (go to **Section 233**)

or Ignore the author and set off to find fame and fortune in the world of musicals (go to **Section 073**)

or You know that the arts and music can bring in good money for the country, hopefully the government will recognise this and support the performing arts (go to **Section 109**)

or Scotland will be stronger with a well informed, scientifically literate public, use the power of musical to educate people about science and the environment (go to **Section 335**)

or Thinking of the SciTech TV show you watched, you dedicate your life to advanced scientific research (go to **Section 255**)

or I don't want to think about all this - just give me something random! (go to **Section 375**)

— Section 314 —

This makes no sense...

You think as you read the following words.

Apple.
Cherry.
Mud.
Pumpkin.
Cow.
Custard.
Cheese and Onion.
Steak and Kidney.
Shepherds.
Hairy.

Just a second... that's sort of ten lots of pie. This must be section 314!

—— Section 315 ——

You make your excuses and try to head off home, but the rest of the debaters are having none of it and insist that you join them in the bar for at least one quickie.

Since they're so persistent you give in and agree.

You've always got time for a quickie. (go to **Section 154**)

—— Section 316 ——

September 18th 2034

Like most of the world, the newly independent Scotland spent most of it's budget firefighting the small day-to-day problems that blight life on Earth.

Like most countries it's government spent too much time scoring points in political fights that meant little to many people. Despite this, like most countries it's peoples' lives slowly improved over time.

Like most of the world every day was much like the last and as most people were pretty well off in the grand scheme of things, there wasn't much impetus for great change.

Like most of the world, day-to-day life on Earth meant that few people ever thought much about the vast universe we sail in.

Then this morning, exactly 20 years to the minute since the poll stations opened on *Yes-Day* a part-time volunteer near-space watcher noticed something that alarmed them. They double checked their readings and then made a call that they hoped they'd never have to make.

Word was passed from government to government, but no official word was said to the public. Hysteria was avoided but a few people noticed the strange spate of sudden suicides amongst government officials around the globe.

Internet rumours started around 20 years after the poll stations closed. But nobody believes internet loons, so it was still a shock to most people when the asteroid struck about 100 miles from Chicago. It was like the world's nuclear arsenal going off at once. Those that didn't die immediately died in the coming days and weeks as the planet entered a severe nuclear winter.

That this happened is not Scotland's fault. It wasn't caused by the referendum (unless the Butterfly Effect was in overdrive) and looking out for threats should be a joint effort, but maybe, just maybe, if the new Scotland had spent more on science and space research, or even just voted 'NO'...

The thing that annoys you most is that you die just as you are considering applying for the 100% money back guarantee refund from that dodgy book that predicted this end.

The End (of life on Earth)

Should it actually happen in your reality, this ending is <u>NOT</u> covered by the 100% money back guarantee. For reasons that should be obvious - you never got around to applying for the refund.

—— Section 317 ——

You wait...

Dum-de-dum. De-dum. Dum. Dum.

This is so incredibly boring. Why oh why do you have to wait so long to be seen by a doctor?

Dum-de-dum.

It's amazing how boring waiting rooms are. Almost as if they are designed to make waiting as bad as possible so as to deter people from bothering hospitals with their petty injuries, illnesses and other life-threatening conditions.

Dum-de-dum-de-dum.

DEAD CAT TIME

I'm too bored to even make up a cat name and some possible fates for the cat. Just pick one of the following three boring options.

Option One (go to **Section 246**)
or Option Two (go to **Section 090**)
or Option Three (go to **Section 236**)

—— Section 318 ——

September 18th 2018 (ish?)

The shows you watched not long after *Yes-Day* persuaded you that there must be a better, more natural way to live than the modern urban existence you've always been used to. A way where you lived in harmony with the planet, nurturing it and helping the plants and animals to thrive, and in return they look after you with a wellness of body and mind that you just can't find in the city.

Two months later you'd already sold all your worldly possessions and arranged to move to a commune on a small island off the Western coast of Scotland.

It's a great, if simple life, on the isle of, well to be honest you've no idea what the island is called on other people's maps, but at the commune you all call it '*Harmony*' and you think the name suits the place.

You think it's about two years after *Yes-Day*, but you can't be 100% certain. You know how long it is since you brought in the harvest and you know it's about 3 moons until Winter Solstice. But without watches and calendars you've no idea exactly what date it is. You've also no idea what happened to the rest of Scotland after the referendum.

You do know that life has been great on the island, away from the chemicals of modern so-called-civilisation, and you've had no problems that your therapist friends couldn't cure.

Most aches, pains and illnesses have been cured by a quick dose of homeopathic solution. The only time that didn't work was when you were mysteriously retaining water for some reason. Then no-one was sure how much you had to water down the water in the carrier water for the homeopathy to work. You ended up having to drink lots of 'cures' and yet still retained more and more fluid. Eventually acupuncture cured it, but only by turning you into a human watering can.

The homeopath still maintains that her solution would have worked but you still hadn't watered it down enough and were using almost neat water.

The End

Should it actually happen in your reality, this ending is covered by the 100% money back guarantee. But we all know that money is just meaningless tokens that 'the man' forces you to use so he can tax you. I'd only be causing you bad karma if I made you accept a refund. I couldn't bear to have that on my conscience, so I'll do us both a favour and keep the money.

—— Section 319 ——

Better safe than sorry...

It could be the same as last time, but why risk it? You only get one life and you'd hate to lose yours just because you were afraid of looking a little bit stupid. No - you'd rather be known as a martyr; the first person who died from *Blue Blood Syndrome* after selflessly travelling to the doctors so that they could study it, develop a cure and save the human race from total extinction.

It'd be nice not to die at all. But at least now you can bravely look death in the eye as a hero in the making. This is your chance to go from patient zero to patient hero.

With no time to lose, you abandon the search for your phone and leave home looking for a taxi. You've no idea how much time you have left on this mortal coil, so are glad when you quickly hail a cab for the 15 minute drive to hospital. It's bad enough to know that your short life is nearly over, but not knowing which part of the hospital you need is just adding to your stress.

Should you go straight to the School of Tropical Diseases? (go to **Section 160**)

or Do you 'waste time' being processed in A&E, like every other non-life-threatening emergency? (go to **Section 389**)

—— Section 320 ——

You enter the examination cubicle and are pleased to be greeted by a doctor of obvious foreign heritage. You're not racist but you know that foreign doctors really know their stuff. Only the best foreign doctors get to come and work in the UK and the ones who were born here but of foreign heritage are even better, as they've worked so hard to escape their immigrant roots. Yes - foreign doctors and foreign-looking doctors are definitely the best and are just what you want to see when you obviously have a deadly disease turning you into blue mush.

Doctor Nassir will have you diagnosed and on the way back to good health in no time. It's a sign of his pure professionalism that he doesn't waste time on small talk but cuts straight to the chase.

"So what exactly is the problem?"

"L-look at my face… I'm blue. I'm leaking. I'm dying."

The doctor looks closely at your face whilst pulling on a pair of latex gloves and picking up a cotton wool swab.

"Hold still this won't hurt."

He daubs at the outside of your cheek then looks at the blue residue.

"Hmmm.. How long have you been displaying these symptoms?"

You tell him since waking this morning.

"And have you been doing anything unusual recently? Maybe a trip to Africa, unprotected sex with prostitutes, eaten any seafood that tasted odd or even… just painted your face because you're a patriot and it's the Referendum today?"

It must be bad for him to obviously diagnose you so quickly. Maybe the Liberian ebola outbreak has put the health service on high alert looking out for similar diseases here. You can't remember where the blue dye was made - could it have been Africa?

"Yes doctor - the last one. What does it mean? Is it serious?"

The doctor looks deadly serious.

"I'm afraid there's not much we can do for you, I just hope I don't catch it."

"Why what is it? How long have I got?"

"Potentially years - you've got an acute case of *cerebral faeces syndrome.* Shit-for-brains to give it its common name. You've painted your face blue and need to go home and wash it off instead of dicking about here wasting my time. Now fuck off."

You've never seen anyone pull off latex gloves and throw them into a bin in such an annoyed manner as this 'so-called-doctor' Nassir.

Stupid foreign idiot - what does he know? You knew you should have had a good Scottish doctor. Someone who knows what's normal over here.

Do you go home since you're not going to get any help here? (go to **Section 294**)

or Will you insist on getting a second opinion? (go to **Section 009**)

—— Section 321 ——

Finally: the results are due...

It's a big occasion. Maybe the biggest in Scottish history. Maybe bigger than the day of the vote itself.

You feel that it's important to be at just the right venue for when you hear the announcement of whether or not Scotland should be independent. After all it's the sort of thing you'll be asked about by friends, your children, their children, possibly even complete strangers children, although you've no idea why your talking to the children of people you don't know.

Where were you when you heard the result?

Everyone will want to know and you'd better have a good story to tell.

You could just stay at home, but is that really the story you want to tell for years to come?

You could go to a big party, there's bound to be some. Or if there aren't then you could throw a big party. That would be a better story to tell.

Or why not go to the headquarters of the Better Together or the Yes Scotland Independence campaign? Or Holyrood? Maybe they'd impress some people, but it's possible that just as many would think you a right weird bastard for that. Although they may already think you weird for talking to so many children.

Maybe it's better to forget about where you should be. You can always lie anyway, and that way you get to chose the most impressive place to be dependent upon who wins. Yeah you could just wait til you read the news tomorrow and make up an impressive story after the fact.

But that doesn't feel right - what if you jinx the result by not doing something special?

Suddenly you realise what an idiot you're being. The votes are all long cast. Where you find out about the results doesn't affect anything and no-one is going to be thrilled by a tale of how you heard about the results.

It's good to eventually come to the same conclusion that the author of this **You Decide!** book came to. He'd already decided not to provide a range of venues from which to watch the result be announced. No he'd already decided that all you really need to decide now is which side won.

Was it won by 'NO' to an independent Scotland, you'll stay with the Union. (go to **Section 153**)

or Was it won by 'YES' Scotland should be independent and pish to the Union. (go to **Section 069**)

or Was it, even after numerous recounts, a draw. (go to **Section 356**)

—— Section 322 ——

The new government realises the importance of spending on science and technology. Some might argue that problems with the economy or education or housing or defence or anything else take priority, but the government was certain that solutions can be found to problems in all those areas if only enough effort is put into R&D.

And so government funding and tax breaks soon made Scotland a hotbed of groundbreaking research, the envy of the rest of the world.

Science advanced at an unprecedented rate and before long the inventions and concrete benefits were filtering down to the ordinary person in the street. Soon Scots were living in a Halcyon age not unlike that predicted by the most-optimistic 20th Century science fictions. It was an age of peace. An age of plenty. An age where disease had been conquered. An age where ageing had been vanquished. An age where war and disharmony had been dispelled as there was more than enough for all.

But something wasn't quite right.

There had been great advances in science and technology, but people yearned for art and creativity to make their lives complete.

Realising this, the government assigned Scotland's best minds to making breakthroughs in arts and creativity. Those geniuses had worked wonders for science and technology, so surely they could work their scientific miracles with entertainment and art.

The scientists were faced with a new problem in a knowledge domain that very few of them were familiar with. However they firmly believed that there's no problem that can't be solved by the correct equations and theories.

So they locked themselves away in seclusion whilst they pondered the problem and carried out their experiments and research and, slowly but surely, progress was made…

December 24th 2033

The whole world was tuned into holovision eagerly awaiting the scientists special performance.

It had been 6 weeks since official word came out from the scientists bunker that they'd cracked the arts and entertainment problem and that they'd unveil their solution to the world on Christmas Eve.

At 19:00 Edinburgh Mean Time the holographic continuity avatar announces that the show is about to start.

The holoscreen shows the programme's title to be *Clever Scientist Theatre presents 'The Nativity'* before it fades away to show a clear blue sky over the ancient city of Nazareth in Galilee.

A boffin, who you vaguely recognise as the aged cybernetically-enhanced professor Heinz Wolff, appears from above the holoview, descending on a cloud and wearing a long white beard and matching robes.

Above the surround-sound choir and harps you hear him call out "Gabriel, vere are you? Com here bitte."

"I'm here boss" says a scientist flying into view, dressed in a white smock that shows off his argyle socks and sandals nearly as well as his wire coat-hanger and tinsel halo and cardboard wings.

Admittedly the flying effects are good. You suspect that they're either using monofilament wires that are too narrow to be seen or they've developed some fancy anti-gravity technology or maybe even just fantastic advances in live holo-fx processing. However they've done it, it's quite an achievement but it can't mask the fact that the scientists are terrible performers. You've never seen an infant school nativity have such bad performances, nor a TV soap have such wooden actors.

Prof Wolff continues "Gut. I vant you to arrange for the holy ghost to impregnate Mary for me. Unt don't call me 'boss.'"

"Sorry God."

That was a step too far.

Around the world people who still believed in 'something' took offence, not so much because Prof Wolff was portraying a supreme divinity but because he was doing it in such a substandard way.

Suddenly Christians could understand why Muslims were so against depictions of their religious figures. This understanding brought the Christian and Muslim faiths together and before the night was over, they'd joined in religious riots across the globe. Each show of force asserting their faith in religion and denouncing the false god of Science that had tried to do so much for them, before it went too far.

Within weeks society was in tatters. Billions died. Virtually nobody who had ever thought of themselves as a scientist survived. Even being able to change a pair of AA batteries in a remote control was enough to mark you out as a tech-savvy heretic deserving of being stoned to death.

Before long the power stations stopped running, food and goods ceased to be transported from place to place and the globe was plunged back into the dark ages.

The very real promise of a technological utopia for all had been reduced to an ignorant dystopia all because the public objected to scientists playing God.

The End

Should it actually happen in your reality, this ending is NOT covered by the 100% money back guarantee. But on the plus side if you pray hard enough for a refund then you might get it. Although it is extremely doubtful that a benevolent omnipotent god does actually exist, as if they did then surely they'd have stopped the author from inflicting the above pun on you.

—— Section 323 ——

You wait...

Dum-de-dum. This is boring. This isn't doing anything to make you like queues or waiting rooms.

Dum-de-dum.

Why do people say they sit twiddling their thumbs? That's worse than just sitting still. For all the hype, thumb-twiddling is a really boring activity.

Dum-de-dum-de-dum.

DEAD CAT TIME

I'm too bored to even make up a cat name and some possible fates for the cat. Just pick one of the following three boring options.

Option One (go to **Section 221**)
or Option Two (go to **Section 384**)
or Option Three (go to **Section 080**)

—— Section 324 ——

The nurse hardly gives you the chance to describe your symptoms as once she gets a good look at your face she goes pale and reaches for a panic button on the desk.

As she hits it, emergency alert lights start to strobe and a terribly loud klaxon starts to screech. Even to a non-medical man like yourself, it's fairly obvious that this is not a good sign.

Within seconds you're surrounded by people in full biohazard protective suits who strap you to a gurney and rush you through several corridors until you finally pass through decontamination showers and enter some sort of isolation ward.

The next few weeks are a blur where you drift in and out of consciousness and the doctors struggle to diagnose your illness and then find a cure.

You do eventually pull through, but you missed the chance to cast your vote, and even worse you missed the chance to have exciting adventures getting dressed, going to the polling station and waiting for the results.

The author spent so much time writing those segments that he didn't really have much time left to write a fuller description of your many weeks of treatment in the isolation ward. It was probably very touch and go and exciting enough to make a film about it, but we'll never know for sure.

Anyway, no point dwelling on what you missed. If you really want to find out what could have happened you'll have to retrace your steps and pick a different path, or even start over again.

At least you manage to get out of hospital when the newly independent Scotland is forming it's policies and shaping the future of your great nation.

Oh yeah - the Yes vote won. Didn't you know? (go to **Section 069**)

—— Section 325 ——

September 18th 2025

Charging across the soaking wet street, you can hear the chasing gang's shouts and shots blaring out from the alleyway you've just flown out of as you pull the 9mm automatic machine pistol out of your inside jacket.

The driver of the car waiting at the red light doesn't see you coming - she's too busy nervously eyeing the street-punks outside the burger shop.

"Out the fuckin' car, motherfucker" you shout at her as you rip open the driver's door. You know the driver won't resist - no-one likes being pistol whipped or shot and the face-full of Uzi you're showing her proves you're serious.

The shouts are getting louder and a fired round zings off the car bodywork. Shit! You glance around and see muzzle flash in the darkened alleyway. They'll be here any second, so you turn your attention back to carjacking your way out of this situation.

But turning back to the driver you're greeted with a good look down the black hole inside the .357 magnum barrel pointed at you. You shouldn't be surprised. Many drivers are armed - in this city they have to be if they don't want to get carjacked at every other set of lights.

"Now close the door, dickhead" says the driver in a sweet-as-pie voice that matches her looks but not her well-armed demeanour.

Raises your hands in a show of surrender you comply, and as soon as the door is shut she burns rubber despite the red light still showing. You don't notice her knock down the young mother and child as she races off, because you're too busy falling to the ground as the first bullets from the alleyway find their target in your back and legs.

You wait for the 'Game Over - Load a Save?' screen to come.

As your life blood mixes with the rainwater sweeping down the street, you reflect upon the ironic hand that fate has dealt you.

To think that you used to be a successful video-game developer. Your violent car-jacking, cop-killing, hooker-shagging, ho-pimping games used to be so popular, and you're sure that they helped disperse violent tendencies amongst players. You even had the research to prove it. Your games could have avoided this situation.

But back in 2018 the new Scottish Government took the opposing view and decided to ban violent games like the ones you made. They made it illegal to develop the games in Scotland and before long your reputation was worse than a blackmarket arms dealer's.

Then the lawsuits started blaming you for past violent crimes and demanding financial recompense. The courts, following government guidance, took the complainants side even when it was clear that your games couldn't have contributed. Finally you were made bankrupt after being ordered to pay reparations for 1990s Serbian warcrimes, the Nazi Holocaust and several Viking invasions.

Your personal downfall was mirrored by the country's decline. It turned out that violent games did lower actual violence - not least because people sat at home playing games aren't out causing crime. Banning all violent games soon turned explosive - without a gaming outlet for aggression it was left to build up, the pressure getting higher and higher until something was going to blow.

Crime went through the roof. The police couldn't cope. Before long Scotland was ruled by gangs. The virtual world of *Car Jacking Hooker Killer* had gone and been replaced by the reality of it.

As the rainwater washes away the blood draining out of you, you think about all this and how different it could have been.

You wait for the 'Game Over - Load a Save?' screen to come.

It never does.

Reality doesn't have that option.

The End

Should it actually happen in your reality, this ending is NOT covered by the 100% money back guarantee. Fuck you, asshole. I'm gonna keep yo greenbacks an go buy me some tasty ass an a new gun. Bitches and punks gotta learn respec, you get me?

—— Section 326 ——

On the way to the polling station you get a few passing cars and vans honking their horns. They virtually all seem pleased to see you and take your dress in good humour. On more than a few occasions people shout out "Auch eye!", "Scotland forever!" or, on one occasion, they stop and deliver a monologue from Braveheart. An interesting journey, but you're here now.

You walk up to the doors and pause.

You've always held the belief that polling stations are places full of wonder and promise for the future. That they're almost-mystical locations that can alter a nations fate. Each one a powerful nexus where all possible destinies of the country intersect, just waiting for the public will to select one single possibility and to transform it into reality. Places of truly amazing, almost miraculous, transformative power.

But really they are just local primary schools that have swapped the kids for a naff sign saying 'POLLING STATION'.

Finally you approach the doors and prepare yourself to step inside.

DEAD CAT TIME

Yes it's time to peek inside Schrödinger's box and see how well Jess is...

Hello Jess. Where's Pat? (go to **Section 395**)

or Hello Pat. Where's Jess gone? (go to **Section 276**)

or That's not a cat that's a shaved dog! (go to **Section 161**)

or Jess is curled up asleep, blissfully unaware of their role in the future of Scotland. (go to **Section 305**)

or Postcat Jess. Postcat Jess. Postcat Jess has left a mess! (go to **Section 039**) or OMG! Jess is dead! Pat will be upset. (go to **Section 209**)

—— Section 327 ——

"I'm half-fuckin' naked..."

You scream as you realise your error.

What will people think of you leaving home with your cock on show? You'll be on a register for sure. People will point and whisper about you behind their hands. You'll spend every night and all weekend removing graffiti from your front door just so people don't think you've accepted the accusations of 'perv' and 'paedo scum'...

You have no chance to wonder how you came to be in this situation as suddenly a strange creature leaps up in front of you.

"Piss-stained Mingedripping!"

That's all you manage to weakly say as the goblin-banshee lunges forward and rips you a new arsehole.

Your dying thought is that you wish the author had put more effort into writing an entertaining demise in this section instead of just tossing off whatever half-arsed ideas he had. But that would have meant him writing when sober - and that wasn't going to happen so close to his deadline. You are especially upset as the author being half-arsed means that, with the new orifice that the goblin-banshee has given you and is the cause of your death, you are exactly four times as arsed as the author. Somehow that just doesn't seem fair.

The End

Should it actually happen in your reality, this ending is <u>NOT</u> covered by the 100% money back guarantee. But what did you expect? It's not like the author can just throw money away to every idiot who gets killed by a goblin-banshee.

—— Section 328 ——

The coin flies up...

Arcing upwards and upwards, until it flies over the barrier between your booth and the next...

"Owww! Who threw that?" you hear the occupant of the next booth say. Suddenly you don't really care which way you vote, since you're still a bit head-achey from last night you just want to get out of the polling station without getting into a fight.

You pick up the teeny tiny pencil and hurriedly scribble a cross in one of the boxes without really noticing which it was, then you fold the ballot paper and quickly exit the booth.

As you walk across the floor the man in the next cubicle comes out, holding his left eye, and looks at you, obviously after his unseen coin-based assailant. You point towards the door and say "I think he ran out". The man races out after the fictional escaping attacker.

You pop the folded ballot in the box and exchange knowing nods with the station attendants. You know and they know that you have got away with coining a stranger.

With everything you have to worry about whenever there's a poll it's really annoying that even coin-tosses are out to complicate things. No wonder people treat votes as a big deal.

You go home and carry on as normal until the results are announced. (go to **Section 321**)

—— Section 329 ——

You look for a hiding spot in the undergrowth to the side of the path. You've just spotted a hollowed out fallen tree that you may be able to squeeze into. Before you do, you glance back towards the path and what you see there surprises you.

As if by magic, the shopkeeper's appeared.

He looks at you disapprovingly, shakes his head and says "Oh I don't know what's up with people these days. You're nowhere near as good at fancy dress escapades as they were in the 1970s. Back then a city gent in a suit and bowler hat could put on a costume and be ready for adventure. You wouldn't find them cowardly crawling into a tree trunk, ready to burst into tears."

You can still hear the beast bearing down on your position from behind you and approaching grunts and snarls from whatever primitives are up ahead.

"For fuck's sake take me back to the shop" you shout.

"Manners really. They were better in the 70s as well."

And with a wave of the shopkeeper's hand you're back in the shop. (go to **Section 310**)

—— Section 330 ——

The Scottish people decide that they want a fresh start without the Windsors ruling them. Besides, monarchies are such an old outmoded idea, suggesting that one family is special, more important than everyone else, chosen-by-divine-powers.

Now is the time to seize the opportunity to become a modern democracy, get rid of the monarchy and replace it with a president.

So today one year after Yes-Day the first Presidential election takes place.

You're excited as the winner is announced to be…

The person who wanted it most (go to **Section 308**)
or A true Scottish hero (go to **Section 205**)
or An ordinary, but loved, Scot (go to **Section 360**)

—— Section 331 ——

You wait...

Dum-de-dum. This is boring. You hate queues at the best of times but it's even worse when you're ill and waiting to be seen by a doctor.

Dum-de-dum.

It's amazing how boring waiting rooms are. Almost as if they are designed to make waiting as bad as possible so as to deter people from bothering hospitals with their petty injuries, illnesses and other life-threatening conditions.

Dum-de-dum-de-dum.

DEAD CAT TIME

I'm too bored to even make up a cat name and some possible fates for the cat. Just pick one of the following three boring options.

Option One (go to **Section 037**)
or Option Two (go to **Section 080**)
or Option Three (go to **Section 163**)

—— Section 332 ——

September 18th 2015

Just one year after *Yes-Day* you decide to do your bit to help Scottish tourism and take advantage of the warm summer to holiday in the wild expanses of your own country.

So today you find yourself out enjoying the sunshine and hiking across the heather-coated hills. Suddenly you come across a large man in a suit with his back to you digging what looks like a shallow grave. Beside him there seems to be some sort of pile of slightly fluffy black and white material.

Not having a clue what may be going on, but knowing that it looks dodgy and that you should probably not disturb the man, you start to back away. It's at this point that you step on a twig that cracks loudly.

The man drops the shovel he'd been using and spins towards you calling "Is someone there?"

As you get to see his face you're struck unable to move from the shock of recognition.

"Alex Salmond?" you ask.

"Err… yes. So I'm Alex Salmond but that…" he points at the black and white material "That is not a panda suit and I'm no buryin' it."

"A panda suit?"

"You've seen it? Well in that case you already know too much" says the leader of the Scottish government pulling out a gun from inside his jacket and pointing it at you.

"But why?"

"Because I'm a patriot. Edinburgh zoo had it's pandas and they weren't breeding as we'd hoped. The males just weren't up to the job. The Independence campaign was behind in all the polls and we knew that the hope and feel-good factor of a Giant Panda birth would help us."

"Because I'm a patriot. A roughly Giant Panda-sized patriot. So I ordered a panda costume, some chocolate-coated bamboo shoots and half a gallon of panda-pheromones and prepared to do my duty."

"Because I'm a patriot. And if that means going balls deep in panda muff night after night for 5 weeks until she conceives, then that's what I'll do."

"And because I'm a patriot I'll be proud to do it, and I *am* proud to *have* done it, for my country. For Scotland."

You remember the pictures you saw on TV after the birth. How Alex Salmond looked like a proud father, no matter how ridiculous that seemed. You thought he was just pleased for the PR it gave him and the Yes Scotland campaign. How wrong you had been.

"So why didn't you get rid of the suit earlier? Why keep hold of the incriminating evidence until now?"

"What a stupid question. I wanted to keep it until exactly one year after *Yes-Day* because every ending in **You Decide! The Future of Scotland** takes place on an anniversary of that day and it was important that disposing of the suit made it into the book."

You don't even wait to be told to kneel by the already dug grave. You don't need to be told as you know it's inevitable. Anyone who is mad enough to screw pandas for Scotland, break 4th walls at the drop of a hat and carries a loaded gun in their jacket isn't going to let you go free.

You neither hear nor feel it when the gun goes off.

The End

Should it actually happen in your reality, this ending is NOT covered by the 100% money back guarantee. Look I've managed to avoid paying out everywhere else, so I don't know why you bother reading the specific terms for each ending. You're not getting your money back.

—— Section 333 ——

"Hmm not really sure… What do you fancy?" you ask Kelly.

"It's getting late and I'm no really hungry, well not for curry anyway. Stimulating conversation's another matter."

"Yeah I'm the same - I think I'll pass, but thanks for the offer" you say to the punning drunk.

"Nae probs - see you round" he says and he and his friend leave the bar.

Now the drunks have gone you and Kelly continue the debate from earlier, but also take excursions into discussing music, hobbies, family and everything else you'd chat about with a friend. You start to feel like there may be real chemistry between the two of you, and you think she feels the same.

You carry on chatting with Kelly until the bar closes when you walk her back to her place. She invites you in for a coffee, but you don't want to push it. So, having exchanged phone numbers, you finally head home alone.

This morning, as you jump into the shower to freshen up, you smile remembering what a good night it was and hoping you'll maybe see Kelly again sometime. (go to **Section 120**)

—— Section 334 ——

You enter the dressing room to try on the caveman costume. It's especially important that it fits well, as, being essentially just a piece of animal print fabric to drape around your torso, if it doesn't fit you'll end up with your knackers on show to one and all and you'd rather not spend the most important day in Scotland's history in a police station for indecent exposure.

You don't need that again, they'll start to think you're doing it on purpose.

You get out of your normal clothes and pop into the costume. The plastic club and fake sabre-tooth tiger teeth on your tribal necklace look good and the fake fur seems to fit okay, but maybe you should try walking about with it on for a minute or two.

You leave the dressing room. (go to **Section 167**)

—— Section 335 ——

September 18th 2019

It took a while but finally, with government funding, you're ready to see your opus ***Science! The Musical*** debut in Edinburgh tonight. It's exciting as, not being a performer yourself, you decided to leave the staging to the director and cast and haven't seen any of the more recent rehearsals.

Two hours later, it's good to hear people leaving the show humming along to the closing number "*There's no matter like anti-matter*", but it does annoy you that it was originally meant to be "*There's no matter like dark matter*" until rehearsals when the dark matter chorus refused to black up for the number.

The musical goes a lot deeper than many people ever went whilst at school, but unfortunately, whilst your original libretto was scientifically correct, you're angry that the director and cast have introduced a range of inaccuracies into the show. You're so angry that you decide to confront the director about it at the after-show party.

The director is quite adamant that all his changes were minor, made the show more accessible and people will remember the core science now.

After all, he argues no normal person knows or cares about the laws of Thermodynamics, superstring theory or the flavours of quark.

Sure C*harm* and *Strange* are fine. The actors loved *Top* and *Bottom* and were fighting over who would be who. But *Up* and *Down*? Far better his idea to go with a pair of dwarf names - people love those little fellas. They'll definitely remember them if they're renamed.

You might have been okay if that was the only change, but aside from what he had *Top* and *Bottom* doing, he made several more changes to make the show more 'adult'. Gravity, magnetism, chemical reactions and anything else involving attractive forces or molecules joining in union seemed to end up in sex.

Which made it particularly strange that the section on biological reproduction was altered to never mention sex but to try explaining the phenomenon through expressive dance with a beach ball and a hula hoop.

There was even a big change made at the start, in the song about Greek philosopher-scientists the director decided to have the cube character and the sphere having sex on stage. The director explains that he thought it made for a better show than using Platonic solids.

Given all the changes, it shocked you that over the next few days and weeks when the reviews and bookings were all phenomenal. People loved your musical and the general level of scientific knowledge was so poor that most people didn't spot the errors. It was even educating people about many scientific theories…

The show was soon winning awards and it wasn't long before it went global.

In the years to come, many many scientists, in Scotland and beyond, cited ***Science! The Musical*** as the influence that first interested them in becoming a scientist.

Years later you look back and you're proud that you helped more people to study science. You're just still a bit miffed that they're all so bad at science, even down to still believing in *Spin*, *Strange*, *Top*, *Bottom*, *Sneezy* and *Doc*.

The End (of science)

Should it actually happen in your reality, this ending is NOT covered by the 100% money back guarantee. Because gravity doesn't allow it. What do you mean that's not right? It's what I learnt from the musicals.

—— Section 336 ——

You always thought that it was a shame that Giant Pandas had become completely extinct, but now, with your time travel machine, you could undo that. You could travel back to a time when Giant Pandas were plentiful, when they roamed every high street, and bring some back to the present. If you brought enough then they would breed and once more the world would know the magnificent bears.

Sadly you don't actually know when or where to go to find a plentiful supply of Giant Pandas and there aren't many places that you know of that had *any* pandas at all.

Stopping only to get a giant bear-sized butterfly net and a bale of bamboo shoots you set the controls for the one time and place that you know for sure had pandas.

Arriving in Edinburgh Zoo in January 27th 2014 it's only a matter of minutes waiting with the net over a pile of bamboo shoots before you've caught the pair of pandas that the breeding programme is trying to get to reproduce. Mere seconds after that, you've brought them back to 2027.

So that's two Pandas, but you need more. Where to find more?

Suddenly you have a brainwave. You can travel back to January 26th

2014, a whole day before you panda-napped the two you already have, and grab them from then.

Within half an hour (of your experienced time) you're standing back in your room with a pair of pandas from January 26th and another identical pair from January 27th.

Not a bad start, but you still need more than just four…

Five hours (of your time) later your house is starting to get a bit crammed. You've got a similar pair of Pandas from every day between January 27th 2014 and December 1st 2013.

But you need more than just 58 pairs of pandas if you're to repopulate the world and this is taking too much time. If only there was a quicker way…

Then it hits you. If you do a small jump back in time, you can bring back the 58 pairs of pandas that were here 10 minutes ago and put them with the 58 pairs that are here now. You'll double the number that you currently have. And then you can wait a few minutes and repeat the process. It's genius and you're fairly sure it's not causing any sort of temporal paradox or you wouldn't be able to do it. You just need to remember to stop before you've got more pandas than there are atoms in the universe.

It's not long before your neighbourhood is surrounded by 59,392 breeding pairs of Giant Pandas and that's when it strikes you that this may not have been a very good idea.

For a start the whole town is starting to stink of panda shit.

Next off, your house is wrecked because, anticipating a lot more Pandas arriving, a few of the bears saw that you only had one keyboard available, and decided to fight over your laptop in an effort to be the Panda that beat the monkeys to writing *Hamlet.*

But finally you realise that in a lapse of planning you totally forgot to order delivery of the worlds entire supply of bamboo shoots.

The Pandas are hungry. Very hungry. Murderously hungry.

It's only a matter of hours before the first Panda snaps at a neighbour and takes a chunk out of her arm. Within minutes the word spreads amongst the cuddly killers that, instead of being loveable vegans living on nothing but bamboo, it might just be possible to live on human flesh.

The bears riot and it's not something the humans were prepared for. In recent years, partly due to programmes like *The Walking Dead*, many councils and governments have had Freedom of Information requests asking about their plans to deal with a zombie apocalypse, but very very few have ever stopped to think about doomsday scenarios involving over 100,000 Giant Pandas. That's the shocking truth. And to think that that's the sort of short-sighted approach that your council tax pays for.

Within months mankind is overrun. Months later mankind is extinct. Of course it's then only weeks before all the Pandas are themselves extinct, partly due to a lack of food but mainly due to a lack of herd resistance to disease as all the male Pandas are genetically identical and all the female Pandas are genetically identical, being, as they were, identical copies of 2 original Pandas.

So remember this next time you see a Giant Panda at a zoo - they're dicks that killed out all human life and themselves. You're fully justified whispering insults at them.

The End

Should it actually happen in your reality, this ending is <u>NOT</u>

covered by the 100% money back guarantee. But in lieu of refund I'll give you a gem of advice: Giant Pandas particularly dislike being called "*stupid black and white cockend bastards*" but don't let the keepers spot you saying that to them or they'll probably throw you out of the zoo.

—— **Section 337** ——

You really hope that you'll get some form of polling station this time.

DEAD CAT TIME

Yes it's time to peek inside Schrödinger's box and see how well Jess is... but since we know you like things to stay normal, without any surprises, we'll give you some hints.

Thankfully everything about the cat looks normal. Totally and utterly normal. (HINT: This is the option that goes to the normal polling station. Honestly.) (go to **Section 372**)

or Where's he gone? (HINT: This is a very pro-independence polling station. Really.) (go to **Section 264**)

or That's a penguin in disguise! (HINT: And this is the pro-Union polling station. It is.) (go to **Section 127**)

or OMG! The cat's dead! (HINT: This is an odd polling station that you probably won't enjoy.) (go to **Section 293**)

—— **Section 338** ——

September 18th 2028

You cast your mind back to that fateful morning soon after *Yes-Day* when you turned on the TV and had a quick one-off-the-wrist to McBabeStation then saw the programme about space exploration. It was that that made you realise that sex is always the way forward for new technology.

You can create a machine that does all housework, educates your kids, makes you money and saves the planet, even price it at £100 and you'd only sell a handful.

But if you stick a couple of vibrating self-lubricating holes and a multi-speed 10" rabbit on it and raise the price to a grand then they'll sell like hot cakes. They'll even sell like hot cakes would if *they* had sex toys attached (*note to self: patent vibrating cock cookies and Victoria sponge quim*). They'll sell so well that you'll be set for life.

You were convinced that the way to make space exploration financially viable, self-sustaining or even profitable was to find a way to meld sex and space into one single venture.

Before long the business plan for the first McBabeSpaceStation had been approved.

By the end of 2019 the first small station opened it's airlock doors for business in orbit around the Earth. It became a roaring success, and was soon expanding to many times it's initial size. It really helped that initial traffic from millionaires keen to be amongst the first people to experience zero-G sex provided enough income to drive down prices and start regular orbital flights to and from the station. Business boomed and space exploration boomed with it.

By 2023 the next few stations had been planned and soon station modules were on course for Mars and Venus. In 2026 your business empire successfully placed a pair of sex-addicts in Saturn's orbit for two whole run throughs of the Karma Sutra before safely returning them to Earth. As more McBabeSpaceStations come online, demand is through the ceiling and keeps rising, especially now that it's affordable to virtually everyone.

Of course you get a lot of PWUSFWEVAEs, *people with unusual and specific fetishes which are equally valid as anybody else's,* if we're using the language of 21st Century politically correctness. Though it's a lot easier to use old English and just call them perverts.

A lot of these pervs come just for zero-G sex with the Wee Jimmy Krankie sexbots. You're not sure which is worse, that they may be into schoolboys, into women dressed as schoolboys or into robots that look like women dressed as schoolboys. Or they could just come for the zero-G and end up up Wee Jimmy because it's '*the thing to do*', in much the same way as how a trip to Las Vegas just isn't a trip to Las Vegas unless you've accidentally killed a hooker.

You think back over all this as you sit back in your executive office on McBabeSpaceStation Mars-69. Your business is still expanding and you don't intend to ever stop exploring all over the whole fucking universe. And you won't have to as long as people don't stop paying you for the chance to keep fucking all over the whole explored universe.

It's all both moving faster than you expected and taking an age, and so, happy that you're ready to move out of the solar system, you gaze out to your next destination you say to your P.A. the words that you never thought you would ever live to say:

"Next stop, the stars!"

"Are we ready for that sir? Or are you joking?"

"No Cindy" you say "It's no joke. It's totally Sirius."

The End

Should it actually happen in your reality, this ending is NOT covered by the 100% money back guarantee. You liked that obvious Sirius pun, didn't you. Admit it, you did. That's worth more than any refund ever could be.

—— Section 339 ——

You leave home with the dogs eager for their morning walk or, probably more precisely, bursting for the toilet.

You love it when you have the time to take them for a long walk to a local park and play fetch with them for an hour or more, but there's no time for that this morning. No - you'll just take them around the block and let them 'do their business' so you can get some breakfast and get cleaned and ready for going out to vote.

You'll make it up to them tomorrow with a special 'Better Together Won' walk, when you'll play with them all day. Or if not tomorrow, Saturday. Or Sunday. Someday soon anyway. Probably.

It may only be a quick walk around the block, but a walk that would take about 10 minutes by yourself still takes you over an hour with Gwen having a leak every couple of minutes.

Eventually you get back home and the dogs seem happy enough, so you can grab some breakfast if you want.

Do you make yourself a breakfast feast at home (go to **Section 257**)

Or Go out to a local cafe for breakfast (go to **Section 114**)

Or Are you so excited you skip breakfast, keen to jump in the shower, freshen up and get ready to go out and vote as quickly as you can. (go to **Section 258**)

—— Section 340 ——

You open the door and almost immediately know that you've entered the wrong room because you are in a room whose walls are filled with photographs of David Cameron. Many of them have been defaced with thick black marker pen and several have been slashed at with knives or have darts sticking out of them.

Sat in the middle of the room, naked except for a cycle helmet, laughing and throwing darts at the photos is the real Boris Johnson.

You exit quickly before he spots you and decide to look for the polling station behind a different door. (go to **Section 083**)

—— Section 341 ——

You can't remember exactly what happened for the rest of the night, but you're pretty sure that at the end of the night you didn't have to go home alone and it wasn't your home you went to.

You try to think of the details. You remember that you'd fancied the hot redhead, Carly or whatever she was called, all night. She looked a right goer and had a great rack. You're sure that, with a body like hers, you could manage to look past her being a boring intellectual who likes to debate.

You try harder to remember the details and have a vague recollection of having a passionate kiss. You cast your mind back as best you can.

'Oh not again' you thought.

What happened next was inevitable.

Sex. Hot sex. Hot sexy sex. Really hot sex. Really really hot sexy sexy sex. Sex so hot it made your chilli laced lamb tindaloo look like plain old gravy. Really really really hot sexy sex so hot and sexy that it can't be described in any greater detail than just 'really really really really hot sexy sexy sexy sex' or this book would be banned under obscenity law.

You make really really hot sweaty sexy physical animal sex for ages until you fall back on the bed exhausted and gently take your partner's brown hair in your hands.

Yes what a ni- just a second. Brown hair? Curly's a redhead, a sexy redhead with really hot sexy long red hair. So how come you remember brown hair?

Short brown hair - sort of mid-brown. Kind of like Andy's.

Oh shit.

Not again. How pissed were you both?

Last time that happened you couldn't look each other in the eye for about a month. It'll certainly make five-a-side difficult next week.

Realising that it's maybe not just the really really hot curry that is making your bottom burn slightly, you jump into the shower to freshen up before you go to vote. (go to **Section 295**)

—— Section 342 ——

SciTech TV is showing an interesting programme about whether such a thing as pure science can ever really exist or whether all discoveries have applications, just that sometimes we haven't yet recognised what they may be.

It looks at numerous cases of theories and discoveries that were initially thought pointless or just 'interesting but useless' that then went on to be the basis of life- and civilisation-changing creations.

Theories such as the Big Bang Theory. Nobody thought that that could be used in any meaningful non-theoretical way, until US TV execs managed to make a popular multi-season sitcom from it, finding an entertaining use for nerds in the process.

Or Gravity. Isaac Newton thought it was just a useful way to get apples out of trees but then it was discovered that the surface of the Earth is moving very quickly as the planet spins on its axis and so gravity was adapted to stop us all being thrown off into space.

Not to mention Quantum Mechanics, which, whilst initially thought too esoteric for any practical applications, is now being used for controlling the number of stray cats in Milan. Well, in boxes really. But the boxes are in Milan.

Truth be told, you are busy on social media on your phone when the programme's on, so you might not have got all of that right, but you're pretty sure it's near enough. Whatever the details, it's pretty clear that science is pretty important. And that means all science, even the science that no-one can see any point in.

You eventually decide to turn off the TV and start to think about your future and the future of Scotland, and where the priorities lie for both of you.

Are you inspired to personally become a scientist on the theoretical boundaries of science (go to **Section 179**)

or Do you think the government should do more to promote scientific research in all disciplines (go to **Section 260**)

or Will you dedicate your life to seeking out the lizard illuminati that David Icke has warned about for years (go to **Section 111**)

or Should science and environmental awareness join to try saving species like Pandas through technology (go to **Section 270**)

or I don't want to think about all this - just give me something random! (go to **Section 375**)

—— Section 343 ——

You enter the examination cubicle and come face to face with the sickest looking doctor you've ever seen. His hair is thin, his skin a sickly colour and his age is impossible to determine. He looks a wreck, a disturbingly sick, almost inhuman, wreck.

Maybe that's a good thing - it's like the best cobbler in town having the worst shoes, or the best barber having the worst hair or the best gynaecologist having a whale of a time.

If this Doctor West looks like he's at death's door then he's probably a brilliant medical genius - like a pallid House.

"Yesss?" he asks.

"Please help me doctor, I think I'm dying."

As you say that you swear that the corners of his mouth start to curl into a slight smile.

"Really?" he says before taking a great sniff of the air. "Ahhh yesss, it seemss you are at Deathsss dooor, well let's help pull you through."

You know that this is only an NHS hospital, but you're still surprised that a weirdo like Dr West can work here. Nearly as surprised as when his skin starts pulling even tighter over his face as his skull seems to lengthen. His skin tone turns even paler and sicklier. His teeth becoming somehow longer and sharper. His hands slowly stretch and warp into hideous predatory claws, fit to rip through soft flesh as if it were nothing but butter.

This can't be real. You think that it must be the blue death starting to affect your mind, making you hallucinate some sort of goblin-banshee.

Almost as you think that, the doctor says "no - thisss **isss** real" before it shrieks *ktheaaaarrrrrr!!!!*

No! This is not the reality you are used to, it must be a nightmare. There's no such thing as goblin-banshees - they're just a fiction for fantasy books and Japanese horror films. You must be having a bad dream… wake up… WAKE UP… **WAKE UP!**

The 'doctor', or whatever it has become, moves in ready to tear you a new arsehole, saying "Did you never learn anything from non-linear adventure booksss?"

WAKE UP!!!!!!!!!! (go to **Section 067**)

—— Section 344 ——

On the independent channel, STV someone who you recognise as David Icke is sat on the sofa of a daytime magazine-show. From the pile of books on the table between him and Brianna and Kieran, the shows hosts, you can tell that he must be promoting some new book, no doubt packed full of wacky theories.

You pay attention. Hopefully you've not missed him being interviewed. He's always been good before when ranting on about the Royal family and world leaders being 8 feet tall shape-shifting lizards. Sometimes he almost makes Scientology look sane.

Almost.

Brianna addresses the camera, "So joining us in the studio now is leading conspiracy theorist and all-round special person, David Icke. He's just popped in to tell us all about his latest theories about how cold-blooded animals are taking over Caledonia."

"So, David, since I've spent so long introducing you, we've not got long, so can you just quickly sum up the main thrust of your new book 'The Caledonian Cabal: The Theft Of Scotland'. If you can do it in a handy soundbite of 15-30 seconds that would be absolutely fan-tastic."

"I'm sorry, I can't do that. It's a complex subject and can't be summed up that easily."

"20 seconds" says Kieran.

"Trying to describe it in a single sentence just because you think that's all your viewers can understand does disservice to both them *and* my book."

"5 seconds."

Worried about the time limit, David panics and shouts out "Alex Salmond's a 7 feet tall shapeshifting Salmon."

"Thank you, David. Still to come after the break we've got advice for anyone out there with children who's worried that none of them are gay or even just a little bit bi."

You think that it's about time you change the channel.

Do you start watching EUSportTV (go to **Section 077**)
or Decide to try Nature TV (go to **Section 378**)

—— Section 345 ——

September 18th 2019

You watch the high-definition 3D image on the screen anxiously - Lt Kelly McKay is servicing the airlock in sector Beta-5-Tau of Moonbase Independence-4.

The outer door of the lock had been intermittently reporting a fault for the past week and Base Commander Campbell had sent his most trusted engineer (and lover) Lt McKay to take a look at the problem. Little did either of them know that the fault was due to the last service droid installing a counterfeit locking mechanism provided by Willie Galbraith - the no-good tearaway youngest son of Shona Galbraith, who runs the base's most popular cafe (the one across the plaza from McButcher's second hand moon buggy lot).

On the monitor, Kelly moves up towards the faulty door and takes a omniscanner from inside her uniform jacket. You zoom in on the scanner and the doorlock she's scanning.

Suddenly a bang rings out. The faulty lock blew as she was scanning it. The outer airlock door flies off, exposing Lt Kelly to the vacuum of space.

Noooo!

Why didn't she wear a pressure suit?

As she grips onto the door frame, desperately trying to stop herself tumbling out into the icy cold nothingness and certain death, the synth drums start.

Dum-dum-dum dumdumdum dumdumdum.

The familiar *Moonbaser's* theme-song plays out over the credits.

Anyone can die in Space,
It's easy as can be,
But living's much harder.
Explosive decompression hurts,
But not as much as life
So let's have a cuppa… tea.
dum dum dumdummm

You sit back in your chair. Happy that you've put out another great episode that'll have the twatterati and media reviewers buzzing.

You remember back to when the seed of Moonbasers was first planted, just after *Yes-Day* when you watched a TV show about the need for space exploration and followed that with a soap opera.

You agreed that serious space exploration was needed for the future of mankind and you wanted your homeland to be seen as a world leader, but there was no way that a country like Scotland could afford to go it alone. Not without private business getting involved.

Then it hit you. People will pay for entertainment, and one of the most popular forms of entertainment for decades had been the TV soaps. All you needed to do was create a soap on the moon! Between Scottish government contributions and money from TV companies chasing awards and projected advertising revenue, you could easily build a working scientific research station cum colony cum TV-set on the moon.

An hour later you'd already written the opening episode of Moonbaser's (loosely basing it on the 765th episode of a popular soap set in London) and you had plot arcs and episode outlines for the next 50 shows. It was actually quite easy to write once you realised you could just rip off plotlines from Eastenders, changing the odd foreigner or homosexual character to being a robot or alien.

The plan worked - within a few years a large base had been established on the moon providing HD-3D sound stages, costume and makeup facilities, editing suites and rehearsal space for thousands of actors and TV crew. And the show's success had provided the finance for 5 or 6 scientists to stay there as well in a small portamodule near the toiletry block.

Yes - this was the way to make space exploration work. Entertain people. You were already working up plans to colonise Mars using the plots of Emmerdale, and beyond that 'Suspended Animation Suite' would recycle Coronation Street stories whilst becoming the first soap to film en route to Alpha Centauri.

All this would take time, of course. You imagine it'll be four or five seasons until you reach Mars, unless you do particularly well with BAFTAs for Moonbasers in which case it could be next year.

Thanks to your idea, the future looks bright for you and for mankind. Though you're not saying whether it looks bright for Lt McKay - you'll just have to tune in tomorrow.

The End

Should it actually happen in your reality, this ending is NOT covered by the 100% money back guarantee. You're a multi-millionaire writer/TV exec/Space-explorer, *and* you probably got the idea from reading this book. So I think it's paid for itself, don't you?

—— Section 346 ——

Oh no! It's a total disaster!

After 6 packs of bacon, you're feeling almost drugged with bacon-narcosis. But like any junkie you still chase after one more fix.

Desperate to get into the 7th pack of bacon, you cut it open with a knife and…

"Owww! Shit!" you exclaim as you slip and somehow manage to drive the knife into the palm of your left hand.

The pain is terrible and you know that you should try and get to hospital to get it looked at. Trying to stem the blood as best you can, you reflect for a moment. Not on how daft it was to try opening the pack of bacon with such a sharp knife whilst holding it in your hand but instead you reflect on how annoying it is that you just bleed red blood. On today of all days you really wish it was red, white and blue.

You hold a tea-towel to your hand and leave home for the hospital A&E department. (go to **Section 381**)

—— Section 347 ——

September 18th 2023

Soon after *Yes-Day* the Scottish Government was persuaded to run trials of alternative therapies by convincing evidence (from practitioners) that they could both help people live healthier and contribute massive budgetary savings. What government wouldn't want that?

Several therapies were given large scale tests with mixed results.

Reflexology helped with many conditions but it wasn't clear whether much of the effect was placebo or psychosomatic as it seemed to relax patients and leave them feeling good. Much debate was had as to whether the treatment really cured the body or whether it was just good for the sole.

Acupuncture seemed to help with muscular pain, but people complained that undergoing treatment made them feel pricks.

Aromatherapy was very relaxing and soothing, but people were naturally suspicious of it. Many said that they thought something about it smelled a bit fishy.

Crystal healing was tried but had no discernible effect above and beyond placebos, except for a small group of test subjects who mistakenly thought they had to take Crystal Meth.

They even trialled the old treatment of medicinal leeches, but it was soon decided that leech suppliers were charging way too much, the bloodsuckers.

The best results were with homeopathy. It didn't seem to heal many more people than the other therapies, but at least it was the cheapest.

Holyrood was able to cut back spending on traditional drugs as once they'd bought a few grams of chemicals all they'd need was lots and lots of water and they could keep diluting it further to create an endless supply of medicine. The best news was that they could put it in the water supply and heal people before they even became ill.

Of course putting it in the tap water meant that many true believers overdosed and had to be put onto a strict regime of bottled water only, but other than that the new alternative health plan worked well.

Many people were saved by the placebo effect, their own immune system or paying for private traditional healthcare. Many people also died from things like cancer and heart disease, but most of them would have died before long anyway and at least the government hadn't spent thousands extending their lives by a matter of weeks. The best effect was that the Scottish NHS drug bill dropped to about £12.57 per month, and most of that was spent on clean bottles to take samples to later dilute in the water supply over the next month.

The Scottish people slowly became a much more naturally healthy people, mainly because all the naturally unhealthy ones died off over time.

The End

Should it actually happen in your reality, this ending is covered by the 100% money back guarantee. If you provide proof of purchase I'll provide a homeopathic refund - the cost of the book watered down until it's practically undetectable. So look at your bank account, if it doesn't appear to have gone up then I must have got the dilution correct before I made the payment.

—— Section 348 ——

You open the door and almost immediately know that you've entered the wrong room because in front of you rolling about naked in an absolutely massive mound of 20 and 50 pound notes are two men.

You know that this isn't the polling station but it takes you a few seconds to recognise the two ginger-haired men, mainly because you've never seen The Proclaimers naked before!

In fact you don't really twig who they are until you hear them boasting to each other in almost Machiavellian voices.

"HA ha haaaa - I would burn 500 pounds, and I would burn 500 more, just to be the person who spends a grand lighting a barbecue even though it's raining and it'll go out again immediately!"

"Ha ha ha haaaaaa!" they both laugh together.

Then they notice you.

"Oh good dinner's here."

They both stand up and grab expensive gold-plated cutlery from a diamond-encrusted sideboard before slowly, but determinedly, moving towards you.

Oh god! Why did you pick a haggis costume?

Before you're eaten alive, you exit the room and decide to look for the polling station behind a different door. (go to **Section 083**)

—— Section 349 ——

On BizBites TV there's a documentary looking at the thorny difficult-to-resolve issue of Scotland's currency, and the knock-on issues of the chosen currencies effects on business and whether to accept a share of the existing UK debt.

You're currently still using the pound as before, but Westminster has made it clear that it won't let you continue using it as it would mean Scotland's independent actions having direct influence on the UK's finances.

This causes all sorts of issues as the people of Scotland don't want a new currency, and certainly don't want the Euro (even though that may have to be adopted if Scotland wants to join the EU - another tricky issue still being discussed). Creating a brand new currency, separate to the British pound Sterling or the Euro could be extremely costly for the new country.

It looks like there's still no easy answers to this problem, but the longer uncertainty continues the harder it'll be for Scottish businesses to compete internationally.

You eventually decide to turn off the TV and start to think about your future and the future of Scotland, and where the priorities lie for both of you.

Do you create a totally new currency for Scotland (go to **Section 210**)

or Hope that Scotland can find some way to create it's own currency without causing too much disruption to Scottish business during the change-over (go to **Section 053**)

or Press forward with using the British Pound Sterling, holding it hostage until England agrees suitable terms (go to **Section 359**)

or Join the EU and adopt the Euro (go to **Section 227**)

or Look elsewhere for possible currency answers (go to **Section 285**)

or A new country needs a new ruler - let's get rid of Queen Elizabeth and find a new monarch (go to **Section 237**)

or Monarchies are so yester-century, let's elect a president! (go to **Section 330**)

or I don't want to think about all this - just give me something random! (go to **Section 375**)

—— Section 350 ——

September 18th 2020

Despite the lack of tax breaks for technology and entertainment companies, the Scottish video game industry in Silicon Glenn keeps competing on the world stage. Though, over time, it slowly loses ground to innovative companies based in countries with more agreeable economic conditions. But despite games from Scotland slowly getting a reputation as 'a bit shit', the sector still tries to create new forms of entertainment that might allow it to .

One of it's most famous attempts at creating a new popular form of entertainment (aside from, the domestic and international failure, real-feel '*I Reamed a Dream-boat*' robosex dolls of SuBo, Gordon Brown and Alex Salmond) was the development of Verses - the VRS Virtual Reality Simulations.

The plan was to provide computer-generated worlds, populated by Artificial Intelligences and other people, that look and feel entirely realistic to the people 'playing' (or more correctly 'experiencing') them. But without government support to enable the much-needed R&D all that they could hope to achieve was a fairly simple world which lags and jerks and usually causes motion-sickness and vomiting within minutes.

Despite knowing it's failings, you can't refuse having a look when your 13 year old nephew asks you to try the new edutainment title '*How Scotland said Yes*' to let him know if it really does capture what it was like voting in the historic referendum.

So it's with some trepidation that that you put on the VR headset attached to his Playstation 6 and the world vanishes to be replaced by a plain white image field with the words 'START NEW EXPERIENCE' floating in front of you.

You raise your virtual-hand to click the START, noticing that it's less-than-glorious 1000 polygon shape lags behind your intention. If that's how bad it lags when there's virtually nothing else in the simulation, you hate to think what you're about to experience.

Half a second after you click the START, the click registers and the start screen fades away.

You wake up...

You feel groggy, from a troubled night of something ill-defined but you think the sim is trying to conjure the feeling of bad dreams. You also have a vague ill-fitting thought that you never ate any blancmange (or maybe it's yoghurt) before bed.

The world looks odd - and part of you that isn't sucked into the sim realises it's because the simulations lighting model is wrong, the number of polygons used is woefully inadequate and everything moves out of sync with your body and head movements. You almost feel like you're seasick and dizzy inside the *Money for Nothing* music video.

"Oh my head. What was I thinking last night? I'm not 18 anymore. I'm not 18 anymore. I need more sleep… another 24 hours should do. What time is it anyway? Hell… What day is it?"

The bedside clock tells you it's only… well it's hard to tell what time it's meant to be as it's too badly pixellated. You move closer to it and concentrate on it until the software increases it's rendered resolution high enough to make out that it says quarter to seven.

Whilst it increases the detail of the clock, the rest of your room becomes more blocky.

All of a sudden, you don't feel too well because of the the visual and experiential aberrations of the Verse.

You rip off the headset…

Returned to reality your nephew asks "So? Is it realistic?"

You don't manage to answer before you start vomiting over him.

This may be the end of your current adventure, but you know that if this is the best effort the newly independent, optimistic Scotland can do then the future is a very dark, scary place. Really scary.

The end of the beginning

Should it actually happen in your reality, this ending is NOT covered by the 100% money back guarantee. This is all just a simulation, so paying out refunds is essentially meaningless.

—— Section 351 ——

You get some funny looks on the way, but most people seem to accept that on such a momentous day some people might dress up and treat it like some sort of party. At least there's no trouble and eventually you get to the polling station, walk up to the doors and pause.

You always thought that polling stations are places full of wonder and promise for the future. The almost-mystical locations that can alter a nations fate. Each one a powerful nexus where all possible destinies of the country intersect, just waiting for the public will to select one single possibility and to transform it into reality. Places of truly amazing, almost miraculous, transformative power.

But really they are just local primary schools that have swapped the kids for a naff sign saying 'POLLING STATION'.

Finally you approach the doors and prepare yourself to step inside.

DEAD CAT TIME

Yes it's time to peek inside Schrödinger's box and see how well Jess is…

Hello Jess. Where's Pat? (go to **Section 013**)

or Hello Pat. Where's Jess gone? (go to **Section 273**)

or That's not a cat that's George Galloway! (go to **Section 177**)

or Jess is curled up asleep and blissfully unaware of their role in the future of Scotland. (go to **Section 029**)

or Postcat Jess. Postcat Jess. Postcat Jess has left a mess! (go to **Section 366**)

or OMG! Jess is dead! Pat will be upset. (go to **Section 288**)

—— Section 352 ——

September 18th 2022

Despite bad weather repeatedly delaying games in the tournament, the World Cup Final is finally here and it just happens to be on the 8th anniversary of *Yes-day*. What a great omen for Scotland, who enter the final with a real chance to win a historic victory on home soil. All they're got to do is beat the United Arab Emirates and that shouldn't be too hard as they've only made it this far by fluke.

Late in the second half and it's still a goal-less game when, in the 3rd minute of stoppage time, McAdam sends a perfect pass straight to your feet at the halfway line. You turn and start running the ball downfield. You beat one man on the turn, a second with sheer pace before flicking the ball up and over the last defender in your way. Racing around him you get to the ball just in time to volley it with a stunning scissor-kick from just inside the penalty spot.

The shot looks good but the UAE keeper's diving towards it. The next couple of seconds seem to last an eternity as the keeper closes in on the ball that is slowly curling away from him. Finally the keeper gets to the ball, but doesn't get enough on it and he only succeeds in pushing it perfectly into the top left corner of the goal.

GOOOAALLL SCOTLANNNNNND!!!!!

That's all it takes to win the cup and in doing so you have guaranteed that you become a national hero whose name is remembered as one of the great Scottish footballers.

You're so glad that you took up football seriously after Scotland was awarded the World Cup Finals back in 2014. To think, it would never have happened without an independent Scotland.

An independent Scotland that believed in investing in peoples health and fitness.

The end of the beginning

Should it actually happen in your reality, this ending is <u>NOT</u> covered by the 100% money back guarantee. It's the end of this read through or exploration of what may happen to Scotland, but it's not the end of your story or the story of Scotland.

It is not the end. It is just the end of the beginning. Or maybe the end of the middle or beginning of the middle or it might be the end of the beginning of the middle or the end of the end of the beginning of the middle.

Winston Churchill made this type of thing look easier than it is. Honest.

—— Section 353 ——

Are you sure this book's really for you?

Sorry to go all fourth wall meta on you but, as you may have gathered by now, this book's not really a serious study of the independence debate. I know, because I had to read lots and lots about the actual independence issues before realising that nobody really wants a humorous book about the real issues. They're just too emotionally loaded.

Some of my Scottish friends[16] are really stressed by the debate and the misinformation being spread, so this book is just meant to be a little light relief.

No. It isn't going to help you make your mind up, it's just a bit of fun. Something to read for a couple of minutes at a time whilst you're on the loo.

That's why it also costs far less than a serious book. If the humour isn't always 100% to your taste you can hardly complain when it (probably) cost less than half a pint or a couple of bags of crisps (if you bought it on Kindle)[17]. But some of those serious books… sheesh! Some of them cost the best part of a tenner on Kindle and they're drier than the Sahara. Reading them is ten years I'll never get back - or at least it feels that way.

So there you are. That's what this book is trying to be. Is it for you or not?

Doesn't sound like it. Wish I'd never bought it now - that half a pint or two bags of crisps would have been a much better purchase. (go to **Section 363**)

or Oh okay - I get it now. I'll have another try. (go to **Section 355**)

—— Section 354 ——

The coin flies up…

And then comes back down again landing clearly on 'Heads'.

That's interesting. You're fairly sure you'd decided that heads is a NO vote, so you pick up the teeny tiny pencil and place a cross in the 'NO' box.

You fold the ballot paper and happily stroll out of the booth, walk across the floor and pop the folded ballot in the box. You exchange knowing nods with the station attendants. You know and they know that you have fulfilled your democratic duty.

It's surprisingly easy when you use a coin and don't worry too much about political arguments. You hardly know why people treat it as such a big deal.

You go home and carry on as normal until the results are announced. (go to **Section 321**)

—— Section 355 ——

Great!

I knew you'd come around. You're obviously the sort of level-headed rational individual that countries need deciding their future. You won't regret this - not one jot.

Let's have another look at what happens when you wake up… (go to **Section 051**)

—— Section 356 ——

It was a draw…

Even after a recount.

Even after two recounts.

Even after three.

Even after numerous recounts.

Even after a single non-spoilt ballot paper had been found and added to the votes to be recounted.

This was odd. This was very odd. This was odder than odd.

In an infinite multiverse of infinite possibilities the author has seen this happen in exactly 19 individual universes. After rechecking each one of these turned out to have been repeatedly miscounted by complete fuckwits who not only can't count very well but are also practically incapable of successfully comparing two numbers and deciding if one of them is bigger than the other. In other words, by economists and statisticians.

So whilst the mathematical probability of there being a draw in such a large scale poll is small but non-zero the actual number of draws observed through infinite trials is zero.

It seems odd that its not happened in any single universe in all the multiverse. Almost as if something is making a nonzero number equal zero, and that's not right.

There must be some odd underlying reason for this, such as it not really happening. (go to **Section 078**)

—— Section 357 ——

You arrive back at the start of time…

B A N G !

The End

Should it actually happen in your reality, this ending is <u>NOT</u> covered by the 100% money back guarantee. It pretty much needs to have already happened according to current popular received wisdom.

—— Section 358 ——

You struggle to open the doors, twisting the doorknob and heaving and shoving and straining for second after second, but the door just won't budge. You put renewed energy into the struggle but still it won't turn. Your energy now fading fast, you give it one last ditch effort before realising, after what feels like forever but must have been about 5 seconds in reality, that you've been turning the doorknob the wrong way.

Why didn't you notice that quicker? Just more evidence that this dreadful disease is addling your brain. Worse than that, you can't even remember whether 'addling' is the right word to use or if you've just compared your mental ability to a way of cooking eggs.

Worried at your continued deterioration you turn the doorknob the other way and shove hard. It still refuses to move. Then you realise you'd tried the same way as the first time, finally you rotate the knob the other way and it opens easily.

As you walk into the School of Tropical Diseases you take some mild comfort from knowing that if you are to die today, at least you won't be remembered as a complete loser but as someone who, if they put their mind to it, could successfully open doors on the fifth or sixth attempt.

Finally, with salvation, or at least pain relief in your dying hours, so close, you give your details to the nurse on reception.

DEAD CAT TIME

You've not heard a noise out of that box for a while… wonder if Holly is still alive?

Shhh… you'll wake her up (go to **Section 006**)

or Oh so that's what a dead cat being eaten by maggots looks like! (go to **Section 093**)

or Does Dr Schrödinger expect you to clean up all that cat shit? (go to **Section 397**)

or The cat's dead and you can't be sure it's face isn't blue… (go to **Section 165**)

or Holly looks pleased to see you, but more pleased to be fed (go to **Section 112**)

or Holly ignores you, upset that her litter hasn't been cleaned (go to **Section 241**)

or Holly died after scratching "J'accuse" into the side of the box (go to **Section 324**)

—— Section 359 ——

September 18th 2015

Finally after a year of very tough negotiations and uncertainty for Scottish business, today sees the currency question solved as Scotland and rUK (the rest of the UK) agree to terms to let Scotland use the British Pound Sterling.

For much of the past year things had been at an impasse. Scotland insisted that it had the right to use the pound and was flatly refusing to honour any of the debt it had shared with rUK whilst part of the Union. Everyone knew that that reflected badly on the new nation, but they also knew that it was very bad for the UK government (especially the PM and Chancellor of the Exchequer).

Finally, after months of wrangling, it was agreed that Scotland would fully honour it's share of the debt and in return it could use the pound as a nearly-equal partner (the Bank of England having a few situations where it could completely override the Scottish influence).

After signing the agreement, Alex Salmond returns to Holyrood a hero. The Scottish government claims it a victory. The UK Chancellor claims it a victory. The UK PM claims it a victory. Everybody claims it as a victory.

International confidence is restored and both Scotland and rUK flourish.

The End

Wait, what? What do you mean that's a fully unsatisfying ending that is fairly realistic and provides neither humour nor a fun narrative.

God! You ungrateful bastards!

Don't you know how bloody hard it is trying to come up with all these endings, and trying not to seem too biased one way or the other? Nearly imfuckinpossible - that's how hard.

What do you mean 'I *chose* to do it, nobody made me'? FFS I understand why more people don't try anymore - you lot are impossible to please. So damn demanding.

Ok - here, will this do you?

A large part of the lengthy negotiations were solely concerned with the images on future banknotes. Alex Salmond wanted to show the importance of Scotland by having his image alongside the Queen on all banknotes. This was a step too far for the representatives of rUK and the Bank of England. They refused point-blank.

Salmond tried a lesser offer and got agreement that he would appear on the £5 notes. A great, great victory for him, even allowing for the stipulation that he's portrayed sat on the toilet, trousers round his ankles and the Queen is smirking.

And that's how having a shit came to be known as going to '*spend a fiver*' in modern English.

The End

Should it actually happen in your reality, this ending is NOT covered by the 100% money back guarantee. You pushed and you pushed didn't you. You see what you drove me to? Not comedy gold, not even comedy tin, but I tried, dammit. I swear you've pushed me to the edge of a breakdown. I'm not paying any refunds - I'm spending all the money on meds and psychotherapy. It's what you did to me. Yes - you. You. YOU!

—— Section 360 ——

The winner of Scotland's first Presidential election is announced on TV as you watch. You don't recognise the name or the ordinary, slightly geeky looking man as he takes to the podium to whoops and cheers. It's only when he starts talking that you realise that he's one of 80s guitar pop-band The Proclaimers. You're not sure which one, but that isn't really important.

He makes a speech and you can see that he's popular with the public and wants to do the best for Scotland. So it's doubly shocking when a shot rings out from the back of the auditorium and the new President falls back with half his head missing.

There's a scuffle at the back of the room and you hear someone shout "Long live the Queen" as security subdue the royalist assassin, accidentally shooting him 128 times in the process.

Everyone in the hall is stunned. Nobody knows what has just happened or what to do. If only the president had walked a few steps to the side the shot would have missed; just a few steps - so ironic when he often boasted about how far he'd walk.

Then the election returning officer takes decisive action and calls The Proclaimer who hasn't been shot forward. He is announced as the new President of Scotland there and then, on the basis that *nobody* could ever really tell them apart.

At least you have now figured out a cunning method to differentiate the pair: the most popular one who won the vote is the one decomposing in a coffin and the less popular one is alive and serving in public office. Easy when you know how.

Viva el Presidente!

The End of the beginning

Should it actually happen in your reality, this ending is <u>NOT</u> covered by the 100% money back guarantee. It's just not, no matter how far you walk or how many complaining missives you send from the US.

—— Section 361 ——

You turn back to the nurse and say "You don't understand - I need *urgent attention*."

Nurse Dean looks at you oddly "Oh urgent? You'd better come with me then."

She leaves the desk and leads you over to a door on the far side of the room. As she opens the door you notice that the room has a 'staff only' sign on it. As the door closes behind you, you ask "Where are you taking me Nurse Dean?"

She turns and pushes you back against the wall before saying "to heaven… and call me Cindy". She then releases her long blonde hair whilst dropping to her knees and unzipping your fly. As her mouth closes around the end of your mighty throbbing manglue-gun you close your eyes. When you open them again, you notice that you've been joined by about a dozen other young nurses, all in various basques, PVC, rubber and other forms of what is presumably non-standard NHS uniform lingerie.

'Oh not again' you think.

What happens next is inevitable.

Sex. Hot sex. Really hot sex. Really really hot sex. Sex that's hotter than the centre of the Earth. Sex that's hotter than the surface of the sun. Sex so hot that it can't be described in any greater detail than just 'really hot sex' or this book would be banned under obscenity law. Suffice to say that you have really really really hot sex with all the really really really hot sexy nurses and over the next 6 hours of really really really really hot sex you find out that there's *nothing* they won't do… and then do again 5 minutes later when you're ready for a repeat performance.

Whilst enjoying pleasuring seven nurses at once, it occurs to you that this type of thing doesn't usually happen to guys like you, ordinary guys. The type of guys who just get on with life trying not to dwell on their amazing powers of lovemaking.

No for people like you this type of thing is normally just a dream as unachievable as… oh, wait a minute… a dream. That explains it. You're dreaming. Of course you are. You haven't had a shag in weeks and it's playing on your sleeping mind.

Oh well hopefully the dream will last for a while longer it'd be a shame if it ended sudd- (go to **Section 106**)

—— Section 362 ——

SciTech TV is showing a gripping-if-you-like-that-sort-of-thing documentary about the solar system and the future of mankind. It makes a convincing case that we should start exploring more and that maybe we need to start colonising other worlds before too long as all it takes is one medium-sized asteroid or comet to crash into Earth and it would wipe us out.

It makes a good case for setting up a moon base and colonising Mars, so that we don't have all our eggs in one planetary basket, but then focusses on our inability to detect near-Earth objects or other (mainly terrestrial) causes of disaster.

The TV show even helpfully includes some really long, realistic cgi sequences of possible ways that human life could be destroyed, showing people screaming and dying in flames, in floods, in meteorite showers, in tornadoes, in nuclear blasts, in a new ice age, by unfriendly alien invasion, by some sort of hemorrhagic disease, from biblical Armageddon and by a mass outbreak of freak accidents involving garden strimmers.

You get the feeling that the whole show is just an excuse for the gory, attention-grabbing, special effects-laden film sequences. To be honest it's quite depressing and not really the sort of thing you want to watch whilst still relatively euphoric and optimistic about the future.

You decide to change the TV channel.

What's on Suds - the TV channel dedicated to soap operas and light drama (go to **Section 176**)

or You think you'll watch HAM TV - the channel of History And Myth (go to **Section 041**)

—— Section 363 ——

Bye then...

Sad to see you go, but if you must.

Still there? I thought you were going?

Yes. *I'm* still here. A bit surprised that you are though.

You close the book. Go on.

You first.

Ok - let's both go after three.
One...

Two...

Three. (go to **Section 191**)

—— Section 364 ——

You pick up the teeny tiny pencil...
And make a decisive cross in the 'YES' box.

It was a no-brainer really. You came out to vote supporting independence and you're convinced it's the right thing to do.

You fold the ballot paper and, trying not to make eye contact with anybody, walk across the floor and pop the folded ballot in the box. You exchange knowing nods with the station attendants. You know and they know that you have fulfilled your democratic duty.

For such a momentous historic vote it all seems like an anticlimax now. You just hope that your countrymen and women all see sense and vote as well as you have.

All you can do is go home and carry on as normal until the results are announced. (go to **Section 321**)

—— Section 365 ——

For the next few hours, points were made by each side. Counter-points were made in answer to them. At times the independence campaigners made great arguments that seemed to beat the opposition to submission. But then, just when the 'Better Together' supporters seemed to be beaten to submission they'd make a stunning counter-argument that left the pro-independence camp floundering.

So many great points were being made from all sides. You even made three or four yourself and at one point you got into a heated exchange with a young redhead who had a pair of particular note. You remember thinking, as the argument thrust back and forth between you how much you were enjoying it and wished it could go on all night.

You could barely believe how interesting and how much fun it was to discuss serious matters with so many people. You decided that this may be the first but it wouldn't be the last time that you mass debate in public.

Back and forth it went. If it was a boxing match then it would have dragged on for all 90 rounds, neither side scoring a knockout, either in open play or by penalty shot. It was too close to call with both teams equal on points after extra time. [*Note to editor - can you check this, I'm not really a big boxing fan so may have got some terminology slightly off.*]

By the time the debate was over, many issues had been discussed but you'd be surprised if floating voters had been drawn 100% to either side. You'd be even more surprised if the points raised had made anybody change their vote if they'd already decided which way they were going.

Ah well. It may not have really changed anything, but it was interesting and stimulating, and at the end of the debate a group of people were going to a local bar for a few drinks and asked you to join them.

Do you apologise and head straight back home (go to **Section 124**) or go to the bar for a nightcap or two. (go to **Section 146**)

—— Section 366 ——

You open the door and as you enter the first thing that you notice is that you can hear what sounds like a cold war numbers station playing from a nearby radio. There are bursts of some classical music interrupted every minute or so by a child's voice reading out a series of 27 numbers and colours. Every minute it is the same sequence that the child says.

Sat behind the desk waiting to hand out ballot papers is a gorilla in a traditional male Greek dress. You walk over to it and once you have confirmed your identity, the gorilla gives you your ballot paper, looks you up and down and then points to the individual polling booths. She then says, in perfect Swahili, "Well it takes all sorts I suppose. You can vote over there, then put the folded ballot paper in this box when you've finished."

Of course that's not the weird bit.

It's not weird that there are 10 pairs of ballroom dancers dancing to the numbers station, each with a number on their back and a man-sized fly judging them. It's not weird that the obviously female gorilla is in male dress and is wearing different colour eye liner on each eye. It's not weird that neither shade matches her skin tone. It's not even weird that the dancers are dancing in 4/4 time but the classical music is clearly a waltz.

The weird bit is that you understood the gorilla perfectly well and you don't even speak Swahili.

As you walk across the room to the polling booth, it is with the weight of a country's destiny bearing down on your shoulders... (go to **Section 119**)

—— Section 367 ——

September 18th 2214

Just twenty years after *Yes-Day*, helped by increased state funding from the new nation, you discovered a medicine that appeared to have a wondrous ability to fight virtually any disease. The drug seemed to boost the human immune system, cell repair and regeneration and soon passed medical trials with flying colours.

For decades the standard advice from doctors for everything had been *take lots of water and paracetamol and come back next week if it hasn't improved.* That had been the automatic response for patients reporting anything from sniffles, rashes and odd lumps to shattered bones, heart attacks and decapitation.

Your discovery changed this advice to *take lots of water and panaceatamol.* There was no need to say to come back if the complaint hadn't improved, as there was virtually no illness that it didn't cure, although decapitation was still troublesome.

Over the next 5 years the number of deaths from disease and old-age dropped to practically zero. The scifi dream of extreme longevity seemed like it may have finally arrived if you could just avoid accidental death and murder.

Panaceatamol was hailed by everybody as a miracle cure.

But that changed overnight when you mentioned in a magazine interview how you'd decided to dedicate your life to medical research after watching a documentary on Med TV. That was fine, but you followed that up by quipping that it's lucky as things could have ended up very different had you not changed channel from Gayer TV.

Suddenly there were protests from right wing Christians and other anti-homosexuality groups. They would have nothing to do with a drug invented by deviants, sinners and freaks (as they liked to describe you).

These groups stopped taking panaceatamol and within a decade their mortality rates increased dramatically. As there was no longer any need for many doctors, getting medical aid if you refused panaceatamol was nigh-on impossible. Nobody needed other drugs, so even the old advice of *take lots of water and paracetamol* had to change to just *take lots of water*, which doesn't really address many diseases. The protesting groups bigotry was leading to their early deaths from what were now totally avoidable causes.

Perhaps wrongly for a medical man, someone who had dedicated their life to saving people, you had to ask yourself *was it such a bad thing that they were dying off due to their own prejudice?*

Lots of people were able to lead happier lives because the bigots who used to cause them much pain and discomfort had all perished…

An idea formed in your head.

Even though you'd developed panaceatamol as a solo effort, under the pretence of addressing the attacks upon you and your drug, you decided to issue a press release detailing the fictional team who created it with you.

You told the public about the massive role that Phillipe the Nigerian midget Muslim played in it's development. How Consuela, the Mexican ex-addict ex-hooker and now proud single-mother, helped. How the disabled Israeli Jew and the Palestinian goth had worked side by side for the good of mankind. Your team had people of every persecuted and hated group you could think of: every skin colour, social class, religion and sexuality.

There were no extremes that you avoided - You even included a nazi, someone with ginger hair and, worst of all to many, a Frenchman.

You issued the press release and waited for the backlash…

Many more groups filled with hate towards a section of society came out in protest and boycotted your wonder drug. You can't say that you were sad when, over the next 30 years these people tended to die out…

Other people, who had been mildly prejudiced started to rethink their views on the basis that if an Israeli and a Palestinian could set aside their differences to help develop the drug, then maybe we could all show a little more tolerance.

Within 50 years bigotry and hate-crime had become a thing of the past.

Not long after the death of hate, governments around the world were adding low doses of panaceatamol to the domestic water supply. With that development peoples life expectancy rose sharply once more.

This universal rise in life expectancy at the same time as the death of hate had some odd knock-on effects, ones that are still happening now. When people don't hate and know that they could live for hundreds of years, their priorities change. Life changes from a rat-race grab for all that you can in the precious few years you're alive to a much more settled longer-term view. International hostilities around the globe wound down and soon the world was in a state of personal, local, national and international peace and co-operation unseen since… well, since ever.

Now, on the second centenary of *Yes-Day*, you remember back to the vote for independence, and muse on how it was an important first step on the road to this new utopia.

The End

Should it actually happen in your reality, this ending is <u>NOT</u> covered by the 100% money back guarantee. You want money back for living in utopia? That's not going to happen - especially as the author needs as much money as he can get to pay for medical treatment in the less-than-perfect reality he's currently residing in.

—— Section 368 ——

Aaaaaaargh!

The stress is too much. How are you meant to decide the future of an entire nation? It's not fair - you're only human. What if you make a mistake? What if you end up wrecking Scotland's future. What if you do that and the press finds out it was all your fault? You'll be hounded in the street. People will throw things at you. You'll probably be regarded lower than Jonathan King or Gary Glitter. OH GOD!

You can't take it…

You pick up the teeny tiny pencil and go to put a cross in a box to get it over with, but instead a sudden panic makes you accidentally draw a big cock and hairy balls spunking across your ballot paper.

Hmmmm… I suppose that counts as a spoilt paper.

You fold the ballot paper and, without making eye contact with anybody, walk across the floor and pop the folded ballot in the box. The station attendants say something, but you ignore them and walk out quickly, embarrassed that they somehow know what you did.

For such a momentous historic vote it all seems like an anticlimax now.

All you can do is go home and carry on as normal until the results are announced. (go to **Section 321**)

—— Section 369 ——

September 18th 2036

You sit back in your chair enjoying the show and the 3 pairs of pert 18-yr old titties pressed against you. You thought that a lap dance might help you forget that it's exactly 19 years today since the accident hit. It's hard to lose those memories though, no matter how much jiggling is done, especially since you'd never have owned such a successful 'adult' club without the catastrophe.

It was 3 years after *Yes-Day* when *it* happened.

After the referendum, the government of the rest of the UK had given assurances that the nuclear deterrent was safe to keep based in Scotland. That it would happily relocate it in England if Scotland wanted. Given these assurances, and knowing that, unlike power stations, there'd never been any serious accidents with nuclear weapons Alex Salmond cleverly used Trident as a bargaining chip to get a good deal on the currency and EU-membership questions.

Salmond had struck a great deal and everyone knew it, and since the chance of a nuclear accident was negligible nobody was worried.

But the funny thing with negligible probabilities is that, no matter how small they are, they're still greater than zero chance.

And so it was that luck decided to fuck you over on September 18th 2017. The day when the Trident warheads somehow went off in dock, killing thousands and creating a cloud of radioactive fallout that dwarfed the 1980s Chernobyl disaster. A cloud that, over the next few days, spread out over all of Scotland and much of Northern England.

Holyrood tried to clean up as best it could and, probably full of shame, Westminster sent as much help as it could - or alternatively as little help as it could get away with.

Nobody knew exactly how much damage had been done. Certainly the cancer rate rocketed over the next few years and, of more interest to you, the radiation caused numerous birth defects in births after the accident.

Whilst most of the populace got angry or upset about this, you remembered back to the TV you watched after *Yes-Day* and planned a long term plan for the future.

So now, 19 years after the accident, you find yourself sat at your club '*Freaks*' enjoying the assorted mutants and deformed oddities and all the womanly configurations that they offer. It was a long term strategy of yours to look after the young defects, but you knew that sex sells and if they survived into adulthood you'd have a unique product that men (and women) would pay for.

Lost in the memories of how you started, you've decided that, for tonight, you've lost interest in the feel of 3 pairs of firm 18-year old tits pressed into your face. So you wave Shona away. Let the 6-titted novelty go and earn some money off the real punters. You signal to your bouncer to send Sue over. You feel up for a real woman. A real woman with 3 legs and more quim than most men know what to do with.

The End

Should it actually happen in your reality, this ending is NOT covered by the 100% money back guarantee. Unless you can get me a freebie with Shona - and don't tell me missus…

—— Section 370 ——

You look around the shop but nothing is really capturing your imagination until you notice what you initially think is an IT nerd costume of nondescript shirt, plain trousers, crap glasses and ginger wig.

Then you notice the guitar next to the outfit and realise that it's not some complete loser from IT, but a costume replica of one of top 80s Scottish band *The Proclaimers*. You can't tell which one of them it's meant to be, but to be honest it doesn't really matter. Nobody can tell them apart anyway.

The outfit is perfect and you have to have it for today of all days.

You pay the shopkeeper and get changed.

Within minutes, what looks like the happiest nerd in Scotland is walking off to the polling station, and it isn't even 500 miles away. (go to **Section 351**)

—— Section 371 ——

September 18th 2025

Anticipating a boom in Scottish property from rich English people tempted by the TV shows and American tycoons trying to make golf courses, you started working on a portfolio as soon as you could after *Yes-Day*.

Granted it felt like it started slowly and took a while to build up, but now just 11 years later you're able to sell up, making such an enormous return on your investment that you're able to move to a beautiful island in the Caribbean.

You're nervous as you travel out to the islands. Even when you're rich it can be hard moving somewhere completely new. Somewhere where you don't know anybody. Somewhere you're alone.

You step off the plane, go through immigration and collect your case. You're travelling quite light as the rest of your stuff is being shipped over, so you decide to grab a drink at a nearby bar before you go to your new home.

Walking into the bar you're surprised to hear someone call your name. You look around and spot two familiar faces, Iain and Scott from back home.

"What youse two doin' here?" you ask.

"Same as you I spect" answers Iain, "Sold up back in bonny Scotland an moved oot here."

"Aye same here" says Scott.

"I thought I'd be all alone - be good to see a friendly face or two."

"Be more than that - there's loads of us here. You should join the footie league we've set up, 20 full teams. Bound to be one that'll have yer."

You soon find out that there are a lot of Scots just sold up and moved to the islands. So many people saw the same BBC property porn that you saw and realised that buying up property to later flog at great profit to rich English Tories would be a good idea.

The funny thing was, like many past property booms, as soon as some rich Tories started buying Scottish property, every other one wanted in and the prices rapidly went through the roof. The key was in getting out before the bubble burst.

Recently the prices went high enough to make it realistic to sell up and move to somewhere sunny where you'd never have to work again. So many Scots did sell up and move.

Now the Caribbean was full of Scots (or more precisely Caribbean bars were full of Scots as they weren't used to so much sunshine that they could stay outside). Scotland was full of rich English Tories and England was full of English who couldn't afford to move and immigrants who had a much easier time with all the rich Tories gone.

Everyone won - except any Scots left in Scotland, obviously. But at least they benefitted a little from the increased taxes levied on the English invaders.

The End

Should it actually happen in your reality, this ending is

covered by the 100% dream back guarantee. Just rewind all your dreams to the beginning and return them for a complete refund of your deposit. Nightmares excluded.

—— Section 372 ——

You open the door feeling slight trepidation that this may not be as normal as you'd hoped; that somehow you'd been tricked into doing something a little bit zany or odd.

And you are suddenly hit by an almost physical underwhelming tsunami of ordinariness. The polling station looks like every other polling station that's ever existed in the past 50 or 60 years in the UK.

Thank you, thank you. Oh thank you!

The sense of relief that rushes over you is dizzying. See there's nothing boring about being normal. Being normal can give you thrills like no other way of life could, after all if you were weird then you'd soon get used to strange things happening and none of them would seem interesting anymore. Whereas by being totally and utterly normal you can get excited just by the slightest thing, such as being given a penny extra change at the shops.

And that really did happen to you once. You were telling everyone about it for weeks afterwards. Your 'bonus penny in the change at the supermarket' anecdote is legendary.

You exchange the briefest of pleasantries with the exceedingly-normal lady behind the desk dealing with addresses including your home. Once you've confirmed your identity, she gives you your ballot paper and points you in the direction of the small individual booths that you can go in to cast your vote in private.

As you walk across the room to the polling booth, it is with the weight of a country's destiny bearing down on your shoulders… (go to **Section 119**)

—— Section 373 ——

You remember that you're waiting to hear back from your MP about the suggestion you emailed him saying that September 18th should be celebrated every year as 'Union Day' bank holiday.

It would be a perfect annual opportunity to remember everything that's so great about all of Britain. Well, all of Britain except Ireland anyway. You could all spend a day just reflecting on how Scotland, England, Wales and Northern Ireland come together to make a union much more powerful and influential than the sum of it's parts.

A day to feel good about how the union enriches all our lives. A day to recall how much we achieve together. And if that's not persuasive enough: A day to not be at work.

You suggested it months ago, but if Westminster moves quickly and gets it in place today there's still a chance it'll help persuade some floating voters that the United Kingdom is worth preserving.

The dogs will wait a minute or so whilst you check your email. They'll understand how important it is to you, today of all days.

You switch on your computer expecting to be greeted by the familiar start-up chimes but instead the screen remains black except for a blinking text cursor in the top-left corner. That's odd you think.

But not as odd as when text starts appearing on the screen without you touching the keyboard.

'WAKE UP' appears, then, on a new line, 'ANSWER THE DOOR'.

You jump as you hear a knock on your front door. Of all the times for someone to call - it's annoying to think you were nearly given the fright of your life by mere coincidence.

Then the cursor jumps to a new line and says 'WELL - ANSWER IT WILL YOU'

That's very strange. And very rude. It could at least say 'PLEASE'. Maybe you better had answer it.

You go to the front door and open it to be greeted by the sight of someone in a white, adult-sized rabbit costume holding a silver platter with an old rotary-dial telephone on it.

Actually, looking closer, you realise that your first impression is wrong. It's not an adult-sized rabbit costume at all. It really is a 6'2" white rabbit, complete with twitchy nose, stood on it's back legs and holding a silver platter on it's right forepaw.

You barely have time to consider how very curious that is, as the old black telephone starts to ring loudly.

"It's for you" says the rabbit in an American accent.

If there's one thing you're proud to say you learnt at school, it's that you should never argue with anthropomorphised animals, especially when they are bigger than you.

You pick up the receiver and put it to your ear.

Immediately you feel very odd, as if being suddenly jolted from a deep sleep. (go to **Section 103**)

—— Section 374 ——

You pick up the teeny tiny pencil...

And make a cross in the 'YES' box.

You fold the ballot paper and, trying not to make eye contact with anybody, walk across the floor and pop the folded ballot in the box. You exchange knowing nods with the station attendants. You know and they know that you have fulfilled your democratic duty.

For such a momentous historic vote it all seems like an anticlimax now.

All you can do is go home and carry on as normal until the results are announced. (go to **Section 321**)

—— Section 375 ——

At this late stage you realise that it's a lot of responsibility making the decisions that will decide your future, the future of Scotland and the future of the United Kingdom, maybe even the future of the whole world.

It's too much for one person to bear on their shoulders.

Far easier to have a final look in the box and see how Schrödinger's Cat is getting on. Let a random quantum state decide the future with either a miaooow or the stench of decomposition.

Having said that, there are unique endings for each of the third TV shows you watch, whereas these are a few odds and sods that are common to all, so don't think that these are all the endings available…

DEAD CAT TIME

Thomas? Thomas? Little tinker Tom - are you okay in there. I hope so as a lot rests on this… You open the lid to check.

Hiya Tommy! Would you like a ball of wool to play with? (go to **Section 149**)

or What about a little mousey? It's got catnip in it… (go to **Section 192**)

or Oh. Dead kitty… (go to **Section 303**)

or Wow look at the sleepy pussy cat! (go to **Section 046**)

or Thomas! Stop that. I've told you before that you are not allowed to shop online with my debit card (go to **Section 280**)

or Ahh has Tommy brought a present for daddy? Has he? Has he? Is it a mousey? Or a birdy? Oh - it's a toddlers arm… (go to **Section 123**)

—— Section 376 ——

You struggle to open the doors but they just won't move no matter how hard you push. God you must be deteriorating quicker than you thought, you may only have minutes before you're too weak to walk. Sure you've not lived a saintly life, but you're hardly the worst sinner. You certainly don't deserve to die here on the pavement, so close to help but what may as well be a thousand miles away if you can't get into the building.

The annoying thing is that a thousand miles is nothing to your usual, fit, self. If you weren't near death you'd happily walk 500 miles, then walk 500 more, quicker than a pair of ginger-haired freaks can pick up guitars and start a sing-song.

But you aren't your usual fit self, so you shove and you shove but they stubbornly refuse to move until you push with all the might you have left in your failing body, at which point the nurse sat on reception notices you and buzzes you in.

Instantly the door flies open and you tumble, arse over tit, onto the floor inside the building. The fall knocks the wind out of you and so, as the nurse rushes over to you, you struggle to speak.

"Wha... wha... what the fuck was that for? Openin' the door as I'm shovin' it? Can't you see I'm a dyin' man?"

It took nearly all your energy, but you feel a little better for getting that off your chest.

Finally, with salvation, or at least pain relief in your dying hours, so close, you give your details to the nurse on reception.

DEAD CAT TIME

You've not heard a noise out of that box for a while... wonder if Holly is still alive?

Shhh... you'll wake her up (go to **Section 006**)

or Oh so that's what a dead cat being eaten by maggots looks like! (go to **Section 093**)

or Does Dr Schrödinger expect you to clean up all that cat shit? (go to **Section 397**)

or The cat's dead and you can't be sure it's face isn't blue... (go to **Section 165**)

or Holly looks pleased to see you, but more pleased to be fed (go to **Section 112**)

or Holly ignores you, upset that her litter hasn't been cleaned (go to **Section 241**)

or Holly died after scratching "J'accuse" into the side of the box (go to **Section 324**)

—— Section 377 ——

You open the door and you are suddenly hit by an almost physical underwhelming tsunami of ordinariness. The polling station looks like every other polling station that's ever existed in the past 50 or 60 years in the UK.

But then what did you really expect?

It looks like a normal polling station because it is a normal polling station. Nobody's going to dress primary schools up in union flags and saltires just because the subject of the vote is Scottish independence.

You exchange the briefest of pleasantries with the normal lady behind the desk dealing with addresses including your home. Once you've confirmed your identity, she gives you your ballot paper and points you in the direction of the small individual booths that you can go in to cast your vote in private.

As you walk across the room to the polling booth, it is with the weight of a country's destiny bearing down on your shoulders… (go to **Section 184**)

—— Section 378 ——

Nature TV is showing a documentary about the pregnancy and birth of the baby giant panda at Edinburgh zoo just before *Yes-Day*.

The whole world had followed both the trouble Tian-Tian had conceiving and then her eventual pregnancy. When she finally gave birth everyone in Scotland was elated at seeing such an endangered creature born in Edinburgh. Giant Pandas should be protected, like independence and democracy and fairness. You like to think that maybe somehow, alongside the Glasgow games, the birth of Indy-Pendy helped contribute something to the national pride that won the Yes vote.

You still remember the day of the birth, when Alex Salmond stood outside the Panda enclosure looking as proud as if he was the new dad himself. Thinking about it, a bit of black and white makeup or a panda outfit and he'd make a quite convincing panda.

He'd made a rousing speech about hope and new life and the importance of bamboo shoots. Although you might have misheard the last bit.

Following *Yes-Day*, Indy-Pendy panda grew rapidly in size, strength and confidence, almost as if she was the living embodiment of the new nation.

It's a story that you know well enough, having seen all the other documentaries about them in the few weeks since the birth. So you decide to see what's on the other side.

You turn over to watch SciTech TV (go to **Section 342**)
or Do you switch to Channel 4 (go to **Section 113**)

—— Section 379 ——

You re-enter the bathroom and start running the shower. You know from past experience that it's going to take hours of scrubbing to get your face back to it's normal colour. Maybe next time you should buy some proper stage make-up instead of bursting open a blue biro and using its ink.

What are you saying? There's never going to be another time. You've learnt your lesson. You'll never paint your face blue again.

Upon thinking this you burst out into laughter. You *know* you'll do it again. There's no avoiding it. All it takes is a decent malt and Braveheart or a Scottish international from Murrayfield and bits of you start turning a patriotic blue almost automatically. It just comes so easily to you that sometimes you wonder if you were a smurf in a past life.

You make a mental note to visit the costume shop and buy some proper makeup on your way back from the polling booth.

Once you're sure you should be pretty much cleaned up you decide it's time for breakfast. But getting out of the shower you look in the mirror and are shocked to see that your face is still a sickly blue. It's hard to tell if it's any better than when you went into the shower - maybe it is just a little. Or is it?

Maybe it would be better for you to go to the hospital and get checked over.

You dry off and pull on some clothes, all the time looking for your mobile phone. (go to **Section 319**)

—— Section 380 ——

You need to go further back in history to be certain that there'll be plenty of Giant Pandas. You're not too sure how far, but Edinburgh Zoo in 2014 isn't early enough. Anytime in the 21st century is probably not early enough. The 1990s won't be early enough. Remembering your history lessons, you're pretty sure that the mid-80s isn't early enough.

What about the 1970s?

"Don't be crazy" you think "I'm not after dinosaurs or the bloody dodo." Added to which the 1970s is a far too dangerous time to visit in case you accidentally turn into a nonce just by being there.

No - you decide to try 1981 as the perfect spot in time, somewhere between the far-too-late mid-80s and the impossibly early 1970s.

Stopping only to get a giant bear-sized butterfly net, a bale of bamboo and your almost-omniscient handheld omnipedia you set the controls for…

August 13th 1981

You arrive somewhere in Edinburgh in a darkened room and quickly look around. By god, you were right! There's Giant Pandas everywhere. But it's obvious that these ones have been maltreated as they all seem to be incredibly malnourished and thin. Even their faces are drawn and you wouldn't recognise them as Pandas if it wasn't for the white faces and black eyes.

The poor beasts are being forced to listen to some outrageous cacophony coming from a band on a brightly-lit stage at one end of the room. What sort of madman would do this to such beautiful animals?

Then you notice that some of the emaciated pandas seem to be dancing and drinking pints of cider and black… odd. You can't remember Pandas having opposable thumbs, but it is a while since you last saw one.

The music from the stage abates for a moment and the trapped animals make some sort of noise that could be a cry for help but is more likely to be a mixture of cheers and applause. You take the audio break to check the omnipedia and soon realise that you've made a mistake. These aren't Pandas - they're goths and you seem to be at a music concert.

Damn! You know that goths died out (partly as a result of being forced out of their natural habitat by the more aggressive emo) but you don't want to save them from extinction. You'd best jump to another time period and try for Pandas again.

But before you open a fresh time portal, the band on stage starts playing a twiddly guitar riff, which is soon joined by a bassline and haunting female vocals. As omnipedia reliably informs you that this is 'Happy House' one of the big goth hits you decide to take in history and hear it live before going who-knows-when.

The front-woman, in startling makeup, soon starts singing proper lyrics:

This is
A charnel house
There's death in here
In our charnel house
A house of pain
Pain Pain woah-ohhhh

Omnipedia is buzzing away in your hand - trying to get your attention. You glance at it and see that the tune is spot-on but these aren't the correct words to the song *Happy House.*

Something odd is going on so you compare the omnipedia image of the lead-singer to the singer on stage. It definitely is Siouxsie Sioux, but then it hits you: It's Siouxsie, but it's not Siouxsie and the Banshees… no. It's far worse. It's *Siouxsie and the Goblin-Banshees*!

Obviously in trying to go back in time you've shifted realities to one slightly different to your home universe. One where goblin-banshees aren't extinct but instead form bands and appear on stage playing modern post-punk genres of music. That's not a universe that you want to live in - you must get out of here.

Suddenly, before you have chance to activate the time portal generator, the 3 male goblin-banshees have leapt from the stage and are upon you. Siouxsie Sioux keeps on singing acapella as the goblin-banshees take turns to each rip you a new arsehole.

At least the song was accurate - for you this is a house of pain for the few minutes it takes you to die.

The End

Should it actually happen in your reality, this ending is NOT covered by the 100% money back guarantee. I've never paid out if it might mean offending a single goblin-banshee do you really think I'll pay out and offend 3 of them? Just be glad that you got to see Siouxsie Sioux performing in her prime.

—— Section 381 ——

Arriving at the busy A&E department you hurry into the hospital and luckily you're surprised to see that there's no queue so you walk straight up to the nurse on reception. You give her your details and are asked to sit in reception.

After a short wait you're seen by Doctor Cook who soon sterilises and bandages your wounded hand.

"I bet you think I'm a right idiot" you say to the doctor.

"Oh don't worry you're not so bad. I see a lot worse in here. It's amazing what idiocy and drink can combine to create."

"I bet" you say.

"I see all sorts - people who've obviously been beaten up and claim it was fighting a gang of special-forces, people with everything from action man to toilet duck stuck up their backsides and people thinking they've got a deadly disease just because they went to sleep with their face painted blue. In comparison you're quite sane and normal."

"I bet you could write a book about it all."

"Aye. And that's only a selection of who I've seen this morning. Honestly, the tales I could tell."

With that he's finished working on your hand and tells you to drink plenty of fluids and take paracetamol if it causes any pain.

You say bye and go home to freshen up in the shower, with a plastic bag tied around your bandaged hand. (go to **Section 258**)

—— Section 382 ——

You open the door and almost immediately know that you're entered the wrong room as you can hear rowdy cheering and what sounds strangely like fighting.

You head on through the dense cigarette smoke and are astonished to see Vladimir Putin bare-chested and bare-knuckle fighting a bear.

Actually that's not really true. You're astonished to see a man fighting a bear and you're astonished to see Vladimir Putin. But if you knew you were going to see Vladimir Putin then you'd half expect him to be in a state of semi-undress doing something befitting a manly manly manly manly man, like fist-fighting a bear.

You exit the room and decide to look for the polling station behind a different door. (go to **Section 115**)

—— Section 383 ——

September 18th 2035

In the ongoing party after winning the referendum, you and many other people concentrated on building the best Scotland that you could. An honourable aim but perhaps just a little too local-minded when the planet was crying out for attention.

The next decades saw the ice caps melt and the sea level rise. Slowly, but surely the plains of Southern England were flooded and rendered uninhabitable.

You and your countrymen managed not to smirk in public as the water crept closer to Westminster, especially when it became apparent that many of the displaced people couldn't bear the thought of living "Oop North" in Northern England and so headed for Scotland.

Before long much of the old Britain had sunk beneath the waves and the Scottish highlands became the centre of life on these once-small-but-now-even-smaller islands. Just over 35 million people fled Southern England to establish home in the place that they once seemed to ignore or deride as a barbarous waste.

That was really annoying.

You thought that you'd managed to escape the bloody self-important Londoners and Home Counties Hoorays. At least this time they were forced to live under Scottish rule.

Payback's a bitch.

Though you'd still have preferred it if you'd looked after the planet and kept the Southerners a decent distance away…

The End (of a scenic, reasonably-empty Scottish

countryside)

Should it actually happen in your reality, this ending is NOT covered by the 100% money back guarantee. You brought it on yourself really. Look after the planet and you won't have to live shoulder-to-shoulder with displaced Conservative voters.

—— Section 384 ——

You wait...

You're already bored of waiting. The only thing to do is worry or watch the other people, but that's just annoying.

Take those two youths over by the blood donor poster for example.

"A pint! That's most of me arm innit!"

"No idea mate - I don't do that old pints and ounces shit. Ain't a pint just under half a litre?"

"No idea - it's just a quote from some old Alfred Hitchcock film me gran told me about once. Hitchcock's in hospital an' he sees a poster asking for blood donors to give a pint an' he says 'A pint! That's most of me arm innit?' Me gran thought it were proper funny."

"I s'pose people used to laugh at anything after the war."

Thankfully at this point your name is called by the nurse from reception and she leads you through to an examination cubicle.

DEAD CAT TIME

Has anyone fed Tiddles today? No? I'll see how he is then.

He's fine and ready to play! (go to **Section 320**)

Or He's fine and ready for some food! (go to **Section 188**)

Or He's fine… if you didn't want a living cat. (go to **Section 133**)

—— Section 385 ——

You climb out of the giant vat of blackberry-flavoured custard feeling lucky to still be alive. You still don't quite understand how you ended up in the vat in the first place.

The last thing you knew was that this section was supposed to be a spare place-holder designed to look like a real section of the book but it was never to be linked to in any way shape or form. So you really are mystified as to how you got to be here. Either you've been flicking through sections without following the links, or you accidentally turned a page too far to get here or the author fucked up when he was having to manually code in all the links…

You think for a moment and decide that the latter is most likely. The author is a total fuckwit so you wouldn't put it past him to bollocks up the manual coding. The worst part is: the author agrees with you.

— Section 386 —

September 18th 2120

The Scottish independence win changed everything for the rest of the UK (rUK).

Part of the reason that Northern Ireland had stayed with the Union for so long was because of it's links with Scotland. An independent Scotland raised new questions and new hopes for a possible unified Ireland.

Wales questioned whether it needed to stay with the Union, although it did admit that choral singing wasn't quite as good a revenue stream as North Sea Oil, so it had more financial answers to find.

Many parts of England saw the Scottish victory as a win over Westminster rule, something which they saw as being as relevant to their regions as it had been to Scotland. Suddenly the North West, North East and Midlands were all looking at the viability of losing the Home Counties and London who took so much and made sure that their spending per head was higher.

It didn't help London that Scotland and it's people were thriving under it's own rule. The country had entered a golden age and other parts of rUK knew that they could do the same.

Within a couple of years there were regular independence protests and riots in Manchester, Birmingham, Liverpool and Newcastle. It was so bad that even the gentlefolk of Harrogate staged an hour-long sit-in at Betty's Tea Rooms.

After a couple of years Westminster relented and let the regional referendums commence. As Yes vote after Yes vote came in and the regions became independent before, invariably, aligning with Scotland, Wales and the New UK, London became more and more insular. Soon it started to favour its own comfort and protection even over the Home Counties that had stood with it for so long.

Then finally, on September 18th 2020, Mad King Boris, the white haired piffle-talker and ruler of Old London Town and the old UK (which was precisely Old London Town) had the London Wall erected. Overnight a 100 feet high wall, topped with barbwire, appeared, shutting Old London Town off from the New UK. From the World.

Left alone and unloved by their old protector, the home counties soon recanted their London-centric past and joined the New UK and the last 100 years have been prosperous for all. With closer ties between all parts of New

UK and even further, to the rest of Europe.

As for London?

Well nothing ever went in or out of Old London. No boats. No cars. No planes - mainly as they never did build Boris Island so there was nowhere for planes to land if they did enter Old London.

So nobody really knows what happened behind the wall. Whether the people of London carried on regardless, believing that betting on whether numbers would go up or down was important or did they all succumb to the mad king's insanity and die in a lengthy bout of cycling and sex. Nobody knows...

But some still believe that if you walk too close to the wall after dark you'll hear the mad king phwoarring and waffling on about wiff waff, crumpet and jolly poor shows.

But reason says that he died long ago, so, surely, that's just superstition.

Isn't it..?

The End

Should it actually happen in your reality, this ending is NOT covered by the 100% money back guarantee. Ooh that turned a bit spooky at the end didn't it... I'm too scared of the (possibly spectral) mad king BoJo to go giving out refunds today.

—— Section 387 ——

You go right again because even though you have remembered reading '*Even More Dragon Gold!*' you know it's not real. There's no such thing as a goblin-banshee in real life.

Is there?

Of course not, but then you remember that there's no such thing as Camelot, King Arthur and the Knights of the Round table either. You stop running, suddenly realising that if they've somehow become a reality then maybe there's nothing stopping the goblin-banshee from doing the same.

No sooner have you thought that than you hear the inhuman wail of a goblin-banshee behind you. You try to turn, but can't as the goblin-banshee is already proving that 20th Century plastic toy armour is no match for a supernatural demon hell-bent on ripping you a new arsehole.

If only there was a 'next time' you'd heed the advice of multiple-choice-stories... but there won't be as you are dead.

The End

This ending is <u>NOT</u> covered by the 100% money back guarantee should it actually happen in your reality. Because the goblin-banshee said so. It's *that* evil.

—— Section 388 ——

September 18th 2025

Running across the rain-sodden street, you can hear the chasing gang's shouts and shots ringing out from the alleyway you've just emerged from as you pull the 9mm automatic machine pistol out of your pants waistband.

The driver of the car waiting at the red light doesn't see you coming - he's too busy nervously eyeing the street-punks outside the burger shop.

"Out the fuckin' car, motherfucker" you shout at the occupant as you rip open the driver's door. You know he won't resist - no-one likes being pistol whipped or shot and the face-full of Uzi you're showing him proves you're serious.

The shouts are getting louder and a fired round zings off the car bodywork. Shit! You're in a hurry, so thoughtfully 'help' the driver out - throwing him into the middle of the road and into the path of both cars and the gang's bullets. His death isn't pretty, but it doesn't bother you as you miss it, too busy slamming the door shut and accelerating off.

Racing through the junction you knock down a pedestrian mother crossing with their young child. Too bad - you weren't hanging around to be killed and they shouldn't have been in the way.

Part of you does feel bad though - a police cruiser spotted you jump the red light and so now you've got a wanted star on you. You hate it when that happens.

You look at the time. Damn - you're not going to make it.

Oh well - You turn off the console and head off to work. You'll just have to carry on playing *Die CrackWhore Die! 3* when you get back home tonight.

Ever since the new Scottish government gave breaks for production of gritty violent games the number of titles like *Car Jacking Hooker Killer V* exploded (though unlike many objects in the games themselves, the explosion was just metaphorical).

Their realism increased and so did their popularity. Before long an unexpected side-effect was noticed. Violent crime seemed to be dropping.

The games let people get rid of their aggressive tendencies.

Of course the boom in violent video games didn't solve all crime. For the first few years there was still a large jump in property theft whenever a new console or triple-A title came out. But that was tackled after the government starting subsidies to make video gaming more easily affordable for all.

Soon school lessons were incorporating the games. Not only did they help disperse playground aggression and halt bullying but the games were realistic enough to teach driving skills and many pupils learnt basic mathematics and chemistry purely by dealing virtual crack and cooking Meth. In some schools it was taken so seriously that you would get detention if it was thought that you were going soft on hoes or purposefully wounding policemen instead of killing them without mercy.

It was happy, peaceful days for everyone - well everyone who wasn't computer-generated anyway. It sucked donkey balls if you were a character in one of the games.

The End

Should it actually happen in your reality, this ending is NOT covered by the 100% money back guarantee. Sorry I've not got time to process refunds at the moment, I've nearly finished this mission. Just need to get to the safehouse before 5-0 pop a cap in my ass.

—— Section 389 ——

Arriving at the busy A&E department you hurry into the hospital and are upset to see a small queue between you and the nurse on reception. You can't wait in a queue, not with time against you. With what could easily be the last of your strength you manage to say weakly "Excuse me, let me through, I think I'm dying."

"Aren't we all - that's why we're at A&E, you prick. Fuckin' wait your turn" says the big guy in front of you with a badly beaten and bruised face. Given the size of him you wonder who could have done that to him. Though maybe he's a mixed martial arts fighter or something.

Luckily for him, you're certainly too weak to enter into an argument with the ill-mannered brick-shithouse who replied, otherwise you'd have shown him who's boss. As it is, you wait your turn and just silently hope he catches whatever it is you are carrying. Eventually you reach the front of the queue.

"Next! Mister..?" Says Nurse Dean, the receptionist, in a welcoming tone before getting a proper look at you and being struck by recognition. "Oh…" her pitch drops "it's you again. I'll bring up your records. Take a seat and we'll be with you as soon as we've dealt with the… real patients."

Do you sit down in the waiting room and wait your turn (go to **Section**

286)

or Try to make the nurse realise that you are far too ill to last a wait of even 10 minutes (and you know it'll be longer than that). (go to **Section 052**)

—— Section 390 ——

Skye Living+1 is showing a guide to alternative therapies and holistic healing available on the Inner Hebrides islands to the West of mainland Scotland.

If you believe the show, then unusual beliefs and complementary therapies can keep you a lot healthier than newfangled so-called medical science can. Instead of paracetamol you should try reflexology or give your chakras a spring clean with reiki. Instead of drinking medicines full of active ingredients with chemical-names you should drink some water that remembers once seeing an illness similar to the one you have. Instead of taking antidepressants you should think about sticking needles in your scrotum.

It's full of all sorts of alternative treatments like these, and you can't be sure that any really work, although you're fairly certain that sticking needles in your ballbag would take your mind off whatever had previously been depressing you.

Well, that's just so long as you weren't getting depressed at the thought of having genitals that look eerily like Pinhead from the Hellraiser films.

Whatever you make of it all, you can tell that the programme makers earnestly believe in alternative therapies and lifestyles. Even the documentary itself is homeopathic. Most documentaries are stuffed full of facts, whereas any facts that were ever meant to be in this documentary must have been watered down so much that they're practically undetectable.

You eventually decide to turn off the TV and start to think about your future and the future of Scotland, and where the priorities lie for both of you.

Move to a remote commune where you can live in harmony with nature and keep healthy through alternative therapies (go to **Section 318**)

or You don't need to live on a commune to be in harmony with nature, just move to a small island (go to **Section 306**)

or The Scottish Government should look into using alternative medicine to complement the NHS and reduce medical expenditure (go to **Section 347**)

or Thinking of the SciTech TV show you watched, you dedicate your life to advanced scientific research (go to **Section 255**) or I don't want to think about all this - just give me something random! (go to **Section 375**)

—— Section 391 ——

You enter the examination cubicle and are shocked to see that it's empty. "Where's the doc-"

You're sentence is cut short as Nurse Dean pushes you back against the wall. clamping her mouth over yours and kissing you deep, her tongue probing your mouth like a probing lump of sensually wiggly flesh.

When you finally get chance to breath you manage to ask "Nurse Dean what th-" before she silences you with a finger on your lips.

"Shhhh - and call me Cindy. I know what you want. Why else would you keep painting your face blue other than for an excuse to come here and see me? I know you want it. You know you want it."

If only you knew what this 'it' was she's on about.

But before you get chance to ask she's let down her hair, undone her top and pulled up her skirt to reveal long stockings and suspenders.

'Oh not again' you think.

What happens next is inevitable.

Sex. Hot sex. Really hot sex. Really really hot sex. Sex so hot you're surprised it doesn't melt the very wall you're shoved up against. Sex so hot that it can't be described in any greater detail than just 'really hot sex' or this book would be banned under obscenity law.

After you've spent what seems like hours rutting like teenage wildebeest you both re-arrange your clothes and leave the cubicle, amazed that no-one else noticed how long you'd been in the cubicle, nor how noisy you'd been.

Of course no-one noticed - it may have felt like hours of hormone-crazed warthog rutting that left you both screaming out loud, but it was actually just 138 seconds of mild hamster moans that left passers by thinking someone had a touch of toothache or a sprained ankle.

Still, it was long enough for you to feel a lot better and realise that maybe you're not dying.

As you wander home you wonder if anybody has suggested that the people who have caught ebola in West Africa have tried shagging it away. It could be the miracle cure for all sorts of ailments. You're not exactly sure how long it'd take you and nurse Cindy to get around a few thousand infected each. It might cure them, but it'd take ages and be knackering. Still, if the World Health Organisation asks you to help out, you'd try as best you can. It's the right thing to do.

You walk home smiling and wondering who you contact to volunteer your services to selflessly shag women in Africa. (go to **Section 118**)

—— Section 392 ——

Sometime in 2014...

You look at the books available to buy. You fancy something a bit different.

'Hmmm - what's that one?' you wonder seeing the cover of some book called **You Decide! The Future of Scotland**. It's claiming to be humorous and not really linked to the upcoming Scottish referendum, but you can't be sure. Why call it that title if it really has nothing to do with the independence poll?

The description worries you. You're not certain that you'd like a puerile mix of hot sex, quantum physics, goblin-banshees, time travel, hot sex, political debate, dinosaurs and all the other oddities the book claims to throw into the mix. That could describe practically anything, but strikes you a bit like when people in the office describe themselves as 'wacky', 'mad' or 'well up for it', it usually just means that they're annoyingly odd with borderline mental difficulties usually only seen in deluded X-Factor contestants. You're not sure you want to read a book like that.

No; on second thoughts, maybe you're better sticking to something from Ricky Gervais or Karl Pilkington.

You decide not to buy the odd **You Decide!** Book and so never read this.

The End (or maybe The Not-Even-Began)

Should it actually happen in your reality, this ending is <u>NOT</u> covered by the 100% money back guarantee. You didn't buy the book so you're not reading this and you get no refund of the monies you never spent.

—— Section 393 ——

You enter the polling booth, close the little privacy curtain and look at the ballot paper. It's such a small piece of paper. Almost too small and unassuming for the role it plays in this historic day.

You turn your attention to the single question on the ballot paper.

Should Scotland be an independent country?

Such a small sentence. Almost too small and unassuming for the massive decision it represents, with all its implications and knock-on effects. Whichever way the vote goes, those six little words play an important role in making history.

Okay - it's time to make a decision and make your mark, so you pick up the pencil ready. It's such a small pencil, almost too small and unassuming for the vital part it plays in this most momentous of days. It's a pencil that would look small in a betting shop and would be dwarfed by the pens in Argos.

It's taking the piss.

If everything today was sized appropriately for the important role they play, then the question should be printed on sheets of A0 paper in letters 6-inch high. You should have to make your mark with a paint roller and the option of just using cowardly yellow paint for voting 'NO' or a mix of colours to create a great big tartan cross in the 'YES' box.

It's too late to change the ballot conditions, so, doing your best to ignore how small and insignificant everything seems, you prepare to cast your vote.

Vote for 'Yes'. (go to **Section 364**)

or Vote 'No'. (go to **Section 243**)

or Wait and think about it a little longer. (go to **Section 180**)

or Flip a coin. That's the way to decide. (go to **Section 279**)

Flip a coin. But what sort of coin? (go to **Section 008**)

And is heads yes or heads no? (go to **Section 139**)

I suppose heads should be 'No' since it shows the queen of the United Kingdom, (go to **Section 212**)

but then she'd still be the queen of Scotland if the 'Yes' vote wins independence. (go to **Section 222**)

Oh this coin flipping is far too confusing, but it's the only way to decide. (go to **Section 328**)

Okay heads is 'Yes', tails 'No'. (go to **Section 354**)

Should it be the other way round? (go to **Section 092**)

or Oh god you can't decide - the stress is too much! (go to **Section 256**)

—— Section 394 ——

The punster's fist surprises you as it arcs towards your head before making solid contact.

"You'll regret that, shithead" you shout at full volume as you start hammering blows down on the guy's head. He soon falls to the floor begging for you to stop, but instead you look around for a weapon and spot one of the 3 feet tall cuddly, anthropomorphised thistles from the Glasgow games. You grab it and start beating him with it as he lies curled up on the floor.

"Think you can bully people do you?" You scream, punctuating every word with a swing of the thistle. "Think that it's alright just because you're bigger than them do you? Do you? Just because you're bigger and older than them? Just because you're bigger, older and shagging their mum? Well you can't 'daddy' and you're not my real dad anyway. You're just a twisted sick fuck. Mummy doesn't really love you no mummy loves me and mummy still loves my real daddy and you can't treat people like this."

Suddenly you realise you're not standing up to your stepdad when you were 13.

The drunk crawls off, being helped to his feet by his mate. You turn and see everybody else in the room staring at you, several of them with disbelieving, open mouths.

"Oh. Sorry about that... don't know what happened."

One of the debate organisers is brave enough to ask you to put down the thistle and leave.

You'd been enjoying debating, and could argue against any political point if you wanted to, but you can't think of any reasonable argument against his request to you.

You go home and cry yourself to sleep.

This morning, as you climb into the shower to freshen up, you almost wish you hadn't remembered what you did last night. (go to **Section 120**)

— Section 395 —

You open the door and you're assaulted by the sound of a music system blasting out 90s pop music. You recognise the track as the biggest hit that *2 Unlimited* had - you think it was called *No Limits*.

It only takes a few moments for you to realise that something's wrong: the CD or record seems to be stuck in a loop. It just keeps repeating part of the chorus.

No no. No no no no. kzt No no. No no no no. kzt No no. No no no no. kzt No no. No no no no. kzt No no. No no no no. kzt No no...

Oh! Suddenly you realise what it is - it's not a broken music player but an intentional loop acting as a slightly less than subliminal hint about how to vote.

Then you notice that the room is decorated with union flags and graphical reminders of the long history that Scotland has suffered under the rule of the rest of the UK. You've obviously stumbled into a polling station set up by Unionists who are trying to persuade people to vote 'No'. Well it's not going to work on you and you're going to try stopping them from having it all their own way. You're going to at least get them to stop that repetitive 'No no' looping away.

You go to the lady behind the desk dealing with the area that includes your address. She's dressed in equal parts of red, white and blue and, seeing your attire, is already scowling at you.

"Eh I don't much like that music - it's trying to influence the vote. Will you change it?"

To your surprise she agrees and goes over to the sound system and changes the CD. Immediately some throw-away 80s pop comes on.

She returns and asks "you don't object to some Rick Astley do you?"

"Auch no" you reply, though you're thinking it isn't that great and that maybe silence would have been better, but at least it isn't trying to make you vote to keep the union.

Once you've confirmed your identity to the attendant, she looks you up and down before saying "You know you ought to be ashamed of yourself, laddy". Then she gives you your ballot paper and points you in the direction of the small individual booths that you can go in to cast your vote in private.

It's only as you're leaving the desk that the music gets to the chorus and, mysteriously, starts looping.

Together forever and never to part kzt Together forever and never to part kzt Together forever and never to part kzt Together forever…

As you walk across the room to the polling booth, it is with the weight of a country's destiny bearing down on your shoulders… (go to **Section 393**)

—— Section 396 ——

September 18th 2019

Yes-Day was when it started.

Nobody realised it then of course. Close to home everybody had been watching the Scottish referendum. Further away people had been busy fighting ebola that had spent months spreading out of Western Africa.

People were definitely interested in the referendum or ebola, nobody was interested in both. Which is why it took a long time for anyone to notice that a new hemorrhagic fever, a mutated form of ebola, had taken hold in Scotland.

Patient Zero was admitted to hospital on the 18th September itself. He showed signs of a blue face and doctors initially thought the patient had merely painted his face with a patriotic saltire. That diagnosis soon proved incorrect and the patient seemed to be leaking blue fluid as his organs bled out.

He died a week later by which time there were already another 276 identified cases in Scotland and another 34 confirmed cases around the rest of the world (mainly in the UK and EU). He was the first death from *St Andrew's Cross Disease.*

Within a month nearly all of those cases had died and there were over 50,000 known cases in 38 countries. So far the disease was killing over 95% of all those infected. The media had dubbed the disease 'eblula' but many called it the Blue Death, which was probably the most accurate name as, in extremis, the disease caused a sort of extreme deoxygenation of haemoglobin that changed blood from it's usual oxygen-bearing red to the blue that was characteristic of the dying.

Luckily the Scottish government had already decided to pour money into medical research and whilst the English NHS, WHO and America's CDC were failing to make any progress, government funded doctors started to better understand the diseases transmission vectors and before long they had a couple of ideas of how to beat the disease.

Not all these ideas were equal. A Dr Cook famously thought that the entire disease was psychosomatic or made up by time wasters and so tried to 'cure' eblula by a mix of rectal endoscopy and sarcasm. Sadly it wasn't that easy, even though he defended his view until he was blue in the face. Literally. He died of the Blue Death soon after his medical trials began. Luckily many other Scottish doctors had much better ideas.

It took many trials, many setbacks, but slowly these initial ideas were turned into successful cures and preventative measures and so today, the 18th of September 2019, the last case of St Andrew's Cross Disease was finally cured.

Eblula took a dreadful toll on humanity. The world population fell to around 350 million before the disease was eradicated.

But it was eradicated, and all thanks to your homelands scientists and doctors and the increased funding they'd received from the new government.

The End

Should it actually happen in your reality, this ending is <u>NOT</u> covered by the 100% money back guarantee. Just be happy that you survived eblula thanks to your wise decision that the government should prioritise health and medicine.

—— Section 397 ——

The nurse takes your details then says "is that it?"

At first you're confused: You've never heard a woman say that before while you've still got your pants on. Then, after the confusion, shock sets in at how very unprofessional she's being, but then you remember that this disease is so debilitating you're probably just misunderstanding her. At least you still have enough wits about you to ask for clarification rather than just fly off the handle.

"What do you mean 'is that it'?"

"Well, you great numpty, it's clear to me that you've only gone and got some sort of paint or pigment on your face. There's nothing else wrong with you, other than maybe being a bit thick to still think you're dying when you're only dyed."

The nurse's words hit you like a jackhammer. She's meant to be part of a caring profession. How can she be so callous to someone at death's door?

"Now why don't you just get off home and get yerself cleaned up? Leave us free to deal with any real emergencies that might happen. Go on. Go."

You trust the nurse, so turn to leave and soon find yourself on the way home. (go to **Section 062**)

or You'd feel a right wally if you let yourself get fobbed off by a nurse and then die. No - you're off to A&E for a second opinion. (go to **Section 212**)

—— Section 398 ——

You open the door and almost immediately know that you've entered the right room because you seem to be in some sort of underground BDSM club.

The air is full of the sounds of hard techno, begging, panting and spanking and the smells of lube, poppers, sweat and sex.

As soon as the door has closed behind you, the music stops and everyone stares straight at you. A woman nearby does a sharp involuntary intake of breath which is echoed by the other revellers around the room.

You know what this means.

'Oh not again' you think.

What happens next is inevitable.

Sex. Hot sex. Really hot sex. Really really hot sex. Really really really hot sexy sex. Really really really hot tied-up submissive sadomasochistic superskin-clad sexy sexy sex. Sex so hot that it can't be described in any greater detail than just '*really* hot sex' or this book would be banned under obscenity law. Suffice to say, it was 'really hot sex'.

Though, in truth, there is only one word to describe it and do it justice and that word is : *hotsexreallyhotsexreallyreallyhotdirtyhotdepravedhotfunhotenjoyablehotbodywreckinghothotsex!*

There's only so much really really really hot sex, like that, that any man can take so after 87 seconds you exit the room and decide to look for the polling station behind a different door. (go to **Section 083**)

—— Section 399 ——

You get some very odd looks on the way and several people shout abuse at you. You take it all in good nature and wave at people you pass but, for some strange reason, many of them wave back with only one or two fingers.

Eventually you get to the polling station, walk up to the doors and pause.

You always thought that polling stations are places full of wonder and promise for the future. The almost-mystical locations that can alter a nations fate. Each one a powerful nexus where all possible destinies of the country intersect, just waiting for the public will to select one single possibility and to transform it into reality. Places of truly amazing, almost miraculous, transformative power.

But really they are just local primary schools that have swapped the kids for a naff sign saying 'POLLING STATION'.

Suddenly you hear a commotion behind you.

"There he is officers - near the school like I said."

You turn to see a little old lady gesticulating in your direction and talking loudly to a pair of policemen.

The two officers start running towards the polling station and one of them shouts "Oi! Stop right there, you pervert!"

You look around to see who they could be shouting at, but can't see anyone or anything suspicious. You hear the police run up to you and turn around to face them just in time to get a face full of truncheon.

"You dead fuckin' nonce bastid. Thank god the kids aren't here today."

You fall to the floor as the second policeman brings a knee up to your crotch and informs you that "You shoulda stayed dead, Jimmy, now were gonna fix it for youse paedo scum."

Of course! You suddenly remember why the costume was so cheap, the recollection striking you hard like the baton being brought to bear on your white-wigged head. But unlike the baton, the realisation only strikes you once and doesn't keep on going until you pass out.

Two days later, as you finally pass away in hospital having never recovered consciousness, your last thought is that maybe you should have gone with the comedy Fred West costume after all.

The End

Should it actually happen in your reality, this ending is <u>NOT</u> covered by the 100% money back guarantee. Really, if you're the sort of person that thinks it's funny to visit schools dressed up as a celebrity sex-pest paedo then, sooner or later, someone will fix it for you spend an eternity in the special hell usually reserved for beloved stars of 70s light entertainment. You're certainly not getting your money back, now fuck off.

—— Section 400 ——

You open the door and almost immediately know that you've entered the wrong room because you walk in on a brightly lit kitchen where two extremely fit naked women are writhing about on the floor, not shy about expressing their lesbian lust for each other.

You can't help but stop and stare.

Suddenly the cheesy wah-wah guitar you can hear stops as someone calls out "CUT! CUT! SHTOP! SHTOP!" in a dodgy European accent that may be an attempt at Dutch (only the author knows for sure).

You look to where the shout came from and from near some video cameras an angry blond-haired man is shouting.

"Vot are you doingk? You are meant to be dressed as plumber viv za dungarees unt a massif shpanner inzem. You haff com to repair za vashink mashine unt vann za lesboes say 'oh haff you brought your big toolz' you drop your clothes unt fukzem viv your hart peeness."

"Vot iz hart to unnershtand abowt zat, Dummkopf?"

You're not sure that you caught a single word that he said, but in your defence you were distracted by the sapphic floorshow that hasn't yet stopped.

"Go owt agenn unt zis time do it right. Unt dont vorgett za 1970s shtyle mustash. Zat iz zo ferry important for za porno."

You exit the room and decide to look for the polling station behind a different door. (go to **Section 083**)

—— Section 401 ——

September 18th 2015

Immediately after seeing the programme on HAM TV you decide to start saving up for the equipment you need to mount a serious search for the Loch Ness Monster.

Through a mixture of determination, credit cards and doing favours for sailors, just one year after *Yes-Day* you find yourself staying on the banks of Loch Ness with a custom-made submersible ready for the search.

You're dismayed to find that amongst the guests of *Hotel Paradise*, you aren't the only Nessie-hunter (or cryptozoologist as some of the more pretentious ones insist on calling themselves). You think that maybe there'll be some sort of camaraderie between the 12 teams hunting Nessie, but you've misjudged how cut-throat the hunt really is.

Every team has it's own custom-made sub. Every team is sure that their sub gives them an advantage. Every team is keeping tight-lipped about the specifics of their sub design and why it'll give them an advantage.

Of course you're not really surprised when you overhear a team talking about just how much money it could be worth if you are the ones to get proof that Nessie exists…

The teams of monster-hunters keep to themselves so much that the only people you really get to talk to all night are the hotel owners. But you are buoyed by the way that the woman is adamant that she's seen Nessie and that she's quite easy to spot if you're patient. She's even sure that there's a whole family of 'Nessies' living in the loch.

With the owners views giving you hope, you sleep well and are up early the next morning. Being careful not to let the other 11 teams see the design of your sub, you leave the hotel and are soon entering the water in your Nessie-shaped sub. It's genius, if you do say so yourself. If your sub looks like Nessie then it won't freak her out and you should be able to get close to her… if you can find her that is.

You search for hours and then suddenly you spot her!

Creeping forward slowly you're amazed - the submarine's disguise works so well that Nessie isn't swimming away from you - far from it, she's actively heading towards you!

Then you notice another 'Nessie' homing in on you. And another. Then another. There *is* a whole family out here!

Before long you're facing a group of 11 Nessies (or Plesiosaurs or whatever they really are). You're mesmerised by the sight, but keep enough of your wits about you to check the cameras (still and video) are all running okay.

After about 5 minutes you decide to head back to shore and report your find to the world before one of the other teams sees a Nessie and beats you to it.

In your rush to race back and call the Associated Press news service, you never notice that the 11 Nessies in front of you are all strikingly similar to your submarine design…

And all 12 of the mechanical monsters (your own included) are so eager to race back to shore and issue a press release that none of them spot the more organic matriarchal plesiosaur in the distance. The one that is keeping hidden near a rocky outcrop to the North and telling her family to stay hidden for now as the silly humans are still out there in their metal vessels.

The End

Should it actually happen in your reality, this ending is <u>NOT</u> covered by the 100% money back guarantee. Surely you don't need a few quid refund when you must be rolling in it from discovering Nessie? What - you missed her? I told you that she was near the rocky outcrop to the North. If you can't even follow the directions given in the text then there's no helping you.

—— Section 402 ——

The blue-faced zombie man gets up close to you just after Tommy and Hamish have both done really massive poos. You're busy bagging one of them up when, with almost laser-guided precision for someone who staggers about without looking where they are going, the bloke steps straight into the other one.

"Oh I'm very sorry - you've stood in the dog mess" you say to the man. You're not sure at first if he's heard you or not as he seems almost shellshocked with a thousand yard stare. Maybe he really is a zombie.

You repeat your apology to him and this time he seems to register it as your words have a profound effect on him. All of a sudden he starts screaming "Why me? Why? What've I done?" and he staggers towards you and looks like he is about to hit you.

You raise your hands to protect yourself, momentarily forgetting that you're holding a bag of steaming-fresh dog shit…

The man brings his fist crashing down at you and slams it into the hand holding the bagged biggie.

The effect is explosive. Dog crap flies everywhere. All over the man. All over you. All over everywhere.

"Why..?" cries the man pitifully, falling to the floor right over the poo he'd stepped in and crying.

You really don't want to be near this blue-faced lunatic any longer than necessary, especially since you're covered in flecks of crap. So you quickly call the dogs to you, put on their leads and head home.

Once there you can't stand the idea of eating, not whilst stinking of poo. So you jump in the shower as quick as you can. (go to **Section 258**)

—— Section 403 ——

You think about all the options available and then decide that you really can't be arsed putting in loads of effort picking something special to wear just so that you can look like a total prick all day. Knowing your luck, it'd only lead to aggro and, as you're still feeling a little less-than-lively after the events of last night, you don't need that. Not today.

So you quickly get dressed in the first pair of trousers and top that come to hand and look at yourself in the mirror.

"Aye - they'll do."

And with that you set off to the polling station. (go to **Section 020**)

Afterword

Hopefully you enjoyed that, or at least some of that. If not, then it's no doubt due to not stumbling upon the right set of choices that delivers you unto your own personal idea of comedy gold, comedy platinum or at least comedy iron pyrite. I can hardly be blamed for that can I?

Oh - you're right. I can. Oh well, no use crying "*over spilt milk!*"

That'd just make everyone around you think you mad. You don't need to have not enjoyed this book *and* to end up on strong medication for unprovoked outbursts of dairy-themed non sequiturs.

I tried to spread things out between good and bad outcomes for both the Yes and No campaigns and to base very little in our reality. There are two main reasons for that:

1 - Where's the fun in sticking to our universe when so many possibilities exist in the eternally infinite multiverse? i.e. It's a lot more fun making weird shit up.

2 - I personally can't vote in the referendum and whilst I have personal views about what is for the best (for both Scotland and the rest of the UK) it's not my place to try persuading anyone which way to vote.

Having said that, bad things are usually funnier than good things, as long as they don't happen to us that is. So I may have a few more bad outcomes, but hopefully they're absurd enough to not be taken as serious comment on what may happen (even though they did really really happen somewhere).

As a quick serious note: I do think it's important that people vote, whichever way they lean, whenever there's a public election (not just in the Scottish referendum). If you don't agree with any party, vote and spoil your paper - at least then the powers-that-be may realise that people don't like any of them but felt strongly enough to turn up at the polling station. Before long 'none of the above' may become an option.

So hopefully this book raised a smile, and possibly this afterword makes someone who wasn't going to vote to think that maybe they should (and not just in case Alex Salmond is planning to spawn in Scottish rivers).

Of course, from my travels through time and other parallel universes I already know whether it worked or not, but I can't tell you now. That would be interference and could lead to a temporal paradox - and they're against all rules of time travel.

And I should know because my 7 year old great-great-grandfather told me that with his dying breath.

Best wishes,
Dave

Judgement Dave
Independent Territory of New Manchester
September 18th 3714AD

Frequently Asked Questions

For the 34th reprint of this book in 2027, JDC News entertainment correspondent Fanny Fiddler interviewed Judgement Dave about some of the many questions commonly asked, by both fans and reviewers, about '**You Decide! The Future of Scotland**'.

FF: Thanks for meeting me. There's a few questions that everybody seems to keep asking about your bestselling series of **You Decide!** Books and especially about the one about the Scottish Independence Referendum that kicked it all off.

JD: Fire away. You've got my complete attention.

FF: Obviously your books have won numerous awards and several have been turned into box-office record-breaking films. Out of all of the accolades and achievements, which would you say is the one you are most proud of?

JD: Oh that's a good question, Fanny. It's not easy picking any one thing but, if you stuck a gun to my head and forced me to answer, which is something I hope you won't do today but in other realities you've already done, then I'd have to say it was 10 months after Scotland gained independence when my first book became required reading in all Scottish schools.

FF: So it's not winning your third Man Booker prize? Becoming the richest man in the world or being McTime Magazine's man of the year 5 years straight?

JD: (laughs) No, not at all. Those were all great times, though I'm afraid that it was inevitable that they happened. But **You Decide! The Future of Scotland** becoming the main textbook for the new subject of *Possible History* in Scottish schools, well, that was something both very special and unexpected.

FF: Talking of possible history, a lot of the futures you described in that first book came true, such as Nessie battling Godzilla over Scottish fishing rights, but a lot of things you described, such as the discovery of a popular 1970s light entertainer who never diddled kids, haven't happened - not yet at least. It raises questions about how much is down to factual research or whether some is pure fiction designed to titillate.

JD: It's all very well researched, it's just that not everything comes to pass in every single universe.

FF: So you really did research the book by extra-dimensional exploration?

JD: Yes. Although you've also got to remember the significant contribution that alcohol and time-travel made. It's the mix of all 3 aspects that really does the trick. That's also how I managed to include this 2027 interview for the 34th reprint in the 2014 first edition.

FF: Were there any realities that were just too raunchy, too sickening or too unbelievable that you couldn't include them in the book?

JD: Oh yes - an infinite number really. Although the one reality I couldn't include that really annoyed me was the revelation about a former Prime Minister. It was all completely true that he often liked to **[REMOVED BY COURT ORDER ON THE REQUEST OF LAWYERS REPRESENTING T.B.]** and get the home secretary to lick it up but his lawyers challenged it under libel law. Sadly proof obtained by time travel isn't yet legally recognised in UK law, so I had to temporarily pull the truth. But you can't libel the dead so it'll be back in any day now, once Cherie finds out about his fondness for autoerotic asphyxiation.

FF: Finally, the ***You Decide! Effect*** has been cited as the main reason Britain has seen 13 years of record-breaking birthrate. Many people have described your hot sex scenes as '*50 shades turned up to 1000 degrees*', '*gusset-moisteningly good*' and '*okay if you like that sort of thing*'. So what everyone wants to know is: How do you come up with them?

JD: Well thank you for the compliments. It's quite easy really as all the really really hot sex scenes are based upon my own personal research. The great sex is based upon my performance and the bad sex is based upon my great imagination of what the opposite of me would be like. Or is it the other way round? I'm always getting mixed up. One way or another it's all based on personal experience though.

FF: Thank you for taking the time out to talk to me.

JD: It's been a pleasure. Say, would you like to meet up later for some hot sex. Really hot sex. Really really hot sex. Really really really hot sexy sex so hot it could boil an ostrich egg in seconds. Sex so really really hot it -

FF: No I'm fine thanks.

JD: Oh not again.

About the Author

Judgement Dave was born David John Buckley but very quickly (after only 40 years) decided that his given name didn't sound right for comedy. That it didn't sound right had never occurred to him mainly because the idea of doing anything other than software/BI development hadn't really been considered.

Given that he loved puns and had already been Judgement Dave online for 6 years (partly due to the City of Heroes MMO and partly due to Terminator 2) that seemed the logical nom de guerre for his comedic exploits.

Now that he's got the name right all he needs to do is to become funny. Hopefully that won't take another 40 years, even though it may presently seem to be an impossible challenge.

Since turning his attention to comedy, Judgement Dave has performed stand up (usually as one of the many *Increasingly Unconvincing Characters of Judgement Dave*, such as Gunther or Mr Dolphin), created many Youtube films, had success with short screenplays and sitcom pilots and has seen his sketches performed on stage, in several podcasts and by London's record-breaking NewsRevue and BBC Radio.

He's currently working on a full length novel, a book of shorter works and assorted projects for live performance and podcast/YouTube.

About the Author (by his Wife)

He's a fucking mentalist.

Does anybody want to take him off my hands?

Please.

Pretty please with sugar on top??

Helneaux Farkier

Helneaux/Farkier was formed in the mid 1990s after Michel Helneaux first saw Alec Farkier in a Montreal police booking area after a raid on the BDSM wife-swapping party they'd been attending. Both had actually met earlier, when Alec tried to swap 2 goats for Michel's wife, but the station was the first time they'd actually seen each other without the leather masks.

Seeing that they both had similar tastes in comedy, literature and strap-ons, the pair quickly bonded and were soon in bed together (in both literal and metaphorical senses).

Either that or it's a bogus name used for producing Judgement Dave's various mindfarts.

Coming Soon from Helneaux/Farkier...

Remember to Wash Your Hands

A collection of humorous short stories, oddities, mindspasms and assorted doodlings from the mind of Judgement Dave. Almost guaranteed to be perfect reading material for visits to the toilet and probably more coherent, better edited and less sweary than **You Decide! The Future of Scotland**.

Don't Do It! The Essential Guide to Procrastination

Ever had things to do that you don't really want to do but couldn't figure out a good way to avoid doing them? Well if so, you need this book. When it's finished, obviously. The first draft should be ready after I've done the dishwasher. Oh look is that a butterfly in the garden?

Coming ~~2010~~ ~~2011~~ ~~2012~~ ~~2013~~ ~~2014~~ Soon

Notes

[1] Admittedly the main thrust of research was in the 'strong alcoholic drinks' area. It's surprising how quickly you can 'research' a subject with homebrew cider.

I recommend SuperBucks: "It gets you Pissed! Fast!"

[2] And by 'broadsword' I mean an actual broadsword and not your genitalia.

Let's face it calling it more than a steak knife is probably hyperbolic boasting.

Although I once saw a man who'd had surgery to turn his penis into a swiss army knife. It made urinating difficult but at least nearby horses never had to suffer with stones in their hooves.

At least, not until after he was trying to help a horse and ended up serving time on charges of bestiality and indecent exposure.

[3] Well it's actually at least 10 possibilities. I know there's that many as I was counting them, but stopped once I'd used all fingers and thumbs.

[4] Of course you may not be roleplaying if you actually *are* a twenty-something Scottish male who lives in Scotland and is eligible to vote in the referendum. Although it's probably best to seek professional help if that does describe you and all the descriptions and choices in this book make perfect plausible sense to you.

[5] Roleplayers are often more than happy to demonstrate hobbit mating rituals, if anyone insists, and can often provide full costumes including oversized hairy-feet.

Still, at least it's not as weird as some Trekkies.

[6] It's even more depressing to realise that 0.00023% of your life was spent working out that the mundanities took up 99.423% of your life. You'd be *really* depressed if you knew exactly what percentage of your life was spent just reading this footnote…

[7] It's odd that this is used to show how unusually tired you are but is the very real state that Mrs Judgement Dave spends her entire waking life in. It pretty much explains why she gets on well with cats.

[8] It's odd that this is used to show how unusually tired you are but is the very real state that Mrs Judgement Dave spends her entire waking life in. It pretty much explains why she gets on well with cats.

[9] The author knows that Guinness is brewed in Dublin, in the Republic of Ireland. But he couldn't think of any breakfast food to represent Northern Ireland in particular and he wasn't going to start researching facts just to get a breakfast right.

[10] I'll happily let people say many things about this book, but I flat out

refuse to let them say that it's been over-researched.

I wouldn't mind but I kept thinking of things to represent Northern Ireland but then realising they were from the Republic of Ireland, and that only left me references to the troubles or the cop-out that I plumped for.

[11] At least it was good, old-fashioned harmless fun as long as we ignore the adverse effects of alcohol, any minor dance-related aches and strains and the trip to the GU clinic that was a direct result of the loving.

[12] At least it was good, old-fashioned harmless fun as long as we ignore the adverse effects of alcohol, any minor dance-related aches and strains and the trip to the GU clinic that was a direct result of the loving.

[13] Mind you… A teenage suicide linked to this book would boost the sales… The poison I was thinking of was **[CENSORED]**. Knock yourselves out, Kiddies!

[14] Just as long as you have a particularly stilted imagination.

[15] Mind you… A teenage suicide linked to this book would boost the sales… The poison I was thinking of was **[CENSORED]**. Knock yourselves out, Kiddies!

[16] Yes I do actually have a few Scottish friends in much the same way that people making jokes about ethnic minorities always have some friends from those same minorities.

I think that probably makes it alright, although part of me worries that a significant section of the Nuremburg rallies was taken up by Hitler pointing out how he had a Black Jewish Gypsy friend who happened to be a homosexual professor.

[17] Admittedly I wrote that this book *(probably) cost less than half a pint* before I'd set a final price for it.

Although I don't specify what it's a pint of. I'm pretty damn certain that whatever price I actually sell the book at it'll still be a lot less than buying half a pint of racehorse or prize pig semen.

www.ingramcontent.com/pod-product-compliance
Lightning Source LLC
LaVergne TN
LVHW052257070426
835507LV00036B/3099
* 9 7 8 0 9 9 3 0 1 2 5 1 8 *